SEVENTH EDITION

HITLER AND NAZI GERMANY

A HISTORY

Jackson J. Spielvogel
The Pennsylvania State University

David Redles
Cuyahoga Community College

Boston   Columbus   Indianapolis   New York   San Francisco   Upper Saddle River
Amsterdam   Cape Town   Dubai   London   Madrid   Milan   Munich   Paris   Montréal   Toronto
Delhi   Mexico City   São Paulo   Sydney   Hong Kong   Seoul   Singapore   Taipei   Tokyo

Editor in Chief: Ashley Dodge
Editorial Assistant: Nicole Suddeth
Director of Marketing: Brandy Dawson
Executive Marketing Manager: Kelly May
Marketing Coordinator: Theresa Rotondo
Program Manager: Kathy Sleys
Senior Operations Supervisor:
 Mary Fischer
Operations Specialist: Mary Ann Gloriande
Art Director: Jayne Conte

Cover Designer: Suzanne Behnke
Cover Photo: War Poster/Alamy
Director of Digital Media: Brian Hyland
Digital Media Editor: Rachel Comerford
Digital Media Project Manager: Tina Gagliostro
**Full-Service Project Management and
 Composition:** Abinaya Rajendran/Integra
Printer/Binder and Cover Printer: Courier
 Companies
Text Font: 10/12, ITC New Baskerville Std

Credits and acknowledgments borrowed from other sources and reproduced, with permission, in this textbook appear on the appropriate page within the text.

Library of Congress Cataloging-in-Publication Data

Spielvogel, Jackson J.,
 Hitler and Nazi Germany : a history/Jackson J. Spielvogel, The Pennsylvania State University; David Redles, Cuyahoga Community College. — Seventh Edition.
 pages cm
 Includes index.
 ISBN-13: 978-0-205-84678-8 (alk. paper)
 ISBN-10: 0-205-84678-5 (alk. paper)
 1. Hitler, Adolf, 1889-1945. 2. National socialism. 3. Germany—Politics and government—1933–1945. 4. Heads of state—Germany—Biography. I. Redles, David. II. Title.
 DD247.H5S648 2014
 943.086092—dc23
 [B]

2013006774

10 9 8 7 6 5 4 3 2

ISBN 10:   0-205-84678-5
ISBN 13: 978-0-205-84678-8

To Diane, the love of my life,
and to my mother, a beautiful woman
who taught me much about her native Germany

Contents

MySearchLab Connections   vii

Preface   x

About the Authors   xiii

1 Introduction   1

Europe in the Nineteenth Century   1
Imperial Germany   2
The Impact of World War I   7
Suggestions for Further Reading   9

2 Beginnings: Weimar Germany and the Rise of Hitler and Nazism   12

Weimar Germany   12
Hitler and the Emergence of the Nazi Party (1889–1920)   26
The Munich Politician and the Early Nazi Party
    (1920–1923)   34
First Attempt at Power   40
Suggestions for Further Reading   43

3 THE GROWTH AND VICTORY OF NAZISM 1924–1934   48

New Beginnings: The Rebuilding of the Nazi Party, 1924–1929   48
The Climb to Power, 1930–1933   58
The Consolidation of Power, 1933–1934   69
Suggestions for Further Reading   80

4 THE NAZI STATE, 1933–1939   83

The Hitler State   84
Economic and Social Developments   89
Anti-Jewish Policies, 1933–1939   100
Instrument of Terror: The SS Police State   107
Legal and Judicial Systems   112
The Churches   114
The Military   118
Public Opinion and Resistance in the Third Reich   119
Suggestions for Further Reading   121

5 THE DICTATOR   125

Hitler's Personality   125
Hitler as Messianic Leader   130
Hitler the Orator   131
Hitler as an Ideologist   134
Propaganda and Mass Meetings   140
Suggestions for Further Reading   147

6 CULTURE AND SOCIETY IN NAZI GERMANY   151

Culture   151
The Manipulation of Youth   162
Education   166
Women in the Third Reich   169
Family and Population Policy   174
Sex and Morals   176
Suggestions for Further Reading   179

7 HITLER'S WAR   184

Prelude to War   184
World War II   200
Suggestions for Further Reading   216

8 NAZI GERMANY IN WARTIME   220

The New Order   220
The Home Front: Civil Life in Wartime Germany   229
Resistance in Wartime Germany   241
Suggestions for Further Reading   249

9 THE HOLOCAUST   253

Hitler's Racial Ideology   253
The Final Solution   255
The Other Holocaust   273
Questions about the Holocaust   276
Suggestions for Further Reading   279

10 CONCLUSIONS   285

The War Crimes Trials   285
The Significance of Nazism   286
Suggestions for Further Reading   288

GLOSSARY   291

INDEX   292

MySearchLab Connections
www.mysearchlab.com

CHAPTER 1
Documents
Adolf Hitler, Excerpt from *Mein Kampf*
The German Act of Confederation, 1814
William Graham Sumner, from *What the Social Classes Owe to Each Other*
   (1883)

Map
The Unification of Germany, 1866–1871

Image
Nazi Rally

CHAPTER 2
Documents
The Covenant of the League of Nations
Heinrich Hauser, With Germany's Unemployed (1933)

Audio
Emergence of the Nazi Party
Adolf Hitler

Activity
Map Workbook Activity: Europe Between Wars,
   1919–1939

CHAPTER 3
Document
Doctrine of Fascism (1932), Benito Mussolini

Videos
Germany: Jewish property destroyed during Kristallnacht—"Night of broken glass"
Adolf Hitler Becomes Chancellor

Images
Nazi Party Congress, Nuremberg
Hitler at Nuremberg Rally, ca. 1928

CHAPTER 4
Documents
Speech to Spaniards (1936), Francisco Franco
Gertrud Scholtz-Klink, "Speech to the Nazi Women's Organization" (Germany), 1935
Neville Chamberlain, In Search of Peace

Closer Look
The Nazi Party Rally

Podcast
Hitler

CHAPTER 5
Document
Adolf Hitler, The Obersalzberg Speech, 1939

Map
German Expansion Under the Third Reich

Images
German Painting Idolizing Hitler
Hitler and Mussolini in Munich, 1940
Hitler at Nuremberg Rally, ca. 1928

CHAPTER 6
Documents
Karl Pearson, "Social Darwinism and Imperialism"
The Rise of Totalitarianism—Propaganda?

Compare & Connect
The Soviets and the Nazis Confront the Issues of Women and the Family

Images
Brandenburg Gate, Berlin, Germany
1936 Berlin Olympics

CHAPTER 7
Documents
Heinrich Himmler, "Speech to SS Officers"
Franklin D. Roosevelt and Winston Churchill, "The Atlantic Charter"

Map
World War II in Europe, 1939–1945

Images
Hitler celebrating French surrender
Nazis executing Russian civilians

CHAPTER 8
Document
Marc Bloch, from Strange Defeat

Videos
Hitler and Roosevelt (Randy Roberts)
Nazi Murder Mills: WARNING: This clip is very graphic.

Images
Civilian refugees in Europe
Nazi Book Bonfire, 1933

CHAPTER 9
Documents
The Holocaust: Memoirs from the Commandant of Auschwitz (1940s),
    Rudolf Hoess

Map
The Holocaust

Closer Look
Envisioning Evidence: Deciphering the Holocaust

Images
The Holocaust I
The Holocaust II

CHAPTER 10
Documents
The United Nations, Universal Declaration of Human Rights, 1948
Israel's Proclamation of Independence, 1948
Winston Churchill, from the Iron Curtain Speech (1946)

Video
The Big Three Confer—Yalta Conference

Images
Tokyo and Nuremberg war crimes trials, I

Preface

Hitler's Third Reich continues to be the object of study of many historians and writers. I am grateful for the opportunity to incorporate new material and suggestions from readers in this seventh edition of my book.

Nazi Germany had its formal beginnings in the appointment of Adolf Hitler as chancellor of Germany on January 30, 1933. Hitler and the Nazis believed that they would create a Third Reich that would last a thousand years. And yet, within a brief twelve years, despite their creation of a powerful Germany and the conquest of much of Europe, they ended up totally destroyed.

The world has not forgotten the enormity of Nazi crimes against humanity. The name *Hitler* and the word *Nazis* have become virtually synonymous with evil. Historians, philosophers, and many others have struggled to explain how and why such a phenomenon as Nazi Germany could ever have occurred in the twentieth century, and especially in a country with such a humanistic cultural heritage. While massive biographies and hundreds of specialized books on various aspects of the Third Reich have been written, my purpose in writing this book has been to provide a brief but comprehensive survey of the Third Reich based on current research findings. It is intended for general readers who want a deeper view of this short period in German history. As seen in the title, I have emphasized the person of Adolf Hitler. Although I do not believe that individuals alone determine the course of history, there is no doubt in my mind that Hitler played a crucial role in the history of the Third Reich. I have sought, however, to present a balanced picture that examines Hitler's role; the economic, social, and political forces that made possible the rise and development of Nazism; the institutional, cultural, and social life of the Third Reich; World War II; and the Holocaust. I have approached World War II and the Holocaust as logical outcomes of the ideology of Hitler and the Nazi movement. I have discussed these subjects both chronologically and thematically.

One of my major interests in writing this book has been in putting the story back in history. I believe that a combination of good analysis and narrative is both possible and desirable. Narrative history conveys well the lessons of the past and is the form that best aids remembrance. I am convinced that an understanding of the Nazi era today is crucial if we are to avoid a repetition of similar events.

NEW TO THIS EDITION

- Section on anti-Semitism in Germany moved from Chapter 9 to Chapter 1 to better reflect chronology and to introduce students to the topic earlier in the book.
- Section on Nazi anti-Jewish policies, 1933–1939, moved from Chapter 9 to Chapter 4 to better reflect chronology of events.
- Increased coverage of the Jewish experiences of, and responses to, Nazi persecution throughout the text.
- New discussion of the importance of Hitler's mentor Dietrich Eckart and the notorious hoax, *The Protocols of the Elders of Zion.*
- Contains a more focused linkage of the Eastern War and the escalation of the Final Solution beginning in 1941.
- Increased focus on the experiences of ordinary bystanders, perpetrators, and victims throughout the text.
- New images added throughout the text.
- Expanded discussion of non-Jewish victims of Nazi aggression, including new material on the persecution of the Sinti and Roma (Gypsies), Slavic peoples, and homosexuals.
- Contains thorough bibliographies throughout the text.

MySearchLab™   www.mysearchlab.com Pearson's MySearchLab™ is the easiest way for students to start a research assignment or paper. Complete with extensive help on the research process and four databases of credible and reliable source material, MySearchLab™ helps students quickly and efficiently make the most of their research time.

This text is available in a variety of formats—digital and print. To learn more about our programs, pricing options, and customization, visit www.pearsonhighered.com.

ACKNOWLEDGMENTS

Many people have helped me in one way or another to write this history of Hitler and Nazi Germany. I wish to thank Timothy Whisler, who first suggested the project and provided research assistance. David Redles, associate professor of history at Cuyahoga Community College, contributed his expertise to the seventh edition by revising and updating the text in accordance with the most recent scholarship in the field. I appreciate the financial and verbal support of my department heads, Gerald Eggert and Charles Ameringer. My colleague Dan Silverman read part of the manuscript and made valuable suggestions. I would also like to thank Ann Carney, Pennsylvania State University, Erie; Jennifer Miller, Southern Illinois University, Edwardsville; Jim Phillips, Highland Community College; Kara Ritzheimer, Oregon State University; and Marynel Ryan Van Zee, University of Minnesota, Morris, for reviewing the manuscript and making helpful comments. The enthusiastic questions and responses of my students have caused me to see many aspects of Nazi Germany in new ways, and I am thankful to them. I am also grateful to colleagues and students for their unsolicited comments about this book. I hope that this seventh edition will continue to assist new readers in making some sense of one of history's most disturbing experiences.

Above all, I thank my family for their support. My sons, Eric and Christian, and daughters, Jennifer and Kathryn, were patient and tolerant of their father's time in his study. In addition to providing editorial assistance, my wife Diane was a loving companion who helped me keep the rigors of writing a book in their proper perspective. In truth, I could not have written this book without her.

Jackson J. Spielvogel

I would like to acknowledge Jackson Spielvogel for mentoring and befriending me all those years ago, and for trusting in me the continuation of this book. Both Richard Landes of Boston University and the Center for Millennial Studies and Charles Strozier of John Jay College and the Center on Terrorism encouraged my work on the apocalyptic, millenarian, and messianic aspects of Nazism. I thank you for all the support over the years. I am indebted to my father Richard for instilling in me a love of history and my mother Duane for a love of life. I dedicate my work to their memory. Finally, Rachel Stehle has given me the love, patience, and support I need to continue my work in a subject that is, at times, all too dark.

David Redles

About the Authors

Jackson Spielvogel is associate professor emeritus of history at the Pennsylvania State University. He received his Ph.D. from the Ohio State University, where he specialized in Reformation history under Harold J. Grimm. His articles and reviews have appeared in such journals as *Moreana, Journal of General Education, Catholic Historical Review, Archiv für Reformationsgeschichte,* and *American Historical Review.* He has also contributed chapters or articles to *The Social History of the Reformation, The Holy Roman Empire: A Dictionary Handbook, Simon Wiesenthal Center Annual of Holocaust Studies,* and *Utopian Studies.* His work has been supported by fellowships from the Fulbright Foundation for Study and Research in Nürnberg, Germany, and the Foundation for Reformation Research. At Penn State, he helped inaugurate the Western civilization courses as well as a popular course on Nazi Germany. He is the author of *Western Civilization,* published in 1991 (seventh edition, 2009). He is the coauthor (with William Duiker) of *World History,* first published in 1998 (sixth edition, 2010), and *The Essential World History* (third edition, 2008).

Professor Spielvogel has won five major universitywide teaching awards. He held the Penn State Teaching Fellowship, the university's most prestigious teaching award, in 1988–1989. In 1996 he won the Dean Arthur Ray Warnock Award for Outstanding Faculty Member and in 2000 the Schreyer Honors College Excellence in Teaching Award.

He has been happily married since 1962 to Diane Laughlin, his high school sweetheart. Jack and Diane have four children and six grandchildren.

David Redles received his Ph.D. in history from the Pennsylvania State University and is currently associate professor of history at Cuyahoga Community College in Cleveland, Ohio. He is author of *Hitler's Millennial Reich: Apocalyptic Belief and the Search for Salvation* (hardcover: 2005, paperback: 2008). He has also contributed essays to the following publications: *The Paranoid Apocalypse: A Hundred-Year Retrospective on the Protocols of the Elders of Zion*, Richard Landes and Steven T. Katz, eds. (2011); *The Oxford Handbook of Millennialism*, Catherine Wessinger, ed. (2011); *The Fundamentalist Mindset: Psychological Reflections on Religion, Violence, and History*, Charles B. Strozier, James W. Jones, and David M. Terman, eds. (2010); *End of Days: Essays on the Apocalypse from Antiquity to Modernity*, Karolyn Kinane and Michael A. Ryan, eds. (2009); and *War in Heaven/Heaven on Earth: Theories of the Apocalyptic*, Glen McGhee and Stephen O'Leary, eds. (2005).

Introduction

The advent of Nazism in the 1920s and 1930s shocked many Europeans who believed that World War I had been fought to make the "world safe for democracy." Indeed, Nazism was only one, although the most important, of a number of similar-looking fascist movements in Europe between World War I and World War II. While Nazism, like the others, owed much to the impact of World War I, it also needs to be viewed in the context of developments in Europe in the late nineteenth and early twentieth centuries.

EUROPE IN THE NINETEENTH CENTURY

Many Europeans perceived the nineteenth century as an age of progress based on the growth of rationalism, secularism, and materialism. One English social philosopher claimed that progress was not an "accident, but a necessity," which would enable humans to "become perfect." By the end of the nineteenth century, however, there were voices who challenged these optimistic assumptions. They spoke of human irrationality and the need for violence to solve human problems. Nazism would later draw heavily upon this antirational mood and reject the rationalist and materialist views of progress.

The major ideas that dominated European political life in the nineteenth century seemed to support the notion of progress. Liberalism professed belief in a constitutional state and the basic civil rights of every individual. Nazism would later reject liberalism and assert the rights of the state over individuals. Nationalism, predicated on the nation as the focus of people's loyalty, became virtually a new religion for Europeans in the nineteenth century. Although nationalism was a liberalizing force in the first half of the nineteenth century because of its stress on the freedom and right of separate peoples to have their own nations, in the second half of the century it became a chauvinistic force that encouraged the right of some nationalities to dominate others. Tied to the new mass politics, popular nationalism came to destroy nineteenth-century liberal values, fostering fanaticism and violence at the expense of reasoned debate and compromise. Along with this extreme nationalism came a virulent racism, commonly in the form of anti-Semitism, that insisted on the right of a race to maintain its purity by excluding the Jews. Nazism would champion nationalism and place anti-Semitism at the heart of its own ideology. Advocating leadership and hierarchy, Nazism would also react against the nineteenth- and twentieth-century development of political democracy with its practice of universal manhood suffrage. The granting of political rights to the masses by the upper- and middle-class leaders of society had been intended to prevent the radicalization of the masses from below. But the advent of new demagogues who knew how to manipulate mass sentiment created the potential for strong antidemo-cratic movements. Another nineteenth-century political ideology, conservatism, played only a moderate role in the development of Nazism, which generally allied itself with conservative forces for purely opportunistic reasons.

Nineteenth-century European civilization underwent a tremendous transformation as a result of the Industrial Revolution. Industrialization led to increased urbanization, a new class structure, and new values. By the end of the nineteenth century, 50 percent of Europeans lived in cities, which were seen by many as places of alienation and deperson-alization. A new industrial middle class emerged and soon allied itself with the traditional conservative landed aristocratic classes. Moreover, the industrial factory system created a huge urban working class. Many workers were eventually attracted to the Marxian socialist movement in the hope of bettering their condition. It is no accident that Nazism would try to win over workers by appealing to both nationalism and socialism (Nazi = National Socialist German Workers' Party), even though its brand of socialism was far removed from Marxian socialist doctrines. Finally, the products of industrialism dazzled Europeans and led to an increased faith in science and technological achievements, further reinforc-ing the feeling of progress. The Industrial Revolution, however, led to social discontent as well. The workers had their socialist trade unions and parties to work for better condi-tions, but often members of the middle class, and especially the lower middle class, felt threatened by the rapid changes in society. Their fear of economic decline and loss in social status to the proletariat would lead many of them to support the Nazis as champions of a hierarchical social order that would preserve traditional class positions. The lower middle class would be one source of support for Nazism, although ultimately they would draw support from all strata of society.

Internationally, Europeans saw themselves as experiencing an age of progress in the nineteenth century. Since 1815, wars had been localized or contained by agreement of the great powers. Europe developed a balance-of-power politics based on alliances that kept the peace but at the same time increased rivalry among the states. After 1870, imperialism added to the competition. European technological progress enabled Europeans to carve up almost all of Africa and dominate the Middle East and Asia. Militarism, expressed especially in the formation of large armies, increased dramatically. Imperialistic adven-tures led to new rivalries, culminating in World War I. It was the results of World War I that spurred the rise of Nazism in Germany.

IMPERIAL GERMANY

Germany entered the nineteenth century as a divided state and did not become united until 1871. An earlier attempt at unification in the revolution of 1848, when the forces of liberalism and nationalism were combined, failed miserably. Unification was finally accomplished under the militaristic north German state of Prussia, whose policies were dominated by its strong and confident minister-president, Otto von Bismarck.

Bismarck and the New Germany

Bismarck unified Germany by force, using the methods of *Realpolitik*—a policy of real-ism. One of the great practitioners of *Realpolitik*, he gave a compelling explanation of the term in his famous address to the Prussian parliament in 1862: "The great questions of the day will not be settled by speeches and majority decisions—that was the great mistake of 1848 and 1849—but by blood and iron."[1] After isolating each of them, Bismarck and Prussia successively defeated Denmark, Austria, and France to achieve a united German state in 1871, with the Prussian king as the new German emperor. Bismarck managed to separate nationalism from liberalism and wed it to his own conservatism, but even German liberals were not unhappy because of his success. One old liberal proclaimed:

> I cannot shake off the impression of this hour. I am no devotee of Mars; I feel more attached to the goddess of beauty and the mother of graces than to the powerful god of war, but the trophies of war exercise a magic charm even upon the child of peace. One's view is involun-tarily chained and one's spirit goes along with the boundless row of men who acclaim the god of the moment—success.[2]

Prussian leadership also meant the victory of authoritarian over liberal–democratic, con-stitutional sentiments in the creation of the German state.

The new German state established in 1871 began with a constitution that provided for a federal system with a bicameral legislature. The upper house, or Bundesrat, contained representatives from the twenty-five states that made up the German Empire. Individual states, such as Prussia and Bavaria, kept their own kings, post offices, and armies in peace-time. The lower house, known as the Reichstag, was elected on the basis of universal manhood suffrage, which created the potential for the growth of political democracy. This potential remained unfulfilled, however, until Germany's defeat in World War I. Ministerial responsibility, an important component part of political democracy, was excluded from the German system. Ministers of government, among whom the chancellor (a position held by Bismarck until 1890) was the most important, were held accountable not to the Reichstag but to the German emperor. The emperor also controlled the armed forces, foreign policy, and internal administration. As chancellor, Bismarck worked to maintain the strong position of the emperor and to prevent the growth of a functional parliamen-tary system and responsible political parties. The German army, a powerful institution, supported the traditional monarchical and aristocratic institutions and operated under a general staff responsible only to the emperor. Thus, the army was independent of the chancellor and the Reichstag, virtually a state within the state and a hindrance to the evolu-tion of German democracy.

The Reign of Wilhelm II

The new imperial German state established by Bismarck continued as an authori-tarian, conservative, "military–bureaucratic power state" during the reign of Kaiser (Emperor) Willhelm II (1888–1918). The young emperor, who cashiered Bismarck in

---

[1]Quoted in Otto Pflanze, *Bismarck and the Development of Germany: The Period of Unification, 1815–1871* (Princeton, N.J., 1963), p. 177.

[2]Ibid, p. 327.

1890, was politically unskilled, intellectually unstable, and prone to verbal aggressiveness and tactless remarks, as evidenced in his rejoinder to young recruits that they must shoot at their parents when their emperor commanded them to do so. The emperor was joined by a small group (about twenty) of powerful men who determined government policy.

During Wilhelm's reign, Germany became the greatest industrial and military power on the Continent. Its population rose dramatically from 41 million in 1871 to almost 68 million in 1914. New social configurations emerged rapidly. By 1910, over 50 percent of German workers were employed in industry; only one-third of the work-force remained in agriculture. As large numbers of workers fled from rural to urban areas in search of jobs, cities mushroomed in size and number. But rapid changes in Wilhelmine Germany led to serious strains, producing a society torn between modern-ization and traditionalism.

With industrial and urban expansion came demands for more political participa-tion and a noticeable shift to the left politically. Two of the major parliamentary groups of imperial Germany, the liberals and conservatives, experienced a decline in Reichstag seats from 1890 to 1912. While the Center Party, dedicated to Catholic interests, maintained a steady 20 percent of Reichstag delegates, it was the Social Democratic Party (SPD) that experienced the most rapid growth to become the largest party by 1912. The SPD claimed the allegiance of many workers and managed to maintain unity despite an ideological split between those Social Democrats who favored Marxian revolutionary activity and those who believed in cooperating with the parliamentary system to gain reforms. The growing strength of the Socialists frightened the elites of imperial Germany, who blamed organized labor for their own problems. Under Wilhelm, the role of the Reichstag and political parties was expanded, as the emperor and his chancellors attempted to gain a parliamentary coalition on crucial issues. But parliamentary authoritarianism did not come easily. There was considerable underlying sentiment for reforms that would lead to greater democratization. Conservative forces were unwilling, however, to permit it, and imperialistic adventures came to be seen as an avenue to maintain their position.

During the reign of Emperor Wilhelm II, Germany pursued *Weltpolitik* (world pol-icy), an activist foreign policy aimed at finding Germany's "place in the sun." Germany felt a need to catch up with other world powers and assumed a natural right to hegemony over central Europe and a share in the colonial, economic, and political division of the world. Imperialism was favored by both the landowning nobility and the representatives of heavy industry, two of the powerful ruling groups in Wilhelmine Germany. For both groups, expansionism would stabilize domestic politics by creating less need for further democratization. However, for underrepresented groups, such as German Jews, further democratization was exactly what was needed.

German Anti-Semitism: Religious, Political, and Racial

In Germany, there were three primary variants of anti-Semitism. One was rooted in medieval Christian opinion, which held the Jews responsible for the death of Christ. This belief developed into what may be characterized as a religious anti-Semitism, or more precisely, anti-Judaism. Medieval Christian policy emphasized converting the Jews to save these unbelievers from eternal damnation. Conversion attempts gradually used more force, especially to separate Jews from Christians. However, the failure of conversion resulted in greater fear of Jews and after the thirteenth century led to the ultimatum to either convert or face expulsion.

In Germany this Christian anti-Semitism was especially virulent in the works of Martin Luther, the sixteenth-century Protestant reformer and national hero. In his earlier years Luther had urged mutual tolerance and brotherly love between Christians and Jews. He came to feel that many Jews would willingly convert to Christianity once the worst abuses in Christianity had been corrected by the Reformation. When they refused to do so, Luther became increasingly impatient. In 1543 he published a bitter tract against them entitled *The Jews and Their Lies*, in which he characterized the Jews as criminals desiring world rule, killers of Christ and Christendom, and a plague to Germany. To smother this "pestilence," he advocated burning Jews' synagogues and schools, destroying their houses, removing their "cash and treasure of gold and silver," eliminating their prayer books and Talmudic writings, abolishing safe conduct for Jews on the highways, and, "if this be not enough, let them be driven like mad dogs out of the land...."[3] Luther's vehement attacks on the Jews were frequently recalled and widely publicized by the Nazis. The original edition of *The Jews and Their Lies* would be exhibited in a special glass case at Nuremberg party rallies.

Another source of anti-Semitism was the powerful ideology of German nationalism, which was awakened by the Napoleonic conquests and which led to a movement in the nineteenth century for the unification of the separate German states. The new imperial German state, created in 1871, tended to view Jews as outsiders, constituting a state within a state. Heinrich von Treitschke, the distinguished professor of history at the University of Berlin, expressed this political anti-Semitism in a phrase coined in 1879, "the Jews are our misfortune," thus assisting the growth of the anti-Semitic movement. The years 1875–1895 saw the formation of German political anti-Semitism. This anti-Semitism had a new foundation. As Hermann Ahlwardt, a member of the anti-Semitic faction in the Reichstag, pointed out, they were fighting the Jews because of race, not religion, "A Jew who was born in Germany does not thereby become a German; he is still a Jew."[4] His solution was to separate the Jews from the Germans. This type of racial anti-Semitism meant that conversion to Christianity could no longer provide a solution to the so-called Jewish Question, as they were seen as being racially Jewish. Therefore, neither conversion nor assimilation could ever make Jews true Germans.

During the two decades prior to World War I, when German imperialism was at its height, political anti-Semitism began to decline and lost its mass appeal. It was revived, however, during World War I. After the war, as we will see, although the constitution of the new Weimar Republic granted complete legal equality to all Jews, anti-Semitism continued to flourish. It would be especially strong among the representatives of the conservative German National People's Party (DNVP) and other right-wing parties such as the National Socialists.

Religious, political, and racial anti-Semitism, then, were prominent features of modern German life. It is, of course, difficult to ascertain how deep and how widespread anti-Semitism was in Germany. It was surely not unique to Germany, as its presence in other countries well demonstrates.

Another related development during the reign of Wilhelm II was Germany's confrontation with new, radicalized, right-wing politics. National Socialism would arise

---

[3]Martin Luther, *Luther's Works* (Philadelphia, 1957–1983), 47, pp. 266–292.

[4]Quoted in Paul Massing, *Rehearsal for Destruction: A Study of Political Anti-Semitism in Imperial Germany* (New York, 1949), p. 304.

from the right-wing, *völkisch*-nationalist groups that had established themselves in impe-rial Germany at the end of the nineteenth century and the beginning of the twentieth century. The concept of the *Volk* (nation, people, or race) had been an underlying idea in German history since the beginning of the nineteenth century. Inherent in it was a feeling of the superiority of German culture and the idea of a universal mission for the German people. This meant that individuals must be willing to sacrifice themselves for the higher claims of the *Volk*. *Völkisch* ideology consequently emphasized the idea of a *Volksgemeinschaft*, a people's community that would unite all Germans in a racially pure community. The Jews—portrayed as an alien people harmful to the community—would be excluded.

In the second half of the nineteenth century, *völkisch* ideology began to stress anti-Semitism in racial–biological terms. The writings of Julius Langbehn, who affirmed that race, or the "power of the blood," was more important than state were especially popular in this respect. He advocated a German elitist state based on race that would exclude the Jews. Biological racism stemmed from a pseudoscientific interpretation of the concepts of Charles Darwin. Races, like species of animals, had evolved through time. Some were superior, others were inferior. Like the struggle for existence in the natural world, racial conflict was considered a part of human societies. The works of the Frenchman Arthur de Gobineau and the Englishman Houston Stewart Chamberlain, who chose to become a German citizen, popularized the idea of race as the crucial factor in human history. Through his book *The Foundations of the Nineteenth Century* (1900), Chamberlain made a special impact on Germany. He argued that the Aryans (a term borrowed from lin-guists, who used it to identify people speaking a common set of languages known as Indo-European), of which the Germans were the foremost element, were the true creators of culture, whereas the Jews were simply parasites who destroyed culture. The Aryan race must be prepared to fight for civilization itself. Because of such biological arguments, the Jews were now viewed in racial terms: All Jews supposedly had immutable characteristics harmful to the *völkisch* state that bore Aryan culture. This identification of nation with race, and the subsequent belief that Jews were therefore not members of the new German nation, occasionally led to acts of extreme anti-Jewish violence. A blend of socioeconomic crisis, radical anti-Semitic agitation, and rumor mongering by scurrilous newspapers gen-erated spasmodic episodes of anti-Jewish violence throughout the nineteenth and early twentieth centuries in Germany.

Völkisch ideology, grounded in racial anti-Semitism, experienced new life during the period of depression and economic upheaval from the 1870s to the 1890s. To a great extent, Jews were scapegoats for the new economic and social problems created by indus-trialization and urbanization. Especially affected were elements of the traditional lower middle class—the farmers, artisans, and shopkeepers—who felt threatened by the new economic forces, which they identified largely with the Jews. Reared on preindustrial social ideals, many members of the traditional lower middle class blamed Jewish capital-ists for all the problems of modern urban-industrial life.

In the 1890s, *völkisch* ideology combined with militant German nationalism to give rise to various nationalist pressure groups that tried to establish mass support for national goals. Groups such as the Pan-German League and the Navy League were strongly anti-socialist and antiliberal. Despite large membership lists, they did not have direct political influence. They did provide an outlet for a considerable minority that was unwilling to participate in the regular political parties. This minority preferred a moral crusade for nationalist ideals to participation in electoral politics, and in the process they radicalized right-wing politics. The Pan-German League was perhaps the best-known pressure group. It was antidemocratic and stressed extreme nationalism and the use of social imperialism to overcome social divisions and unite all classes. The Pan-German League attacked Socialists and especially the Jews as the destroyers of national community. The traditional conservative right, fearing the tremendous growth of the Socialists and unable to gain a mass following, found itself making common cause with these radical right-wing groups, giving them respectability and keeping anti-Semitism alive in German politics. During the war, radical right-wing groups, a new force in themselves, pushed for territorial annexations. Nazism would emerge as one among a number of radical, right-wing, anti-Semitic *völkisch* groups motivated by Germany's defeat in the war to struggle even further for expansion and against "pernicious world Jewry."

THE IMPACT OF WORLD WAR I

The imperial Germany of Wilhelm II came to an end with its defeat in World War I (1914–1918). The war had caused a declining standard of living for the Germans, although there were noticeable gaps between rich and poor. While defense industries and the skilled laborers who worked in them prospered, price controls hurt both farmers and producers of consumer goods. Civil servants also suffered noticeably. Because the value of the mark fell by 50 percent during the war, middle-class plans for postwar financial security from lifetime savings and the purchase of war bonds were dashed, adding to the growing insecurity of middle-class individuals. National Socialism would make vigorous appeals to these groups adversely affected by the war.

World War I shattered the liberal, rational, democratic society of nineteenth- and early twentieth-century Europe. The enormous suffering and the death of almost 10 million people shook traditional society to its foundations and destroyed, for many, the whole idea of progress. New propaganda techniques manipulated entire populations into maintaining involvement in a senseless slaughter. The suffering of the masses in turn intensified their demands for greater material and political rewards, which evoked a fear of social revolution on the part of the established classes. This anxiety manifested itself in the red scare, or the fear of communist revolution. Nazism would appeal to these fears and project itself as the savior of the German nation from the evil force of communism.

World War I was a total war, the first of its kind. Total war meant complete mobilization of resources and populations and increased government centralization of power over the lives of citizens. The need for quick decision making seemed to necessitate an authoritarian system unhindered by democratic debate, and political rights became limited. World War I made the idea of strong central authority a way of life and certainly one that the Nazis would later advocate. Civil liberties, such as the freedoms of speech, press, assembly, and movement, were restricted in the name of national security. Military censorship of war news often kept the German populace ignorant of the true course of the war, and the sudden capitulation in 1918 shocked many, feeding into the myth that the war had not been lost, but that victory had been stolen. Lack of knowledge of atrocities committed by the German army in both the Western- and Eastern-occupied territories also made the harshness of the Versailles Treaty difficult for most Germans to comprehend. Economic freedom was curtailed by the desire of governments to plan production and distribution, allocate raw materials, and ration consumer goods. Food shortages became rampant toward the end of the war. Twelve-year-old Elfriede Kuhr of Schneidemühl, Germany, wrote in her journal on September 10, 1917:

> Everyone is talking about food at the moment—and about the need to stock up. No one wants to go through another winter like the last one, the "turnip winter." Fortunately they have a cellar full of potatoes at Alte Bahnhofstrasse 17 (they bought a whole load off Herr Kenzler), as well as turnips. They have almost no bread, however, nor cooking fat. Their diet is utterly drab and monotonous.

A year later the monotony turned to tragedy for Elfriede. Writing in the third person on August 17, 1918:

> A summer's night. Warmth. He is dead now, that little boy of six months who had been Elfriede's favourite. The emaciated child died in her arms yesterday: "He simply laid his head, which seemed much too big for his skeletal body, on my arm and died without as much as a rattle or a sigh."[5]

Thousands of other Germans would starve to death as the war sputtered to an end.

World War I created a lost generation, consisting of war veterans who had become accustomed to violence and a culture of mass killing. Military life had seemed exciting and offered a comradeship that gave meaning to life. Unable to adjust to peacetime conditions, some veterans joined paramilitary groups, such as the Nazi Stormtroopers, which seemed to offer the discipline, adventure, and camaraderie of their war years. These men and many of their countrymen were fiercely nationalistic and eager to restore the national interests they felt had been betrayed in the peace treaties. The myth of the war experience, which promoted the notion of German soldiers united at the front for defense of the nation, no longer divided by class, estate, and religion, later would be exploited by postwar nationalists, including the Nazis, as a vision of the coming new Germany.

Finally, World War I ended the age of European domination of world affairs. The transition point was 1917, when the Russian Revolution created the new Soviet Union and the United States entered the war. The termination of this European age was not apparent to all, however, for it was obscured by two developments—American isolationism and the Soviets' withdrawal from world affairs and nurturance of their own socialist system. These developments were only temporary, but they created a political vacuum that was filled by Nazi Germany's attempt to establish European and world hegemony. This attempt failed only with the reentry of the United States and the Soviet Union into European affairs.

Events moved quickly in the fall of 1918 to produce the end of the imperial German state. To avoid certain defeat as a result of the entry of fresh American troops into the war, army leaders Paul von Hindenburg and Erich Ludendorff sought an armistice even though German armies were still fighting outside Germany. It was realized that the Allies would grant better terms if German imperial authoritarianism were eliminated, so democratic reforms designed to establish a liberal, democratic monarchy were instituted. Implicit among the Allied demands, however, was the abdication of the emperor. But Wilhelm II refused to abdicate, and it took a revolution of soldiers, sailors, and workers (November Revolution) to force him to do so. Workers' and soldiers' councils (German versions of the Soviets of the Russian Revolution) were formed throughout Germany and began to

---

[5]Quoted in Peter Englund, *The Beauty and the Sorrow: An Intimate History of the First World War* (New York, 2011), pp. 392, 474.

supervise civilian and military administrations. Wilhelm II finally agreed to abdicate, and the Social Democrats under Friedrich Ebert took control and established a new republican government on November 9, 1918. Two days later, an armistice was signed to end the war. Unhappy with the course of the revolution, radical left-wing Socialists formed the German Communist Party (*Kommunistische Partei Deutschlands* or KPD) and staged a pitiful attempt at revolution in January 1919. This "second revolution," bloodily suppressed by the republican authorities, created a deep fear of communism among many Germans. After decades of authoritarian rule, Germany shakily embarked upon an experiment in democracy.

SUGGESTIONS FOR FURTHER READING

The history of Europe in the nineteenth century can be pursued in three valuable surveys by Matthew S. Anderson, *The Ascendancy of Europe 1815–1914,* 3rd ed. (Harlow, England, 2003); Robert Gildea, *Barricades and Borders: Europe 1800–1914,* 3rd ed. (Oxford, 2003); and Robin W. Winks and Joan Neuberger, *Europe and the Making of Modernity, 1815–1914* (Oxford, 2005). General surveys on modern Germany include Dietrich Orlow, *A History of Modern Germany, 1871 to Present,* 7th ed. (Boston, 2012); Gordon Craig, *Germany, 1866–1945* (Oxford, 1978); and David Blackbourn, *History of Germany, 1790–1918: The Long Nineteenth Century,* 2nd ed. (New York, 2003). Also useful are the essays found in Jonathan Sperber, ed., *Germany, 1800–1871* (Oxford and New York, 2004).

On the background to imperial Germany, see Otto Pflanze, *Bismarck and the Unification of Germany: The Period of Unification, 1815–1871* (Princeton, N.J., 1963). On the history of imperial Germany, see Wolfgang J. Mommsen, *Imperial Germany 1867–1918, Politics, Culture, and Society in an Authoritarian State* (New York, 1995); Volker Berghahn, *Imperial Germany, 1871–1914, Economy, Society, Culture, and Politics,* Revised and Expanded ed. (New York, 2005); Hans-Ulrich Wehler, *The German Empire, 1871–1918* (New York, 1997); Michael Stürmer, *The German Empire 1870–1918* (New York, 2000); Edgar Feuchtwanger, *Imperial Germany, 1850–1918* (London, 2001); Stephen J. Lee, *Imperial Germany 1871–1918* (New York, 1998); David Blackbourn, *Class, Religion, and Local Politics in Wilhelmine Germany* (New Haven, Conn., 1980); Thomas Rohkrämer, *A Single Communal Faith? The German Right from Conservatism to National Socialism* (New York, 2007); and Geoff Eley, *Reshaping the German Right: Radical Nationalism and Political Change After Bismarck* (Ann Arbor, Mich., 1991) and *From Unification to Nazism* (Boston, 1986). See also the essays in James Retallack, ed., *Imperial Germany, 1871–1918* (Oxford and New York, 2008); and Sven Oliver Müller and Cornelius Torp, eds., *Imperial Germany Revisited: Continuing Debates and New Perspectives* (New York, 2011).

For good introductions to the political world of Wilhelm II's Germany, see Thomas A. Kohut, *Wilhelm II and the Germans: A Study in Leadership* (New York, 1991); John C.G. Röhl, *The Kaiser and His Court: Wilhelm II and the Government of Germany* (New York, 1994), *Germany in the Age of Kaiser Wilhelm II* (New York, 1996), and *Wilhelm II: the Kaiser's Personal Monarchy, 1888–1900* (New York, 2004). German foreign policy of the imperial period is covered in Imanuel Geiss, *German Foreign Policy, 1871–1914* (Boston, 1976). On the growth of anti-Semitism as a political force, see Paul W. Massing, *Rehearsal for Destruction: A Study of Political Anti-Semitism in Imperial Germany* (New York, 1949); Peter C. Pulzer, *The Rise of Political Anti-Semitism in Germany and Austria,* rev. ed. (Cambridge, Mass., 1988); and Richard Levy, *The Downfall of the Anti-Semitic Political Parties in Imperial Germany* (New Haven, Conn., 1975). On the role of the Pan-German League, see Roger Chickering, *We*

Men Who Feel Most German: A Cultural Study of the Pan-German League 1886–1914 (London, 1984). On the connections between German nationalism and anti-Jewish violence, see Helmut Walser Smith, *The Continuities of German History: Nation, Religion, and Race Across the Long Nineteenth Century* (Cambridge, Mass., 2008) and his case study, *The Butcher's Tale: Murder and Anti-Semitism in a German Town* (New York, 2002). Also instructive are the essays in Christhard Hoffmann, Werner Bergmann, and Helmut Walser Smith, eds., *Exclusionary Violence: Antisemitic Riots in Modern Germany* (Ann Arbor, Mich., 2002).

On religious anti-Semitism, see Joshua Trachtenberg, *The Devil and the Jews: The Medieval Conception of the Jew and Its Relation to Modern Anti-Semitism* (Philadelphia, 1993); James Carroll, *Constantine's Sword: The Church and the Jews* (New York, 2001); and Robert Michel, *Holy Hatred: Christianity, Antisemitism, and the Holocaust* (New York, 2006). On the history of anti-Semitism in general, see Phyllis Goldstein, *A Convenient Hatred: The History of Antisemitism* (Brookline, Mass., 2012); Robert Wistrich, *Antisemitism: The Longest Hatred* (New York, 1992) and *A Lethal Obsession: Anti-Semitism from Antiquity to the Global Jihad* (New York, 2010); John Weiss, *Ideology of Death: Why the Holocaust Happened in Germany* (Chicago, 1996); Marvin Perry and Frederick Sweitzer, *Antisemitism: Myth and Hate from Antiquity to the Present* (New York, 2002); and Walter Laquer, *The Changing Face of Antisemitism: From Ancient Times to the Present Day* (New York, 2006). On the association of Jews with capitalism, see Matthew Lange, *Antisemitic Elements in the Critique of Capitalism in German Culture, 1850–1933* (Bern, 2007).

There is an enormous literature on World War I. A good starting point on the causes of the war can be found in the work by James Joll and Gordon Martel, *The Origins of the First World War,* 3rd ed. (New York, 2007); Richard F. Hamilton and Holger H. Herwig, *Decisions for War, 1914–1917* (Cambridge, Mass., 2004); Holger Afflerbach and David Stevenson, eds., *An Improbable War?: The Outbreak of World War I and European Political Culture Before 1914* (New York, 2007); William Mulligan, *The Origins of the First World War* (Cambridge, 2010) and Jack Beatty, *The Lost History of 1914: Reconsidering World War I* (New York, 2012). Especially important is the work of Fritz Fischer, who revived the question of German war guilt in *Germany's Aims in World War I* (New York, 1967); *World Power or Decline: The Controversy over Germany's Aims in World War I* (New York, 1974); and *War of Illusions: German Policies from 1911 to 1914* (New York, 1975). There are two good accounts of World War I in Martin Gilbert, *The First World War* (New York, 1994); and the lavishly illustrated book by Jay M. Winter, *The Experience of World War I* (New York, 1989). See also the brief work by Neil Heymann, *World War I* (Westport, Conn., 1997). For a history of the war that includes an extended discussion of the immediate postwar years see Eric Dorn Brose, *A History of the Great War: World War One and the International Crisis of the Early Twentieth Century* (New York, 2010). There is an excellent collection of essays on all facets of World War I in Hew Strachan, ed., *The Oxford Illustrated History of the First World War* (New York, 1998). On World War I and the effects on the German home front, see Roger Chickering, *Imperial Germany and the Great War, 1914–1918,* 2nd ed. (Cambridge, Mass., 2004); Benjamin Ziemann, *War Experience in Rural Germany: 1914–1923* (Oxford, 2006); Belinda Davis, *Home Fires Burning: Food, Politics, and Everyday Life in World War I Berlin* (Chapel Hill, N.C., 2000); Peter Englund, *The Beauty and the Sorrow: An Intimate History of the First World War* (New York, 2011); and Michael S. Neiberg, *Dance of the Furies: Europe and the Outbreak of World War I* (Cambridge, Mass., 2011). On the brutal German occupation policy in the Eastern and Western Fronts, see Vejas Liulevicius, *War Land on the Eastern Front: Culture, National Identity and German Occupation in World War I* (Cambridge, Mass., 2000), and Larry Zuckerman, *The Rape of Belgium: The Untold Story of World War I* (New York, 2004). On World War I as a deliberate war of cultural annihilation, both material and human, see Alan Kramer, *Dynamic of Destruction: Culture and Mass Killing in the First World War* (Oxford, 2007).

MySearchLab™ Connections

Study and Review

While the rise of Nazism shocked some observers, the movement had its roots in political trends in Continental Europe: nationalism, politicization of the social classes, and imperialism. These trends, combined with severe economic conditions, created conditions in the Weimar Republic in which Nazism could grow and flourish.

Read the Document

1. **Adolf Hitler, Excerpt from *Mein Kampf***
   This excerpt shows Hitler's rationale and the reasoning behind his anti-Semitic views and policies.

Read the Document

2. **The German Act of Confederation, 1814**
   This document is a prime example of the stirrings of the nationalism that would sweep Europe in the nineteenth and early twentieth centuries.

Read the Document

3. **William Graham Sumner, from *What the Social Classes Owe to Each Other* (1883)**
   This excerpt recommends the political approach of "minding one's own business." Many in the intellectual elite dismissed working-class demands for improved conditions as unnecessary, and argued and that the best position was to deal with problems as they occurred.

RESEARCH AND EXPLORE

Fascism evolved partly from the frustrations of the working class. The demand for improved living and working conditions exploded as a result of severe postwar inflation and shortages in Germany. This unfocused anger and a search for national pride after a humbling defeat allowed what had been a fringe movement to emerge as a real political force.

1. How did the workers' movements in post–Industrial Revolution Europe influence nationalistic policies in Germany? How did this contribute to the rise of fascism in Germany?

2. In which ways can German anti-Semitism be traced to Martin Luther? Without the writings of Martin Luther, might Catholic attitudes to the Jews have led to an equally high level of anti-Semitism among Germans?

3. Had Germany and Austria/Hungary won World War I, would Nazism have developed in Germany? In which ways were the extreme socioeconomic conditions of postwar Germany essential for the development of the Nazi party?

ADDITIONAL RESOURCES

The Unification of Germany, 1866–1871

Nazi Rally

2

Beginnings

Weimar Germany and the Rise of Hitler and Nazism

As a result of World War I, Germany experienced considerable internal disorder. Military defeat was especially devastating to the German people after four years of sacrifice and the assurances of their leaders that Germany was on the verge of victory over all foes. A humiliating peace treaty, which burdened Germany with enormous war reparations and total responsibility for the war, left Germans bitter and vengeful. Soon, new political parties arose to feed on the discontent. A small Bavarian rightist party known as the Nazis, under an obscure Austrian rabble-rouser named Adolf Hitler, created a stir in 1923 when it attempted to seize political power in southern Germany. Although it failed, this coup projected Adolf Hitler and the Nazis into national prominence. This rise of Hitler and the Nazis was directly related to the crises that beset the Weimar Republic from its very beginnings.

WEIMAR GERMANY

The Weimar Republic, Germany's experiment in parliamentary democracy, was established at the end of the war under arduous circumstances. The early Weimar Republic was beset with difficulties that a people unused to democratic practices could barely handle.

Repercussions of Defeat in Early Weimar

The new republican government, led by a coalition of Social Democrats (SPD), the Catholic Center Party, and German Democrats (DDP), was forced to accept the Treaty of Versailles in June 1919. This treaty was written by the victorious Allies without German involvement. The Germans thought it a harsh peace settlement and were especially dissatisfied with several provisions. In Article 231, the so-called war-guilt clause, the Germans had to accept responsibility for all the damage to which the Allied governments and their people were subjected as a consequence of the war "imposed upon them by the aggression of Germany and her allies." Consequently, the treaty required Germany to pay enormous reparations in both goods and money. Military provisions of the treaty also rankled: Germany was forced to reduce its army to one hundred thousand men, limit

Germany after World War I

its weapons, reduce its navy, and eliminate its air force. Germany was virtually disarmed. German territorial losses included colonies in Africa to Belgium, islands in the Pacific to Japan, the cession of Alsace and Lorraine to France, and large sections of Prussia to the new Polish state. German land west and as far as fifty kilometers east of the Rhine was established as a demilitarized zone, stripped of all offensive or defensive armaments or fortifications. Although the new democratic government vowed at first to resist such a dictated peace, it had no alternative but to accept the treaty imposed by the Allies. Rejecting it meant a renewal of the war, and even the army counseled against that.

  The German army played an important role in undermining the foundations of the Weimar Republic. The army had been instrumental in bringing an end to the war and the

German Empire. But army leaders publicly shunned any involvement in these events and helped to foster the "stab in the back" theory, later used so effectively by Hitler and the Nazis. According to this theory, the invincible German army had not really been defeated in the field, but stabbed in the back by civilian traitors. After all, no Allied soldier had entered German territory during the war. It was the new government, composed of unpatriotic Socialists (many of them Jews, according to Hitler's version of the myth), who had arranged the armistice, written the new democratic constitution, and signed the peace treaty. That such a myth could readily be accepted by millions of Germans did not augur well for the new German democracy. To many Germans the Weimar Republic appeared only as a temporary alternative. Radical leftists awaited a communist revolution that would overthrow the republic; army and aristocracy awaited the restoration of the Hohenzollern monarchy; extreme nationalists and racists such as the Nazis awaited an authoritarian order that would wipe out the shame of Versailles and establish a mighty German Empire. Although a majority of Socialists, many workers and Catholics, and a minority of the middle class supported the republic, they were faced with the other elements of society who were openly hostile to it.

Political Uncertainties

Initial difficulties might have been overcome, but the Weimar Republic was continually plagued by problems. One serious political problem was a dearth of truly outstanding democratic leaders. The republic's early leaders were actually quite able. Friedrich Ebert, who served as the first president, was a pragmatic politician whose socialist background did not prevent him from working with the former military elites. Gustav Stresemann, founder of the German People's Party (DVP), served as chancellor in 1923 and then as foreign minister until his death in 1929. Both Ebert and Stresemann were strong leaders who ably supported the republic, but both died in the 1920s. Upon Ebert's death in 1925, Paul von Hindenburg, a World War I military hero, was elected president. The Weimar constitution had established a democratic system in which the chancellor and cabinet ran the government but were responsible to the Reichstag, which was directly elected by universal suffrage. Fearing political instability, the architects of the new constitution had provided for a president, elected by the people for a seven-year term, who could dissolve the Reichstag, appoint and dismiss chancellors, and control the armed forces. Most important, however, in Article 48 the Weimar constitution provided that the president could rule by decree in an emergency, adding considerably to his or her potential power. Hindenburg was a traditional military man, monarchist in sentiment, and at heart distrustful of the republic and party politics.

Weimar Germany's political weakness was evident in party politics and resulted in a failure by politicians to achieve any effective party collaboration in ruling Germany. Each of the major parties that had formed the original Weimar ruling coalition—the SPD, DDP, and Center Party—suffered problems that weakened its effectiveness in governing. Although the SPD, the largest party in Weimar Germany, adhered to Marxist revolutionary theory, few members actually believed in revolution. The SPD was democratic in practice and remained loyal to the republic. But as a working-class party that continued to use Marxist slogans, it frightened the German middle classes, who feared communism. The SPD became increasingly a party of old men; in 1930, only 10 percent of its members were under twenty-five years of age. The DDP was unable to define themselves clearly enough to the electorate and had already experienced a serious decline in Reichstag seats by the early 1920s. In the late

1920s, they became increasingly antidemocratic in sentiment. The Center Party, predominantly Roman Catholic, cut across both class and regional lines by appealing to Catholics from all social groups and sections of the country. By the end of the 1920s, the new leadership of this party was also becoming increasingly antidemocratic.

Two other political parties, the German People's Party (DVP) and the German National People's Party (DNVP), moved in an authoritarian direction by the end of the 1920s. The DVP, founded in 1919 by Gustav Stresemann, was predominantly a middle-class party that was occasionally willing to work with the Socialists in the Reichstag to avoid political instability. The DVP was eventually taken over by extremely conservative business circles who tended to favor antidemocratic positions. Until the advent of the Nazis, the DNVP was the strongest right-wing opponent of the Weimar Republic. Its followers came from the landed aristocracy, the upper middle class, and big business. With the election of Alfred Hugenberg, who controlled much of the press and film industry, as party chief in 1928, the DNVP became unalterably opposed to Weimar democracy and wished to establish a strong, nationalistic, authoritarian state that would eliminate the Communists and Socialists from German political life.

The existence of numerous political parties, no one of which had a majority, necessitated the formation of coalition governments to create ruling majorities. This system was inherently unstable. Between February 1919 and June 1928, there were fifteen separate cabinets, none lasting longer than eighteen months and some less than three months. The original Weimar coalition of the SPD, DDP, and Center Party dissolved upon the decline of the DDP. There was a deeper problem as well. Political parties in Germany were tightly knit organizations that cared primarily about the specific interests of the people represented by them; they made little attempt to appeal to others. Party politics tended, then, to reflect the serious divisions already prevailing within German society. The revolutionary period from 1918 to 1920 left the socialist working class divided between those who supported the SPD and the new republic, and those who followed the Communists, and hoped to destroy it. Supporters of the Communist Party tended to be younger, less skilled, and more unemployed than those of the SPD. Labor groups, while designed to foster solidarity, had the effect of increasing social segmentation among workers. The working classes in general often found themselves in conflict with the interests of the middle class. For its part the middle class was also fragmented. The old middle class, centered on craftsmen and shopkeepers, was hit hard by the postwar economy as income decreased and prices increased. Politically it often found itself at odds with the new middle class of white-collar workers who had greater status and wealth and perceived themselves as distinct from the working classes. The various social classes became radicalized, as tensions created political divisions not only between classes, but also within them. These differences left little room for flexibility and made the political parties unwilling to compromise the interests of their constituencies. One man who became a Nazi at this time was frustrated by such party factionalism, complaining:

> One government alternated with another. Marxist mass gatherings! The citizenry was splintered into smaller and smaller parties. Program upon program swirled through the air. A completely uniform and clear direction was lacking. It appeared impossible in this witch's temple to find one's way from one slogan to another. The Volk was fissured in interests and opinions, in classes and estates—a plaything of enemy powers and nations.[1]

[1]Quoted in David Redles, *Hitler's Millennial Reich: Apocalyptic Belief and the Search for Salvation* (New York, 2005), p. 20.

The ensuing difficulties in forming a coalition from among such factions resulted in continual cabinet crises and stalemated parliamentary politics. Frequently, coalitions depended on the support of the conservative parties, which were actually opposed to the republic. It was no surprise that by 1930 President Hindenburg, who with much reluctance tried to work with this system of petty party politics, became willing to avoid the stalemate in the Reichstag by allowing a new chancellor, Heinrich Brüning of the Center Party, to form a government that relied on the emergency decrees of the president instead of a parliamentary majority. This ominous precedent signaled the beginning of the end for German democracy.

The young republic suffered additional political turmoil in the form of attempted uprisings and attacks from both the left and the right. On the left, the German Communist Party (KPD) espoused a Marxist revolutionary orthodoxy that called for the overthrow of the decadent Weimar government. A Communist putsch (coup) was attempted early in 1919, but was quickly crushed. In April 1919, a group of Communists established a Soviet Republic (in imitation of the Soviet Union) in Bavaria. By May, it had been bloodily suppressed by the regular army and the *Freikorps* (Free Corps). The latter were bands of World War I veterans who were unable to give up fighting and adjust to civilian life. The Free Corps were recruited by the army and government to provide armed forces that could maintain law and order. The story of Josef Schulz, a veteran and later Nazi, reflects this process. The end of the war, which Josef clearly believed Germany had not really lost, and the forced reduction of the military by the Versailles Treaty left him unemployed, with little assistance from the much-vaunted Weimar welfare state. The sight of the Allied occupation, coupled with bands of German communists, called Spartacists, roaming the streets, left him angry and frustrated:

> 1918—collapse. Instant unemployment. There was no assistance. The "victor" marched in. The Rhineland occupied. Americans in Linz. In unoccupied Spartacists raged. I came as a volunteer orderly with a medical transport to Stettin in early 1919. Upon the return journey I saw on a placard in Berlin a proclamation: "Who will save the Fatherland? Freikorps Lützow! Join Freikorps Lützow!" Rootless and jobless, without even returning home, I joined Freikorps Lützow in Berlin.[2]

In truth, many such Free Corps units became "roving bands of armed killers," who fought not to save the republic but to crush communism and protect their German fatherland.

An attack on the Weimar Republic from rightist political forces occurred in the Kapp Putsch in 1920, led by a Prussian civil servant named Wolfgang Kapp and a former general, Walther von Lüttwitz. This putsch was an attempt by right-wing elements to overthrow the government and install a rightist dictatorship. It failed miserably when the trade unions called for a general strike, which brought life in Germany to a sudden stop. Hitler's Beer Hall Putsch in 1923, examined later in this chapter, was another example of a rightist attempt to overthrow the republic. These uprisings, from both the left and the right, made civil war seem a real possibility. The civil peace of 1914 was all but dead, and in its place stood a fragmented Germany, politically and socially.

[2]Ibid., p. 18.

Free Corps Recruitment Poster. "Who Will Save the Fatherland?" reads this poster for the Lützow Free Corps, formed in Berlin in 1919 and named after a famous Prussian volunteer force that fought Napoleon a century earlier. The Lützow Free Corps took an active part in violently repressing the communist revolution in Munich in 1919. *(Library of Congress Prints and Photographs Division [LC-USZC4-11641])*

Basic Structural Problems

One of the lessons learned by the government in these revolts was that it could rely on the regular army (the Reichswehr) only when it was in the interests of the army to lend its support. This illustrates another of the republic's problems—its unwillingness or inability to change the basic institutional structure of Germany. The army was never really controlled by the republican government and operated virtually as a state within a state. Army officers received higher salaries than their civil service counterparts, and the army itself retained much of its traditional prestige. Institutions other than the military failed to serve the new democracy faithfully. Judges, teachers, and government bureaucrats had not been ousted from office by the new government and replaced by individuals favorable to the republic. Teachers in universities and elementary and secondary schools continued to teach the values of the old imperial German system to the young. Judges and bureaucrats stayed in power and not only talked against the republic but used their positions to undermine democracy from within. One intellectual, Kurt Tucholsky, observed:

> When the Republic was created these same judges held over from the monarchy found it impossible to transfer their allegiance to the new organization of the state. Thus they entered into opposition and began to serve their own independent ideas of what they desired the state to be. They created a private law and subverted the public law of the Republic by refusing to administer justice in an equal manner to all people.[3]

In short, judges were not politically neutral, as is evident in a comparison of sentences imposed upon left- and right-wing revolutionaries in the Weimar Republic. In twenty-two cases of murder committed by the left, German judges sentenced ten people to death and seventeen to lengthy prison terms. Of the 354 cases of murder committed by the right, judges sentenced no one to death and one person to a long jail term.

Economic and Social Chaos

The Weimar Republic was faced with serious economic and social problems for most of its existence. Reparation payments constituted a burden that many Germans considered simply impossible, especially when the Inter-Allied Reparations Commission announced in 1921 that Germany's bill would be the staggering sum of 132 billion gold marks (equivalent to $35 billion at that time), payable in forty-two years. The government responded by developing a policy of fulfillment. By appearing to try in good faith to satisfy these reparation demands, the Germans hoped to prove to the Allies that the provisions were unfulfillable. They mistakenly thought that the Allies would then back down. This policy of fulfillment was especially unpopular with right-wing elements, who resented attempts at any cooperation with Allied governments. A staunch republican follower of this policy and foreign minister, Walter Rathenau, was assassinated in protest by right-wing extremists. Rathenau was also Jewish, and right-wing groups were especially fond of charging that it was the Jews who created and dominated the Weimar Republic.

Germany experienced runaway inflation in 1923. This was caused largely by war debts and the payment of reparations, but was intensified when the French occupied the industrial Ruhr region, ostensibly in retaliation for Germany's defaulting on reparation payments. To support a policy of passive resistance to the French, the government subsidized the idle population by printing more money. The inflation of the German mark soon became catastrophic. In 1914, 4.2 marks equaled $1; in 1919, it was 8.9 marks to the dollar. But by November 1, 1923, the ratio had reached 130 billion to 1, and by the end of November of the same year it had skyrocketed to an unbelievable 4.2 trillion. Evidence of runaway inflation was everywhere; housewives even used the worthless currency to light their household fires.

The social effects of the great inflation were devastating. People on fixed incomes, such as widows and orphans on pensions, retired elderly couples, army officers, teachers, and civil servants, watched their monthly stipends become worthless or their lifetime savings disappear. The government finally moved to stabilize the currency by creating the Rentenbank, which issued a new temporary currency, the Rentenmark, equal to 3 trillion

---

[3]Quoted in Paul Bookbinder, *Weimar Germany: The Republic of the Reasonable* (New York, 1996), p. 113.

The Effects of Inflation. By 1923, the value of the German mark had fallen so disastrously that the German housewife pictured here was using the worthless currency to light a fire in her cooking stove. *(Bettmann/Corbis)*

old marks. But even after extreme inflation ended, psychological scars remained. Many who were initially wary of democracy now distrusted it more than ever.

Shortly after ending the inflation madness, Germany experienced some relief from reparations. An international commission chaired by Charles Dawes, an American banker, reduced and stabilized Germany's reparation payments. The Dawes plan called for large loans to be granted to Germany to finance the payments. After the Dawes plan was enacted, American bank loans began to flow into Germany, helping to initiate a period of prosperity from 1924 to 1929. These loans financed the construction of public works, such as roads, stadiums and town halls, and other public buildings, and made possible the reconstruction of German industry through the building of new plants and machinery. By 1928, the German economy was operating at virtually full employment.

This period of prosperity was notable for political stability and foreign policy successes. The latter were due primarily to the efforts of Gustav Stresemann, leader of the DVP, who served as foreign minister until his death in 1929. Stresemann had first been opposed to the republic, but he came to feel that the collapse of the Weimar government would simply lead to a dictatorial regime by the extreme left or right. Dedicated to German nationalism, Stresemann wished to eliminate some of the restrictions placed on Germany by the peace of Versailles and to reestablish Germany as a strong power by peaceful cooperation with the Allied powers. In 1925, he signed the Locarno Treaties, which guaranteed Germany's new western borders with France and Belgium and opened the door to a new spirit of international cooperation. In the next year, Stresemann reestablished normal relations with other European countries when Germany entered the League of Nations.

Political stability paralleled these foreign policy achievements. A center-right coalition government lasted for four years. The 1928 elections resulted in a shift away from the right that benefited the SPD, which now took responsibility for forming a new coalition government. The election of Hindenburg as president in 1925 added to the political calm. Although a monarchist, Hindenburg accepted his new role and worked to uphold the Weimar system. The presence of the venerable war hero at the head of government reassured many Germans and created a grudging acceptance of the republic. It soon became apparent, however, that the newfound political stability was highly dependent on economic prosperity.

By 1929, Weimar Germany's brief period of prosperity was beginning to wear thin. Unemployment had already started to rise some time before the crash of the American stock market in October 1929. Germany was especially affected by the stock market failure because its prosperity was based on short-term loans, which were now hastily recalled by American bankers. German industrialists were forced to slow down their operations and fire workers. Public works projects were severely curtailed. Unemployment increased to 3 million in March 1930 and to 4.38 million by December of the same year. The coalition government led by the Socialist Hermann Müller resigned in March 1930 over the issue of funds for unemployment compensation. Heinrich Brüning now formed a new government that relied on Hindenburg's decrees rather than parliamentary democracy. The depression opened the door to social discontent, fear, and extremist parties. It was certainly not an accident that the Nazis and the Communists, extremists of right and left, respectively, had become two of the largest parties in the Reichstag by the end of 1930.

Weimar's Divided Culture

In *The Journey to the East*, Hermann Hesse, one of the greatest novelists of Weimar Germany, spoke of "this period since the world war, troubled and confused, yet, despite this, fertile."[4] Indeed, historians speak of Weimar Germany as a "cradle of cultural modernity." Germany after the war experienced an outburst of creative activity in art, music, literature, theater, and science that was second to none in German history. While many of the movements associated with Weimar culture, such as Bauhaus architecture, expressionism, psychoanalysis, and atonal music, really began in pre–World War I Germany and Austria, it was in the Weimar era, and especially in the decade of the 1920s, that these new ideas and practices directly influenced large numbers of people.

This cultural revolution was a product of both circumstances and policy. World War I had shattered German society, uprooting traditional values and freeing Germans to adopt new perspectives, which were soon generated by a large number of talented individuals. In addition, the republican government created a climate of freedom and encouragement for artists and intellectuals unlike that in any other European government.

Right-wing intellectuals, who favored a strong authoritarian state and opposed democracy, did not think much of the unprecedented political and cultural freedom fostered by the republican government. To them, "modern" Weimar culture was simply decadent. Some right-wing intellectuals, pointing to the relatively large number of Jewish avant-garde artists and intellectuals, portrayed Weimar's cultural decay as a conspiracy by world Jewry. Oswald Spengler, author of the influential book *The Decline of the West*,

---

[4]Hermann Hesse, *The Journey to the East* (New York, 1956), p. 4.

emphasized the decadence and decline of his society and encouraged anti-intellectualism and violence. In doing so, Spengler, like other right-wing intellectuals, prepared the way for Hitler, even if they themselves rejected Hitler once he came to power.

Left-wing intellectuals especially owed much to the tolerant environment provided their works by the new democratic system. But even some of these intellectuals rejected the Weimar Republic. They expected change and planned to play an important role in the new state. The *Weltbühne*, the most influential of the left-wing journals, espoused their fundamental causes: pacifism and an attack on militarism, sexual reform and freedom, and the abolition of capital punishment. When the government ignored these cherished goals, some left-wing intellectuals shrilly denounced the republic in attacks that further sapped the strength of the Weimar government. Even the intellectuals who accepted the republic did so grudgingly. The historian Hans Delbrück expressed it well: "One serves the Republic but one does not love it."[5]

Weimar's modern culture was evident in art, literature, theater, and music. Dadaism and expressionism in art gave rise to new forms and unconventional techniques that mirrored inner experiences and aroused emotional involvement. Perhaps the most original artistic style to emerge at this time was the *neue Sachlichkeit* (New Objectivity). An offshoot of the expressionist movement, these artists deliberately used cartoonish and occasionally grotesque styles to simultaneously portray and satirize Weimar society. Otto Dix, a World War I veteran and postwar social critic, painted in this style. His work often centered on disfigured veterans, street prostitutes, and other social outcasts. Some art critics found this style fitting for the times. Carl Einstein wrote that "Dix gives this era—which is only the caricature of one—a resolute and technically sound kick in its swollen belly, wrings confessions of vileness from it, and produces an upright depiction of its people, their sly faces grinning an array of stolen mugs."[6] Conservative critics, however, were repulsed by this style, which only seemed to glorify the cultural degeneracy they saw around them. Paul Schultze-Naumberg characterized the Weimar scene in this way:

> Were one to name the symbols that find expression in the majority of the paintings and sculptures of our period, they would be the idiot, the prostitute, and the sagging breast. One has to call things by their right name. Spreading out here before us is a genuine hell of inferior human beings, and one sighs in relief upon leaving this atmosphere for the pure air of other cultures—[7]

Typical of much of Weimar culture, critics and patrons were divided between those who saw in the new style a penetrating critique of the many ills facing the new republic and those who saw it as simply another sign of the times, an era of degeneracy and chaos.

Among the numerous writers was Hermann Hesse, whose novels reflecting the influence of Carl Jung's psychological theories and Eastern religions made a large impact on German youth in the 1920s. The New Objectivity movement also played a role in literature, primarily in the use of reportage, a style that employed the short, clipped sentences popular in newspapers and magazines. This style was meant to reflect a detached, non-sentimental accounting of the darker aspects of modern, primarily urban, life. Topical

---

[5]Quoted in Walter Laqueur, *Weimar: A Cultural History* (New York, 1974), p. 4.

[6]Quoted in Anton Kaes, Martin Jay, and Edward Dimendberg, eds., *The Weimar Republic Sourcebook* (Berkeley, 1994), p. 490.

[7]Ibid., p. 498.

novels, such as Alfred Döblin's *Berlin Alexanderplatz*, stressed important social issues such as the emergence of the white-collar workers, the trauma of mass unemployment, or life in the metropolis. These works were characterized by an emphasis on factual accuracy and used a straightforward language. Döblin believed that traditional narrative forms were inadequate modes for expressing the chaos of modernity. He preferred the stream-of-consciousness style of Joyce's *Ulysses*: "A part of today's image is the disconnectedness of his activity, of his existence as such, the fleeting quality, the restlessness."[8] However, for many others, finding the chaos of modern life depicted in disconnected and seemingly meaningless writing was hardly comforting. They desired order and respite from chaos, not its celebration.

More traditional novels, of course, were still being written. Their subjects were often escapist in nature, and given the many traumas of the Weimar era, perhaps this is not surprising. The topical themes of the New Objectivity, with its emphasis on exposing the seamy, brutal, and often mindlessly dull nature of modern life, portrayed an existence that many would rather forget. Nationalist and populist novels turned to myth as an escape from such harsh realities. New genres, such as science fiction and fantasy, appeared. Significantly, this literature was often utopian or dystopian, frequently exhibiting a telling blend of racism, apocalypticism, and messianism. Antiwar novels, in particular Ludwig Renn's *Krieg* (*War*) and Erich Maria Remarque's *Im Westen nichts Neues* (*All Quiet on the Western Front*), were not only popular but also much hated. Their initial success was soon eclipsed after 1930 by works glorifying war, including those by Franz Schauwecker, Hans Zöberlein, and Ernst Jünger. Many readers, seeing a world collapsing around them, yearned for their adolescent heroes, their battle-hardened saviors. The myth of the war experience, with its emphasis on masculine virtues and an appeal for national unity, became a desired, if not altogether real, world.

The New Objectivity, with its emphasis on exposing the ills of society and its desire to appeal to the masses, also found resonance in musical composition. The so-called *Gebrauchsmusik* (utilitarian music) was intended for practical ends, as composed for film, radio, or popular theater. The emphasis was on music for the masses, rather than high-brow music for the social elite. Like the art of the New Objectivity, *Gebrauchsmusik* blended social consciousness with new forms of expression. In classical music, composers such as Arnold Schönberg, Anton Webern, and Alban Berg created radically new forms of musical expression, using a twelve-tone scale and deliberately employing dissonance and atonality. Performances of Berg's 1925 opera *Wozzeck* caused near riots with its subject matter, the exploitation of the poor, and its revolutionary musical forms.

Other composers, such as Paul Hindemith, Kurt Weill, Hanns Eisler, and Ernst Krenek, attempted to translate the new music to a wider audience through the use of film, radio, the gramophone, and popular theater. Weill collaborated with writer Berthold Brecht to create *Zeitoper* (topical or contemporary opera), musical dramas that blended popular music, especially jazz, with so-called serious music. Weill condemned the usual separation of the smaller operatic audience from the larger theater audience, and hoped to bring these two together. The combination of new music with topically relevant librettos was designed to expose a naïve and corrupt bourgeois world. Theodor W. Adorno, writing about the Brecht/Weill opera *The Rise and Fall of the City of Mahagonny*, which satirizes capitalism above all, likened it to the novels of Kafka, where "the bourgeois world appears

[8]Ibid., p. 514.

absurd and displaced in that it is viewed from the hidden perspective of redemption, the bourgeois world is unmasked in Mahagonny as absurd when measured against a socialist world that itself remains concealed."[9] For Adorno, it was precisely the shocking nature of the music and the text that peels away the veneer of bourgeois sensibility. Out of the apocalypse of the bourgeois world, therefore, the new socialist world could be reconstructed. At its Leipzig premiere in 1930, and in subsequent debuts in Frankfurt and Berlin, chaos did in fact ensure, as riots orchestrated by the Nazis broke out. The dream of a socialist utopia was soon to fade as a different millennium, the thousand-year Reich, was soon to unfold.

Of all the fine arts, architecture exercised the most lasting influence internationally. The Bauhaus school of art, architecture, and design—founded in 1919 at Weimar by Walter Gropius, a Berlin architect—exerted a major influence on the design of modern buildings and furniture. Gropius urged his followers to foster a new union of arts and crafts in order to create the buildings and objects of the future. According to Bauhaus philosophy, modern buildings should be functional, simple, yet beautiful structures, unencumbered by superfluous decoration. While the simple functionality led to a severity of form that was off-putting to many, it was largely successful in achieving its stated aims. Increasingly, Bauhaus moved in the direction of utilitarian housing projects, as well as the mass production of furnishing for those units. However, for many critics, the new architecture was nothing more than cultural Bolshevism, a soulless monstrosity reflective of a sterile world.

Weimar Germany also established the norms of modernism in popular culture. Germany produced more films than all the other European countries combined, including the expressionistic classic *The Cabinet of Dr. Caligari* and the early sound film *The Blue Angel*, which catapulted Marlene Dietrich into her film career and brought the Berlin cabaret scene to the masses. By the early 1930s radio stations had been established in all of Germany's major cities, and consumer purchase of radios had increased dramatically. Advances in photography made illustrated magazines especially popular. The mass press was one of the first expressions of the new mass media during the Weimar period. By 1928 there were 3,356 newspapers in Germany, with Berlin accounting for 147 alone. Such an abundance of coverage allowed for a tremendous diversity of voices to be heard. This diversity was not always welcomed however. National papers were seen by the right as the stifling voice of the left. Spectator sports, such as soccer, boxing, and tennis, also mushroomed. These new forms of popular entertainment generated much mass enthusiasm, a phenomenon not lost on Adolf Hitler and the Nazi leadership.

In theater the use of new forms to reach a mass audience made great strides. Revues, many featuring near-nude dancers, were increasingly popular, but many individuals found them immoral. Deliberately chaotic and fragmented like the world in which they were born, these revues, with colorful sets, new music influenced by American jazz and Broadway tunes, and precisely timed dance routines, provided light entertainment for the masses. Cabaret was another attempt to lampoon modern life, albeit with a sharper tongue and more biting wit than the revue. Beginning in late nineteenth-century France, cabaret mixed entertainment with nonconformist attitudes and a deliberate flaunting of traditional values. Especially popular in Berlin and among homosexuals, cabaret continued throughout Weimar as a center of nonconformist, or more properly, nontraditionalist, expression. For some critics it was precisely cabaret's ability to reveal the pretensions and absurdities of modern life that justified its existence. Many others, however, saw cabaret as just another seedy example of how far German society had fallen.

[9]Ibid., p. 588.

While many artists and critics considered serious contemporary theater eclipsed by revues, cabarets, and new media such as film and radio, for others it still had an important function in the new, modern, socialist Weimar era. Leopold Jessner, in a 1919 plea to other theater directors, proclaimed that "at the dawn of Germany's rejuvenation, a new time has also come for the German stage, perhaps even *the* time." Critic Siegfried Jacobsohn agreed, explaining that theater, "the expressive organ of this world," must reflect "the revolutionary bustle of the new age." But how best to represent this new age, this fragmented and dissolute modern world? Herbert Jhering noted perceptively that "the horrors of the last few years were not the collapse of a nation, but the inability to experience the elemental things elementally. People's energy was so exhausted that they accepted apocalyptic events like everyday inconveniences. Pain is not the worst thing, lack of sensitivity to pain is." Jhering found this sensitivity in the work of Berthold Brecht:

> Brecht's nerves, Brecht's blood, are filled with the horrors of the times . . . Brecht physically feels the chaos and the putrefaction. This is the reason for the unparalleled pictorial strength of his language. This is a language that you feel in your tongue, your palate, your ears, your spine. It omits links and opens up perspectives. It is brutally sensual and melancholically tender. It contains sordidness and deepest mourning, grim humor and plaintive lyricism.[10]

While Jhering found in Brecht the voice of an era, for many others the last thing they wanted to see in the theater was an expression of their own anguish. They wanted salvation, not catharsis.

Topical theater, socialist multimedia spectacles, bawdy revues, and cabarets were seen as evidence of a nation collapsing from within and without. This perspective was especially prevalent among those who eventually turned to the Nazis for that desired salvation. The seeming degeneracy of German social and cultural life was seen as resulting from the poisonous effects of foreign cultures, whether French, American, or for some, Jewish. The reflections of one Nazi party member exhibit this viewpoint as well as the search for a scapegoat for the alleged collapse:

> Meanwhile Germany further decayed. In unpleasant ways an entire people was alienated from itself. A new society spread out which only recognized the majesty of one's own ego. Sinister poison gushed forth into the brains and blood of German men in theaters and cinemas, in varieties and in dance halls. German youth, often still children carried in one's arms, moved about this hideous depravity, as all that was great and holy in our people drifted away. An unbelievable sensual orgy had seized Germany and a people danced a death dance to the rhythm of foreign music—and the Jew held the baton.[11]

For this man, the Weimar Republic resembled Sodom and Gemorrah far more than it did the powerful, united, and moral society he so desired.

Social Divisions

The sense of a society divided against itself was experienced during the Weimar years as being something as potentially dangerous as the political divisions that crippled the new

---

[10]Above quotations by Jessner, Jacobsohn, and Jhering, as found in Ibid., pp. 533–555.
[11]Quoted in Redles, *Hitler's Millennial Reich*, p. 34.

democracy. Most of these divisions were rooted in fundamental demographic shifts that accompanied the industrialization, urbanization, and modernization of German society. These shifts generated divisions between generations and sexes. The German population had experienced a high growth rate in the decades before war, with a significant baby-boom generation around the turn of the century. After the war, this generation flooded the job market, which was stagnant at its best, spirally downward at its worst. It is not surprising that there arose at this time a call for more *Lebensraum* (living space) to satisfy a *Volk ohne Raum* (people without space). This apparent excess of people versus living space, combined with the fact that the population was simultaneously aging (with birthrates falling since 1900), made fears of a *Volkstod* (death of the people) seem plausible. With the previous surplus of births to deaths beginning to reverse, the calls for women to do their "natural" duty and to leave work and give birth became commonplace.

That German youth after the war faced a saturated job market only exacerbated the traditional conflicts that occur when a younger generation attempts to make its place in society. Some of these youths joined the so-called *wilde cliques*, rebellious associations that simultaneously rejected and mocked bourgeois life. That the model for many such groups was deemed "American" (in terms of fashion, music, and even language) led some to see them as "un-German" and polluting. Adult-sponsored youth groups were set up to both control and socialize young people, as free time was considered the main cause of youth excesses such as drinking and promiscuity. Many German youth found themselves divided between being supporters of a vibrant new culture and defenders of an embattled traditional one. The proliferation of youth groups during a time of high unemployment provided the parties of the extreme left and right, the Communists and the Nazis, with plenty of potential recruits.

For women the situation was somewhat similar to that of the youth. There were new opportunities and freedoms on one hand, and unfortunate and largely false associations that many saw as the darker aspects of modernity. While the number of women in the workforce rose only slightly during the Weimar years, there was a decline in what was considered traditional "women's work" and a rise in new "modern" jobs. For example, from 1907 to 1925, the proportion of women working as domestics and farm laborers declined, whereas that of women working in the industrial and white-collar sectors rose significantly. That women were increasingly predominant in modern jobs, many of which had previously been dominated by men, also was a cause for both celebration and anger, depending on one's perspective. Jobs such as shorthand typist, assembly-line worker, shop assistant, primary-school teacher, and social worker were more and more assumed by women. Such occupations were considered appropriate for single or widowed women, whereas a married woman who worked was considered a *Doppelverdiener* (double earner), and therefore a threat to the earning capabilities of men. In response the 1932 Law Governing, the Legal Status of Female Civil Servants and Public Officials allowed women to be dismissed from public service if their husbands were employed.

The organized women's movement in Germany began, like other developments discussed here, during the Wilhelmian age. German feminists pushed for a greater role for women in society, arguing that women could bring a special "motherliness" to the heretofore overly masculine society. World War I provided German women with new opportunities to contribute to society, and with the coming of the Weimar Republic they gained the right to vote and run for political office. Women also received greater educational opportunities, especially in universities, although male exclusivity in fraternities and social clubs limited such opportunities. While many applauded these new freedoms and opportunities, many conservative men and women saw them as socially dangerous. That the new modern woman was often wrongly associated with the image of the morally suspect American flapper only exacerbated the tensions. Unfortunately, rejections of modernity and the mythic "new woman" often went hand in hand.

Like other Western countries, Weimar Germany underwent a modern revolution in manners and morals. Undoubtedly, defeat in war and the continuing postwar instability created by inflation, depression, and political problems fostered an atmosphere of revolt against traditional society. Parents and schoolmasters faced rebellions by their children and students. Female liberation grew dramatically. Women could vote and had greater educational and professional opportunities. While some expressed their freedom in premarital sexual relationships, the use of tobacco and alcohol, and short hair and short skirts, most women remained committed to the traditional roles of wife and mother. An overwhelming number of the women who voted supported the political parties that expressed the old values.

Postwar Germany manifested an openly permissive sexual climate in its large cities, where nude shows, nude cabarets, periodicals such as *Free Love*, and hard-core pornography competed for attention. A number of books, films, and plays focused on the identification and analysis of sexual problems. Police regulation in Berlin consisted of the issuance of cards that permitted female and male homosexual prostitutes to freely practice their trade.

Berlin, the Weimar capital, was the entertainment center of Europe. Theaters, cabarets, cinemas, and jazz clubs provided a wealth of high and low cultural opportunities. It was also the scene of incredible decadence, glaring contrasts of conspicuous wealth and abject poverty, every imaginable sexual perversion, experimentation with drugs (sniffing cocaine was the rage for a time), and violent crime. Many observers commented on the feverish pace of life in the capital. It was as if time was short, and indeed it was. One political party, above all others, maintained a constant criticism of all aspects of Weimar culture. "Cultural bolshevism," the Nazis proclaimed; "a junkyard," Hitler said. Hitler and the Nazis would dramatically alter the cultural landscape of Germany when they came to power.

HITLER AND THE EMERGENCE OF THE NAZI PARTY (1889–1920)

The economic, social, political, and cultural difficulties that characterized the Weimar Republic made possible the rise of extremist parties such as the Nazis. Such political groups flourish in times of turmoil and extreme dissatisfaction. But it is important to remember that the Nazi Party was more effective than the others in appealing to the discontented and in capturing popular support. Much of the Nazi success was due to the charismatic leadership of the Austrian provincial, Adolf Hitler, who was convinced of his own greatness.

Early Life

Adolf Hitler was born on April 20, 1889, in the Austrian village of Braunau-am-Inn, near the Bavarian frontier. His father, Alois, was an Austrian customs official. The Hitler family was of peasant stock, although Alois, through his petty bureaucratic position, was the first to break the pattern and enter the lower middle class. Adolf was the fourth child of Alois's third wife, Klara Pölzl. There is no real evidence to support the assertion of some that Alois's father and hence Adolf's grandfather was Jewish.

Adolf's father, who was stern and had a bad temper, wanted Adolf to follow in his footsteps and become a civil servant. The young Adolf was contemptuous of his father's wishes for himself, and the two had a tense and stormy relationship. Adolf was much closer to his mother, who was described by her doctor as "a simple, modest, kindly woman [with] . . . a long, oval face with beautifully expressive grey-blue eyes."[12] To compensate for her husband's harshness toward the children, Klara smothered them with love. After Alois's death in 1903, she indulged every wish of the teenaged Adolf. Hitler returned his mother's affection and later wrote, "I had honoured my father, but loved my mother."[13]

Young Adolf was a willful, indulgent child with strong opinions. His early education was satisfactory, but he was a total failure in the secondary, technical school in the city of Linz, where Alois had settled his family. The family continued to live there after Alois's death. Claiming illness, Hitler left school in 1905. The real reason was his failing grades. Even in geography and history, which he claimed in his autobiographical *Mein Kampf* (*My Struggle*) were his "favorite subjects" in which he led his class, he received only mediocre marks.

After dropping out of high school, the teenaged Hitler idled away the next two and a half years in Linz, drawing, painting, writing poetry, going to the theater, and day-dreaming. In many ways, this period of Hitler's life, especially as revealed by his youthful Linz friend and companion, August Kubizek, foreshadows much of his later life pattern. According to Kubizek, Hitler was a dreamer who preferred creating fantasies to doing any real work. His mania for redesigning and reconstructing cities appears in his grandiose plans for the rebuilding of Linz. As Kubizek related, "the more remote the realization of a project was, the more did he steep himself in it. To him these projects were in every detail as actual as though they were already executed."[14] Hitler believed that one day he would carry out his projects.

According to Kubizek, the young Hitler was impatient, moody, irritable if contradicted, and prone to outbursts of temper. He disdained regular work, preferring to live what he considered the life of an artist. He was a compulsive talker, inclined to giving dramatic speeches in which he was carried away by his own emotions. He was extraordinarily serious: "He approached the problems with which he was concerned with a deadly earnestness which ill suited his sixteen or seventeen years."[15] Willful and determined, the young Adolf, contrary to the wishes of his mother and brother-in-law, decided to pursue art as his career.

The Years in Vienna

In September 1907 Hitler left Linz to go to Vienna, where he applied to the Vienna Academy of Fine Arts. His painting samples were declared unsatisfactory and he was refused admission. The director suggested architecture, but Hitler needed a diploma

[12]Quoted in Ian Kershaw, *Hitler 1889–1936: Hubris* (New York, 1999), p. 12.

[13]Ibid.

[14]August Kubizek, *The Young Hitler I Knew*, translated by Geoffrey Brooks (St. Paul, Minn., 2006), p. 106.

[15]Ibid., p. 42.

from secondary school to enroll in a school of architecture. He did not have one and was certainly unwilling to take the final exams to get one. He returned briefly to Linz for his mother's death in December 1907, a deeply emotional experience because "he had lost the only creature on earth on whom he had concentrated his love and who had loved him in return."[16] In February 1908, he returned to Vienna and remained there until 1913.

He was joined in Vienna by his friend Kubizek, who enrolled as a music student in the Vienna Conservatory and roomed with Hitler for almost six months. Kubizek has given us an account of how Hitler spent his days in Vienna, frequenting museums and libraries. At night he went to the opera, especially to see the works of Richard Wagner. He saw his favorite, *Lohengrin*, ten times. As in his Linz days, Hitler continued to create fantastic projects. He began an opera, started a play, and drew up detailed architectural plans for the reconstruction of Vienna. When Kubizek asked him one day what he was doing, Hitler responded, "I am working on the solution of the housing problem in Vienna, and I am doing certain research for this purpose; I therefore have to go around a lot."[17]

Kubizek left Vienna in July 1908 for an army stint. When he returned in November planning to room again with Hitler, he discovered that his friend had moved without leaving a forwarding address. From late 1908 to 1913, Hitler's Viennese years were spent in the shadowy world of public shelters and hostels for men. Increasingly, as his early sources of income dried up, Hitler's financial circumstances became more difficult. During these years, Hitler pieced together the fragments of a *Weltanschauung* that he would never change: "In this period there took shape within me a world picture and a philosophy which became the granite foundation of all my acts. In addition to what I then created, I have had to learn little, and I have had to alter nothing."[18] This "world picture" was based on the political ideas and movements and the social conflicts of early-twentieth-century Vienna. What were the influences that Hitler experienced there?

Influences on Hitler's Development

In *Mein Kampf*, Hitler refers to two of the political figures who made a significant impact on him, Georg von Schönerer and Karl Lueger. Schönerer was an extreme German nationalist who desired the union of all Germans in one national state and hence opposed the continuing existence of the Austrian multinational state. Schönerer's movement was also anti-Semitic. The rabid Pan-German nationalist turned anti-Semitism from a religiously and economically motivated movement to one that was politically and racially oriented. Hitler criticized Schönerer, however, for his inability to understand the "social question," since Schönerer neglected the masses by directing his attention to the middle classes.

Karl Lueger was the mayor of Vienna and leader of the anti-Semitic Christian Social party. Hitler, with his usual lack of moderation, referred to him as "the greatest German mayor of all times" and a "statesman greater than all the so-called diplomats of the time."[19] He especially admired Lueger's demagogic methods, including his ability to

---

[16]Ibid., p. 138.

[17]Ibid., p. 169.

[18]Excerpts from *Mein Kampf* by Adolf Hitler, translated by Ralph Manheim, p. 22. Copyright © 1943, renewed 1971 by Houghton Mifflin Harcourt Publishing Company. Reprinted by permission of Houghton Mifflin Harcourt Publishing Company. All rights reserved.

[19]Ibid., pp. 55, 69.

use propaganda to appeal to the masses. Hitler believed that Lueger understood the politics of a mass party formed with the aid of emotional slogans. Part of Lueger's appeal lay in his clever manipulation of anti-Semitism, although Hitler felt that Lueger merely used it for political purposes without correctly understanding the racial significance of anti-Semitism. Lueger also failed, in Hitler's eyes, to grasp the significance of German nationalism, since he continued to support the multinational Austrian state. Hitler concluded his assessment of Schönerer and Lueger with these comparisons:

> The Pan-German movement was right in its theoretical view about the aim of a German renascence, but unfortunate in its choice of methods. It was nationalistic, but unhappily not socialistic enough to win the masses. But its anti-Semitism was based on a correct understanding of the importance of the racial problem. . . The Christian Social movement had an unclear conception of the aim of a German reawakening, but had intelligence and luck in seeking its methods as a party. It understood the importance of the social question, erred in its struggle against the Jews, and had no notion of the power of the national idea.[20]

In these comments, Hitler established the contours of his own Nazi party. It would be based on a strong German nationalism, socialism (or at least Hitler's version of it in his attempt to win over the masses), and extreme anti-Semitism.

Hitler's attitudes toward anti-Semitism were probably most influenced by an ex-Catholic monk named Adolf Lanz who called himself Lanz von Liebenfels. Liebenfels founded the quasi-religious Order of the New Templars, whose primary purpose was to foster Ariosophical doctrines. Ariosophy was a combination of occult ideas, German *völkisch* nationalism and anti-Semitism. Liebenfels established a New Templars castle on the Danube in 1907 and proudly flew a swastika flag over it. He wrote a series of occult works that presented his Ariosophical philosophy, although his major work, *Theozoologie* (*Theo-zoology*), written in 1904, contains the essence of his thought. That philosophy was based on the supposed superiority of the Ario-Germans. The Aryan was an exalted spiritual being: "The Aryan hero is on this planet the most complete incarnation of God and of the Spirit."[21] Jews, as well as other allegedly inferior races, were characterized as "animal-men" who must someday be eliminated by genetic selection, sterilization, deportations, forced labor, and even "direct liquidation." The elimination of the "animal-man" made possible the coming of the "higher new man," the Aryan superhero. Liebenfels also propagated his occult racial views in a magazine called *Ostara*, which was one of the periodicals that Hitler read to enlighten himself on the racial problem.

Richard Wagner was another important influence on the ideas of the early Hitler. Hitler once claimed that he had "heard Tristan thirty or forty times, and always from the best companies."[22] He was also influenced by the composer's life and political ideas and later claimed that he had no forerunners except Richard Wagner. One of Wagner's appeals to the young Hitler was the myth of the outsider, who follows his own rhythms and is forced to oppose the straitlaced social order of his day determined by tradition. In Wagner's *Rienzi* and *Lohengrin*, Hitler could see aspects of his own rejection by the

[20]Ibid., p. 122.

[21]Quoted in Wilfried Daim, *Der Mann, der Hitler die Ideen Gab* (Munich, 1958), p. 180. Unless indicated otherwise, translations from German are the authors'.

[22]*Hitler's Secret Conversations*, translated by Norman Cameron and R. H. Stevens (New York, 1961), p. 271.

world. The need to dominate is also an underlying theme in much of Wagner's music, and from this urge came Hitler's attempts to overwhelm through imposing demonstrations of power. The later public ceremonies of the Third Reich, with their massive stage effects, owe much to the influence of Wagner's operas on Hitler.

If his time in Vienna was the formative period of Hitler's world picture and philosophy, what then were the basic ideas that he had absorbed and made into an ideology that he would adhere to for the rest of his life?[23] Racial anti-Semitism was clearly at the core of his ideas. Moreover, Hitler had become an extreme German nationalist who favored the union of all German peoples. Anti-Semitism and nationalism were, of course, stock ideas in the bourgeois world of both Linz and Vienna. Viennese mass politics gave Hitler practical examples of the effective use of propaganda and terror by political parties. Finally, underlying all of his beliefs was a strong conviction of the need for struggle. The world was a brutal place filled with a constant struggle for existence in which only the fit survived. Hitler may have gathered this view of life from his experiences in Vienna, but these Social Darwinist ideas were also prevalent both in the bourgeois circles of Vienna and in the works of people such as Lanz von Liebenfels.

Hitler's years in Vienna served as the foundation for his later experiences. There he developed an ideology from which he deviated little for the rest of his life. He had the conviction of the closed-minded fanatic who sees no need to pursue new ideas in response to new situations. Adolf Hitler never doubted that the world could be seen in only one way—his way. Vienna had been a time of despair because of his frustration in not being recognized as the great artist and genius that he believed himself to be. The rejected Hitler projected his anger and hatred against the Jews, the bourgeois world, the rich, and the aristocrats. He could blame everyone for his personal disasters except the one person actually responsible—himself. Adolf Hitler left Vienna in 1913 with no real purpose, hating a world that had rejected him but convinced that he would someday be recognized.

Munich and World War I

In May 1913 Hitler moved to Munich. He claimed that he had made the move because of his passionate dislike of the Austrian Empire and his longing for the art capital of Bavaria. His real reason was to escape Austrian military obligations. Although the authorities caught up with the draft dodger, he was rejected as physically unfit for military service.

Munich brought no real change to Hitler's life. He continued to sell his paintings to keep alive. The escape from Vienna and the move to Germany had solved nothing. He had no real future in sight. The outbreak of World War I proved to be his salvation: "To me these hours seemed like a release from the painful feeling of my youth . . . overpowered by stormy enthusiasm, I fell down on my knees and thanked Heaven from an overflowing heart for granting me the good fortune of being permitted to live at this time."[24] Hitler volunteered

---

[23]See the discussion of Hitler as an ideologist in Chapter 5.

[24]Excerpts from *Mein Kampf* by Adolf Hitler, translated by Ralph Manheim, p. 161. Copyright © 1943, renewed 1971 by Houghton Mifflin Harcourt Publishing Company. Reprinted by permission of Houghton Mifflin Harcourt Publishing Company. All rights reserved.

Hitler and the Outbreak of World War I. In this extraordinary photograph taken at the Odeonsplatz in Munich on August 2, 1914, the twenty-five-year-old Adolf Hitler can be seen celebrating the outbreak of World War I. *(Heinrich Hoffmann/Hulton Archive/Getty Images)*

for the Bavarian army and was accepted on August 3, 1914. At the age of twenty-five, Adolf Hitler had at last found a purpose for his life. The formerly undisciplined Bohemian now accepted a grueling regimen for the sake of serving a greater purpose—Germany's greatness. Hitler threw himself into the war with great energy. As a dispatch runner, he distinguished himself by his courageous acts and received the Iron Cross, First Class, seldom awarded to enlisted men. He was, however, promoted only to corporal. His dedicated patriotism and willingness to sacrifice his personal interests for higher ideals made him unattractive to his fellow soldiers. A loner who shunned common vices, Hitler simply did not fit in with the other soldiers. But the military with its clear-cut system of order and values and its sense of male camaraderie made a great impact on Hitler's later lifestyle. So, too, did the excitement and discipline of war.

The news of Germany's defeat, which he heard while being treated at a military hospital for temporary blindness from a gas attack at the front, touched Hitler to the core of his being. Although he grieved for Germany, his own newfound existence was also jeopardized. The war had brought purpose and meaning to his life. He could not return to his wretched prewar condition. To Hitler, the war could not have been lost by the army. Defeat had been caused by the weakness of the home front; the army had suffered a Jewish–Marxist "stab in the back." As a result of a vision he claimed to have had while blinded, he decided early in November 1918 that he would go into politics to redress these dreadful wrongs. His rabid anti-Semitism was certainly evident at this time, as documented in a letter to a superior military officer in 1919:

> Antisemitism based on purely emotional grounds will always find its ultimate expression in the form of pogroms. A rational antisemitism, however, must lead to the systematic legal fight against and the elimination of the prerogatives of the Jew which he alone possesses in contradistinction to all other aliens living among us . . . Its ultimate goal, however, must unalterably be the elimination of the Jews altogether.[25]

Hitler and the German Workers' Party

Upon his return to Munich, Hitler remained in the army during the postwar turmoil in Munich that saw the temporary establishment of the Soviet Republic in April 1919. Hitler's German nationalistic enthusiasm led his superiors to appoint him as an information officer who could indoctrinate his fellow soldiers with German ideals. His job also entailed observation of small right-wing parties that might ultimately be of assistance to the German army. On one occasion, in September 1919, Hitler wound up in a Munich beer hall as an observer at a meeting of one such right-wing party, the German Workers' Party (DAP).

The DAP was merely one of many right-wing *völkisch*-nationalist parties in Munich. The Bavarian capital was especially conducive to extreme right-wing politics. In 1919, the army and Free Corps groups had crushed the Soviet Republic and reestablished the moderate Socialist government in Bavaria. But in 1920, at the time of the Kapp Putsch in Berlin, a coup replaced the Socialist government with a right-wing regime under the conservative Gustav von Kahr. Because the Weimar constitution granted control of the police to the governments of the individual federal states rather than to the central government, the Bavarian rightist regime provided a haven for the extremist activities of right-wing *völkisch*-nationalist groups. One of the most important of these groups was the Thule Society.

The Thule Society was basically a continuation of the Germanic Order, whose first lodge was established in Berlin in 1912. Modeled after the organization of Freemasonry, the aims of the Germanic Order were to achieve German racial purity (a result of its *völkisch* nationalism), attack the Jews, and establish Germans as the leaders of Europe. In 1917, Rudolf von Sebottendorf was made head of the order's Bavarian province. To provide a cover for the order's activities, he founded the Thule Society in January 1918. The Thule Society essentially combined occult racial philosophy (in the tradition of Lanz von Liebenfels) with a belief in militant action. The Thule Society preached Aryan supremacy and acted to achieve it. Although the society functioned outwardly as a "German studies" group, it was actively involved in the counterrevolution against the Bavarian Soviet Republic, which the Thule Society felt was dominated by the Jews.

In his 1933 book *Bevor Hitler Kam* (*Before Hitler Came*), Sebottendorf claimed that the Thule Society was of great importance to the founding of Hitler's National Socialist movement: "It was Thule people to whom Hitler first came and it was Thule people who first united themselves with Hitler."[26] No doubt, Sebottendorf exaggerated his own

---

[25]Quoted in Eberhard Jäckel, *Hitler's Weltanschauung*, translated by Herbert Arnold (Middletown, Conn., 1972), p. 48.

[26]Rudolf von Sebottendorf, *Bevor Hitler Kam* (Munich, 1933), dedication page.

significance. There is no evidence that he and Hitler ever met. Nevertheless, the DAP, which Hitler joined and later renamed, was founded by the railway mechanic Anton Drexler early in 1919 under the chairmanship of Karl Harrer, a journalist and member of the Thule. In fact, the DAP had a number of close links with the Thule Society. Hitler also had intimate ties with Thule members. Dietrich Eckart, whom Hitler accepted as his mentor and praised as the father of the Nazi movement, Alfred Rosenberg, eventually the Nazi Party's ideologist, and Rudolf Hess, Hitler's future second-in-command, were all members of the Thule Society.

In *Mein Kampf*, Hitler gave his own version of his relationship with the DAP. After attending a meeting at which Gottfried Feder spoke on finance capital and the elimination of capitalism, Hitler was prevailed upon to join the party as member number fifty-five and at the same time member seven of the executive committee. This small party of mediocrities gave Hitler an outlet for his own political interests and especially an opportunity to play a leading role. As propaganda chairman of the party, Hitler was able to develop his organizational skills, but above all to discover his oratorical talents. A month after joining the party, as a result of his first major speech, on October 16, 1919, he found that he "could speak." Thereafter, he spoke regularly at DAP gatherings as well as to other *völkisch* groups outside of Munich. From his position on the executive committee, Hitler began to gradually change the DAP from a mere discussion group to a noisy, publicity-seeking party of struggle, a mass political party.

On February 24, 1920, the DAP held its first authentic mass meeting in the Hofbräuhaus, a large Munich beer cellar. Hitler was overjoyed by the attendance of almost two thousand people and used the opportunity to announce a twenty-five-point party program composed by himself and Drexler. The program made clear that the new movement opposed capitalism, democracy, and especially the Jews. The latter were, in fact, to be excluded from German citizenship (point 4: "No Jew can be a member of the nation"). The party program was strongly nationalistic and imperialistic (point 1: "We demand the union of all Germans in a Greater Germany upon the basis of the self-determination of the people"; point 3: "We demand land and territory [colonies] for the nourishment of our people and for settling our excess population").[27] The influence of Hitler on the party program was evident in the call for the revocation of the Treaty of Versailles and the stress on the unalterable nature of the program. Both the party program and Hitler's early speeches provided simple explanations for the German misery: the Jews, Marxists, the Versailles treaty, and the "November criminals"—the democratic leaders who had stabbed the army in the back.

In Hitler's eyes, the Hofbräuhaus mass meeting was a turning point for the new movement: "By it the party burst the narrow bonds of a small club and for the first time exerted a determining influence on the mightiest factor of our time, public opinion."[28] The party's name was changed to the National Socialist German Workers' Party (NSDAP), or Nazi for short, to distinguish itself from the socialist parties while gaining support from working-class and *völkisch*-nationalist circles alike. In April 1920, Hitler

[27]The twenty-five points appear in Ernst Deuerlein, ed., *Der Aufstieg der NSDAP in Augenzeugenberichten* (Düsseldorf, 1968); points 1, 3, and 4 are listed on p. 108.

[28]Excerpts from *Mein Kampf* by Adolf Hitler, translated by Ralph Manheim, p. 359. Copyright © 1943, renewed 1971 by Houghton Mifflin Harcourt Publishing Company. Reprinted by permission of Houghton Mifflin Harcourt Publishing Company. All rights reserved.

took the decisive step of quitting the army and dedicating himself completely to politics, which was a logical step. Politics proved to be the ideal vocation for one who had no vocation and was certainly not trained for any. The Nazi movement had begun.

THE MUNICH POLITICIAN AND THE EARLY NAZI PARTY (1920–1923)

In the spring and summer of 1920, Adolf Hitler was basically a local Munich politician who spoke night after night in rowdy beer halls to win people over to National Socialist ideas. Hitler perceived the need to separate the NSDAP from the numerous small-time nationalist-*völkisch* groups vying for attention in the postwar Bavarian capital. Hitler possessed one advantage in his pursuit of popular attention. He had absolutely no scruples. He was willing to use any method, including brawls and riots, to get attention. As he said in *Mein Kampf,* "At that time I adopted the standpoint: It makes no difference whatever whenever they laugh at us or revile us, whether they represent us as clowns or criminals; the main thing is that they mention us, that they concern themselves with us again and again, . . ."[29] To some people attracted to the Nazi party, Hitler was a "mass drummer" who could be used to popularize *völkisch*-nationalist policies. One of the keys to Hitler's rise to effectiveness as a politician would be his ability to use people who planned to use him. In his early years as a Munich politician Hitler seemed willing to play the role of "drummer" to gain mass support for the nationalist cause. Eventually, however, he would be satisfied with nothing less than complete leadership.

Hitler's Assumption of Party Leadership

Hitler's position as propaganda director of the party enabled him to exert considerable influence within the new party. Other party leaders, such as Chairman Drexler, had regular jobs and could not devote the time and energy to the party that Hitler could. Hitler's abilities as a speaker and his frenetic activity on behalf of the party brought in new members and made Hitler indispensable.

A party crisis in 1921 enabled Hitler to push for more control of the party. Some party leaders, including Drexler, advocated the coalescence of the NSDAP with other national socialist and *völkisch* groups such as the German Socialist Party (DSP). They believed such a union of the *völkisch* movement would create a more productive political instrument. Hitler strongly disagreed, thinking such a move might swamp the Nazi Party and imperil his own important position within it. When Drexler attempted to merge the NSDAP with a *völkisch* party in Augsburg during Hitler's absence, Hitler reacted dramatically and forcefully. On July 11, 1921, he announced his resignation from the party. He demanded the acceptance of two conditions before he would rejoin: (1) election of a new executive committee with himself as first chairman of the party "with dictatorial powers" and (2) complete primacy of the Munich local branch over all other Nazi groups in and outside of Bavaria. Although the old-line members of the party objected, they also realized Hitler's indispensability to the party and capitulated to his demands. Hitler was now able to begin constructing his

[29]Ibid., p. 485.

leadership as the central principle of the party. He called himself "leader of the NSDAP," and others now began to speak of the Nazi movement as the Hitler movement.

Early Organization of the Nazi Party

By the end of 1921, the Nazi Party was rapidly becoming the instrument of Adolf Hitler. Its organizational structure became authoritarian after Hitler's establishment of dictatorial party leadership. The leader principle and a military command structure constituted the essence of the National Socialist party organization. Hitler was thus unwilling to compromise or fuse with other nationalist-*völkisch* parties and groups in southern Germany and Austria. For Hitler, others could join the NSDAP if they were willing to submit to the authoritarian structure of the party.

In *Mein Kampf*, Hitler had emphasized the importance of propaganda and organization in the development of a mass political movement:

> The function of propaganda is to attract supporters, the function of organization to win members . . . Propaganda works on the general public from the standpoint of an idea and makes them ripe for the victory of this idea, while the organization achieves victory by the persistent, organic, and militant union of those supporters who seem willing and able to carry on the fight for victory.[30]

In the "years of struggle," as the Nazis referred to the party's early efforts to survive and grow, Hitler placed much emphasis on developing a strong organizational structure.

Hitler perceived clearly the importance of physical trappings in the organization of the NSDAP. Symbols could unify the party by making members feel important and create a wider appeal by drawing attention in mass demonstrations. Hitler chose the swastika as the official party emblem. The swastika was an ancient occult symbol invoking the power of the sun. It had been adopted in Germany and Austria by occult *völkisch* groups as a symbol of Aryan anti-Semitic movements. The Templars of Lanz von Liebenfels, the Germanic Order, and the Thule Society of Rudolf von Sebottendorf had all used it. It was not Hitler's invention, despite his claim to the contrary in *Mein Kampf*, but it was his decision to use it officially for the party. He instructed the heads of local groups that members were to always wear party badges carrying the swastika.

In 1920, Hitler introduced the out-raised arm *Heil* salute, which he had borrowed from Austrian *völkisch* parties. The wearing of uniforms with party badges and the use of flags and standards at meetings became commonplace. Reviews, parades, and the use of ceremonies with flag dedications became visible symbols of growing Nazi strength. Hitler appreciated physical symbols and mass meetings as methods of achieving a sense of identification and a feeling of belonging by party members.

Mass meetings served another purpose as well: unleashing mass propaganda techniques for winning public support. These meetings were very emotional and included a major speech as well as a panoply of flags, standards, parades, and martial music. With his free time and enormous energy, Hitler was able to hold a mass meeting every week. Between November 1919 and November 1920, he spoke at thirty-one meetings out of the forty-eight that were held. In his speeches, Hitler railed against the peace of

---

[30]Ibid., pp. 581–582.

Versailles, Marxism, international capitalism, the November criminals, and of course the Jews. A recording secretary summarized one of his speeches:

> The lecturer [Hitler] spoke on Judaism. Everywhere one looks, he said, there are Jews. Jews rule all of Germany. What dishonor, that German workers, both white collar and manual laborers, allow themselves to be so harassed by the Jews. Of course, because Jews have the money . . . Germans should unite and fight against the JEWS . . . The lecturer's final words: We must struggle until the last Jew is removed from the German Reich, even if it comes to a coup and even more, to another revolution.[31]

Hitler always emphasized the need to reduce ideas to simple slogans for mass consumption. The Nazi Party's mass meetings with Adolf Hitler as chief speaker became increasingly effective. Crowds of hundreds grew to thousands in the early 1920s.

To reinforce his mass propaganda techniques, Hitler and the Nazi Party realized the importance of a party newspaper. The *Münchener Beobachter* (*Munich Observer*), the racialist organ of the Thule Society, was purchased by the party with the help of army funds. Renamed the *Völkischer Beobachter* (*People's Observer*), it became the official party newspaper. Hitler, as the party's propaganda chief, exercised considerable control over the paper's editorial content.

Role of the Sturmabteilung (SA)

Under Hitler's direction, the Nazi Party was becoming one of the most noticeable of the numerous right-wing *völkisch* groups in Bavaria. These groups shared a basic belief that their eventual goal was the overthrow of the Weimar government. Hitler, too, shared this goal, and by the beginning of 1923, he had rejected the participation of the NSDAP in electoral activity in favor of a cooperative armed uprising. For that reason, the party's paramilitary unit, the SA, came to be increasingly emphasized.

The SA had been established as a Gymnastic and Sports division within the Nazi movement during the summer of 1921. As the "armed part of the movement," it was organized along military lines and used primarily to defend the party in meeting halls and on the streets as well as to break up the meetings of other parties. In October 1921, after a series of victorious brawls, Hitler labeled the party militia as the *Sturmabteilung*, or Storm Troops. The SA added an element of force and terror to the growing Nazi movement. Hitler believed that terror had its own magnetic power and could be used not only to intimidate people but also to attract new followers.

The SA grew rapidly by recruiting ex-soldiers and volunteers from the Free Corps. Some entire units of Free Corps—such as the Free Corps Rossbach under Edmund Heines, subsequently a brutal SA group leader—joined the SA. Increasingly, young people were attracted to a group that offered adventure in secret meetings, parades, the painting of slogans on buildings, and fighting with opponents. In February 1921, a National Socialist student organization with its own SA troop was founded at the University of Munich. From its founding in 1921, the SA had grown to fifteen thousand members by 1923. The adoption of the official Brown Shirt uniform that same year gave the SA its distinctive military appearance.

---

[31]Ernst Deuerlein, "Hitlers Eintritt in die Politik und die Reichswehr," *Vierteljahrshefte für Zeitgeschichte*, 7 (1959), pp. 177–227. This quotation appears on pages 211–212.

Early Party Leaders

Although Adolf Hitler soon became the unquestioned leader of the Nazi Party, a number of individuals played important roles in the early history of the party. Some eventually became prominent leaders in Nazi Germany.

The two who achieved more for the early Nazi Party than anyone except for Hitler were Ernst Röhm and Dietrich Eckart. Röhm came from an old Bavarian family of civil servants. A captain in the Reichswehr, he joined the DAP in November 1919. He promoted Hitler's political career by providing followers, arms, and financial support for the struggling young party. As a military officer, Röhm could introduce Hitler to nationalistic officers and politicians. The support of the army was crucial to the early survival of the Nazi Party. Röhm's skills as a military organizer enabled him to help build up the SA as party troops.

Dietrich Eckart was a mediocre poet and dramatist who blamed the Jews for his lack of success. Eckart was an associate of the Thule Society and came to the DAP through it. Eckart interpreted the immediate postwar years in apocalyptic terms, as a time of tribulations that would elicit the coming Third Reich. Writing in his anti-Semitic periodical *Auf gut deutsch*, Eckart proclaimed in 1919:

> Signs and wonders are seen—from the flood a new world will be born. These Pharisees however whine about wretched nest eggs! The liberation of humanity from the curse of gold stands before the door! It's not simply a question of our collapse—it's a question of our Golgotha! Salvation is to befall our Germany, not misery and poverty. No other people on Earth are so thoroughly capable of fulfilling the Third Reich than ours! *Veni Creator spiritus!* [Come Holy Spirit Creator].[32]

The appearance the previous year of the notorious hoax *The Protocols of the Elders of Zion* was seized upon by Eckart as proof that the Jews were behind Germany's apocalyptic collapse. A faked document originally produced within the Russian Empire around 1903, the *Protocols* purported to be the secret minutes of a meeting of Jewish elders at the first Zionist Congress in Basel, Switzerland, in 1898. It detailed the supposed plans of the Jews to mount a vast conspiracy to foment world war and revolution, topple the royal houses of Europe, and use both capitalism and communism to takeover the world. For Eckart, and later Hitler and other key Nazis, the loss of World War I, the end of the German and Russian monarchies, and the rise of communism were all the proof they needed that *Protocols* were real and that the Jews were on the precipice of world dominion. Eckart concluded: "The hour of decision has come: between existence and non-existence, between Germany and Jewry, between all or nothing, between truth and lies, between inner and outer, between justice and caprice, between sense and madness, between goodness and murder. And humanity once again has the choice!"[33] It was for this reason that in 1919 Eckart had prophesied the coming of a national savior for Germany. By the following

---

[32]Quoted in David Redles, "The Nazi End Times: The Third Reich as Millennial Reich," from *End of Days: Essays on the Apocalypse from Antiquity to Modernity* © 2009, p. 173. Edited by Karolyn Kinane and Michael A. Ryan by permission of McFarland & Company, Inc., Box 611, Jefferson, NC 28640. www.mcfarlandpub.com.

[33]Quoted in David Redles, "The Turning Point: *The Protocols of the Elders of Zion* and the Eschatological War between Aryans and Jews," in Richard Landes and Steven T. Katz, eds., *The Paranoid Apocalypse: A Hundred-Year Retrospective on* The Protocols of the Elders of Zion (New York, 2011), p. 117.

year, he was touting Hitler as this messiah. He and Hitler established a close relation-ship. Eckart took responsibility for polishing Hitler socially by improving his German and introducing him to wealthy Munich society. Through Eckart's efforts, Hitler became the darling of society matrons such as Elsa Bruckmann, wife of a renowned publisher, and Helene Bechstein, wife of a famous piano manufacturer. These rich women sup-ported Hitler financially and essentially tried to mother him. It was also Eckart who made the financial arrangements for the purchase of the *Völkischer Beobachter* and then became its editor. He authored the Nazi battle cry "Deutschland Erwache!" (Germany Awake!). Hitler acknowledged the importance of Eckart when he called him the "spiri-tual cofounder" of Nazism and dedicated *Mein Kampf* to that man, who was "one of the best, who devoted his life to the awakening of his, our people, in his writings and his thoughts and finally in his deeds . . ."[34]

Alfred Rosenberg and Max Erwin von Scheubner-Richter were Baltic Germans who made their way to Munich and into the Nazi Party. Rosenberg was born in Estonia and studied architecture at the University of Moscow. After the Russian Revolution, he came to Munich, met Dietrich Eckart, and joined the DAP in 1919. He began writing for Eckart's *Auf gut deutsch* and later the *Völkischer Beobachter*, succeeding Eckart as editor of this newspaper in 1923. Rosenberg considered himself an intellectual and tried to construct an underlying ideology of Nazism from a mixture of anti-Semitism, anti-Slavism, anti-Bolshevism, and an anti-Christian version of world history. Later he came to be viewed as the chief ideologist of the Nazi Party.

Max Erwin von Scheubner-Richter joined the Nazi Party in 1920 as a friend of Alfred Rosenberg. Scheubner-Richter served as an important liaison between Hitler and the World War I commander General Erich Ludendorff. He also organized con-tacts with industrial and monarchist circles and brought enormous sums of money into the early party. Scheubner-Richter was the only important Nazi to be killed in the Beer Hall Putsch.

One of Hitler's earliest party comrades and a dominant figure in his immedi-ate entourage was Hermann Esser. Esser was a crude person who indulged in sinister accounts of Jewish activities. Nevertheless, he was an effective rabble-rouser and Hitler used him as an editor of the *Völkischer Beobachter* and as chief of party propaganda begin-ning in 1921.

Rudolf Hess, an early party comrade, was outstanding in his slavish devotion to Hitler. A student of political science at the University of Munich, Hess joined the Nazi Party in January 1920 after hearing a Hitler speech. He became a rabid believer in Nazi ideology and established a student group of SA Stormtroopers at the university. His intense need for a strong authority figure led to his complete and unwavering devotion to Hitler.

Hermann Göring, who later became the number two man in the Third Reich as Hitler's designated successor, was not typical of the early Nazi leadership. He came from an upper-class background and married the daughter of a wealthy Swedish aristocratic family. The last commander of the famous Richthofen fighter squadron in World War I, Göring was a much-decorated pilot and war hero. Although Göring was a strong German

---

[34]Excerpts from *Mein Kampf* by Adolf Hitler, translated by Ralph Manheim, p. 687. Copyright © 1943, renewed 1971 by Houghton Mifflin Harcourt Publishing Company. Reprinted by permission of Houghton Mifflin Harcourt Publishing Company. All rights reserved.

nationalist and anticommunist, he cared little for Nazi ideology; he joined the Nazi Party because of his need for action, adventure, and comradeship and a hunger for power. Hitler was delighted with the respectability Göring brought to the Nazis as an aristocrat and genuine war hero. He was made leader of the SA in 1922.

A Social Analysis of the Party

Since the 1930s historians have frequently asserted that the Nazi movement was a lower-middle-class phenomenon. Recent sociological analyses of the composition of the Nazi movement, however, has shown that, while the lower middle class was somewhat overrepresented regarding membership and votes cast, the Nazi party also drew significant support from the working classes and social elites. It was, in many ways, a true "people's party."

The Nazi Party appealed to all segments of the German population. As seen in the party's title, Hitler and the early Nazi leaders tried to attract workers away from the Social Democratic and Communist parties. Before 1925, however, they were only partially successful. Although workers (both skilled and unskilled) constituted 36 percent of the party's membership in 1923, they were underrepresented in comparison with the entire German population of which workers constituted 55 percent. However, in the six weeks just prior to the failed Hitler Putsch, discussed later, in some cities workers actually made up the majority of new members. This was true of Vilsbiburg (59 percent), Starnberg (58.3 percent), Augsburg (55.9 percent), Pappenheim (54 percent), and Memmingen (51.3 percent).[35]

The lower middle class was somewhat overrepresented in the party as a whole. Constituting 43 percent of the entire population, the lower middle class made up 52 percent of party membership in the fall of 1923. Especially visible were urban and later small-town and rural merchants and artisans who had suffered from the war and thought of themselves as victims of the republic's economic policies. Although coming late to the party, office clerks and lower civil servants, attracted to Nazism because of their dislike of the Weimar government and fear of Marxism, made up 18 percent of party memberships. Another section of the lower middle class, the farmers, did not begin to join the party in significant numbers until 1923, when they constituted 11 percent of the total. For all of these lower-middle-class groups (be they merchants, craftspeople, office clerks, lesser civil servants, or farmers), Nazism was especially attractive because of its anti-Semitism. Jews were seen as owners of large department stores and hence a threat to lower-middle-class merchants and artisans. Farmers were also susceptible to a firm tradition of rural anti-Semitism and were inclined to accept the stereotypes of the Jewish cattle dealer and the Jewish–Marxist revolutionary in the city.

The upper classes of German society were overrepresented from the very beginning of the Nazi movement. Only 3 percent of the entire German population, they totaled 12 percent of Nazi membership in the fall of 1923. In Munich, 50 percent of the upper-class members consisted of university students. Many of these youths, as disillusioned former frontline soldiers, were strongly attracted by the Nazi appeal to

---

[35]Statistics found in Detlev Mühlberger, *The Social Bases of Nazism 1919–1933* (Cambridge, Mass., 2003), p. 44.

German nationalism and action. Universities and university fraternities also possessed a strong anti-Semitic tradition. Many early Nazi students were drawn to the militaristic SA within the NSDAP. Other members of the elite, such as manufacturers, publishers, and aristocrats, were attracted to the Nazis as an instrument for the restoration of the old imperial order. Even some academics and intellectuals, especially in Munich, joined the party. Indeed, as historian Michael Kater has concluded, "from 1919 to 1923 the Nazi Party, far from being a perfect mirror image of the social profile of the nation, contained, albeit in varying proportions, elements of every important social segment in the country so that it potentially assumed an integrative function in German society."[36]

Two other characteristics stand out in a social profile of rank-and-file membership. The Nazi Party was a youthful party. If the men who founded the original Nazi Party were in their early thirties, the men who joined tended to be even younger. In 1923, the mean age of newcomers was twenty-seven and almost 50 percent of all joiners were twenty-three or under. Most of these new members were also male. Hitler and the early Nazi leaders believed in male supremacy and reflected this belief by formally excluding women from party leadership positions as of January 1921. The 10 percent female membership in the Nazi Party in 1919 had declined to 5 percent by 1923 as women realized that the party was controlled by male values and militaristic ideals.

FIRST ATTEMPT AT POWER

In its early years, the Nazi movement had been only one among many radical right-wing political groups in Bavaria. The crises of 1923, however, brought a dramatic increase in the growth of the Nazi Party, which became the strongest of the nationalist-*völkisch* parties in southern Germany. In the same year, Hitler made his first and last attempt to seize power solely by force.

Background: Bavarian Politics and the Crises of 1923

Hitler's attempt to seize power in 1923 was played out against a backdrop of crises for the democratic Weimar government. As we have seen, the French and Belgian occupation of the Ruhr in January 1923 due to Germany's inability to pay reparations was met by a government-inspired policy of passive resistance that led to runaway inflation and economic chaos. These crises created fertile soil for right-wing dreams of overthrowing the Weimar democracy and establishing a right-wing dictatorship.

Nowhere were these dreams more pronounced than in Bavaria and its capital, Munich. A right-wing regime had been established in Bavaria in 1920. Since the police under the Weimar constitution were responsible to the federal states and not to the central government, the Bavarian police had used their power to protect radical

---

[36]Michael Kater, *The Nazi Party: A Social Profile of Members and Leaders 1919–1945* (Cambridge, Mass., 1983). Percentages in this section, unless otherwise noted, are drawn from Kater's book, especially from the tables on pp. 241–243.

right-wing groups such as the Nazis. The police chief of Munich, Ernst Pöhner, had openly helped Hitler's party, and one of his aides, Wilhelm Frick, later became a prominent Nazi. Bavarian courts were notoriously harsh to left-wingers while coddling right-wing extremists.

The army in Bavaria likewise opposed the republic and aided right-wing groups. General Ritter von Epp, who had played a leading role in the liberation of Bavaria from its Soviet Republic, was a Nazi sympathizer. His staff officer Ernst Röhm, as we have seen, joined the Nazi Party and provided it with considerable material support. General Otto von Lossow, head of the Bavarian military district, also demonstrated pronounced right-wing sympathies. In 1923, the army began protecting extremist paramilitary groups such as the Nazis' SA.

In 1923, the Nazi Party clearly became the leading party among the extremist right-wing groups. Party membership swelled to fifty-five thousand and the SA grew to fifteen thousand members. Hitler became head of the *Kampfbund* (Combat League), an umbrella organization for various right-wing paramilitary groups including the SA. The *Kampfbund* found itself sympathizing with Gustav von Kahr and other conservative Bavarian leaders. Following the example of Mussolini's march on Rome in October 1922, both parties favored a "march on Berlin" to overthrow the Weimar government and establish a new nationalist, right-wing government. They hoped to achieve this goal with the support of right-wing groups in northern Germany and elements of the regular German army that had never really accepted the new democratic system. Even an excuse for the military march on Berlin was at hand—the necessity to suppress the leftist governments in the states of Thuringia and Saxony that had been created by the cooperation of Socialists and Communists. In the spring and summer of 1923, Hitler's SA and other right-wing paramilitary groups held a series of mass demonstrations in Munich, exciting the paramilitary units with calls for a national uprising. Expectations of action soared among the enthusiastic rank and file.

The Beer Hall Putsch of 1923

In the fall of 1923, events came to a head. A new Weimar government under Gustav Stresemann had ended the policy of passive resistance against the French. This new government came into conflict with the Bavarian authorities. On September 26, the Bavarian government had proclaimed a state of emergency and given Gustav von Kahr dictatorial authority. The new Weimar government likewise declared a state of emergency in Germany and conferred executive powers on the head of the Reichswehr, General von Seeckt. The government tried to force the Bavarian government to control the Nazis by banning the party newspaper, the *Völkischer Beobachter*. When the head of the Bavarian military district, General von Lossow, rejected this order, he was relieved of his command. The Bavarian government insisted that Lossow remain in his post. A clash between the Weimar and Bavarian governments seemed inevitable.

Unfortunately for the conspirators, Hitler's *Kampfbund* and Kahr's government now began to divide on the best way to proceed. When the Stresemann government used the army to crush the leftist governments in Saxony and Thuringia in October, the Bavarian conspirators lost their justification for a march on Berlin. Kahr became very reluctant to pursue a coup. Likewise, north German right-wing groups counseled against precipitous action. General von Seeckt, certainly no fan of the Weimar Republic and a believer himself in a right-wing coup, now became hostile to the idea. His primary concern was the independence of the Reichswehr, the regular army, and he feared that a rightist putsch could create a civil war that would ultimately harm the army. By the end of October the idea of a march on Berlin was beginning to appear less feasible, and on November 6, Kahr cautioned Hitler and the *Kampfbund* against any hasty military action.

Hitler was left in a difficult position. He had aroused the paramilitary forces with great expectations. To fail to act threatened his own leadership position with these men. Moreover, it was evident that the crises of 1923 were ending with the Weimar government in ever-growing control. To wait longer would eliminate any hope of success. Hitler decided to try to force Kahr and other Bavarian leaders to join the *Kampfbund* in a march on Berlin.

Hitler seized the first opportunity for action. On November 8, a rally was held in one of Munich's large beer cellars, the Bürgerbräukeller, to honor Kahr. Kahr was the featured speaker, along with General Lossow and Colonel Seisser, head of the police. Hitler surrounded the building with SA troops, broke in, took over the meeting, and melodramatically proclaimed: "The national revolution has broken out." Taking Kahr, Lossow, and Seisser into an adjoining room, Hitler pressured them to join him in overthrowing the national government. They refused until General Erich Ludendorff, who in Hitler's scheme for the new government was to be head of the army, came in to apply new pressure. Ultimately the three agreed and returned to the beer cellar with Hitler and Ludendorff to the acclaim of the audience.

Hitler accepted their promises of support and allowed them to go free, much to his undoing. Circumstances changed dramatically for Hitler overnight. Although Ernst Röhm had seized the local army headquarters, the leadership of the army refused to support Hitler. Lossow, upon his release, telephoned Bavarian army headquarters for new troops to be sent to Munich to crush Hitler's revolt. Kahr also reneged on his promise. Hitler, faced with the complete collapse of his plans, tried a last desperate gamble by marching with Ludendorff and two thousand supporters through Munich to gain popular support for the coup. Their march was stopped by police barricades, and after a brief gun battle, the Hitler group, with the noticeable exception of General Ludendorff, fled. The Beer Hall Putsch had collapsed. The leaders, including Hitler, were later arrested. Some observers considered it the end of the upstart Austrian.

The treason trial against Hitler, Ludendorff, and other leaders of the *Kampfbund* took place in February and March 1924. Considerable public attention became focused on the trial and gave Hitler the opportunity to establish his name outside of Bavaria. He used the publicity brilliantly to transform defeat into propaganda victory.

At the trial, Hitler did not deny that he had planned to overthrow the national government. But he refused to admit that this had been an act of high treason. The real criminals, Hitler proclaimed, were the betrayers of Germany who had signed the Versailles treaty and perpetuated the Weimar Republic. Hitler also attacked the credibility of the state's chief witnesses, Kahr, Lossow, and Seisser, saying that they all wanted the same thing he did. Hitler portrayed himself as the real patriot opposing the Weimar Republic, since he had had the courage to act: "I consider myself not a traitor but a German, who desired what was best for his people." But he was more than just a patriot, for he pictured himself as Germany's man of destiny who from the beginning wanted to "become the destroyer of Marxism." Regardless of the judge's verdict, concluded Hitler, history's judgment would be positive:

> Gentlemen, judgment will not be passed on us by you; judgment will be passed on us by the eternal court of history. This court will judge the accusations that have been made against us. That other court, however, will not ask, "Did you or did you not commit high treason?" That court will pass judgment on us, . . . as Germans [who] wanted the best for their people and their country, who were willing to fight and die for it. Even if you find us guilty a thousand times over, the goddess of the eternal tribunal of history will smilingly tear apart the proposal of the Prosecutor and the sentence of the Court, because she will acquit us.[37]

Hitler need not have worried; the right-wing judges were sympathetic to his words. Ludendorff was acquitted and Hitler was given the most lenient sentence possible for treason—five years in prison with an understanding of early probation.

The putsch had failed, but Hitler had not. He would have time in prison to mull over the lessons of the past months and would emerge convinced that the real struggle for the soul of Germany was just beginning.

SUGGESTIONS FOR FURTHER READING

Although not comprehensive, two guides to the historical literature on Weimar Germany are Peter D. Stachura, *The Weimar Era and Hitler 1918–1933: A Critical Bibliography* (Oxford, 1977); and the annotated bibliography on periodical literature in *The Weimar Republic* (Santa Barbara, Calif., 1984). An important collection of documents is Anton Kaes, Martin Jay, and Edward Dimendberg, eds., *The Weimar Republic Sourcebook* (Berkeley, Calif., 1994).

For a sound survey of Weimar Germany, including a lengthy bibliography, see Eberhard Kolb, *The Weimar Republic*, 2nd ed. (New York, 2005). See also Matthew Stibbe, *Germany, 1914–1933: Politics, Society, and Culture* (New York, 2010); Hans Mommsen, *The Rise and Fall of Weimar Democracy* (Chapel Hill, N.C., 1996); Richard Bessel, *Germany after the First World War* (Oxford, 1993), which focuses on the immediate aftermath of the war; Detlev Peukert, *The Weimar Republic* (New York, 1992); E. J. Feuchtwanger, *From Weimar to Hitler* (New York, 1993); Paul Bookbinder, *Weimar Germany* (New York, 1996); Ruth Henig, *The Weimar Republic 1919–1923* (New York, 1998); and Stephen J. Lee, *The Weimar Republic,* 2nd ed. (New York, 2010). Good collections of essays are Anthony McElligott, *Weimar Germany* (Oxford and New York, 2009); and Richard Bessel and E. J. Feuchtwanger, eds., *Social Change and Political Development in Weimar Germany* (London, 1981). The relationship between state and military in Weimar Germany can be examined in F. L. Carsten, *The Reichswehr and Politics 1918–1933* (New York, 1966); Gaines Post, Jr., *The Civil-Military Fabric of Weimar Foreign Policy* (Princeton, N.J., 1973); and Harold Gordon, *The Reichswehr and the German Republic 1919–1926* (Princeton, N.J., 1957). On the use of paramilitary forces in Weimar Germany, see Robert Waite, *Vanguard of Nazism: The Free Corps Movement in Postwar Germany, 1918–1933* (Cambridge,

[37]Printed with permission from the Continuum International Publishing Company Group. Klaus P. Fischer, *Nazi Germany: A New History* © 1995, pp. 161–162.

Mass., 1952); and Nigel H. Jones, *A Brief History of the Birth of the Nazis* (New York, 2004). On the psychology of paramilitary fighters, see Klaus Theweleit, *Male Fantasies*, 2 vols. (Minneapolis, Minn., 1987–1989). Good studies of prominent individuals in Weimar history are Anna von der Goltz, *Hindenburg: Power, Myth, and the Rise of the Nazis* (New York, 2009); Andreas Dorpalen, *Hindenburg and the Weimar Republic* (Princeton, N.J., 1964); H. J. P. Harmer, *Friedrich Ebert: Germany* (London, 2008); Henry A. Turner, *Gustav Stresemann and the Politics of the Weimar Republic* (Princeton, N.J., 1963); and Jonathan Wright, *Gustav Stresemann: Weimar's Greatest Statesman* (Oxford, 2002). The foreign policy of the Stresemann era is examined in John Jacobsen, *Locarno Diplomacy, Germany and the West, 1925–1929* (Princeton, N.J., 1972). Aspects of Weimar's political parties can be studied in William Smaldone, *Confronting Hitler: German Social Democrats in Defense of the Weimar Republic, 1929–1933* (Lanham, Md., 2009); Richard N. Hunt, *German Social Democracy 1918–1933* (New Haven, Conn., 1964); Richard Breitman, *German Socialism and Weimar Democracy* (Chapel Hill, N.C., 1981); Donna Harsch, *German Social Democracy and the Rise of Nazism* (Chapel Hill, N.C., 1993); and Lewis Hertzmann, *DNVP Right-Wing Opposition in the Weimar Republic* (Lincoln, 1963). A concise, but informative discussion of Weimar economics can be found in Theo Balderston, *Economics and Politics in the Weimar Republic* (Cambridge, Mass., 2002). On the French invasion of the Ruhr valley, see Conan Fischer, *The Ruhr Crisis, 1923–1924* (Oxford, 2003). On the hyperflation that followed, see Gerald Feldman, *Iron and Steel in the German Inflation, 1916–1923* (Princeton, N.J., 1977); Fritz Ringer, ed., *The German Inflation of 1923* (New York, 1969); and Gerald Feldman, *The Great Disorder: Politics, Economics, and Society in German Inflation, 1914–1924* (New York, 1997). On the effects of the inflation on German society see Bernd Widdig, *Culture and Inflation in Weimar Germany* (Berkeley, Calif., 2001). On the cultural and intellectual environment of Weimar Germany, see Eric D. Weitz, *Weimar Germany: Promise and Tragedy* (Princeton, N.J., 2007); John Willett, *Art and Politics in the Weimar Period: the New Sobriety, 1917–1933* (New York, 1996); Walter Laqueur, *Weimar: A Cultural History* (New York, 1974); Peter Gay, *Weimar Culture: The Outsider as Insider* (New York, 1968); Barbel Schrader, *The Golden Twenties: Art and Literature in the Weimar Republic* (New Haven, Conn., 1988); Michael Brenner, *The Renaissance of Jewish Culture in Weimar Germany* (New Haven, Conn., 1996); Jeffrey Herf, *Reactionary Modernism: Technology, Culture and Politics in Weimar and the Third Reich* (New York, 1984); David Durst, *Weimar Modernism: Philosophy, Politics and Culture in Germany, 1918–1933* (Lanham, 2004); and Istvan Deak, *Weimar's Left-Wing Intellectuals* (Berkeley, Calif., 1968) and the essays found in John Alexander Williams, ed., *Weimar Culture Revisited* (New York, 2011); and Kathleen Canning, Kerstin Barndt, and Kristin McGuire, eds., *Weimar Publics/ Weimar Subjects: Rethinking the Political Culture of Germany in the 1920s* (New York, 2010). On the intellectual crises in academic circles, see Fritz Ringer, *The Decline of the German Mandarins: The German Academic Community, 1890–1933* (Cambridge, Mass., 1969). On youth, see Luke Springman *Carpe Mundum: German Youth Culture of the Weimar Republic* (Frankfurt am Main, 2007). On specific areas of Weimar culture, see Peter Jelavich, *Berlin Cabaret* (Cambridge, Mass., 1993), and *Berlin Alexanderplatz: Radio, Film, and the Death of Weimar Culture* (Berkeley, Calif., 2006); Valerie Preston-Dunlop and Susanne Lahusen, eds., *Schrifttanz: A View of German Dance in the Weimar Republic* (London, 1990); and Janet Ward, *Weimar Surfaces: Urban Visual Culture in 1920's Germany* (Berkeley, Calif., 2001). On the perception of the Weimar collapse as apocalypse, see Klaus Vondung, *The Apocalypse in Germany* (Columbia, Calif., 2000); and Jost Hermand, *Old Dreams of a New Reich: Volkish Utopias and National Socialism* (Bloomington, Ind., 1992). On the importance of such perceptions on the origins of the Nazi movement, see David Redles, *Hitler's Millennial Reich: Apocalyptic Belief and the Search for Salvation* (New York, 2005).

There is an enormous literature on Nazi Germany. Useful bibliographical guides are Helen Kehr and Janet Langmaid, *The Nazi Era, 1919–1945* (London, 1982), a selected bibliography of published works to 1980; and *The Third Reich, 1933–1939* (Santa Barbara, Calif., 1984), an annotated bibliography on periodical literature published between 1973 and 1982. Also of much value are a number of basic reference tools, Roderick Stackelberg, *The Routledge Companion to Nazi Germany* (New York, 2007); Tim Kirk, *The Longman Companion to Nazi Germany* (New York, 1995); Louis L. Snyder, *Encyclopedia of the Third Reich* (New York, 1976); Malvin Walker, *Chronological Encyclopedia of Adolf Hitler and the Third Reich* (New York, 1978); Robert Wistrich, *Who's Who in Nazi Germany* (New York, 1982); Christian Zentner and Friedemann Bedurftig, eds., *The Encyclopedia of the Third Reich*, 2 vols. (New York, 1991); Michael Freeman, *Atlas of Nazi Germany*, 2nd ed. (London, 1995); and James Taylor and Warren Shaw, *The Third Reich Almanac* (New York, 1987). Detailed works on the various historical interpretations of Hitler and National Socialism include Pierre Aycoberry, *The Nazi Question* (New York, 1981); Ian Kershaw, *The Nazi Dictatorship: Problems and Perspectives of Interpretation*, 4th ed. (London, 2000); John Hiden and John Farquharson, *Explaining Hitler's Germany: Historians and the Third Reich* (London, 1983); and Klaus Hildebrand, *The Third Reich* (London, 1984), which includes a brief history and a discussion of problems and trends in research.

On the origins and rise of the Nazi movement, see Richard J. Evans, *The Coming of the Third Reich* (New York, 2004). On the Thule Society, see David Luhrssen, *Hammer of the Gods: The Thule Society and the Birth of Nazism* (Washington, D.C., 2012). An excellent analysis of why the Nazis found increasing support as the Weimar Republic collapsed is found in Peter Fritzsche, *Germans into Nazis* (Cambridge, Mass., 1998). General works on Nazi Germany include Karl D. Bracher, *The German Dictatorship: The Origins, Structure, and Effects of National Socialism* (New York, 1970); Joseph Bendersky, *A Concise History of Nazi Germany*, 3rd ed. (New York, 2007); Tim Kirk, *Nazi Germany* (New York, 2007); Klaus Fischer, *Nazi Germany: A New History* (New York, 1995); Jost Dülffer, *Nazi Germany 1933–1945: Faith and Annihilation* (New York, 1996); Michael Burleigh, *The Third Reich: A New History* (New York, 2000); Donald Wall, *Nazi Germany and World War II*, 2nd ed. (Belmont, 2003); and Roderick Stackelberg, *Hitler's Germany: Origins, Interpretations, Legacies*, 2nd ed. (New York, 2009). Three brief studies are D. G. Williamson, *The Third Reich*, 4th ed. (New York, 2011); Dick Geary, *Hitler and Nazism*, 2nd ed. (London, 2000); and Stephen J. Lee, *Hitler and Nazi Germany*, 2nd ed. (London, 2009). Older works still of value are Friedrich Meinecke, *The German Catastrophe* (Boston, Mass., 1963); and Franz Neumann, *Behemoth: The Structure and Practice of National Socialism, 1933–1944* (New York, 1963). An excellent collection of essays covering various essential topics can be found in Jane Kaplan, ed., *Nazi Germany* (New York, 2008). Also useful are Panikos Panayi, *Weimar and Nazi Germany: Continuities and Discontinuities* (New York, 2001); Peter Stachura, ed., *The Shaping of the Nazi State* (London, 1978); Henry A. Turner, ed., *Nazism and the Third Reich* (New York, 1972); and Thomas Childers and Jane Caplan, eds., *Reevaluating the Third Reich* (New York, 1993). On women in Weimar and Nazi Germany, see Renate Bridenthal, Atina Grossmann, and Marion A. Kaplan, *When Biology Became Destiny: Women in Weimar and Nazi Germany* (New York, 1984); Katharina von Ankum, ed., *Women in the Metropolis: Gender and Modernity in Weimar Culture* (Berkeley, 1997). Jeremy Noakes and Geoffrey Pridham have edited a valuable collection of documents in *Nazism, 1919–1945: A Documentary Reader*, 4 vols. (Exeter, 1983–1998). Also valuable are the single volumes edited by Benjamin Sax and Dieter Kunz, *Inside Hitler's Germany* (Lexington, 1992) and Roderick Stackelberg and Sally A. Winkle, *The Nazi Germany Sourcebook: An Anthology of Texts* (New York, 2002).

The best biographies of Hitler are Alan Bullock, *Hitler: A Study in Tyranny* (New York, 1964); Joachim Fest, *Hitler,* trans. Richard and Clara Winston (New York, 1974); and especially Ian Kershaw, *Hitler 1889–1936: Hubris* (New York, 1999); and *Hitler 1936–1945: Nemesis* (New York, 2000). Other studies include Helmut Heiber, *Adolf Hitler* (London, 1972); Norman Stone, *Hitler* (London, 1980); Werner Maser, *Adolf Hitler: Legend, Myth, Reality,* trans. Peter and Betty Ross (New York, 1973); Rainer Zitelmann, *Hitler: The Politics of Seduction,* trans. H. Bogler (London, 2000); David Welch, *Hitler: Profile of a Dictator* (New York, 2001); and Frank McDonough, *Hitler and the Rise of the Nazi Party,* 2nd ed. (New York, 2012). Popular biographies are A. N. Wilson, *Hitler* (New York, 2012); Robert Payne, *The Life and Death of Adolf Hitler* (New York, 1973); and John Toland, *Adolf Hitler* (New York, 1976). Two works that examine the enormous literature on Hitler are John Lukacs, *The Hitler of History* (New York, 1997); and Ron Rosenbaum, *Explaining Hitler* (New York, 1998).

On the early Hitler, see William Jenks, *Vienna and the Young Hitler* (New York, 1960); Franz Jetzinger, *Hitler's Youth* (London, 1958); Bradley Smith, *Adolf Hitler: His Family, Childhood and Youth* (Stanford, Calif., 1967); and Brigitte Hamann, *Hitler's Vienna: A Dictator's Apprenticeship* (New York, 1999), a detailed examination of the Vienna years. On Hitler's war years, see John F. Williams, *Corporal Hitler and the Great War, 1914–1918: The List Regiment* (New York, 2005) and Thomas Weber, *Hitler's First War* (Oxford, 2010). The early Munich years are covered in David Clay Large, *Where Ghosts Walked: Munich's Road to the Third Reich* (New York, 1997). On the importance of Richard Wagner on Hitler, see Joachim Köhler, *Wagner's Hitler: The Prophet and His Disciple* (Cambridge, UK, 2000), trans. Ronald Taylor. For another overlooked influence, see Steven F. Sage, *Ibsen and Hitler: The Playwright, the Plagiarist, and the Plot for the Third Reich* (New York, 2006). On important religious aspects of early Nazism, see Derek Hastings, *Catholicism and the Roots of Nazism* (New York, 2010); David Redles, "Nazi End Times: The Third Reich as Millennial Reich," in Karolyn Kinane and Michael A. Ryan, eds. *The End of Days: Essays on the Apocalypse from Antiquity to Modernity* (Jefferson, N.C., 2009), pp. 173–196. The *Protocols of the Elders of Zion* are discussed in Norman Cohn, *Warrant for Genocide: The Myth of the Jewish World Conspiracy and the Protocols of the Elders of Zion* (London: 1996); Stephen Eric Bronner, *A Rumor About the Jews: Reflections of Anti-Semitism and "The Protocols of the Elders of Zion"* (New York, 2000); and David Redles, "The Turning Point: *The Protocols of the Elders of Zion* and the Eschatological War between Aryans and Jews," in Richard Landes and Steven T. Katz, eds. *The Paranoid Apocalypse: A Hundred-Year Retrospective on The Protocols of the Elders of Zion* (New York, 2011), pp. 112–131. The role of the SA is considered in Otis C. Mitchell, *Hitler's Stormtroopers and the Attack on the German Republic, 1919–1933* (Jefferson, N.C., 2008); Nigel Jones, *A Brief History of the Birth of the Nazis* (New York, 2004). For an interesting account by an unrepentant storm trooper himself, see Wilfred von Oven, *Hitler's Storm Troopers: A History of the SA: The Memoirs of Wilfred von Oven* (Barnsley, 2010). A detailed examination of the Beer Hall Putsch is found in Harold J. Gordon, Jr., *Hitler and the Beer Hall Putsch* (Princeton, N.J., 1972).

MySearchLab™ Connections

Study and Review

After World War I, Germans had to confront heavy war reparations, a peace treaty that assigned Germany total responsibility for the war, and the humiliation of their national pride. The Weimar Republic was ill-equipped to deal with the public's resentment and support for the political extremes on the left and the right. In this chaos, the Nazis attempted to seize power in a coup d'état in Bavaria. Despite the coup's failure, the Nazi Party was projected into national prominence.

Read the Document

1. **The Covenant of the League of Nations**
   This document illustrates the international community's attempts to build cooperation among its member nations and to ensure world peace.

Read the Document

2. **Heinrich Hauser, With Germany's Unemployed (1933)**
   This document presents the testimony of Heinrich Hauser (1901–1955) about his time in a German shelter for the homeless and destitute.

View the Map

3. **Map Workbook Activity: Europe between Wars, 1919–1939**
   This activity shows the geopolitical condition of Europe following World War I. The sprawling Austro-Hungarian Empire had broken up, and Germany lost a great deal of its borderlands, causing a great deal of political instability.

RESEARCH AND EXPLORE

Despite moderate popular support for the Weimar Republic, unfair peace demands, a weak post-war economy, and poor leadership toward the end of the republic created a situation that would ultimately result in the collapse of the government.

1. What role did the German army play in the collapse of the Weimar Republic? In what ways were the army's attitude toward the republic and public reaction to the republic's policies used by extremists for political gain?

2. What did the hyperinflation of the mark do to German morale? Did American intervention in the German economy improve the financial situation?

3. What effect did the Brüning administration have on the efficiency of the Reichstag? What effect did this administration have on German morale?

ADDITIONAL RESOURCES

Emergence of the Nazi Party

Adolf Hitler

CHAPTER 3

The Growth and Victory of Nazism, 1924–1934

The Beer Hall Putsch and Hitler's subsequent imprisonment proved a significant turning point in his career. Hitler saw clearly the need for a change of tactics. The Nazis could not achieve power by a frontal assault on the Weimar Republic but would have to work within constitutional or legal means. This meant the creation of a mass political party that would actively compete for votes with the other political parties in Weimar Germany. Hitler, having regained faith in himself and ever the opportunist, guided the Nazi Party through this transformation.

NEW BEGINNINGS: THE REBUILDING OF THE NAZI PARTY, 1924–1929

Hitler was sentenced to a five-year term in Landsberg prison, fifty miles west of Munich. He was treated like a distinguished guest and established a pleasant daily routine. Hitler now had time to reflect on the lessons of the Beer Hall Putsch. Disillusioned by the weakness of the Bavarian authorities, he became convinced that he alone would have to lead the national revolution and that it no longer sufficed to play the role of "drummer" for nationalist forces in Bavaria. The German army would have to be courted more carefully and subtly. Its opposition had meant certain failure for the putsch. If the Nazis had any hope of gaining power, it would have to be with the support or, at least, the neutrality of the army. Most important, Hitler perceived that he and the Nazis would have to seek power by legal or pseudolegal means, within the framework of the Weimar political system. Once in power, the Nazis could dismantle the republic by using the agencies of the state itself.

Mein Kampf

The most immediate and tangible result of Hitler's stay in prison was the first volume of *Mein Kampf* (*My Struggle*). (The second volume was completed in 1926.) Rudolf Hess, one of Hitler's most devoted followers, had voluntarily joined his leader in prison and served as his secretary. Hitler began his book by creating an official Nazi version of the Beer Hall Putsch. The fiasco was transformed into a myth of the revolutionary hero Hitler leading his band of dedicated followers, who wanted only "the resurrection of their people." Those who had fallen in the streets of Munich were heroes and martyrs for the Nazi movement and the German nation. This revolutionary event was later remembered each year in a commemorative ceremony in Munich on November 9.

In *Mein Kampf*, Hitler discussed the roles of theoretician and politician in the creation of a significant political movement. "The theoretician of a movement must lay down its goal, the politician strive for its fulfillment. The thinking of the one, therefore, will be determined by eternal truth, the actions of the other more by the practical reality of the moment." But, "in long periods of humanity, it may happen once that the politician is wedded to the theoretician."[1] There is no doubt that Hitler saw himself as this rare combination of theoretician and politician. Consequently, *Mein Kampf* is basically a statement of the goals or fundamental ideas of the Nazi movement. These ideas predate Hitler and are certainly not original. German nationalism, a virulent anti-Semitism, and anti-Bolshevism are linked together by a Social Darwinian theory of struggle that emphasizes the right of the stronger in racial conflict, the right of superior nations to gain *Lebensraum* (living space) through foreign expansion, and the right of superior individuals to establish authoritarian leadership over the masses.

As historians have pointed out, the only originality in *Mein Kampf* is Hitler's discussion of effective methods of propaganda, mass psychology, and mass organization of peoples. What is remarkable about *Mein Kampf*, however, is Hitler's elaboration of a set of ideas that would guide his actions once he achieved power. That others failed to take Hitler and his ideas seriously was one of his greatest advantages over his opponents. However bizarre those ideas may have been, it was Hitler who brought them to their frightening logical fruition in the Third Reich.

Rebuilding the Nazi Party: Hitler's Control, 1925–1926

On December 20, 1924, after only a year of his five-year sentence, Hitler was released from prison. He found the Nazi Party in a state of disorder. The NSDAP had been officially banned across Germany. Hitler had chosen Alfred Rosenberg, the self-styled ideologist of the party and editor of the *Völkischer Beobachter*, to be the party leader while he was in prison. Rosenberg, as Hitler knew, was no leader, and the party had disintegrated into factions. Hitler had no wish to see the party flourish while he was in prison.

Hitler formally refounded the party in Munich on February 27, 1925, and proclaimed that it would fight Marxism and Jewry. After he promised to function within the republican system, the Bavarian state lifted its ban on the Nazis. A number of Nazi supporters who had been in the *völkisch* movement now joined the reconstituted party. They were attracted to Hitler because of the reputation he had established during his trial as a man of action. Hitler was now viewed as the leader of the *völkisch* cause in southern Germany.

Although Hitler quickly reestablished his control over the party in Munich and in Bavarian districts outside of Munich, he was faced with opposition to his rule from other

---

[1]Excerpts from *Mein Kampf* by Adolf Hitler, translated by Ralph Manheim, pp. 210, 212. Copyright © 1943, renewed 1971 by Houghton Mifflin Harcourt Publishing Company. Reprinted by permission of Houghton Mifflin Harcourt Publishing Company. All rights reserved.

parts of the party, especially in northern and western Germany. In March 1925, Hitler had authorized Gregor Strasser to organize the Nazi Party in north Germany. Strasser, who had been an officer in the German army during World War I, joined the Nazi Party in 1921 and took part in the Beer Hall Putsch. A man of great energy, Strasser was an excellent organizer who quickly built up hundreds of local branches for the Nazi Party in north Germany. Gregor and his brother Otto tended to take the socialist part of the Nazi program seriously and especially hoped to obtain support for the party from the working classes in western and northern Germany. Late in 1925, a group of party leaders from the north and west formed the National Socialist Working Association with Gregor Strasser as director and Joseph Goebbels, an intellectual and unsuccessful novelist, as secretary.

This group differed from Hitler and the Munich party leadership on four issues. They objected to the control and domination of the party by the Munich leaders. They supported the Socialist demand for the expropriation of the property of the royal princes. Hitler labeled this demand a Jewish swindle, fearing that the party's support from business-men would be harmed if it pushed the expropriation bill in the Reichstag. The Working Association also opposed participation in election campaigns and favored instead the use of strikes by the urban masses, another reflection of its socialist orientation. Goebbels, in fact, had even called for the expulsion of the "petty bourgeois Adolf Hitler" from the party. Finally, the actions of the Working Association implied that regional party organiza-tions should participate in the framing of major lines of policy. Hitler, on the contrary, believed that discussion of any of the policies within the party's program, the twenty-five points of 1920, would encourage doctrinal disputes within the party, endanger party unity, and impede the ability of the party leader to act as needed for the good of the party. The Working Association posed a threat both to Hitler's leadership as the ultimate source of authority and to the Munich leadership of the party.

Hitler realized he had to move decisively. He called a meeting of party leaders in the city of Bamberg on February 14, 1926. He spoke for five hours and emerged victorious. He denounced the expropriation of the princes' property, disagreed with the opening to the left, and refused to allow any tampering with the twenty-five-point program of 1920. The program of 1920, Hitler said, "was the foundation of our religion, our ideology. To tamper with it would constitute treason to those who died believing in our Idea."[2]

This success was followed by a number of measures designed to reinforce Hitler's sole control over the party. In May 1926, at a national membership meeting, the NSDAP program was declared unchangeable. Other party meetings outlawed working asso-ciations such as that of Strasser and Goebbels. Further centralization of the party was achieved when local Nazi groups were ordered to gain approval from party headquarters before making any local changes, and local committees on propaganda were instructed to report to and receive instructions from the Munich leadership. Party tribunals known as *Uschla* were established in 1926 under Hitler's direction to settle internal party differ-ences. Since the *Uschla* judges were appointees loyal to Hitler, this new organization gave him the opportunity to control the party without direct involvement. *Uschla* could expel individuals or even entire local groups from the party.

Joseph Goebbels, whom Hitler recognized as a man of considerable talent, was completely won over to Hitler's side. Hitler gave him the important position of

[2]Quoted in Dietrich Orlow, *The History of the Nazi Party: 1919–1933* (Pittsburgh, 1969), p. 70.

regional party leader in Berlin in November 1926. Goebbels responded to Hitler's personal attention with great joy, as expressed in his diary:

> We drive to Hitler. He is having his meal. He jumps to his feet, there he is. Shakes my hand. Like an old friend. And those big blue eyes. Like stars. He is glad to see me. I am in heaven . . . I arrive. Hitler is there. Great joy. He greets me like an old friend. And looks after me. How I love him! What a fellow! And he tells stories the whole evening. I could go on listening forever. A small meeting. He asks me to speak first. Then he speaks. How small I am! He gives me his photograph. With greetings from the Rhineland. Heil Hitler! . . . I want Hitler to be my friend. His photograph is on my desk. I could not bear it if I had to despair of this man.[3]

Goebbels submitted to the Hitler cult with extreme emotionalism. But he was intelligent and clever enough to realize that his future with the party was more secure with Hitler than with anyone else.

In July 1926 in Weimar, the NSDAP held its first party congress since the Beer Hall Putsch. It was apparent that the party was now unified under the control of Adolf Hitler and the Munich party branch. All final decision-making powers rested in Hitler's hands. His position was clear, and he wanted no discussion of ideas in the party: "A good National Socialist is one who would let himself be killed for his Führer at any time."[4] The party had established the *Führerprinzip*, the leader principle. It was a single-minded party under one leader and only one leader. Even Gregor Strasser, after the Bamberg meeting, had hailed Hitler as the outstanding leader to whom party members would be loyal until death.

Rebuilding the Nazi Party: Organization, 1925–1929

As an extremist party, the Nazis faced their most serious challenge in the late 1920s with the return of political and economic stability to Germany. The year 1924 had witnessed economic recovery and the beginning of relative prosperity. Extremist attacks on the Jews and Communists were much less convincing while the economy was growing. The Weimar government seemed more acceptable to Germans with the election of the conservative military hero Paul von Hindenburg as president in 1925 and the participation of the rightist Nationalists (DNVP). Through the efforts of Gustav Stresemann, Germany's international position seemed greatly strengthened. Problems remained, such as the refusal of the largest party, the Social Democrats (SPD), to join in governing. But the domestic crises seemed mastered and the remaining problems manageable. In such circumstances radical political groups of both the left (Communists) and the right (Nazis) lost influence.

Hitler was not dismayed by the return to stability in Germany. He did not believe it would last and worked to establish a highly structured party that could compete in elections throughout Germany and attract new recruits when another time of troubles arose. The organization of the Nazi Party was established on a regional basis. Germany was divided into regions called *Gaue*. At the head of each *Gau* stood a *Gauleiter*, or regional party leader. Originally, *Gauleiter* owed their position to their superior effectiveness in their regions. But after 1926, they were officially appointed by Hitler and served as executive agents for their districts. Basically, *Gauleiter* became bureaucratic agents subject to

---

[3]Helmut Heiber, ed., *The Early Goebbels Diaries* (London, 1962), pp. 47, 50.

[4]Quoted in Joachim Fest, *Hitler*, translated by Richard and Clara Winston (New York, 1974), p. 241.

control by Hitler and the party leadership in Munich. The physical size of the *Gaue* was originally determined by circumstances peculiar to each district, but in 1928, the *Gaue* were reorganized to correspond more closely to the thirty-five Reichstag electoral districts.

Each *Gau* was divided into smaller units known as *Kreise* (districts) under the control of *Kreisleiter* (district leaders). These units were subdivided into *Ortsgruppen* (local branches or chapters) led by *Ortsgruppenleiter* (branch or chapter leaders). At least fifteen members were required to form a local branch. Local branches were responsible to district leaders, who in turn were responsible to regional leaders. Although the various administrative units of the Nazi Party were allowed some freedom to exploit issues unique to their areas, they were supposed to be totally obedient to the policies established by Hitler and the Munich leadership. The *Uschla*, the party court system, gave the leadership the means to expel members and thus enforce obedience to a rigid authoritarian order.

By 1929, the NSDAP had created a national party organization. The party itself had experienced considerable growth since being refounded by Hitler in 1925. In that year the party had 27,000 members, slightly less than half of its membership in 1923. After a modest expansion to 35,000 members in 1926, the party grew to 75,000 in 1927 and 108,000 in 1929. The regional, district, and branch leaders of the Nazi organization were relatively young men, mostly between twenty-five and thirty-five, who had been uprooted after the war from normal family ties and jobs. They were committed to Hitler as their leader because he gave them the kind of active politics they wanted. Instead of democratic debate they favored brawls in beer halls and streets, enthusiastic speeches, and comradeship in a struggle on behalf of a new Germany. One new, young Nazi member expressed his participation in the party in these words:

> For me this was the start of a completely new life. There was only one thing in the world for me and that was service in the movement. All my thoughts were centred on the movement. I could talk only politics. I was no longer aware of anything else. At the time I was a promising athlete; I was very keen on sport, and it was going to be my career. But I had to give this up too. My only interest was agitation and propaganda.[5]

Such enthusiasm created tremendous dynamism for the party when turned against Nazi opponents.

But this energy could also result in passionate internal conflicts resulting in struggles for leadership positions. As a dedicated believer in struggle and the victory of the fittest, Hitler rarely interfered in leadership conflicts. For him, the strongest and hence best leaders would emerge as the victors. When party conflict got out of control and created chaos, then Hitler and the Munich leadership would intervene. In 1926, disintegration of the Berlin and Hamburg parties led to the replacement of the *Gauleiter* there by Joseph Goebbels and Albert Krebs, respectively. Goebbels proved especially competent in transforming the energy that had created internal chaos into a dynamic movement against the Communists.

As part of the Nazi Party's organizational overhaul, the SA was refounded in the fall of 1926 under a new leader, Franz Pfeffer von Salomon. In reestablishing the SA, Hitler stressed that it was no longer connected to any other paramilitary group and that it was, in fact, not a pseudomilitary force, but an instrument of propaganda and strong-arm tactics led by the party. Its function was to make war on Marxism and Jewry by mass

---

[5]Quoted in Jeremy Noakes and Geoffrey Pridham, eds., *Nazism 1919–1945* (Exeter, 1983), vol. 1, pp. 50–51.

demonstrations and the conquest of the streets. The growth of the SA made it useful for the campaigns of terror and propaganda, especially in the cities. But Hitler feared that it could get out of control, which might lead the government to ban the party again. Responding to these fears, Hitler appointed himself supreme leader of the SA in 1930 and recalled Ernst Röhm from Bolivia to make him chief of staff. In 1925 and 1926 an elite group known as the *Schutzstaffeln* (SS—protection squads) was established within the SA for special duties. It remained insignificant until Heinrich Himmler was appointed its leader in 1929 (see Chapter 4).

In addition to its paramilitary forces, the NSDAP established a series of auxiliary organizations in the late 1920s. For the young there were the Hitler Youth, the Student League, and the Pupils' League. Professional groups, such as teachers, lawyers, and doctors, had their own auxiliary units. The National Socialist Women's League offered female supporters some involvement in a predominantly male party. With its numerous auxiliary organizations, the Nazi Party created an all-inclusive movement that met the needs of many different groups.

Hitler and the SA. The SA was first established in 1921 and then refounded in 1926 after it had been banned as a result of the failed Beer Hall Putsch. Hitler is shown here addressing some members of the SA in the late 1920s. *(National Archives and Records Administration[242 HAP-1928-11C])*

Hitler and the Blood Flag. The Blood Flag was a banner stained with the blood of Nazis killed during the Beer Hall Putsch. New flags were officially consecrated for use by touching them to the Blood Flag. *(National Archives and Records Administration[242-HAR-2-30B])*

Moreover, various departments with specific responsibilities were created within the party. The Reich Directorate had overall administrative responsibility for the party. Departments were created for such areas as foreign policy, the press, labor, agriculture, the economy, the interior, and justice. These departments virtually constituted a miniature state bureaucracy within the Nazi Party itself, making it, in Hitler's words, "the germ of the future state." This party bureaucracy, then, not only provided Hitler with a powerful instrument for controlling the party but also created a shadow government that could govern the state when the Nazis achieved power.

During these years of organization increased use was made of special uniforms and titles. And in 1927 the annual party rally was held in Nuremberg for the first time. This city was one of the party's substantial growth areas, and as the center of the medieval German Reich, it had a rich historical tradition that helped to root Nazism in the German past.

Turning Point to a Mass Movement, 1928–1929

During these years of rebuilding, and especially from 1925 to 1927, the Nazi Party pursued an "urban plan" designed to win industrial workers away from the traditional labor parties, the SPD and Communists (KPD). But the strategy was only partially successful, with gains in certain areas such as the city of Berlin and the highly industrialized Ruhr region.

In other areas German workers remained class conscious and bound to their traditional socialist orientation. Like Catholics, who were often immune to Nazi propaganda, they were a closely knit group conscious of their differences from other groups. It did not help Nazi urban strategy that Hitler was never fully committed to the working-class plan. Despite the statements in the twenty-five-point party platform, Hitler himself believed in private property and capitalist enterprise and remained hostile to the idea of a party-sponsored trade union movement.

This pro-working-class strategy had other repercussions. It led many middle-class Germans to see the NSDAP as a socialist working-class party. It alienated business leaders, whose subsequent withdrawal of financial support created money problems for the party. For a while, the Nazis were forced to rely upon members' dues, contributions at rallies, and other such sources of support that were insufficient for the expansion of the party.

In 1928, the Nazis began a shift in strategy, one that was accentuated after their failure in the Reichstag elections in May of that year. The Nazis received only 800,000 votes, or 2.6 percent of the total vote, and gained only twelve seats in the Reichstag. The NSDAP lost heavily in the urban areas—precisely those areas designed to be won by the urban plan. The party did relatively well in rural areas, such as Schleswig-Holstein in northwest Germany, where it had tried early in 1928 to appeal to the growing discontent among farmers and to small towns dependent on agriculture. These electoral results solidified the need for a shift in strategy.

In the summer of 1928, Hitler told a leadership conference in Munich that the party had to concentrate more on rural and small-town areas, especially in northern, central, and eastern Germany. Although Munich and Bavaria in southern Germany remained the organizational headquarters, the party had limited appeal in an area dominated by the Catholic Bavarian People's Party (BVP). The Nazis now pursued a propaganda program aimed at rural voters and the interests of lower-middle-class inhabitants of small towns, although in some areas, such as Berlin, they continued direct appeals to the working classes.

Farmers were especially vulnerable to Nazi propaganda because of the economic difficulties they began to experience in 1927 as a result of a worldwide agricultural depression. Falling prices and harvests, high expenses, and indebtedness had resulted in growing numbers of foreclosures. The Nazis identified Jewish bankers and capitalists and the Weimar government controlled by Marxists (the SPD) as the cause of the farmers' economic distress. They promised to eradicate indebtedness and tax relief once in power. Nazi ideological emphasis on "blood and soil"—the belief that the products of German soil grown by the noble farmers and eaten by the people created a pure German blood and thus a pure *Volk*—made an effective impact on rural areas. Appeal to German nationalism, as the Nazis discovered, also played well with both farmers and the middle classes.

In the small towns Nazis appealed to the middle classes, which were composed of small businessmen, artisans, white-collar workers, and civil servants, in a variety of ways. They downplayed the anticapitalist slogans of their urban plan and became defenders of private property. They attacked the Marxists (whether the SPD or KPD variety) as revolutionaries who wanted to destroy private property. In order to defend private property, Hitler officially reinterpreted point 17 of the twenty-five-point program, which called for expropriation of agricultural estates. Now, he explained that this meant only the estates owned by Jews. The Nazis assailed large department stores, especially those owned by Jews, as an economic threat to small businessmen. The Nazis presented an antimodernist image to the middle classes, claiming to embody traditional German values and to oppose the decadent values of the Weimar Republic. By promising to destroy Marxism and the Weimar political party system, they implied a return to the authoritarian order of imperial Germany, when the traditional middle class had supposedly been secure and honored.

The new propaganda barrage was aimed also at university students, veterans' organizations, and professional groups. The Nazis were particularly successful with university students, many of whom were attracted by the Nazi emphasis on German nationalism, especially the idea of a unified national community. By 1930, the Nazis had infiltrated the chief student self-governing organization. In shifting his focus to new sources of votes, Hitler was eager to find people who could bring professional skills to the party's bureaucracy. Hitler perceived correctly that if the Nazi Party were to emerge as an effective mass party, it would need intelligent, well-trained members who could organize election campaigns and membership drives and activities. *Gauleiter* would need to be efficient bureaucrats who could be counted on to secure votes and members in their region.

By 1929, the party had successfully shifted to its new political strategy. In that year, the Nazis joined in a right-wing attack on the Weimar Republic that brought them considerable success and foreshadowed the impressive breakthrough they would make in 1930.

Prelude to Power, 1929

This right-wing attack focused on the issue of the Young Plan. This was a new reparation payment plan, which scaled down the amount Germany owed but still required annual payments until 1988. Alfred Hugenberg, the wealthy press and film magnate who had become head of the German Nationalists (DNVP) in 1928, seized upon this issue to gain support for the DNVP and recoup some of the losses sustained by his party in the election of 1928. Hugenberg was a staunch German nationalist who wished to destroy the Weimar Republic and establish a conservative authoritarian state. In the fall of 1929, he organized a national referendum to reject ratification of the Young Plan. Hugenberg was joined by a coalition of big business, right-wing political groups, and nationalist organizations. The Nazis were also invited to join. Hugenberg believed that he could take advantage of Hitler's movement. The DNVP was a very respectable and wealthy party, but it lacked mass popularity. Hitler's party was dynamic and offered considerable mass support. Although Hugenberg viewed the Nazis as too radical to ever govern, he believed that they and especially Hitler could be manipulated to attract mass support for the rightist–nationalist cause. Hitler perceived that he was being used, but realized the advantages of joining in a coalition with these rightist forces.

Although the referendum to reject the Young Plan, voted on in November 1929, failed miserably, the Nazis gained considerably from the affair. They were now seen as less radical and more acceptable, especially by the middle classes. As allies of Hugenberg, the Nazis received national attention and attained respectability. They acquired financial resources that enabled them to wage an efficient and dynamic political campaign. Hitler's speeches alone generated enormous enthusiasm and added to the general impression of a dynamic, young, spirited movement. Consequences were immediate and impressive. The party made gains in local and state elections in November and December 1929. In the December elections in Thuringia, the Nazi vote grew from 4.7 percent to 11.3 percent of the total. Party membership increased dramatically. By the end of 1928, the NSDAP had 108,000 members; by the end of 1929, it had grown to 178,000, almost doubling its membership in one year. The SA had grown to 100,000 men, the size of the German army. The year 1929 was a good one for the Nazis, even before the effect of the October 1929 stock-market crash, which would have dramatic repercussions in Germany. Before examining the impact of the depression, though, we need to take another look at the social composition of the Nazi Party.

Nazi Members and Leaders, 1925–1930

Between 1925 and 1930, the NSDAP continued to attract elements of every important social group in Germany. Despite the party's urban plan, workers remained slightly underrepresented in the party as a whole. However, the lower classers were very well represented in the SA, the SS, and the Hitler Youth. Leadership of these groups remained dominated by the middle class and the elites.

Historians distinguish an old and a new lower middle class in twentieth-century Germany. The old lower middle class consisting of artisans, shopkeepers, and independent merchants (in general, small businessmen) joined the party in large numbers. They were especially attracted by the Nazis' attack on large department chain stores and their blame of the Jews for the problems of small business. Farmers, who were underrepresented in the party from 1925 to 1927, began flocking in after the NSDAP began to direct its propaganda toward their problems. In fact, by 1928 they were overrepresented in the party compared with their percentage of the total population. The new lower middle class was slower in opting for Hitler, but also became overrepresented in the party as the economic crisis worsened. This group included white-collar salaried employees in industry and commerce, lower civil servants, and elementary school teachers. These groups consistently faced economic uncertainties.

Elite and upper-middle-class membership in the Nazi Party was not large in number; nevertheless these segments of society were overrepresented in the party after 1925. Already in 1926, a small group of discontented students under Wilhelm Tempel at Leipzig had founded the National Socialist German Student Union. By 1930, half of the entire German university student body had joined the Nazi Party. Managers and entrepreneurs joined the party in large numbers as well. The frequent assertion that a significant number of industrial leaders became party members or contributed large amounts of money to the Nazis seems not to be true. The party did gain support from smaller manufacturers and entrepreneurs who resented the tycoons. Although fewer academic intellectuals were attracted to the NSDAP after 1924, this group was still overrepresented in the party. Higher civil servants also remained overrepresented and increased in proportion after 1924.

During its rebuilding phase, then, the NSDAP retained the allegiance of the lower middle class and the elite but was unable to attract larger numbers of workers, with the exception, as already noted, of memberships in the SA and the Hitler Youth. It remained a young man's party in terms of membership, although less so among voters. The average age of joiners between 1925 and 1928 was twenty-nine and of those in 1930, thirty. The percentage of party members eighteen to twenty-nine remained considerably greater than the proportion of that age group in the German population. The party was thus much more youthful than the German population—undoubtedly a crucial factor in understanding the dynamism of the Nazi movement. An openly radical party, the Nazis attracted young people who were turned off by the inertia of the established parties and who welcomed the constant activity of the Nazi Party. Women continued to remain conspicuously absent from the party, constituting between 5 percent and 6 percent of total membership. Nevertheless, many of the new voters attracted to the Nazi Party were women.

The social profile of the Nazi Party's leaders differs somewhat from that of the rank and file. The elite was heavily overrepresented. The higher the rank of the leader, the higher the class. In 1930, for example, 40 percent of the *Gauleiter* had upper-middle-class backgrounds. By that time, Hitler was seeking more highly skilled functionaries, and party leaders were coming ever more from the elite. The more skill required, the more qualified the administrators—a basic characteristic of industrial societies. Leaders, as would be expected, were generally older than members. It does not appear that Nazi leaders were social outcasts who used Nazism simply to advance and enrich themselves. Indeed, many Nazi leaders became impoverished as a result of their work for the party. Such men were motivated by an ideal rather than by opportunism or greed. Some *Gauleiter* had to depend on handouts to survive. It was not until 1929 and 1930 that *Gauleiter* were put on the party's payroll.

THE CLIMB TO POWER, 1930–1933

The Young Plan referendum in 1929 had given Hitler and the Nazi Party new respectability and national stature. But 1929 was significant for another reason as well—the beginning of a worldwide depression. The subsequent economic chaos and misery gave the Nazis the opportunity they had been waiting for. They made the most of it and emerged as the largest mass party in Weimar Germany.

The Great Depression: Parliamentary Paralysis and Presidential Government

Even before the famous New York stock-market crash on October 24, 1929, business activity in Germany had experienced a slowdown resulting in 1.3 million unemployed by the fall of that year. The stock-market crash, however, had an even greater effect on the German economy because it led to the recall of short-term American loans that had helped fuel Germany's economic prosperity in the late 1920s. Business failures multiplied and unemployment rose dramatically—to 3 million in 1930, 4.35 million in 1931, and 6 million by the winter of 1932. The last figure meant that one in three of the working population was out of work. This economic crisis created a climate of despair for many Germans. Many workers, especially hard hit by unemployment, remained committed to the left but turned increasingly away from the democratically oriented SPD toward the more radical KPD, which desired the overthrow of the Weimar Republic.

The middle classes, who remembered what the inflation of 1923 had done to them economically and socially, were alarmed. Although not unemployed, they feared the eventual loss of their jobs and their social prestige and status. As the workers became more radicalized and joined the KPD in larger numbers, the middle classes grew apprehensive at the thought of a communist revolution. Small businessmen resented big business and big labor. As the depression progressed from 1930 to 1932, the middle classes, like the workers, tended to become radicalized.

Unlike the workers, however, they found the answers to their insecurity in the messages of the NSDAP. Nazi propaganda provided simple but apparently understandable reasons for the economic collapse. The Nazis blamed the Versailles settlement and reparations, the Weimar system itself, the "November criminals" who created it, and the political parties that perpetuated it. They blamed the Communists, who wanted a revolution that would destroy the traditional German values. They blamed big business and the economic profiteers who were ruining the middle classes. And they blamed the Jews, who allegedly stood behind Marxism, the Weimar system, much of big business, and economic profiteering. The Nazi accusations were unsophisticated but effective. Lower-middle-class unemployed and employed embraced a Nazi Party that promised to eliminate this corrupt Weimar system.

The economic, social, and psychological crises created by the Great Depression had dire political consequences for Weimar democracy. Beginning in 1928, the "Great Coalition," which included the left-wing SPD and the conservative People's Party (DVP), had governed Germany. This unlikely combination worked largely because of the economic recovery and the political acumen of the DVP leader Gustav Stresemann, the primary architect of Germany's progress between 1924 and 1929. His death in October 1929 and the simultaneous economic decline severely tested the coalition. It fell completely apart in March 1930 over the issue of the rising cost of unemployment benefits. The DVP, representing the interests of industrialists, wished to reduce unemployment benefits. On the other hand the SPD, unwilling to see any loss in the benefits gained by labor since 1918, favored an increase in unemployment funds with employers shouldering half of the burden. Neither side was willing to compromise, and the government resigned.

The collapse of the Great Coalition and the continuing economic chaos created a parliamentary crisis that opened the door to the so-called presidential system, built upon the extension of the president's constitutional powers. Article 48 of the Weimar constitution gave the president emergency powers to restore law and order in a crisis, including use of the army if necessary. However, the Reichstag had the right to revoke these emergency measures. Because of the imprecision of Article 48's wording, it was left to the Reich president himself to determine when a threat to law and order existed. This power had been invoked by the first Weimar president, Friedrich Ebert, to defend the republic against armed attacks. It had, in fact, saved Weimar democracy on a number of occasions.

This power of the president to rule in an emergency was now enlarged to cover the crisis created by the depression and the failure of the parliamentary parties to form a majority government that could deal with the economic difficulties. The president would form a new government composed of a chancellor and cabinet ministers. The government would not be affected by the interests of the political parties but would rule by emergency decrees issued by the president in lieu of laws passed by the Reichstag. Such a government would depend on presidential support rather than on the Reichstag.

Several forces converged to create this presidential system. Reich president Paul von Hindenburg, at heart a monarchist, had never fully accepted the republican system of party politics and had come to detest the squabbling of the parties. The president was old (he had been first elected in 1925 at the age of seventy-eight) and was easily persuaded by his advisers to pursue a new course because of the political stalemate. The president's state secretary, Otto Meissner, and other members of the state bureaucracy favored a change to a more authoritarian system that would be "above parties" and, through use of the president's emergency power, independent of the Reichstag.

The army favored the change as well. It felt that the Weimar system, especially because of the power of the pacifistic left, had never created a climate favorable to army growth. The army's political expert, General Kurt von Schleicher, was the foremost exponent of a presidential system. Because of his intimate ties to Hindenburg's advisers and to Hindenburg himself, he was able to manipulate the appointment and dismissal of chancellors and cabinets behind the scenes. But Schleicher was not a right-wing fanatic; he wished to use the presidential system not to destroy but to maintain the life of the republic.

Despite Schleicher's objectives, it is easy to see in hindsight that the presidential system meant the demise of democratic rule. The Germans were politically inexperienced, and to many of them democracy seemed merely a sham anyway. A more authoritarian system, reminiscent of imperial Germany, was envisioned as Germany's salvation. In many ways, Weimar democracy ended in 1930 with the establishment of the presidential system. It prepared people for the dictatorial rule of the Nazis.

Upon Schleicher's recommendation, the first chancellor under the presidential system was Heinrich Brüning, one of the leaders of the Catholic Center Party. Brüning tried to deal with the depression by applying traditional economic theory and submitted a balanced budget to the Reichstag in July 1930. When the Reichstag failed to pass it, Brüning had Hindenburg invoke Article 48 and implement his program by presidential decrees. The Reichstag, acting within its constitutional rights, overrode the chancellor and revoked these decrees. Normally, upon this vote of no confidence, Brüning and his government should have resigned. But, considering his government a presidential one and above parliamentary politics, Brüning had Hindenburg dissolve the Reichstag and establish new elections for September 14, 1930. Meanwhile, Brüning continued to run the government and even reinstated his economic agenda through the use of Article 48.

Brüning believed that the forthcoming election would vindicate his efforts at strong leadership and produce a parliamentary majority that would bolster his presidential chancellorship. But he was very wrong. The economic crisis in Germany had spawned fear and insecurity. Supporters of the republic attacked the government for destroying the constitution. Others blamed the government for the economic crisis. The extremists of left and right saw new possibilities in the midst of crisis. In the end, they were right.

The Reichstag election of September 14, 1930, proved to be the decisive breakthrough that Hitler and the Nazis had planned for. Even Hitler was surprised by the magnitude of the Nazi victory. The Nazi vote went from 800,000 in the 1928 election to 6.5 million, or 18.3 percent of the total, giving the Nazis 107 seats and making them the second largest party in the Reichstag after the Social Democrats. The NSDAP made its best showing among farmers and the middle class, especially the lower-middle-class voters in rural, small-town Protestant areas in northern, central, and eastern Germany. The Nazis also gained support from considerable numbers of new voters and pulled middle-class voters away from center and right-wing parties such as the People's Party (DVP), the Democrats, and the Nationalists (DNVP). The last three parties lost sixty-seven seats in the Reichstag.

The Nazi shift in strategy in 1928 had proved to be a master stroke. The party had been organized so well that the Nazis easily made the transition to a mass movement. Within three months of the election, they added another 100,000 members, and the SA began to mushroom. The Nazi Party had become a formidable force.

Hitler and the Nazis believed that more electoral victories would eventually produce a majority that would give them power. Although this did not happen, Nazi electoral successes were an important factor in Hitler's eventual claims to the chancellorship. In turn, a crucial element in the party's election successes was its superior use of mass propaganda.

Elections and Nazi Propaganda, 1930–1932

The Nazis became adept at propaganda. Hitler emphasized its importance and established the principles on which it should be based. Propaganda must be addressed to the masses and not to the intellectuals. Its function was to call the attention of the masses to certain facts, not to educate them. Since the masses were influenced more by emotions than by reason, propaganda must be aimed primarily at the emotions. Given the limited intelligence of the masses, propaganda had to focus on constant repetition of a few basic ideas, eventually establishing these ideas as truths in the minds of the masses. In addition, mass meetings were psychologically important in creating support for a movement. They offered a sense of community, gave meaning to life, and created the emotional effects that gave people strong convictions.[6]

The man responsible for putting Hitler's principles into practice was Joseph Goebbels, the master propagandist of the Third Reich. Goebbels, the son of a Catholic working-class family in the Rhineland, had received a Ph.D. in German literature from the University of Heidelberg in 1921. After failing in his attempts at a professional career and writing a novel, Goebbels joined the Nazi Party in 1924 and became a collaborator of Gregor Strasser. A cynical opportunist and shrewd realist, Goebbels switched to Hitler's side in 1926 and was rewarded with the position of *Gauleiter* of Berlin. His tremendous success in Berlin, achieved through the brilliant use of propaganda and his oratory (many thought he was as good an orator as Hitler), brought a new appointment by Hitler in 1929 as Reich propaganda leader of the NSDAP. In this position, Goebbels played a crucial role in the electoral campaigns from 1929 to 1932.

The Reich Propaganda Office under Goebbels maintained control over the propaganda activities of the party. Propaganda departments were set up at each level of party offices. Although subordinate to the political leadership at each level, propaganda offices had their own chain of command as well. Information on local activities was collected and passed up to higher levels. The Reich Propaganda Office sent out specific directives to lower levels by means of a monthly magazine. These directives specified the themes and slogans to be used at mass rallies and underscored the necessity of adapting subjects to the interests of the local audience. The Reich Propaganda Office printed standard posters and pamphlets for all districts and distributed patriotic and party movies.

The most effective regional and national speakers were used on more important occasions. Through posters and leaflet campaigns controlled from above, local groups mobilized people for mass rallies of varying sizes. The Nazis used a technique of saturation advertising. They would schedule 70–200 rallies in the space of one to two weeks in one district. These rallies were carefully planned to make maximum use of party groups. This saturation strategy was used particularly where there was hope for a major electoral breakthrough for the party. This type of campaign usually made use of Hitler as the featured speaker.

In fact, the Nazis were pioneers in modern electioneering techniques. They covered Germany in whirlwind campaigns by car, train, and airplane. "Hitler Over Germany" was the name attached to one of Hitler's campaign tours, which covered fifty cities in fifteen days. The Nazis also established voter recruitment drives that continued both during and between elections.

Undoubtedly, there was a relationship between the number of young people in the Nazi Party and the dynamism of its electoral politics. As we have seen, young people were especially attracted to Nazism. It offered a politics of activism, clear-cut lines of authority, and opportunities for leadership at an early age. Compared with the other political parties

---

[6]See the section on propaganda and mass meetings in Chapter 5 for more detail on this subject.

(except for the Communists, who attracted working-class youth for similar reasons), Nazism certainly offered a break with old conventions and a hope of restoring German greatness. Nazism gave young people a chance to actually be part of this process, to feel a part of historical destiny. In a sense, Nazism liberated in young people the tremendous energy that comes from participating in a politics based on the belief that one is indeed going to create a new world or a new age. Many observers have commented on how the Nazis, regardless of the size of their local group, seemed to do more in election campaigns than all the other parties combined.

The mass meetings of the election campaigns were carefully organized to the smallest item. Marching bands, swarms of fluttering flags, shouts of *heil*, the play of spotlights all were precisely orchestrated to produce the maximum emotional effects on the crowd. Hitler's own rallies were exceptionally well managed. A Hamburg schoolteacher gave this impression of a rally she attended:

> "The Führer is coming!" A ripple went through the crowds. Around the speaker's platform one could see hands raised in the Hitler salute. A speaker opened the meeting, . . . A second speaker welcomed Hitler and made way for the man who had drawn 120,000 people of all classes and ages. There stood Hitler in a simple black coat and looked over the crowd, waiting—a forest of swastika pennants swished up, the jubilation of this moment was given vent in a roaring salute. Main theme: Out of parties shall grow a nation, the German nation. He censured the system ("I want to know what there is left to be ruined in this state!") . . . When the speech was over, there was roaring enthusiasm and applause. Hitler saluted, gave his thanks, the Horst Wessel song sounded out across the course . . . Then he went.—How many look up to him with touching faith as their helper, their saviour, their deliverer from unbearable distress.[7]

This schoolteacher's impressions reveal the emotional impact of these rallies on the onlookers. They also disclose the approach Hitler took to campaign themes. What were the Nazis telling the German people that made them so attractive to certain groups?

The Nazis successfully managed two fundamentally opposite approaches to the German voters. First of all, in their election campaigns they specifically geared their themes to the needs and fears of different social groups. In working-class areas, they campaigned against capitalism, offering to protect workers by destroying international high finance, or exploited the economic issues of unemployment. One Nazi campaign poster directed to the working class shows a Nazi destroying the stock exchange, which is labeled "International High Finance." Another poster, entitled "Work and Bread," pictures an arm with a Nazi armband, the hand offering tools to the outstretched hands of the unemployed. For the middle classes, the Nazis exploited fears of the communist revolutionary threat to private property. A Nazi poster portrayed a hideous skeleton in a Communist uniform against a red background with the caption "Only one man can save us from Bolshevism—Adolf Hitler." To appeal to lower-middle-class businessmen, the Nazis attacked big department stores as a threat to shopkeepers, stressing that the attacks were really aimed at the Jews who controlled these stores. The Nazis were flexible, however. In areas where anti-Semitism was not popular, the Nazis would drop the attacks on Jews and focus instead on anticommunism, nationalism, and the defense of religious values. The last of these issues was important for Protestant voters.

[7]Quoted in Noakes and Pridham, *Nazism 1919–1945*, vol. 1, p. 74.

The second half of the Nazis' dual approach blatantly contradicted the first. The Nazis denounced conflicts of interest and claimed to stand above classes and parties. They promised to overcome the old class and caste spirit and build a *Volksgemeinschaft*, a national community, a new Germany based on social equality. To create the new Germany, the Nazis would have to replace democracy with the principle of leadership. The Nazis also appealed to traditional militarism, national pride, and national honor, denouncing the Versailles treaty and the "traitors" who accepted and upheld it. Hitler believed that human beings are motivated by more than economic forces, that idealism, national honor, sacrifice, and dedication struck chords of emotion in his listeners. While his Nazi speakers in various regions of Germany could appeal to the specific interests of different groups, Hitler claimed to stand above it all. Hitler's only promise was to create a new Germany, a nation great and proud again, devoid of class differences and party infighting, a nation where all could work after the turmoil of Weimar democracy. Hitler struck a note to which many Germans responded from the depths of their souls.

Political Maneuvering

Since the unsuccessful Beer Hall Putsch, Hitler had pursued a legal strategy of working within the system to achieve power. The campaigns of 1930 to 1932, in which the Nazis sought power through victories at the ballot box, reflected this strategy. But Hitler and the Nazis did not plan to govern democratically. The Nazis made it clear that they intended to establish a new order under their sole direction once they came into power legally. Indeed, in the oath of legality Hitler had taken at a trial of young army officers in Leipzig in 1930, he had stated that the Nazis were entering the legal arena in order to make their party the ruling power. Once they possessed constitutional power, they would mold the state into "the shape we hold to be suitable." Parliamentary elections, however, proved to be a stumbling block, and the Nazis were forced to become involved in the intricate political maneuvering within the presidential system in order to come to power "legally."

Heinrich Brüning had failed miserably in the elections of 1930 to gain a center-right majority to support his presidential regime. Brüning's government, relying upon Hindenburg's use of Article 48, did survive, but only because the Social Democrats were unwilling to face new elections. Although that party considered Brüning's presidential regime a violation of the constitution, it was unwilling to bring down the government.

During 1931, Brüning's government proved unable to cope with Germany's problems. His difficulties were exacerbated by Nazi tactics. SA troops marched through the streets challenging Communists and engaging them in pitched battles. Themselves the instigators of this civil violence, the Nazis nevertheless blamed the government for being unable to curb the lawlessness on the streets of Germany. While claiming to work within the constitutional system to gain power, the Nazis worked at the same time within the Reichstag to undermine the parliamentary system and create additional chaos. Eighty-eight percent of the Nazi delegates were newcomers to the parliament; 60 percent were under forty years of age. Nazi delegates were effective obstructionists in the Reichstag. They boycotted sessions and disrupted parliamentary debates with shouting and calls for discussion of points of order. They did not want the system to work, but demanded its protection while pursuing a legal path to power.

Within the Nazi Party one group in particular, the SA, stressed the path of revolution. Indeed, in April 1931 a group of SA leaders in Pomerania reproached Hitler thus: "the NSDAP had departed from the revolutionary course of true National Socialism for

Germany's freedom, had pursued the reactionary line of a coalition party, and consequently had given up—purposely or accidentally—the pure ideal for which [SA leaders were] fighting."[8] Many SA members resented the control exercised over them by the political wing of the party while they were carrying out the strenuous and even life-threatening work of the party. Hitler was faced with a serious dilemma. Although he shared their ideals, he wanted to keep the SA on the legal path. He did not want to alienate the authorities and was especially fearful after his Beer Hall Putsch of creating a situation where the army would be used to crush his movement. At the same time, he had to conciliate the militants within the SA who wanted action. For the time being, Hitler managed to keep the SA in line by personal appeals for loyalty and vague promises of the SA as a reservoir of the future national army.

In October 1931, Hitler attempted to convince Hindenburg that the Nazis should be allowed to form a government. Hindenburg had a very low opinion of Hitler and refused. With Hindenburg's term as president coming to an end in the spring of 1932, Hitler was confronted with a new decision—whether or not to run for the presidency. Both Hindenburg and Hitler were reluctant to run. The old field marshal was eighty-four years old and would have preferred retirement. But he was warned that only he could prevent the election of Adolf Hitler, and reluctantly he agreed to run. He was supported not by the parties of the right, as in the election of 1925, but by the left and by moderate supporters of democracy, who now saw Hindenburg as their last hope to preserve the Weimar system against the Nazis. This was not a reassuring development for the future of the republic, since Hindenburg had once been an opponent of the republic and was now approaching senility. Hitler was not eager to run against the popular Hindenburg, knowing he would certainly lose. But as leader of the second largest party, he thought it crucial that the Nazis contest the election. Since he was an Austrian citizen, the tiny state of Brunswick, which had a considerable number of Nazi officeholders, made Hitler a state councilor, a position that automatically bestowed German citizenship upon him. Despite an intensive and exhausting campaign, Hitler gained only 30 percent of the vote. But since Hindenburg failed to gain an absolute majority (he had 49.45 percent of the vote), a second ballot was required, pitting Hitler against Hindenburg without the Nationalist candidate Theodor Duesterberg. This time Hindenburg achieved his absolute majority with 53 percent. Hitler's vote increased to almost 37 percent.

The reelection of Hindenburg set the stage for another change in the presidential system. Three days after the election, Hindenburg accepted Chancellor Brüning's recommendation for a ban of the SA because of its illegal activities during the election. General Kurt von Schleicher, originally a supporter of Brüning, now began to agitate against him. He was especially anxious to harness the Nazis to a new right-wing government and opposed the ban on the SA. Through Hindenburg's son Oskar, Schleicher put pressure on the Reich president to dismiss Brüning.

Hindenburg had already grown increasingly disenchanted with Heinrich Brüning. He blamed him for a political situation in which the Social Democrats and other moderate parties had been his chief support in the recent election. Moreover, Brüning had failed to solve the economic crisis, and his deflationary policies had led opponents to label him the Hunger Chancellor. The final and decisive strike against him, in Hindenburg's eyes, was his plan to carve up the estates of bankrupt Prussian landlords and distribute the land to landless farmers. The Junkers, or Prussian landed aristocrats (of whom Hindenburg was

[8]Heinrich Bennecke, *Hitler und die SA* (Munich, 1962), p. 165.

one), objected, and Hindenburg agreed with them. By the summer of 1932, Hindenburg was willing to let go of Brüning. Brüning, having neglected to win favor in the Reichstag because he had ruled by presidential decree, had no support left. Hindenburg's only condition was a suitable replacement, and General Schleicher arranged that.

Schleicher's choice as the new chancellor was Franz von Papen, a Catholic aristocrat who had defected from the Center Party because his political views were considerably closer to those of the DNVP. Schleicher considered Papen a person who could easily be controlled from behind the scenes. He hoped that Papen, a dedicated right-winger, would win back conservative support for the presidential government. Schleicher negotiated with Hitler to gain Nazi toleration of a Papen government. Fearing a civil war if the Nazis were not won over, Schleicher agreed to lift the ban on the SA and to call new Reichstag elections in return for Hitler's consent. Hitler agreed. Brüning was dismissed on May 30 and the Papen government installed. Reichstag elections were set for July 31, and the ban on the SA was lifted on June 14.

Papen now entered the German political arena as a figure who played a crucial role in Hitler's accession to power. A cunning man, he proved to be dangerous not because of his craftiness but because he did not really have the political ability to play the role he thought he could. He entered big-time politics as a small-time player and was eventually outclassed by his opponents, especially Hitler. Papen was a reactionary who planned to end the democratic system by instituting an authoritarian order. To prove that his government could be effective and win rightist support in the forthcoming elections, Papen used emergency decrees to depose the anti-Nazi Prussian state government run by a coalition of Social Democrats and the Center Party. He purged the Prussian civil service, replacing government officials loyal to the Weimar Republic with Nationalists. Since Prussia constituted almost three-fifths of Germany, this action was a serious blow to the republic. It provided an example to the Nazis of how to take over power in the federal states by pseudolegal means. The relative ease of the Papen takeover convinced Nazis that the process could be easily repeated.

The Nazis waged a vigorous campaign for the July 31 elections that was conducted in an atmosphere reminiscent of civil war: Frequent street battles took place between Nazis and Communists after the ban on the SA was lifted. Almost hundred men were killed and over a thousand wounded in one month's battles in Prussia alone. The Nazis again stressed the inability of the government to maintain law and order.

On July 31, 1932, the Nazis won their most impressive victory to date. The party advanced from 108 to 230 delegates and was now the largest party in the Reichstag. The Nazis had won 37 percent of the vote and yet had failed to gain the majority they thought they could win. Goebbels commented in his diary: "Conclusion: we must come to power. Since the last presidential election we have greatly increased our votes. We'll drop dead from winning elections."[9]

Hitler now demanded that he be made chancellor and that the Nazis be allowed to fill the major cabinet positions. Hindenburg refused and suggested that Hitler take the vice-chancellorship and enter a coalition government. Hitler rejected this offer, believing that he must hold out for the top position if the Nazis were to achieve their goals. The morale of the Nazi Party began to suffer badly. Great expectations of success had not materialized. The SA began again to agitate for a revolutionary course of action since the path of legality seemed at an end. Hitler, ever fearful of army suppression of the movement, rejected any illegal action.

[9]Joseph Goebbels, *Vom Kaiserhof zum Reichskanzlei* (Munich, 1936), pp. 135–136.

Hitler believed that the Nazis still occupied a good position. The Nazis and Communists now made up 52 percent of the Reichstag. Although these extremist parties of the left and the right would never make a coalition government, they could essentially cripple the parliamentary system. Hermann Göring had, in fact, been elected president of the Reichstag. Since the Reichstag had the right by Article 48 to repeal any presidential emergency decrees, the Nazis and Communists could also wreak havoc with a presidential government by coordinating their efforts.

Faced with this dilemma, Papen called for a new election when the Reichstag met in September. Aware of sagging Nazi morale, he hoped that a loss of votes would make the Nazis more cooperative. The Nazis feared another election campaign. After the July 31 Reichstag elections, they were psychologically and financially unprepared for another vigorous campaign. The Nazis' fears seemed justified: Their vote fell from 37 percent to 33 percent, with a corresponding decrease in Reichstag seats to 196. It was a costly defeat for the Nazis. It broke the myth of invincibility that they had fostered. It appeared to contemporaries that the Nazis had peaked in July and then had lost much of their political momentum. By the end of 1932 the Nazi Party seemed at an important crossroad.

The Nazi Party on the Eve of Power

Although the Nazis had failed in elections to achieve a majority in the Reichstag, they had managed to gain control of five German federal states: Anhalt, Oldenburg, Mecklenburg, Thuringia, and Brunswick. In addition, they had gained a fair number of offices throughout Germany. These Nazi officeholders presented a taste of what national rule would be like. They politicized all aspects of life under their control. In the state of Anhalt, they expelled the Bauhaus School of Design from Dessau because of its modern approach to architecture.

For all its efforts, it was apparent by the end of 1932 that the Nazi Party was in considerable trouble. As Joseph Goebbels remarked in his diary: "The year 1932 was one eternal run of bad luck. One must beat it into pieces . . . The past was difficult and the future is dark and gloomy; all prospects and hopes have completely disappeared."[10] The NSDAP had many problems. In addition to the psychological tests of apathy and depression, the party was faced with seemingly insurmountable debts. Rumors continued to circulate about incipient SA revolts. There were additional losses in the state and local elections in November and December, and it was clear that the Nazis had reached a limit with their voting constituency. They could not break the refusal of Catholic and working-class voters to vote for them. Economic improvement in the winter of 1932 made the Nazis realize that they might lose even more of the protest vote that had made their electoral successes possible. Finally, a minority within the party was critical of Hitler's unwillingness to enter a coalition. Hitler's demands, even after the election reversal, remained the same—the chancellorship for himself and a Nazi-dominated cabinet. Gregor Strasser, in particular, feared that the Nazis would miss their chance unless they entered a coalition and tried to gain power through the "back door." Hitler disagreed, believing that progress to full Nazi control through this approach would be too slow and the SA would get out of control from impatience. Strasser's position, however, was shared by others, creating the

---

[10]Ibid., p. 229.

possibility of a split in the party. But renewed political maneuvering led indirectly to the salvation of the Nazi movement and the appointment of Hitler as chancellor.

The Chancellorship, January 30, 1933

After the November Reichstag elections, Franz von Papen contemplated creating an authoritarian presidential government. This would have meant eliminating the Weimar constitution, curtailing the Reichstag and political parties, and possibly banning both extremist parties—the Nazis and the Communists. In Papen's eyes, the new authoritarian order would be run by the "best people," the traditional right-wing elites. Although Hindenburg seemed willing to support Papen, General Schleicher, now minister of defense, vehemently objected to Papen's scheme. He informed Hindenburg that the plan would create a civil war and that the army could not handle both the SA and the Communists. Schleicher, who was influenced by young, right-wing intellectuals, was not a reactionary like Papen. He realized that Papen had no mass support—a crucial element in a modern industrial state. Without mass support, no government could unify the state and push for the renewal of military strength, as the army wished. Consequently, Schleicher persuaded Hindenburg to drop Papen and proposed that he himself be made chancellor with the goal of creating a new popular majority in the Reichstag in support of the government. Schleicher's general scheme was to create a new coalition majority by winning over labor and the Social Democrats, the Catholic Center Party, and the left wing of the Nazi Party under Strasser. In addition, he would seek popular support by solving the economic crises with an imposing program of economic and social reform. Reluctantly, Hindenburg appointed Schleicher chancellor on December 2, 1932.

It did not take long for Schleicher to realize that he could not succeed in his grand plan. He initiated a make-work program of public works and repealed the wage and benefit cuts instituted by Papen. But he failed to work a deal with the left and the Nazis. The Social Democrats were too suspicious of this political schemer and forced the trade unions to stop their negotiations with him. Schleicher's overtures to the left frightened the right, which now feared his Socialist leanings. In order to split the Nazi Party, the new chancellor offered the vice-chancellorship to Gregor Strasser. Although Strasser was personally willing to accept, Hitler rejected the offer. Strasser then resigned from the party. Hitler would never forget Strasser's "treachery," and Strasser would be murdered in June 1934. Schleicher had failed to split the Nazis.

In the meantime, Papen decided to get even with Schleicher and made the initiative that now saved the frustrated Nazis. Papen knew that to get Hindenburg's support he would have to promise him mass support, which could come only through one group—the Nazis. Papen arranged a meeting with Hitler at the beginning of January 1933 at the house of the banker and Nazi Party member Kurt von Schroeder. Hitler was now willing to negotiate with Papen and the German right. The Nazis could not come to power through elections. The party had serious debt, and there was much dissatisfaction within the ranks. Hitler was therefore open to making a deal. Papen suggested a new government that would revive the alliance of the Nazis and the conservatives first formed in the Young Plan referendum. Hitler would be chancellor, Papen vice-chancellor. Hitler compromised on his previous demands and allowed most of the cabinet ministers to be Nationalists instead of Nazis. Papen had only to convince Hindenburg to form a new government with Hitler as chancellor.

Hindenburg had grown quite willing to dismiss Schleicher. He had never forgiven him for unseating his favorite, Papen. When Schleicher proposed to revive Brüning's plan to settle peasants on the estates of bankrupt Junkers, Hindenburg, as a Junker, was further angered. Schleicher's activities, especially his courting of the Socialists, had cost him the favor of right-wingers, who now became more willing to support the Nazis.

Schleicher made one last attempt to keep the Nazis from power when he heard of the proposed Hitler–Papen government. He asked Hindenburg to use his emergency powers to ban the Nazi and Communist parties, suspend the Reichstag, and establish a presidential government under himself, Schleicher. Hindenburg refused after reminding Schleicher that this request was similar to the one by Papen that Schleicher had warned him against. Schleicher resigned on January 28.

Hindenburg was still reluctant to accept Hitler as chancellor. But Papen managed to persuade him that the arrangement he had worked out would render Hitler harmless. After all, there would be only three Nazis in the cabinet—Hitler as chancellor, Wilhelm Frick as minister of the interior, and Hermann Göring as minister without portfolio and also minister of the interior in Prussia. Conservative Nationalists, such as Alfred Hugenberg as minister of economics and agriculture and Franz Seldte as minister of labor, would occupy the remaining nine ministries. In his negotiations, Papen had also secured the right to be present at Hitler's conferences with Hindenburg. Papen evidently believed what he finally convinced Hindenburg of—that Hitler would be boxed in by conservatives. In response to a person who tried to warn him about Hitler, Papen replied, "You are mistaken, we've hired him." When reproached by a conservative opponent of Hitler for opening the door to Hitler, Papen responded angrily, "What do you want? I have the confidence of Hindenburg. In two months, we'll have pushed Hitler so far into a corner that he'll squeal."[11] Papen had also assured Hindenburg that the new government would achieve a parliamentary majority and eliminate the need for a presidential government. Hindenburg, eighty-five, tired of his responsibilities, finally capitulated to Papen and the other right-wing voices. Hitler achieved his goal on January 30, 1933, when he was sworn in as chancellor of Germany.

Hitler had come to power legally and within the system, even if the system had been seriously flawed since 1930. Several observations are pertinent. At the time Hitler became chancellor, the Nazi Party was already declining in strength. Politicians such as Schleicher and Papen, who naïvely believed they could use Hitler, soon found out that he was a considerably more accomplished and infinitely more ruthless politician. In addition, it was the acceptance of Hitler at the last moment by the right-wing elites that made possible his accession to the chancellorship. Startled and frightened by Schleicher's opening to the left, industrial magnates, higher bureaucrats, the army, and landed aristocrats accepted Hitler as the man who had the mass support for an authoritarian regime that would save Germany and their privileged positions from a Communist takeover. They, too, thought Hitler could be used. In retrospect, it is remarkable how deceiving appearances can be and how many otherwise intelligent people underestimated the political abilities of Adolf Hitler.

Hitler, ever the tactician, made a few final compromises to become chancellor. They were calculated risks, but having seen his opponents first-hand, he probably believed that he had all the power necessary to achieve complete Nazi domination. The speed of his conquests would lead one to think that he was right again.

[11]Both quotes are in Henry A. Turner, Jr., *Hitler's Thirty Days to Power* (New York, 1996), pp. 147–148.

THE CONSOLIDATION OF POWER, 1933–1934

The achievement of the chancellorship was for Adolf Hitler only the first step in the Nazi transformation of Germany. Hitler had no intention of ruling Germany as a prisoner of the conservatives. Within the two months in which Papen claimed Hitler would be contained, the new chancellor established the foundations for a Nazi dictatorship. The very speed of the process was undoubtedly a factor in overwhelming his opponents. But the German yearning for stability after years of uncertainty played a crucial role in allowing the Nazis to establish their rule. Although there was much illegality in the Nazi rush to power, Hitler maintained his posture of legality. He had been appointed chancellor under Article 48 and as chancellor used Article 48 to issue emergency decrees, especially against civil liberties. He claimed (correctly) that he was only doing what his predecessors had done. Even if it was contrary to the spirit of the constitution, Hitler liked to claim his National Socialist revolution had been a legal one.

The "Legal Revolution," January–March 1933

When Hitler took his oath of office on January 30, 1933, there was no certainty that he could achieve his goal of sole rule by the Nazis. After all, only three out of twelve cabinet positions were held by Nazis. Nor did Hitler have a working majority in the Reichstag. And Reich president Paul von Hindenburg, who did not like Hitler, could dismiss him as easily as he had appointed him.

But Hitler had clearly arranged his position to give himself some advantages as well. He was, after all, chancellor. As minister of the interior in Prussia, Hermann Göring had control over the police in Prussia, which constituted three-fifths of Germany. Wilhelm Frick as Reich minister of the interior had influence over the remaining police forces. General Werner von Blomberg, the minister of defense, was a Nazi sympathizer and could at least ensure that the army would not actively oppose Hitler. Hitler also had the advantage of knowing that there was little alternative to the Nazis. Only the forces of the right— the Junkers, army, higher bureaucrats, and big industry—offered any option, but they had failed from 1930 to 1932 to find a government acceptable to them that could garner mass support. Finally, one cannot underestimate Hitler's own role. Hitler was a clever politician who had the advantage over his conservative opponents of knowing precisely what he wanted and the ability to be absolutely ruthless in pursuit of it. Although it is doubtful that Hitler had a precise schedule for his seizure of power, he did have a general idea, and as a skillful opportunist he could also take advantage of unfolding events.

The first stage of the Nazi conquest involved the exercise of executive power by presidential decree, as previous chancellors had done. The Reichstag was dissolved on February 1, giving Hitler seven weeks of rule by presidential decree. This, and the scheduling of new elections for March 5, had been one of Hitler's conditions for becoming chancellor. Papen and other non-Nazis in the cabinet had insisted in the first cabinet meeting on January 31 that this election should be the last and should not mean the return to a parliamentary system. Clearly Hitler hoped, with the power of the state behind him, to achieve an absolute majority in the Reichstag that would enable the Nazis to "legally" secure power by eliminating the parliamentary system itself. Electoral success would also give the impression of mass support for the Nazis and their eventual assumption of power.

On January 31, 1933, Hitler made an "appeal to the German people." He described the previous fourteen years of the Weimar Republic as a catastrophe for Germans and stressed how he and the Nationalist leaders had united under Hindenburg's appeal to save the nation by forming a national government. The task of this national government was to create a "national revolution," emphasizing a unity of mind and will of all Germans in restoring the economy and regaining their freedom. All Germans had to unite to build a new Reich that would eliminate the insanity of classes and class warfare. Hitler denounced the Communists as enemies of this new Reich.

The phrase "national revolution" was another one of Hitler's magic formulas to attack his opponents and deceive his allies. Hitler's right-wing collaborators could accept the idea of a national revolution as the fulfillment of their own conservative and nationalist wishes. Since the national revolution was a call for unity, it was above parties, and any opposition to it could be labeled treasonous and hence injurious to the German people and their search for a new Germany. Labeling the Communists enemies enabled Hitler to exploit the fear of a Communist revolution.

Using this fear of communism, Hitler got Hindenburg to issue an emergency decree on February 4 curtailing freedom of the press and outlawing public meetings that posed a threat to the vital interests of the state. The decree was used to suppress the Communist press and legally disrupt Communist gatherings.

Supported by their slogan of the national revolution, the Nazis entered the election campaign. They were well financed as a result of large contributions now coming in from industrialists. In their appeals to the industrial magnates for financial support, Hitler and Göring emphasized that this would be the last election in Germany for the next ten years or even "for the next hundred years." In their campaign, the Nazis made effective use of the power of the state. State-directed public radio, a new and powerful political instrument, was monopolized by the Nazis. Hitler's speeches were transmitted throughout the country. The Nazis could also command the police for their campaign, and nowhere was this done more effectively than in the state of Prussia.

Hermann Göring, as minister of the interior in Prussia, took charge of the police there. His first action was to purge unsympathetic police officials. In a directive to the Prussian police on February 17, Göring ordered that they were to support "patriotic associations" such as the SA and attack Communists. Five days later, the SA and the SS were made auxiliary police and allowed to operate independently. If a Nazi opponent asked for police protection in Prussia, he could have a Nazi policeman himself as his "protector." Göring was blunt about his lack of scruples.

> I declared then, before thousands of my fellow-countrymen, that every bullet fired from the barrel of a police pistol was my bullet. If you call that murder, then I am the murderer. Everything has been ordered by me; I stand for it and shall not be afraid to take the responsibility upon myself.[12]

Göring's words and actions illustrate what could easily be overlooked about the "legal revolution." Contrary to Nazi claims of a "bloodless revolution," the Nazi seizure of power involved considerable violence. Although the SA and SS were the primary agents of Nazi fury, local Nazi organizations throughout Germany often interfered forcefully with state administrations and commercial activity.

Hitler and the Nazis were especially brutal with the Communists. In general, the political left in Germany was unsure how to react to the Nazis. It enjoyed little unity, since

---

[12]Hermann Göering, *Germany Reborn* (London, 1934), p. 125.

the Socialists and Communists had been at odds throughout the Weimar Republic. Many on the left were victims of their own theory that National Socialism was the last gasp of monopoly capitalism. They believed that the new government was actually dominated by Hugenberg and his fellow reactionaries and that it would collapse and open the door to a revolution. Moreover, the SPD maintained the fiction that the government had been installed constitutionally. If they used violence against it, the government would use this as an excuse to crush the Socialist movement. The reality was that the SPD had not only given up its revolutionary Marxist heritage but was unwilling to use force to defend its democratic practices. The Weimar experience had demoralized the Socialists, and they were truly unprepared to resist the Nazis. As a result of Nazi intimidation, increasing numbers of Socialists resigned from their party.

On February 27, one week before the election, the Nazis received another advantage. The Reichstag building went up in flames. A young, demented Dutch Communist, Marinus van der Lubbe, was arrested at the scene. The Nazis immediately exclaimed that this was the beginning of a Communist revolution. The convenience of this opportunity has led many historians to conclude that the Nazis set the fire. Other historians have claimed that van der Lubbe acted by himself. The problem has never been resolved. Regardless of its cause, the Reichstag fire prompted Hitler to get Hindenburg to issue a Decree for the Protection of People and State on February 28. This decree provided the foundation for the creation of a police state. It suspended such basic civil liberties as freedom of the press and the right to assemble. Moreover, it provided that the Reich central government could take over supreme power in any federal state that was unwilling or unable to restore public safety and order. The Nazis used this decree to round up Communists and harass rallies and meetings of other political parties as well. Anyone could now be imprisoned without trial or redress. The Decree for the Protection of People and State was another stunning example of the "legal" source of a reign of terror.

The Reichstag election of March 5, 1933, was a qualified Nazi success. The Nazis received 43.9 percent of the vote and 288 Reichstag seats. But they did not achieve an absolute majority. Nazi support came again not only from the lower middle class in agrarian and small-town Protestant regions but also from the upper class in the cities as well as from some workers. Millions of new voters had also been attracted to Hitler and the prospect of a new Germany. Since the DNVP won fifty-two seats, they and the Nazis did arrive at a majority (51.7 percent). Although that may have created the illusion for the Nationalists that they were still important and in control of Hitler, Hitler had no intention of being limited by his Nationalist allies. To rid himself of that burden he began to plan the passage of an Enabling Act that would free him of any parliamentary restraint.

Meanwhile, in March, both before and after the election, Nazis throughout Germany were busy taking control of local and state governments. The procedure was similar in most states. The SA would create disorder and local Nazi groups would then request intervention from the Reich minister of the interior, Wilhelm Frick, one of the three Nazis in the cabinet. As we have seen, the decree of February 28 had given the Reich government the right to take control in states where order was threatened. Using this decree freely, Frick would then appoint a local Nazi as Reich police commissioner in the federal state. With police support, local Nazis would then force state governments to resign and would form a Nazi government.

The state of Württemberg provides an example of how this procedure worked. The Württemberg state government was headed by the Center Party under Eugen Bolz. In the March 5 elections, the Nazis remained a minority in the state government. On March 6, the Nazis created disorder by staging a mass rally in Stuttgart, the capital city of Württemberg, and the following day they placed swastika flags on all public buildings. The Nazis asked the central government to reestablish order, and Frick appointed a local Nazi, Dietrich von Jagow, as Reich police commissioner on the basis of the emergency decree of February 28. Having secured control of the police, the Nazis forced the election of Nazi *Gauleiter* Wilhelm Murr as president of Württemberg. The Nazis classified this action as a "legal" seizure of power. The real nature of this legality can be seen in Murr's victory speech on March 15: "The government will brutally beat down everyone who opposes it. We do not say an eye for an eye, a tooth for a tooth; no, he who knocks out one of our eyes will get his head cut off, and he who knocks out one of our teeth will get his jaw smashed in."[13]

The Nazi seizure of power in the federal states was accompanied by considerable violence, especially from the SA. During the attempt to gain power legally, the SA had at times been forced to play a subordinate role. Pent-up frustrations were now vented in acts of violence, especially against opponents on the left. Communists and Socialists were singled out for attack and arrest. Party offices were raided and smashed and members beaten, arrested, and sent to concentration camps, which were first established in early March. Since the violence was aimed primarily against the left, other Germans rationalized its necessity and accepted Hermann Göring's pithy comment that "you can't make an omelette without breaking eggs." Actually, by these attacks on the Socialists and Communists, Hitler had assured himself of the support of the right wing, especially his Nationalist allies. What these supporters never considered at the time was the possibility that Hitler might someday use force against them. When they did realize it, it was too late.

The Nazis were also busy bolstering the image of a "bloodless" national revolution. They put on a magnificent day of national celebration at Potsdam on March 21 to inaugurate the opening of the new Reichstag session. The spectacle was coordinated by Joseph Goebbels, the newly appointed cabinet minister of people's enlightenment and propaganda. The cleverly contrived spectacle emphasized German traditions and loyalty and paid special homage to Hindenburg and the German army. This appeal to the traditional values of nationalism and militarism further seduced the conservative forces into believing that Hitler had become one of them. It was a way of helping them to overlook the violence and the true nature of the Nazi seizure of power.

Two days later, on March 23, Hitler sought passage of the Enabling Act. He and the Nazis aimed to eliminate the role of the Reichstag and the parliamentary system altogether. The Enabling Act, officially called the Law for the Removal of the Distress of People and Reich, would give the government the right to issue laws without the consent of the Reichstag. Such laws could even deviate from the constitution. Hitler asked for this power for only four years in order to solve Germany's economic and social problems, to create political stability, and to establish the new Germany.

Since the Enabling Act constituted a change in the constitution, it needed a two-thirds majority to pass. The Nazis and their Nationalist allies, who favored the Enabling Act as a way of eliminating the parliamentary system, held 340 seats. Hitler needed an additional fifty votes, which he could get from the Center Party's bloc of seventy-three. Intimidated by threats to Catholic civil servants and reassured by promises to respect the rights of Catholics, the Center Party capitulated. Center Party leaders argued that by doing so they might have some influence with the Nazis. If they did not accede, they would wind up like the Communists. In this atmosphere of intimidation, created by the SA and the SS,

---

[13]Quoted in Max Miller, *Eugen Bolz* (Stuttgart, 1951), p. 440.

only the Socialists had the courage to vote against the Enabling Act. The bill passed, 444 to 94. Parliamentary democracy had been destroyed by parliamentary means.

Hitler no longer needed the Reichstag. Although his Nationalist allies believed that President Hindenburg, and through him the army, could still control Hitler, they failed to see that Hindenburg was becoming senile and was not inclined to interfere. After all, Hitler had stayed within the limits of the constitution. On March 21, at Potsdam, Hitler had honored Hindenburg's own values. There would be no interference from the president. The "legal" passage of the Enabling Act also gave civil servants and judges some justification for their support of the regime despite its excesses. Since Hitler's government had been established in a legal fashion, technically it was their duty to assist the government. In effect, the Enabling Act legally made Hitler a dictator.

Gleichschaltung: Internal Consolidation of Power, Spring–Summer 1933

With the Enabling Act, Hitler and the Nazis entered another stage in their seizure of power—the establishment of a single-party regime. This step focused on *Gleichschaltung*, or coordination, which really meant the elimination or nazification of the social and political institutions of Germany—the political parties, state governments, bureaucracies, and trade unions. These institutions would need to be controlled just as the central government was now. The policy of *Gleichschaltung* was carried out in the spring and summer of 1933.

As a result of Nazi actions in March, most state governments had already fallen under the control of the Nazis. Hitler made this control official by a March 31 law that regularized the reorganization of the state governments. The new state governments could now issue laws without the approval of state legislatures. Finally, a law of April 7 appointed special Reich governors (*Reichsstatthälter*) to the states. Most of these positions were given to the Nazi *Gauleiter* in those areas. State governments had lost their independence and were now units of a centralized, authoritarian political system.

Coordination was also imposed upon the government bureaucracy. The April 7 law for the restoration of the professional civil service legalized a purge of the civil service and courts, especially of Jews and democratic elements. This was not, however, a wholesale purge, especially at the higher levels. Hitler knew that he needed the traditional civil service elite in order to achieve his foreign policy goals. Initially, he kept these bureaucrats, despite opposition within the party by those who wanted all of them replaced by Nazis. Since German teachers and professors were civil servants, Jews and leftists were removed from university and school positions.

Hitler especially feared the reaction of the trade unions. In 1920, a general strike called by the trade unions had stopped the rightist Kapp Putsch. But the trade unions had been considerably weakened by the depression and the subsequent unemployment. Although trade union leaders were strongly supporting the republic, they hesitated to oppose the Nazis by calling a general strike, which they feared would be ineffective. They, like the other elements of the left, the SPD and the KPD, simply hoped and believed that the Nazis would somehow fall and they would survive.

Hitler handled the trade unions and workers with considerable finesse. In his first few months as chancellor he had concentrated his attacks on the left, thus winning the favor of the right and the middle class. But in April he began to accentuate once again the socialist planks of the Nazi program. Then he declared May 1 the Day of National Labor, making it a paid national holiday. May Day was traditionally a day for the celebration of labor by the left in Europe. German workers had long agitated unsuccessfully for a paid national holiday on that day. The Nazis organized celebrations throughout Germany for the new Day of

National Labor in which the SA, the SS, workers, and employers paraded together. Hitler and other party leaders spoke of the new *Volksgemeinschaft*, the new Nazi national community that would finally eliminate class distinctions and create a real national unity.

The trade unions were now unsure how to react to the regime. But Hitler had merely lulled them into inactivity. On the very next day, May 2, the SA and the SS occupied

Coordination of Labor. This poster exclaims, "Then as today, we remain comrades. The German Labor Front." The soldiers in the background reflect the belief that in the trenches Germans from all classes and occupations fought together united as one people. In the foreground an engineer holds hands in solidarity with a manual laborer, promoting the German Labor Front as a force for worker unity, rather than class antagonism. *(Paul Dwight-Moore/Fotolibra)*

trade union offices and arrested union officers across the country. Without leaders and demoralized by Hitler's duplicity, the unions acquiesced. A law issued on May 10 broke up the trade unions and proclaimed the formation of the German Labor Front under Robert Ley. A pilot in World War I, Ley had joined the Nazi party in 1923 and become *Gauleiter* of the South Rhineland in 1925. The Labor Front, consisting of 8 million workers, was supposedly created to protect the economic interests of the workers. In fact, it was a compulsory organization subject to the party that served to regulate labor and imbue workers with Nazi ideals.

Farmers, like workers, were also coordinated. This was considerably easier, since farmers had provided much support for the Nazi movement. The farmers were organized under Nazi local, regional, and state farming leaders in the Reich Nutrition Estate under Walter Darré, the chief theorist of Nazi farming ideology as the Reich farmer's leader. Darré had fought on the western front in World War I. After studying agriculture at the University of Halle, he wrote several books emphasizing the doctrine of "Blood and Soil," which argued that farmers were the life source of a pure German race. Like workers, the farmers had their day of honor on October 1, when the Harvest Festival was held at the Bückeberg near Hamelin.

The Nazis' elimination of the other political parties finally made possible the one-party state. The KPD had already been banned in March. The conservative allies of Hitler had long favored the elimination of both the KPD and the SPD. Hitler was willing to oblige. The SPD was severely weakened by a split in its ranks in May. After the dissolution of the trade unions, some SPD leaders had fled abroad and issued calls for resistance by the left against the Nazis. The SPD leaders remaining in Germany refused and tried to remain an opposition party, still believing that the Nazis would fail and that they would be able to pick up the pieces. Hitler officially banned the party on June 22 on the pretext that its leaders outside Germany were involved in treason against the state. Hitler's Nationalist allies applauded the move, but they were next. Alfred Hugenberg, leader of the DNVP, was dismissed from the cabinet on June 26 and the Nationalists disbanded the day after. The two Liberal parties did the same at the end of June, and the last remaining republican party, the Center, followed suit on July 5. A Center Party member, Karl Bachem, explained that there was no hope of resistance since they would have been crushed. Besides, democracy was no longer capable of finding solutions to Germany's crises. To avoid a communist revolution and a terrible civil war, force had to be used, and the Nazis could do that best. Therefore,

> It is right to let the new men, particularly the leaders of the National Socialists, go ahead and not put unnecessary obstacles in their way. There are a lot of dubious things in the National Socialist movement, particularly so far as principles are concerned. But that has to be put up with for the time being. Today there is no point in being fussy about legal subtleties. What matters is first to let a strong, efficient government grow and then to support it wholeheartedly in order to suppress Bolshevism.[14]

With all parties eliminated, the law of July 14, 1933, stated the obvious. The NSDAP "constitutes the only political party in Germany." The one-party state had been established. And it had taken less than six months.

Why had it been so easy? Even Hitler was amazed. "One would never have thought so miserable a collapse possible,"[15] he declared at the beginning of July. There is no

---

[14]Quoted in Noakes and Pridham, *Nazism 1919–1945*, vol. 1, p. 165.
[15]Fest, *Hitler*, p. 415.

doubt that people had lost faith in democracy. The depression was the final blow in a series of setbacks that were especially difficult to handle for a people as inexperienced in democracy as the Germans. The loss of faith in the system created a mood of fatalism and resignation. "What could we do?" was a frequently heard comment. Germans had grown to feel that it was useless to worry about the things that were being abolished—they no longer mattered. Of course, the Nazis had also been ruthless in their use of force, and opposition could be costly. The Nazis were ready for power. Hitler had impregnated his movement with his own positive approach. Hitler and the Nazis believed that their time had come. Undoubtedly, the bandwagon effect was important as well. There were those who perceived that they could best preserve their jobs and advance their careers by joining the Nazi Party. Between January 30 and early spring, 1 million new members entered the party. Certainly this added to the impression that the Nazis had created a popular mandate and that anyone opposing it would be swept aside.

But one cannot use only negative factors to explain the Nazi success. To many Germans, the Nazis did offer a regeneration—a national awakening. "Germany Awake!" was an effective call to a people who had been psychologically crushed by World War I. The Nazis presented a compelling image of a strong, virile, dynamic new Germany that was above parties and above classes.

Finally, one must emphasize the role of Hitler. Hitler was a ruthless but clever politician. Of course, one of the keys to his success was that others' consistent underestimation of him gave him opportunities he might not otherwise have had. The KPD, DNVP, and Center Party at one time or another all believed Hitler's promises. They all found out, as European leaders discovered in the 1930s, that the real Adolf Hitler was a cruel, petty, ruthless, and cunning tyrant. For whatever reason, many people, both bright and stupid, did not want to believe that. Under those circumstances, it was easy for Hitler to work his political magic.

The Revolution Devours Its Own, Summer 1934

By the end of the summer of 1933, the *Gleichschaltung* of German social and political institutions was virtually complete. There were only three possible sources of opposition to the regime Hitler and the Nazis had imposed on Germany. President Paul von Hindenburg had the formal right to depose the chancellor. But this was not a real danger to the Nazis. Hindenburg was pleased that order had been restored to Germany and especially happy that he no longer had to play an active role in politics. Old and weary, his chief wish was for quiet and peace. He paid little or no attention to complaints about the Nazis and their tactics. Second, Hitler was concerned about the power of the army because of his 1923 Beer Hall Putsch experience. But Minister of Defense Blomberg was pro-Nazi, and there were obvious pro-Nazi sympathies among the junior officers as well. The army maintained neutrality, with the understanding that the military would not lose its privileged position. But the third source of possible trouble for the Nazis came from within their own party, from the ranks of the SA. The SA also constituted a challenge to the army, a situation that could spell danger for Hitler's power. The clash of the SA and the army and Hitler's resolution of this problem in the summer of 1934 completed the Nazi seizure of power.

By the summer of 1933, the SA had become unhappy with the progress of the Nazi revolution. A number of SA members had always taken seriously the socialist, anticapitalist aspects of the party's program. Now they felt that Hitler's regime had not gone far enough to create fundamental economic and social change. There had been too much compromise with existing institutions. Even the material rewards of power, such as jobs, had not come their way. For some SA members and especially their leader, Ernst Röhm, the National Socialist revolution was not over. As Röhm put it in a Nazi journal article in June 1933:

> If the bourgeois simpletons believe that it is enough that the apparatus of state has obtained a new sign, and that the "national" revolution has already lasted too long, so we agree with them. It is really high time that the national revolution ceases and becomes the National Socialist one. Whether that pleases them or not—we will continue our struggle. If they finally grasp what it is about—with them. If they are unwilling—without them. And if it must be—against them.[16]

To Röhm and other SA members there was need of a second revolution.

Hitler was not sympathetic to the SA position. He feared alienating the army and even other traditional groups such as big business and the civil service. More disruption could hinder Germany's economic recovery and endanger public support for the regime, thus imperiling his planned mobilization of the nation for foreign policy adventures. On July 6, 1933, in a speech to state officials, Hitler pronounced emphatically that the revolution was over.

> Revolution is no permanent condition, it must not develop into a permanent condition. One must guide the liberated stream of revolution into a secure bed of evolution. The education of people is therefore the most important consideration. The current state of affairs must be improved and the people, who embody it, must be educated in the National Socialist conception of the state. We must not dismiss a businessman if he is a good businessman, but not yet a National Socialist; especially not if the National Socialist that we put in his place understands nothing about business.[17]

The issue was clear to Hitler. It was foolish and dangerous to speak of a second revolution. Evolution, not revolution, was the key word. Hard work, compromise, gradual change— these, and not a foolhardy disruption of traditional economic and social institutions, were the prerequisites for economic recovery.

The SA was dissatisfied with Hitler's words. In the fall and winter of 1933, it continued in many places to act independently of state and local authorities. In turn, many Germans grew resentful of these undisciplined activities and the apparent unwillingness or inability of authorities to do anything about them. Party leaders, moreover, resented SA members' insubordination.

The SA presented a second problem to Hitler and the Nazis. Ernst Röhm was quite emphatic about the desire of the SA to become the core of a new German army. He was, in fact, fairly indiscreet in expressing how he felt.

> Adolf is rotten. He's betraying all of us. He only goes around with reactionaries. His old comrades aren't good enough for him. So he brings in these East Prussian generals. They're the ones he pals around with now . . . Adolf knows perfectly well what I want . . . Not a second pot of the Kaiser's army, made with the same old grounds. Are we a revolution or aren't we? . . . Something new has to be brought in, understand? A new discipline. A new principle of organization. The generals are old fogies. They'll never have a new idea.[18]

---

[16]Hans-Adolf Jacobsen and Werner Jochmann, eds., *Ausgewählte Dokumente zur Geschichte des Nationalsozialismus, 1933–1945* (Bielefeld, 1961), p. 2.

[17]Ibid.

[18]Printed with permission from the Continuum International Publishing Company Group. Klaus P. Fischer, *Nazi Germany: A New History* © 1995, pp. 285–286.

The regular army was alarmed by the aspirations of the SA. By the beginning of 1934, the SA numbered 2.5 million men, compared with the regular army of 100,000. General Blomberg, the minister of defense, had had the army adopt a neutral attitude toward the new Nazi regime. But he and other army officers made it clear to Hitler that they and Hindenburg would not tolerate the replacement of the regular army by the SA. The army was being encouraged in its hostility toward the SA by the SS. The latter, led by Heinrich Himmler, was busy expanding. It had already taken control of the political police forces throughout Germany and resented being subordinated to the SA leadership.

Hitler was strongly opposed to the SA's demand to be the core of a new German army. Hitler feared the power of the regular army to force him from office. He genuinely respected the regular army and considered it far superior to the fat old men of the SA rank and file. Hitler's foreign policy plans were to be implemented by a well-disciplined regular army. In any event, even if the army did not react against him, he did not want the SA with its millions of men to become the new army. It would be a threat to his own power. At a meeting of army and SA leaders on February 28, 1934, Hitler made it clear that Röhm's idea of the SA as the new army was not acceptable.

Hitler's statements failed to solve the problem. The strained relationship between the army and the SA continued to grow. Hitler remained indecisive until he learned that Hindenburg was ailing and would soon die. If he wished to assume the office of president, he would need the favor of the army. However, the army was making it clear that it could no longer tolerate the aspirations of the SA. At the same time, conservative circles in the bureaucracy and business were obviously becoming more disgusted with the excesses of the SA and its leaders' talk of a second revolution. Conservatives plotted with Hindenburg to restore the monarchy upon Hindenburg's death as a last desperate gamble to avoid Nazi despotism. On June 17, Franz von Papen, as spokesman for these conservative circles, even dared to give a speech at the University of Marburg in which he warned against any second revolution. The danger to Hitler's power was apparent. The army combined with the conservatives could hinder Hitler's succession to Hindenburg's position. However valuable an instrument the SA had been in the Nazi seizure of power, Hitler knew by June 1934 that it posed a threat to his power.

Once Hitler resolved to deal with this crisis, he moved quickly. The SS had been trying to convince Hitler that the SA was planning a revolution against his leadership. There was little evidence to support this claim, especially since Röhm had agreed on June 7 to have the SA leaders go on leave in June and the rank and file to do the same in July—hardly the actions of a man planning a revolt. Nevertheless, Hitler chose to accept the story and prepared secretly to suppress the leadership of the SA with his elite guard, the SS. The army collaborated by providing arms and trucks to the SS and by preparing to crush any SA resistance.

Hitler struck in the early hours of June 30. He took personal command of the arrest of Ernst Röhm, Edmund Heines (SA chief for Silesia), and other SA leaders staying at a resort at Bad Wiessee in Bavaria. In his diary, Alfred Rosenberg provided an account of Röhm's arrest:

> With an SS escort detachment the Führer drove to Wiessee and knocked softly on Röhm's door: "Message from Munich," he said with disguised voice. "Well, come in," Röhm called to the supposed messenger, "the door is open." Hitler tore open the door, fell on Röhm as he lay in bed, seized him by the throat and screamed, "You are under arrest, you pig." Then he

turned the traitor over to the SS. At first Röhm refused to get dressed. The SS then threw his clothes in the Chief of Staff's face until he bestirred himself to put them on. In the room next door, they found Heines engaged in homosexual activity. And these are the kind who want to be leaders in Germany, the Führer said trembling.[19]

The arrested SA leaders were taken to Stadelheim prison in Munich and shot by the SS. Another group of executions was carried out in the Berlin SS barracks. The "blood purge" of the SA was also used to settle some old scores. Gregor Strasser, who had angered Hitler by his resignation from the party in 1932, was murdered. So were Gustav von Kahr, the former Bavarian state commissioner who had throttled Hitler's Beer Hall Putsch; General Kurt von Schleicher and his wife; and Edgar Jung, the conservative intellectual who had written Papen's Marburg address. Papen himself was put under house arrest. Altogether over hundred were shot.

There were mixed reactions to the Night of the Long Knives, as the purge came to be known. Some people were shocked by the brutality of the Nazi regime. To justify his actions, Hitler had his cabinet issue a law on July 3 legalizing the purge retroactively as a necessary act in defense of the state. In his public speech before the Reichstag on July 13, Hitler claimed that he had acted to save Germany from revolt. But even if some people were dismayed by Nazi violence, there were many others who welcomed this purge of the SA. The radical wing of the Nazis had been curbed. There would be no second revolution. Some even believed that by taming its irresponsible wing, the Nazis would become a respectable government. The army was also pleased. Although upset by the murder of General Schleicher, the army was reassured that it alone would be the bearer of the nation's arms. On July 1, General Blomberg publicly thanked Hitler on behalf of the army. Hindenburg thanked the Nazis for saving the German nation from treachery.

The SS did not publicly thank Hitler, but it gained much from the purge of the SA. On July 20, 1934, Hitler freed the SS from the SA and made it an "independent organization" within the NSDAP. SS power would now rise, while the SA would be increasingly confined to ceremonial roles.

Final Step: Führer of Germany

In purging the SA leadership, Hitler had fulfilled the wishes of the army command. In addition to public thanks, the army was soon able to repay Hitler more concretely. On August 2, 1934, President von Hindenburg died. Hitler immediately announced that the offices of Reich chancellor and president would be combined in Hitler's new position as Führer and Reich chancellor. The army and the conservative forces quickly acquiesced. Public officials and soldiers were all required personally to take an oath of loyalty to Hitler as the "Führer of the German Reich and People." This title represented a new form of authority. Hitler was now in control. The Third Reich had been established. An August 19 plebiscite gave Hitler the approval of 85 percent of the German people.

Only eleven years before Hitler achieved complete power, he had been a Bavarian beer hall rabble-rouser, a "drummer" for the nationalist-*völkisch* cause. The crushing of the Beer

---

[19]Hans-Günther Seraphim, ed., *Das politische Tagebuch Alfred Rosenberg* (Göttingen, 1956), pp. 33–34.

Hall Putsch had forced him and the Nazis to change directions and work within the legal system to become the rulers of Germany. The new direction had succeeded. In the midst of a depression, Hitler and the Nazis had molded a political party into a mass movement. The Nazis had worked within the system, and once in control of it, they had proceeded to demolish it and erect a new authoritarian order. Hitler had had collaborators, especially from the right, who believed that their ideal of a new state was the same as Hitler's. But once they had completed their seizure of power, Hitler and the Nazis could unfold the true nature of their regime. The Nazi total state would ultimately be far removed from what the conservatives had envisioned.

SUGGESTIONS FOR FURTHER READING

A valuable collection of essays on the rise of Nazism is Charles S. Maier, Stanley Hoffmann, and Andrew Gould, eds., *The Rise of the Nazi Regime: Historical Reassessments* (Boulder, Colo., 1985). There is a good summary of the rise of Nazism in Martin Broszat, *Hitler and the Collapse of Weimar Germany* (Leamington Spa, 1987); and Conan Fischer, *The Rise of the Nazis,* 2nd ed. (New York, 2002). On the neglected but significant role of Russians fleeing the Bolshevik revolution on the formation of the Nazi movement, see Michael Kellogg, *The Russian Roots of Nazism: White Émigrés and the Making of National Socialism, 1917–1945* (Cambridge, Mass., 2005). On the development of the Nazi Party, see Dietrich Orlow, *The History of the Nazi Party,* 2 vols. (Pittsburgh, 1969–1973); and Joseph Nyomarkay, *Charisma and Factionalism in the Nazi Party* (Minneapolis, 1967). For sociological analysis of the Nazi Party, see Michael Kater, *The Nazi Party: A Social Profile of Members and Leaders, 1919–1945* (Cambridge, Mass., 1983); William Brustein, *The Logic of Evil: The Social Origins of the Nazi Party, 1925–1933* (New Haven, Conn., 1996); and especially Detlev Mühlberger, *Hitler's Followers: Studies in the Sociology of the Nazi Movement* (London, 1991) and *The Social Bases of Nazism, 1919–1933* (New York, 2003). Another facet of Nazi Party organization is examined in Donald M. McKale, *The Nazi Party Courts: Hitler's Management of Conflict in His Movement 1921–1945* (Lawrence, Kans., 1974). Also of value is Peter Merkl, *Political Violence Under the Swastika: 581 Early Nazis* (Princeton, N.J., 1975); and Theodore Abel's still insightful sociological analysis of those same early party members, *Why Hitler Came to Power* (New York, 1938).

Regional studies of the Nazi Party's rise to power include William S. Allen's *The Nazi Seizure of Power: The Experience of a Single German Town,* rev. ed. (New York, 1984); Jeremy Noakes, *The Nazi Party in Lower Saxony, 1921–1933* (London, 1971); Donald M. Douglas, *The Nazi Party in Hannover, 1921–1923* (Wichita, Kan., 1976); Geoffrey Pridham, *Hitler's Rise to Power: The Nazi Movement in Bavaria, 1923–1933* (London, 1973); Johnpeter H. Grill, *The Nazi Movement in Baden, 1920–1945* (Chapel Hill, N.C., 1983); Rudy Koshar, *Social Life, Local Politics, and Nazism, Marburg 1880–1935* (Chapel Hill, N.C., 1986); Walter Rinderle and Bernard Norling, *The Nazi Impact on a German Village* (Lexington, Ky., 1993); Claus-Christian Szejnmann, *Nazism in Central Germany: The Brownshirts in 'Red' Saxony* (New York, 1999); Peter Fritzsche, *Rehearsals for Fascism: Populism and Political Mobilization in Weimar Germany* (New York, 1990); and Shelly Baranowski, *The Sanctity of Rural Life: Nobility, Protestantism and Nazism in Weimar Prussia* (New York, 1995).

Voting patterns are examined in the fundamental study by Thomas Childers, *The Nazi Voter* (Chapel Hill, N.C., 1984). See also the massive quantitative study by Richard F. Hamilton, *Who Voted for Hitler?* (Princeton, N.J., 1982). There is a valuable collection of essays on the appeal of Nazism to voters in Thomas Childers, ed., *The Formation of the Nazi Constituency, 1919–1933* (Totowa, N.J., 1987). On Ernst Röhm, see Eleanor Hancock, *Ernst Röhm: Hitler's SA Chief of Staff* (New York, 2008). On the SA in general, see Peter Merkl, *The Making of a Stormtrooper* (Princeton, N.J., 1980); Conan Fischer, *Stormtroopers: A Social, Economic, and Ideological Analysis, 1929–1935* (London, 1983); Richard Bessel, *Political Violence and the Rise of Nazism: The Storm Troopers in Eastern Germany, 1925–1934* (New Haven, Conn., 1984); Bruce Campbell, *The SA Generals and the Rise of Nazism* (Lexington, Ky., 1998); and Otis C. Mitchell, *Hitler's Stormtroopers and the Attack on the German Republic, 1919–1933* (Jefferson, N.C., 2008). The development of the Nazi cult of martyrs is discussed in Jay W. Baird, *To Die for Germany: Heroes in the Nazi Pantheon* (Bloomington, Ind., 1990). The role of the principal spokesman of the Nazi left wing is discussed in Peter Stachura, *Gregor Strasser and the Rise of Nazism* (London, 1983). The standard work on the relationship between German big business and Hitler is Henry A. Turner, *German Big Business and the Rise of Hitler* (New York, 1985). The Nazi appeal to workers is examined in Max Kele, *Nazis and Workers: National Socialist Appeals to German Labor, 1919–1933* (Chapel Hill, N.C., 1972). On other aspects of the Nazi rise to power, see James Diehl, *Paramilitary Politics in Weimar Germany* (Bloomington, Ind., 1977); Robert J. O'Neill, *The German Army and the Nazi Party* (London, 1964); Donna Harsch, *German Social Democracy and the Rise of Nazism* (Chapel Hill, N.C., 1993); and Conan Fischer, *The German Communists and the Rise of Nazism* (London, 1991). A detailed examination of the political maneuvering that led to Hitler becoming chancellor can be found in Henry A. Turner, Jr., *Hitler's Thirty Days to Power: January 1933* (New York, 1996) and Hermann Beck, *The Fateful Alliance: German Conservatives and Nazis in 1933: The Machtergreifung in a New Light* (New York, 2008). Also informative in this regard is William L. Patch, *Heinrich Brüning and the Dissolution of the Weimar Republic* (New York, 1998).

Two aspects of the Nazi consolidation of power are discussed in Fritz Tobias, *The Reichstag Fire* (London, 1963); and the popular study on the June 30, 1934, SA purge by Paul R. Maracin, *The Night of Long Knives* (Guilford, Conn., 2004).

MySearchLab™ Connections

Study and Review

After the failure of the Beer Hall Putsch and Adolf Hitler's resulting imprisonment, the Nazi Party made a conscious decision to seize power legally via control of the Reichstag. In the five years that followed Hitler's release from Landsberg Prison, the Nazis transformed themselves from a street gang into a powerful German political party, and they eventually were able to transform Germany into a totalitarian state.

Read the Document

1. **Doctrine of Fascism (1932) Benito Mussolini**
   This document presents the key political ideology of Benito Mussolini, an ally of Adolf Hitler. Mussolini's fascism, a contemporaneous movement with Nazism, incorporated similar ideology in its postwar nationalist movement in Italy.

View the Image

2. **Nazi Party Congress, Nuremberg**
   This image—a scene from the film "Triumph of the Will" (1934)—is a striking piece of political propaganda. The Nazis used the film to inspire enthusiasm and to solidify their hold on power.

Watch the Video

3. **Germany: Jewish property destroyed during Kristallnacht—"Night of broken glass"**
   This video presents an overview of Kristallnacht, the coordinated attacks against Jewish homes and businesses in November 1938. Before this event, the Nazis had limited their public displays of hostility to Jews for fear of losing popular support.

RESEARCH AND EXPLORE

With differing leaders and conflicting ideologies, the Nazi Party in 1924 had to unify, commit to a single political direction, and convince Germany of its republican intentions if it hoped to gain political power. With Hitler's rhetoric and fierce determination, the Nazis flourished, despite a return of economic and political stability in Germany in the mid-1920s.

1. How were the lower classes represented in the Nazi Party, and why did they join the party? Did the Nazi leadership truly represent the values and concerns of the lower classes?
2. What was the Nazi Party's stance on the Young Plan? In what ways did the Young Plan prepare the party for the events of October 1929?
3. What was the Reich Propaganda Office's effect on the elections of 1940? In what ways did the Nazis use saturation advertising?

ADDITIONAL RESOURCES

Adolf Hitler becomes Chancellor

Hitler at Nuremberg Rally ca. 1928

4

The Nazi State, 1933–1939

The Weimar parliamentary state had been smashed. A new authoritarian order under Hitler and the Nazis had been established. But to Hitler, the real task was at hand. Already in July 1933 he had proclaimed to the SA: "We have the power. Today nobody can offer us any resistance. But now we must educate German man for this new state. A gigantic project lies ahead."[1]

Hitler's aims had never been simply power for power's sake or a tyranny based on personal power. Hitler had larger ideological goals that were shared by many of the "old fighters" of the Nazi Party. At their core was the development of an Aryan racial state that would dominate Europe and possibly the world for generations to come.[2] Hitler and the Nazis had realized that the party's violent anti-Semitism in the 1920s had not brought any significant electoral success. Their massive support in the early 1930s came after they downplayed radical anti-Semitism in favor of nationalism, anticommunism, and economic issues. These themes struck positive responses, especially from middle-class citizens caught in the fear of the Great Depression.

The real task, then, was clear. To achieve their larger mission, Hitler and the Nazis needed a deep movement in which the German people would be actively involved, not passively cowed by force. As Hitler stated:

> We must develop organizations in which an individual's entire life can take place. Then every activity and every need of every individual will be regulated by the collectivity represented by the party. There is no longer any arbitrary will, there are no longer any free realms in which the individual belongs to himself . . . The time of personal happiness is over.[3]

This was Hitler's description of what other Nazis called their new "total state."

The Nazi total state developed gradually. Hitler felt the need to cooperate with the forces that had made the Nazi conquest possible—the conservative forces of the army,

---

[1]Quoted in Joachim Fest, *Hitler*, translated by Richard and Clara Winston (New York, 1974), p. 433.

[2]On Nazi ideological goals, see Chapters 5 and 7.

[3]Quoted in Fest, *Hitler*, p. 434.

big business, the civil service, and the landed aristocracy. Compromises were inevitable. However, by 1937 and 1938, as his foreign policy goals became more radical, Hitler took steps to finally cut free of those conservative forces as well.

THE HITLER STATE

The Nazi state was, first of all, a dictatorship based on the personal power of Adolf Hitler. Hitler had already exercised absolute power as the charismatic Führer of the Nazi Party. When Hitler was designated Führer and Reich chancellor (later shortened simply to Führer) in August 1934, his base of charismatic power was simply transferred to the state. As Ernst Huber, the foremost constitutional theorist of Nazi Germany, put it, the office of Führer "has grown out of the movement into the Reich." Huber defined Hitler's position in terms of "Führer power," meaning that all public political power came from the Führer. He was the embodiment of the nation's common will, and his power was total, unlimited, and free. No conditions or controls could be attached to it.

The Nazi Party, 1933–1939

The Nazi state was also a one-party state. Success had made a large impact on the Nazi Party. After January 30, 1933, when many Germans began to sense the inevitability of Nazi control of the government, there was a dramatic influx of new party members until enrollments were closed on May 1. During those three months, 1.6 million people joined the party, constituting almost 65 percent of its total membership. Nazi leaders debated whether the party should be the elite cadre of the nation or a mass organization. Enrollments were closed until 1937, when the need for money prompted a brief reopening of membership rolls. They were opened once more in 1939, when Hitler settled on a rule that 10 percent of all Germans should belong to the party.

After assuming power, Hitler, assisted by Robert Ley (head of the party's Political Organization), Rudolf Hess, and Martin Bormann, enlarged the party hierarchy. Hitler as absolute leader was assisted by a relatively small group of distinguished party leaders (*Reichsleiter*). These leaders were nominally superior to the regional party leaders (*Gauleiter*). In reality, the *Reichsleiter* had little control over the *Gauleiter* since the latter reported only to Hitler through Hess and Bormann. The *Gauleiter* did have authority over district leaders (*Kreisleiter*), who in turn directed chapter leaders known as *Ortsgruppenleiter*. An *Ortsgruppe* (chapter) encompassed 1500 households—usually a city suburb or a few villages. Chapter leaders directed cell leaders (*Zellenleiter*), responsible for 160 to 480 households. *Zellenleiter* had control over the lowest local leaders, *Blockleiter*, who had charge of one block consisting of 40 to 60 households. The cell and block leaders at the bottom of the hierarchy gave the party a strong hold on the civilian populace. These party officials invaded the private lives of families by visiting them regularly and making reports to their superiors. From 1933 to 1939, the Nazi Party experienced a tremendous expansion from 750,000 to 1.7 million full- and part-time leaders. Most of this expansion came from the proliferation of new leaders below the level of *Ortsgruppenleiter*.

The top leadership positions—*Reichsleiter*, *Gauleiter*, and *Kreisleiter*—were filled mostly by Nazi veterans who questioned the sincerity of the new members who flocked to the party after the Nazi victory and were cynically labeled the March converts. These high leadership positions were characterized by the presence of the social elite, although the lower middle class was highly visible in all leadership groups, and representatives from the working class were most notably absent. From 1933 to 1939 there was little turnover in the top leadership positions, leading to a noticeable increase in the age levels of those leaders. Young recruits were discouraged from pursuing party careers because of the domination of the higher offices by party veterans unwilling to make room for new people.

Hard-core Nazi leaders shared Hitler's vision of Nazism as a "spiritual crusade" that would save Germany and create a new national community that would overcome the divisions generated by the Weimar system. The leadership cadres were dedicated to Hitler as their leader and shared his ideological goals, especially his ideal of an Aryan state that would make possible a new European order. To them, Hitler was the embodiment of the German *Volk's* basic mission. They—the leaders—were his instruments for guiding the state, whose task was to preserve the racial interests of the *Volk*. The party should command the state to achieve Nazi goals. Once power was seized, however, the relationship between party and state became considerably more complicated than the old Nazi leaders had ever dreamed.

Party–State Relations: The Problems of Dualism

The fundamental political problem after the Nazi takeover was whether the party would dominate the state or vice versa. This dualism was never really settled, because of the special position Hitler occupied as a charismatic leader. Neither state nor party possessed sovereign power; both depended ultimately on Hitler. Hitler's demand for loyalty and his own method of governing created numerous party and state offices that competed for power, creating constant conflict and administrative chaos.

The bulk of government business at the national level was done by the cabinet, composed of the Reich ministries of state. These offices were staffed by professional bureaucrats under leaders of generally high quality. At the beginning of the Nazi seizure of power, there were only two Nazi ministers—Wilhelm Frick, minister of the interior, and Hermann Göring, minister without portfolio. The other ministries, such as Defense, Economics, Labor, Agriculture, and Finance, were held by non-Nazis. By 1935, with the addition of Joseph Goebbels as minister of propaganda, Walter Darré as minister of agriculture, and Hans Kerrl as Reich minister for ecclesiastical affairs, the Nazis held five of twelve ministries but were still a minority. After the seizure of power, the ministers continued to run their departments' affairs for the country. But Hitler made a significant change. Once in power, he returned to his Bohemian political lifestyle. He did not like bureaucracies and he certainly did not enjoy a daily routine of administrative responsibility. Consequently, Hitler eliminated the day-to-day routine of government. Fewer cabinet meetings of all the ministers were held. In 1933, there were seventy-two; by 1936, there were only four, and the last one was held in February 1938. Hitler's withdrawal from regular participation in the ministers' day-to-day handling of the government left a political vacuum at the head of government that was filled by the Reich Chancellery under its state secretary, Hans Heinrich Lammers, who had been a member of the DNVP until he switched sides and joined the Nazi Party in 1932. The Reich Chancellery became the liaison between Hitler and the Reich ministers. Lammers brought ministerial business and state papers to Hitler, who increasingly did not even bother to stay in touch with his Reich ministers. Collegial government was replaced by a system of separate ministries carrying on business as best they could.

The power of the Reich Chancellery and the Reich ministries in carrying out the business of government was undermined in other ways as well. The Reich Chancellery was faced with competition from two other chancelleries. Although the formal office of president had died with Hindenburg, the Presidential Chancellery under Otto Meissner continued. An even greater challenge to the Reich Chancellery came from the Office of the Führer's deputy, Rudolf Hess. Renamed the Party Chancellery, this office was developed by Martin Bormann, Hess's chief of staff, into an important competitor with the Reich Chancellery.

Already in 1933 Hitler had begun to undermine the powers of the Reich ministers by appointing special deputies for specific commissions. On June 30, 1933, Fritz Todt was appointed general inspector for German roads. Trained as an engineer, Todt was an officer in World War I and joined the Nazi Party already in 1922. Todt became one of the first supreme Reich authorities. His task was to build a large-scale network of autobahns (superhighways). Although this work would normally be the responsibility of the Ministry of Transport, Todt operated independently and was even permitted to take over some of the ministry's functions if they were relevant to his work. Todt's budget came directly through the Reich Chancellery, since he was subordinate only to Hitler and was outside the regular Reich government. Todt's office could issue administrative decrees like the other ministries. He had the power to create gigantic state building concerns and his office could make any administrative arrangements needed to complete their jobs. Hitler felt that a special grant of authority of this kind would cut through red tape and expedite accomplishing a task. But it also undermined the regular state bureaucracy and created conflict over proper spheres of authority.

Todt illustrates a practice in Nazi Germany that had far-reaching consequences. A leader with a special commission was subordinate only to Hitler. As long as he maintained good relations with the Führer, he could build the foundations for independent power that undermined regular state authorities, virtually creating states within a state. This development further blurred the already-troubled relationship between party and state.

Duplication of function was another feature of the dualism of party and state. The Foreign Ministry under the leadership of the conservative Konstantin von Neurath had competition from special party offices established by Alfred Rosenberg and Joachim von Ribbentrop. Rosenberg created a foreign policy office, believing that he would transform German foreign policy along Nazi ideological lines. Basically he made a fool of himself and was no threat to Neurath. Ribbentrop, a wine exporter admired by Hitler, organized his own office for foreign policy. Ribbentrop's entry into foreign affairs placed him in direct competition with the foreign minister. In 1938, Hitler ended the rivalry by cashiering Neurath in favor of Ribbentrop. Clashes between party and state offices in the same sphere did not always end in such a clear-cut fashion, however.

The problem of the relationship between party and state began as soon as the Nazi one-party state was inaugurated. Hitler seemed uncertain about how to deal with this question. A basic problem in this conflict between party and state was that Hitler and other leading Nazis realized that the party's harassment of the government bureaucracy, which was responsible for running the state, would undermine the effectiveness of the government. Since Hitler's goals included economic recovery and military rearmament, he was fearful of weakening the bureaucratic structures of the state. Consequently, as we saw, after an initial purge of Jews, Communists, and Socialists in April 1933, there was no wholesale replacement of civil service personnel by party members. The civil service continued to follow its own legal and bureaucratic rules. At the same time, Hitler countered its independence by creating Special Reich Authorities, which gave special executive functions to party leaders and allowed party members to create new departments in competition with state departments. In doing so, Hitler fostered an enormous degree of "authoritarian anarchy." This dualism, however, enabled him to stay in the background and play the role of final arbiter when conflict occurred.

One of the factors that complicated the party's ability to control state agencies was the administrative confusion within the party itself. Once in power, the Nazi Party tended to crumble into various constituencies such as the SA, the SS, Hitler Youth, Labor Front, National Socialist Physicians' League, and numerous others. These organizations sought to grow and go their own way. Although Hitler stood absolute at the top, there was no central administrative authority to maintain a unified political foundation. Robert Ley had been made head of the Political Organization and Rudolf Hess head of the Political Central Commission, but both were largely disregarded by the *Gauleiter*, who considered themselves responsible only to Hitler. The lack of centralized control created a fundamental problem: Numerous Nazi organizations interfered in state affairs while the government bureaucracy attempted to play off one group against another to solidify its power. Hitler sought to rectify this confusion by establishing order within the party, especially in its connection to the state. He appointed Rudolf Hess as the Führer's deputy for party affairs and gave him the power to make decisions within the party. Hitler chose Hess because he was totally dedicated to him and did not threaten his position. Hess was not given control over party organizations, however. Robert Ley remained chief of state of the Political Organization, and Hess continually struggled with him and the *Gauleiter* within the party.

In his new position as the Führer's deputy, Hess was given responsibility for representing the party's interests in its relations with the state, but his new office seemed unable to handle these responsibilities until Martin Bormann became its chief of staff in July 1933. Bormann had been a regional director of the SA Insurance Office and a business manager of the National Socialist German Workers' Party (NSDAP). He had good administrative skills, was a workaholic, and was ruthless and eager for power. He perceived correctly that the key to power in Nazi Germany was proximity to Adolf Hitler. As Hess's chief of staff he was in a good position to achieve that closeness. He managed Hitler's personal finances and directed the development of the Berghof, Hitler's residence at the Obersalzberg near Berchtesgaden.

As chief of staff of Hess's office, Bormann pursued two major goals. He attempted to downplay the various special authorities within the party and to assert the authority of Hess's office over the party. This was a difficult task in which little was achieved, especially in supervising the *Gauleiter*, until the war years. In addition, Bormann worked to subordinate the state to party control. The party, he believed, should be the creator of policy, and the state, the administrator.

As it grew in power under Bormann, the Office of the Führer's Deputy (Party Chancellery) began competing with the Reich Chancellery under Hans Heinrich Lammers, since both had roles in domestic policy. Ultimately, victory belonged to the person who had personal access to Hitler. After 1935, Bormann's position as controller of Hitler's finances gave him a distinct advantage over Lammers. By 1936, Bormann had begun to assume the right to pass on Hitler's instructions to ministers and party officials. Bormann's power became all-encompassing during the war.

The dualism and conflict of party and state at the national level was evident in regional and local governments as well. As we saw in Chapter 3, the coordination of the federal states had first occurred through the cooperation of local Nazi Parties and the Reich minister of the interior. The law of April 7, 1933, though, resulted in the appointment of Reich governors (*Reichstatthälter*) in those federal states, whose function was to supervise the policy established by the Reich chancellor in the state governments. Most of the Reich governors were party *Gauleiter*. The old heads of state governments, the minister-presidents, were left in place, however, creating serious conflicts of authority at the regional level.

Local governments also showed a pattern of conflict of interest between party and state, especially in the 40 percent of German towns and cities where the mayor was not the local Nazi Party leader. Moreover, district party leaders interfered in the mayor's running of local government.

Hitler's Leadership

Our examination of the Hitler state has revealed a high degree of stress between state and party at all levels of government. In the 1930s, many people, even in the West, believed the Nazi propaganda that the Third Reich was an efficient dictatorship superior to democracy. But, as we have seen, Nazi Germany was instead a system of almost constant personal and institutional conflict resulting in administrative chaos. Even the dissemination of propaganda was a source of struggle. One would expect Joseph Goebbels's Ministry for Public Enlightenment and Propaganda to have sole responsibility for this important task. Yet he faced constant interference from Alfred Rosenberg and his party organization, the Combat League of German Culture, Otto Dietrich as Nazi press chief, Max Amann as Reich leader of the press, and even Joachim von Ribbentrop, who tried to monopolize foreign propaganda. When Goebbels tried to gain clarification from Hitler over spheres of influence, Hitler refused to become involved. Incessant struggle characterized relationships within the party, within the state, and between party and state.

Why this occurred and what effect it had on domestic and foreign policy are sources of controversy among historians. One group of historians, known as structuralists, assumes that Hitler's dislike of making decisions resulted in the chaos that undermined his own authority and made him a "weak dictator." These same historians believe that the more radical measures of the Hitler regime, including the extermination of the Jews, were not Hitler's ideological intentions but simply ad hoc responses to events. These responses became ever more radical as the institutional anarchy worsened.

Another group of historians, known as intentionalists, also believes that Hitler's style of leadership created his regime's administrative chaos. There is no doubt that Hitler disliked bureaucracies. He took it for granted that he had the temperament of the artist, and he detested administrative routine. Since problems could be solved by inspiration and will power, Hitler came to rely upon simply expressing his expectations to his associates, giving rise to the so-called Führer order. The Führer order had the power of law and bypassed normal channels of government business. Hitler's unwillingness to be involved in administrative routine created additional confusion.

Intentionalist historians assume that Hitler deliberately created this institutional confusion. Following the principle of divide and rule that he had used repeatedly in his career, Hitler fostered rivalry within the party and between party and state so that he would be the ultimate decision maker and absolute ruler. This system meant that the key to power for anyone in Nazi Germany was direct access to the Führer. Martin Bormann is the outstanding example of this practice. The *Gauleiter* who had access to Hitler could be more important politically than a Reich minister who rarely got to see him. It is also important to remember that Hitler was a believer in Darwinian struggle. "Struggle is the father of all things," he had said in *Mein Kampf*.[4] The Third Reich as an institutional jungle in which the ruthless and cunning rose to the top and the weak succumbed accorded perfectly with Hitler's belief in the importance of struggle.

Intentionalist historians concede that the institutional chaos that Hitler created may have affected the domestic goals of the Third Reich. However, it did not stop him from pursuing the major ideological goals that he had clearly expressed in *Mein Kampf* in the 1920s—the creation of a *völkisch* state that would eliminate the Jewish threat and the acquisition of *Lebensraum* that would permit the *Volk* to expand. And at the same time, the institutional chaos that resulted from Hitler's own mode of operation left lesser officials with much latitude in following policies that they believed were in accord with the Führer's wishes. In 1934, one state official in Prussia said to a group of local officials:

> Everyone with the opportunity to observe it knows that the Führer can only with great difficulty order from above everything that he intends to carry out sooner or later. On the contrary, until now everyone has best worked in his place in the new Germany if, so to speak, he works toward the Führer . . . it is the duty of every single person to attempt, in the spirit of the Führer, to work towards him . . . [and] the one who works correctly towards the Führer along his lines and towards his aim will in future . . . have the finest reward of one day suddenly attaining the legal confirmation of his work.[5]

"Working towards the Führer" became an important aspect of the Hitler state and in the process enabled Hitler's aims to take concrete form.

ECONOMIC AND SOCIAL DEVELOPMENTS

During their quest for power, the Nazis did not have a consistent economic program. The economic planks of their twenty-five-point party platform, which were antagonistic to big business, big financiers, and big department stores, had been based primarily on the interests of the lower middle class. But by 1932 and 1933, they realized that they needed to consider the economic interests of those groups more favorably, especially in view of their role in Hitler's appointment as chancellor and in bankrolling the last election of March 1933.

Once in power, Hitler understood that he had to solve Germany's economic problems, especially those related to the depression, if the Nazis were to stay in power. Resolving these problems was crucial to him because of his foreign policy goals. To Hitler, economics was clearly subordinate to politics. The purpose of economic policy was to provide the material resources for political and military goals. These goals could not be accomplished without a unified nation behind him, and that required a certain level of material progress.

Hitler opposed the demands of those in the party who favored a radical economic program to implement the twenty-five-point platform and carry out the promise made to middle-class groups to break up large department stores. Hitler was no socialist. He knew that to fulfill his foreign policy goals he needed the technological skills of the

[4]See Chapter 5 for Hitler's ideas on struggle.
[5]Quoted in Ian Kershaw, *Hitler 1889–1936: Hubris* (New York, 1999), p. 529.

industrialists and capitalist industry itself. Besides, he thought that distinctions among economic systems were irrelevant as long as National Socialist goals were dominant. A capitalist system, built on the principle of competition, accorded perfectly well with Hitler's own Social Darwinian belief in struggle. Why frighten people with unnecessary tinkering with the economy?

Early Nazi Economic Policy

When Hitler was appointed chancellor, he shied away from a definite economic program in order to avoid alienating any significant bloc of voters before the March elections. In March 1933, he appointed Hjalmar Schacht the new president of the Reichsbank. Schacht had a Ph.D. in economics and became director of the National Bank for Germany (a private bank). Although Schacht was a founder of the German Democratic Party (DDP) in 1918, he moved increasingly to the right and wound up supporting the appointment of Hitler as chancellor. Schacht was a staunch defender of capitalism, which certainly reassured business and industrial leaders about Hitler's economic direction. Fortunately for Hitler, Schacht was also an astute financier willing to use his many talents to benefit the Nazis.

After seeking advice from leading industrialists, Hitler had instituted an economic program known as the Reinhardt Plan by the summer of 1933. One billion Reichsmarks were allocated for public works projects, such as the building of roads, canals, public buildings, and bridges, as well as for "pump-priming" grants to private construction firms to renovate old buildings and create new housing. Tax breaks were given to encourage industrial plant expansion. Business leaders approved these measures and were particularly enthusiastic about the government's program to construct autobahns, which was directed by Fritz Todt. The building of the autobahns was a highly visible and popular activity. It offered jobs for construction workers and engineers as well as stimulation of the automobile industry and related products.

The Reinhardt economic plan was accompanied by considerable Nazi propaganda. Hitler realized that ending the depression would have psychological as well as economic dimensions. He participated in frequent groundbreaking and laying-of-cornerstone ceremonies. These "let's get to work" spectacles emphasized working not just for money but also as part of building a new *Volksgemeinschaft* (national community) that cared about its citizens. Work had great value. As Hitler said, it was an honor to clean the streets as a citizen of this Reich. The Nazis, of course, benefited enormously from this propaganda. Germans could believe that the Nazis were really trying to solve the economic crisis even if problems remained.

The Reinhardt Plan had more than just psychological effects, however. Although the economy had already begun to improve in 1932, even before the Nazis came to power, the Reinhardt programs probably helped to speed up economic recovery and reduce the number of unemployed. It is difficult to know whether the plan would have had long-term effects, since it was soon overshadowed by rearmament and its impact on the economy, especially after 1936.

Early in February 1933, Hitler had spoken with military commanders and his cabinet about his desire to begin rearming in order to bolster Germany's political position, but cautioned against acting too quickly for fear of repercussions from the Allied nations. In 1934, however, there was a dramatic increase in spending for rearmament. To achieve this goal, Hjalmar Schacht used deficit financing, but once Germany publicly announced rearmament in 1935, the more conventional public methods of taxes and loans were used. Expenditures on rearmament rose dramatically: 1933, 1 billion Reichsmarks; 1934, 3.4 billion; 1935, 5 billion; 1936, 9.3 billion; 1937, 9.5 billion; 1938, 13.6 billion; and 1939, 30 billion.

Closely connected with rearmament was Hitler's acceptance of autarky or economic self-sufficiency as another economic goal for Germany. Hitler was well aware of the effectiveness of the British blockade of Germany in World War I and knew the dangers of dependence on others for raw materials. Already in 1934, he had become interested in developing synthetic materials. Since economic officials felt this was unnecessary because of the expense involved, Hitler ordered his special economic adviser Wilhelm Keppler to create an agency to conduct basic research on the creation of synthetic rubber, metals, and fats. Support for such a program came from the military, which realized the possible advantages of synthetic fuels and metals for the military machine. Colonel Georg Thomas, who directed the army's Defense Economy and Weapons Bureau, was the most outspoken exponent of autarky and synthetic fuels. Although Thomas was not an ardent supporter of Hitler, he believed in the necessity of German rearmament and advocated mobilization of all economic resources for defense, including the construction of plants for synthetic materials and the stockpiling of strategic materials.

Germany's economic recovery and "armaments boom" after 1936 helped reduce the number of unemployed. Unemployment figures dropped from 6 million people in 1932 to 4.5 million in 1933, 2.6 million in 1934, 1.7 million in 1935, 1 million in 1936, and less than 500,000 in 1937. There was virtually full employment thereafter. Not all sectors of the economy benefited from rearmament. Consumer goods industries and certain export trades suffered. Government contracts tended to go to the largest, most technologically advanced companies. Small producers and retailers were often hurt by the centralization of industry and the creation of monopolies by large firms. There is no doubt, however, that the decline in unemployment brought the Nazi regime a high degree of popularity. Nevertheless, serious economic problems remained.

Rearmament created a very unfavorable balance of payments. It required the importation of enormous quantities of raw materials such as metals, fuel, and rubber. Germany, however, had inadequate foreign exchange to pay for its imports, largely because it did not export enough goods. By the summer of 1934, in the midst of the emergency over the SA, Hitler's government was faced with an economic crisis in the form of inadequate foreign exchange to import the raw materials needed for rearmament. Hitler responded in August of that year by making his successful Reichsbank president the Reich minister of economics with dictatorial powers in economic affairs. Schacht rose to the occasion by creating the so-called New Plan.

This New Plan, instituted in September 1934, meant, first of all, an increase in state control of the economy. The government was now empowered to establish quotas on imports. Moreover, the New Plan attempted to increase German trade through agreements with other countries. Governments agreed to accept credit for German purchases and to use it to buy in German markets. Schacht made agreements with twenty-five countries, especially in South America and the Balkans of southeastern Europe. The latter was an area of special interest to Germany in its drive for autarky. By gaining sources of raw materials in adjacent southeastern Europe, Germany could be more independent in case of war. Germany used its New Plan trade policies to establish economic influence over the Balkan countries, and after it occupied Austria and Czechoslovakia in 1938 and 1939, respectively, it established a dominant position there.

Schacht's New Plan increased the German export trade 19 percent by 1935 and brought temporary relief to the balance-of-payments problem. But it was not enough. After Germany repudiated the disarmament clauses of the Treaty of Versailles in March 1935, it increased its importation of raw materials even more. A new economic crisis loomed by 1935.

The fundamental problem was a traditional one—how to provide "guns and butter" (large military and consumer goods) simultaneously. By the end of 1935, Germany was facing a shortage of foodstuffs. Attempts to increase agricultural production had limited success. There was now a need to import foodstuffs, especially fats, or else establish food rationing. The latter was not an acceptable alternative since it entailed a loss of prestige for the regime. At the same time, the demand for increasing the tempo of rearmament meant the importation of even greater quantities of raw materials or, as Hitler now favored, even greater emphasis on creating synthetic materials. And some suppliers, such as the Soviet Union and Romania, were demanding cash payment for their oil. With an exchange deficit of over 500 million Reichsmarks, Germany faced an even greater balance-of-payments crisis. Schacht now argued that Germany could not meet the needs of both rearmament and food imports. If the Nazi regime wanted "butter," it would have to cut "guns." He also believed it was foolish and uneconomic to pursue the production of synthetic raw materials. Hitler, however, had no intention of cutting the pace of rearmament, especially after the Nazi occupation of the Rhineland in March 1936 (see Chapter 7). Convinced as usual that where there is the will there is a way to solve any problem, Hitler shifted to another new plan, the Four-Year Plan, under a new economic dictator, Hermann Göring.

The Four-Year Plan

The theoretical foundation for the Four-Year Plan was laid in August 1936 in a memorandum on economic policy and rearmament composed by Hitler while at the Berghof. In it, Hitler expressed the absolute, fundamental need for Germany to rearm. Germany faced a crucial challenge to its very existence. The Soviet Union under the Bolsheviks, he believed, sought to place the world under Jewish domination. If Germany did not bring its army "to the rank of premier army in the world" as rapidly as possible, then Germany would be lost. Hitler acknowledged that with its increase in employment Germany could not meet its requirements for foodstuffs without importing them. Yet, it also needed the raw materials for rearmament. There were two solutions to this dual need, a long-range final solution and a temporary solution. The final solution would be the acquisition of *Lebensraum* (living space) and new lands that would provide raw materials and foodstuffs—a problem that would be solved eventually by the nation's political leadership. The temporary solution was an economic mobilization of the nation to bring Germany to "political and economic self-sufficiency." In order to save foreign exchange for crucial areas, Germany had to step up production of synthetic materials. The fuel problem must be solved in eighteen months; the production of synthetic rubber, fats, and light and high-grade metals must be achieved with similar urgency.

Hitler's demand, then, was total concentration on the policy of autarky, and he threatened to use force against anyone who failed to cooperate fully. If private industry could not do the job, he warned, the Russian example of total state control of the economy would have to be followed. He ended with a sense of urgency: "The German Army must be operational in four years. The German economy must be fit for war within four years."[6]

---

[6]*Documents on German Foreign Policy* (Washington, D.C., 1966), Series C, vol. 5, p. 862.

Hitler announced the Four-Year Plan in the fall of 1936. Hermann Göring was put in charge of it and given sweeping powers to issue legal decrees and administrative orders to all state and party agencies. The overconfident Göring, who was not inclined to details or hard work, underestimated the difficulties involved. His attempt to coordinate the offices of the Reich ministries of Labor, Agriculture, and Economics into the Four-Year Plan led him into conflicts with Seldte, Darré, and especially Schacht, who objected to Göring's undermining of their ministries. Schacht, in fact, resigned at the end of 1937 and was replaced by the more agreeable Walther Funk. The Ministry of Economics was subsequently coordinated with the Four-Year Plan.

Since the chief objective of the Four-Year Plan was to spur production of raw materials to achieve German self-sufficiency, the most important department involved in the plan was the Office for German Raw Materials. In 1938, this office was replaced by a Reich Agency for Economic Consolidation under Carl Krauch, a director of the chemical company IG Farben. This agency downplayed the general production of raw materials in favor of strategic items for rearmament, such as oil, rubber, explosives, and light metals.

The Four-Year Plan forced the German economy into concentrating on the production of synthetic raw materials and increasing the development of Germany's own natural resources. Between 1936 and 1942, 50 percent of total industrial investment was sunk into Four-Year Plan projects. Of the various production targets established by the plan, the only ones reached were those for brown coal and explosives. The most glaring failure occurred in the target goal for synthetic oil. Although 50 percent of Four-Year Plan investment funds were poured into the creation of synthetic fuels, production by 1939 covered less than 20 percent of demand. In fact, the synthetics program failed to reach the goals of autarky. By 1939, Germany still relied on foreigners for one-third of its raw material needs, and foreign exchange remained in critically short supply.

The Four-Year Plan had other results. It reinforced the existing concentration of economic power by large firms. IG Farben became particularly prominent in the area of synthetics and earned large profits. The appointment of Krauch as head of the Reich Agency for Economic Consolidation established a precedent for the employment of corporate executives in state positions. No doubt men like Krauch provided valuable expertise, but they also weakened the government bureaucracy since they were responsible only to Göring. This does not mean, however, that big business defined economic policies. Those policies were determined by the Nazi state, although big business certainly made enormous financial gains.

Nazi Germany's program of massive rearmament created a military machine greater than that of any of its neighbors. In the long run, however, it proved inadequate for Hitler's aims. Colonel Thomas of the army's Defense Economy and Weapons Bureau had stressed the need for a more comprehensive program—greater state control of the economy, more stockpiling of goods, and added regulation of wages and allocation of labor. The Nazi leadership, however, was unwilling to pursue such admittedly totalitarian goals. Top Nazis, especially the *Gauleiter*, convinced Hitler that many Germans and in particular the working class would not tolerate the sacrifices needed to create a true war economy. The Nazi regime managed to sustain massive rearmament without drastically curtailing consumer goods and managed to keep people reasonably contented. By 1939, however, a new economic crisis was becoming apparent. Hitler did not go to war to solve that crisis, since he had planned war from the beginning. But the war itself was convenient. With the territory it would conquer, Germany could begin to pursue the long-term final solution to the need for raw materials and foodstuffs that Hitler had pointed to in his 1936 memorandum.

Germany's economic needs would be met in part by the plundering of other nations. Of course Hitler's solution would have no meaning if Germany did not win the war.

The Working Class

One of the tasks of the NSDAP had been to win the workers away from Marxism and socialism and steer them toward nationalism. But the workers remained mostly within the Social Democratic Party, with the more radical ones joining the Communist movement. The establishment of a Nazi trade union, the National Socialist Factory Cell Organization (NSBO), had not been overly successful in gaining adherents in the factories. After their seizure of power, the Nazis moved to coordinate labor by destroying the trade unions on May 2, 1933, and establishing the German Labor Front (DAF) four days later. German workers did not resist the destruction of their unions.

By the fall of 1933, the DAF had taken on a new appearance. It was now defined as the organization for all working people regardless of economic or social position. Employers as well as workers belonged, making the DAF a symbol of the German national community. Its fundamental aim was to educate all working Germans "to support the National Socialist state."

Although the DAF was given an insignificant role in labor relations, it continued under Robert Ley to be a powerful organization supporting the Nazi regime's economic and rearmament aims. To encourage worker support for the regime, the DAF established two new organizations, the Beauty of Labor and Strength Through Joy (KdF). Through the Beauty of Labor, the DAF encouraged employers to create better working conditions in factories and provide a more pleasing environment with music, plants, clean washing facilities and changing rooms, canteens, good lighting, and even sports facilities such as swimming pools.

The purpose of KdF was to coordinate the free time of the working class by offering a variety of programs. Leisure activities included concerts, variety shows, operas, films, guided tours, and sporting events. An especially popular KdF feature was the availability of relatively inexpensive vacations. Robert Ley leader explained the vacation philosophy of the Nazis:

> When someone arrives at a beach resort, he must be able to forget his past right away. I would like to arrange things in such a way that he is swept off his feet immediately by a general mood filled with excitement, so much so that it will take his breath away and he will not come to his senses with all the music, dancing, theater visits, and so on . . . Starting with the first hour, the vacationer must be submerged in an intoxicating environment up to the very last second, when he climbs back onto his train to go home. This is also the wish of the Führer, and so we want to construct this beach resort with these leisure principles in mind: a theater, a movie, evening shows, music, dance locales and so on.[7]

As a consequence of this philosophy, the KdF introduced the modern package tour. This could be a cruise to Scandinavia or the Mediterranean or, more likely for most workers, a shorter trip to various sites in Germany. Cruises were, of course, more expensive, and in

---

[7]Quoted in Frederic C. Tubach, *German Voices: Memories of Life during Hitler's Third Reich*, p. 24. © 2011 by the Regents of the University of California. Reprinted by permission of University of California Press.

Coordinating Free Time. This poster reads, "With Strength through Joy in the sunny Rheingau." The Kraft durch Freude (KdF) program was designed to promote worker happiness by providing laborers with access to inexpensive vacations such as the river cruise promoted here, and even affordable automobiles such as the new Volkswagen (the People's Car). *(INTERFOTO/Alamy Limited)*

1938 only 130,000 workers were able to take advantage of them, compared with the almost 7 million who took short trips. To make these vacations possible, the regime increased the number of paid holidays for workers from three in 1933 to twelve in 1939. Probably the most popular of all KdF-sponsored programs was the mass production of a "people's car" (Volkswagen), which all workers could buy through a weekly savings plan. The first Volkswagen factory was dedicated by Hitler in 1938.

Through its KdF programs and other activities, the Labor Front tried to combat worker dissatisfaction over wage rates, which rose little in relation to the growth of the economy. Of course, the Nazi policy of pushing rearmament meant some restraint on consumption. The Labor Front concentrated, then, on intangibles to convince workers that they were happy. Nazis waxed enthusiastically about the new community spirit in Germany and even the egalitarian features of Nazi rule. Rudolf Hess stated:

> It is of much importance that we should assess the social position of the German worker, not on the basis of "an increase in wages or no increase in wages," but from a consideration of what position the workers, the employees or the small tradesmen now hold within the national community. And in this case we need only go through Germany with eyes open to discover that the ordinary citizen can do things in Hitler's Germany which in other countries are open only to a privileged class but never to the workers . . .[8]

Nazi leaders never tired of pointing out that workers, like the rich, could now take cruises and own a car—examples of Nazi egalitarianism. Reality tended to fall short of promises, however. The money that workers contributed every week for the purchase of a Volkswagen would ultimately be used to build tanks instead.

The Labor Front continually stressed how a revived Germany was creating a new national community in which class distinctions were disappearing. Work was portrayed as a noble activity, a true service to the community and the real reason to live. Of course, all these intangibles were designed to keep workers happy, and in some cases they probably did. However, they were not provided in and for themselves, but to secure the ultimate goal of maintaining the "war economy."

Similar psychological arguments about the nobility of work and the creation of a national community were used to justify another labor institution, the Reich Labor Service (RAD). This was not a new institution but one taken over by the Nazis when they came into power. In 1935, six months of service in the RAD was made compulsory for all males between eighteen and twenty-five. Labor Service men were usually put to work in the countryside on land-reclamation projects. The Nazis used the Labor Service for several purposes. Political indoctrination was a regular feature of the daily routine, with special emphasis on manual labor. "Work ennobles" was the slogan. Premilitary training was emphasized in two-and-a-half-hour daily drills. The Labor Service was also used to further the Nazi ideal of a national community by breaking down class barriers. As Hitler expressed it, "We want to contribute to the mutual understanding of the different classes in order to reinforce the tie which binds together the community of the people . . ."[9] Young men of all social backgrounds participated together in the RAD's daily activities and work. Despite its ideological function, the Labor Service served a very material end as well: it provided a source of very cheap labor for projects that would otherwise have cost much more.

---

[8]Quoted in Gerhard Starcke, *Die Deutsche Arbeitsfront* (Berlin, 1940), p. 143.
[9]Norman H. Baynes, ed., *The Speeches of Adolf Hitler, 1922–1939* (Oxford, 1942), vol. 1, p. 893.

Regardless of what the Labor Front offered in terms of supplementary benefits, the workers had lost their fundamental rights. They no longer negotiated labor conditions and wages with their employers, who were now heads of their factories without any trade union interference. The eight-hour working day was stretched, resulting in much over-time work. The "work book," introduced for all workers in 1935, provided detailed job qualifications and supplied the precondition for the Nazi control of labor. Agricultural workers were required to get approval before they could work in industry. Increasingly, the Nazi regime controlled and finally even conscripted labor. In 1938, in order to build the West Wall, a defensive barrier along the border with France, the Nazi government resorted to the conscription of labor. Over 1 million workers were drafted to construct Four-Year Plan factories and to work in munitions plants wherever needed. But this stimulated so much dissatisfaction that Hitler decreed in 1939 that workers should be allowed to work in their hometowns.

This concession points once again to some of the limitations in the Nazi regime's relationship with the working class. Nazi policy toward the working class was determined by two overriding concerns: the need to pursue rearmament to fulfill its major tasks of foreign policy and the need for worker acceptance of the regime to make rearmament possible. Workers' responses to the regime were mixed. Wages alone gave workers cause to be unhappy. The government, fearing a wage-price inflation spiral, was generally successful in limiting increases in wages, and between 1933 and 1939, workers' wages barely rose. Price increases in basic food-stuffs and clothing were offset by a decline in the cost of heating, light, and rents. Because of a skilled-labor shortage that began in 1936 and had become especially acute by 1939, skilled workers tended to be paid considerably higher wages. By taking advantage of vocational training, workers could always hope to advance to skilled-labor positions and hence earn a higher income. Workers responded positively to the Labor Front's benefits, especially the KdF projects, even if they did not always accept the propaganda about the national community. Perhaps most important in the workers' response to the regime was the overwhelming belief that the Nazis had ended the insecurity of unemployment. If they had lost their rights, then, as one worker expressed it, "it's all the same to us; at least we have work." For those who could not contain their discontent, there were always the Gestapo informants in the factory to answer to. Their presence led to less and less fraternizing and considerable apathy.

Regardless of their successes with workers, the Nazis were aware of the workers' mixed feelings about the regime. This awareness was an important ingredient in the tension that existed between the army and government offices, which pushed for rearmament, and the Labor Front and party leaders, who worried about winning the workers' confidence. The military, the Ministry of Labor, and the Ministry of Food and Agriculture wanted more control of workers, even longer hours, and a lower standard of living so that a total economic mobilization could be achieved. Although Hitler shared this ultimate goal, he sided with the Labor Front and party *Gauleiter*, who argued that Nazi support among the workers would be questionable if these measures were carried out. Hitler was never really prepared to pay that price for total economic mobilization. And although his reasons were sound, his decision may have cost him the war.

Business

After seizing power, the new Nazi government had to concern itself with the diverse interests of the business classes. Nazi electoral propaganda had supported the interests of the traditional lower-middle-class business groups—the small retailers and artisans. Once in control, the regime began to favor big business interests over those of small business. Certainly big business was of far greater value to the Nazis in restoring the economy and rearming Germany. Nevertheless, small retailers and artisans had constituted an important part of the party's support and could not be disregarded.

Nor did the rank-and-file Nazis initially allow the party to forget its campaign promises. The Nazis had campaigned against large department stores, chain stores, and consumer cooperatives, all of which threatened the prosperity of small retailers. At the local level, members of the party and SA tried to implement these election demands in the spring and summer of 1933. They boycotted department stores and consumer cooperatives and obstructed businesses. But the Nazi fear of creating more unemployment through economic disruption brought swift reaction. All Nazi groups were forbidden to harass businesses. The state even loaned money to one large department store owned by Jews. In 1934, a policy of general state licensing allowed the government to control the number of new retailers. Artisans' guilds were organized hierarchically under the leadership principle, giving the Nazis a means of controlling the artisans.

Although the government did make some concessions to small business interests, overall the position of small businessmen either remained the same or deteriorated. Despite Nazi claims about helping the little person, small businessmen did not experience such aid. They fell behind economically, especially in comparison with big business, which profited immensely from German rearmament.

Big business interests had not been particularly significant supporters of the Nazis before their seizure of power, and Nazi campaign slogans, especially those geared to workers and the lower middle class, had not reassured those interests. After Hitler became chancellor, there was more enthusiasm, but certain sections of big business, especially firms focusing on exports, opposed Nazi plans for deficit financing and autarky. However, the profits of rearmament brought most of big business to support the Nazis.

Big business had been little affected by the policy of *Gleichschaltung*, or coordination, in the spring and summer of 1933. Hitler was well aware of the importance of big business in reviving the German economy. Desiring more control over the business community, the Nazis organized a unified system of businesses divided by sector (such as commerce, banking, insurance, and energy) and region (such as East Prussia and Bavaria). These groups provided for "self-regulation" of business. Since each group was led "according to the principles of the National Socialist state," the system gave the government a means of influencing the business community without excessive bureaucratic controls. The government did place restraints on foreign exchange, imports and exports, prices, wages, and the allocation of labor. It determined the quantity and nature of what should be produced. Profits were limited and directed by the government back into reinvestment for expansion or for the acquisition of government bonds to provide more capital for rearmament. When businesses refused to work with the government on a project that would be unprofitable, the government moved in and established its own factories. For example, the refusal by industrialists to process low-grade iron ores resulted in the creation of a state concern named the Reich-Works–Hermann–Göring.

These government controls and restrictions, however, did not stop big business from maintaining a certain degree of independence. After all, the state was dependent upon the business groups for the ultimate success of its rearmament drive. And, as we have seen in the case of the production of synthetic fuels, the use of businessmen in official posts (as in the Four-Year Plan organization) because of their expertise meant a high degree of government–business cooperation and interdependence. Despite controls, then, big business remained in private hands. Cooperation with the government also produced massive rewards. The large chemicals firm IG Farben provides a stunning example. Between 1933 and 1939 IG Farben profits increased almost 400 percent. In fact, between 1928 and 1939 the profits of big business in general rose from 1.3 billion Reichsmarks to 5 billion, again almost a 400 percent increase.

In the realm of economic policy, ideology played a small role. Hitler's goals of rapid economic recovery, autarky, and rearmament—all in the interests of pursuing his foreign policy goals—meant compromises and expediencies and not the nazification of the economy. In the area of the economy, the total state was rather imperfectly realized.

Agriculture

The agrarian community had been one of the chief pillars of Nazi support between 1930 and 1933. The Nazis had made strong appeals in areas depressed by agricultural crises. Hitler promised from the very early days of his chancellorship to help the farmers. He did this not only for political reasons but also for ideological ones. Nazi agricultural policy had been expressed by the party's Agrarian Policy Apparatus under Walter Darré. Darré, like Hitler and SS leader Heinrich Himmler, was a strong believer in the racial "blood and soil" theory, which touted the farmers as the backbone of the pure Aryan race. Only they could grow on German soil the food that would produce strong and healthy Germans.

Because of strong farmer support, the Nazis had been able to infiltrate the chief associations of farmers even before they seized power. Once in power, however, they wasted no time in coordinating the old peasant associations under the direction of Darré, who was proclaimed Reich peasant leader in May 1933. In the next month, after Alfred Hugenberg's resignation from the cabinet, Darré took over his position as Reich minister of food and agriculture. Believing in the importance of the farmers in the Nazi racial scheme, Darré worked to reinvigorate German agriculture.

Under Darré's direction, Nazi agricultural policy consisted of two major innovations: the Reich Food Estate and the Reich Hereditary Farm Law. The Reich Food Estate was established in the fall of 1933. It was a compulsory organization for anyone connected with agriculture. Under Darré, it was organized hierarchically with peasant leaders at state, district, and local levels. The Food Estate had the power to regulate the production, distribution, and prices of all agricultural products. Certain items, such as grain, milk, eggs, cattle, and fats, were subject to a high degree of state supervision and price fixing. Beginning in 1936, farmers were given precise production quotas for products such as milk and eggs.

The Reich Hereditary Farm Law of 1933 was enacted for ideological rather than economic reasons and was intended to ensure the continued existence of small farmers as the "blood spring of the German nation." The law stipulated that medium-size farms (under 300 acres) were guaranteed as an indivisible family holding. The owner of the hereditary farm had to be of pure German blood and would be designated by the honorific title of *Bauer* ("peasant" as opposed to *Landwirt*, "agriculturalist"). The farm could not be encumbered by debts and could not be sold but only passed on undivided to a single heir.

The new farm law was generally viewed as a failure by farmers themselves, since it basically bound them to the land. Farmers could no longer use their hereditary farm as collateral for loans. They were thereby prevented from modernizing and could no longer compete with large landowners. Since there could be only one heir, the farmer's other children suffered. Because hereditary farms could not be sold, the price of other farmland tended to rise, discouraging small farmers from buying and creating a flight from the land to the cities, where there seemed to be an abundance of better-paying jobs.

Nazi agricultural politics had very mixed results. The ideological praise of farmers as the "blood spring" of the German nation enticed many farmers to continue to support the regime. Some farmers, however, became unhappy with Nazi policies. Hereditary farmers had a specific set of grievances. Others complained too, mainly about the effect of controls on production and prices. Darré's hope of achieving self-sufficiency in foodstuffs failed, especially in certain areas, such as fats. Food consumption by the population increased only slightly from 1933 to 1939. Agricultural income certainly did not keep up with the general growth in national income, encouraging agricultural workers to leave the land to seek jobs in industry. In turn, this and the demands for labor and military service created a genuine agricultural labor crisis. It is estimated that the number of agricultural workers dropped by 500,000 from 1933 to 1938. The crisis would be solved only by the use of slave labor from occupied Europe during the war.

ANTI-JEWISH POLICIES, 1933–1939

Soon after they had secured power by the Enabling Act in March 1933, Hitler and the Nazis began to translate the anti-Jewish planks of their party program into action. The first anti-Jewish policy was initiated in 1933 with a boycott of Jewish businesses on April 1. For many German Jews this was a shocking development. Writing in her diary on April 3, Mally Dienemann expressed her disbelief:

> On Saturday there was a boycott of all Jewish stores, doctors, lawyers. Black slips of paper with white dots were posted on Jewish stores and SA men stood in front of the buildings and stopped people from entering the stores or going to lawyers or doctors. [. . .] I thought, how unvarying is our fate; now we are [supposedly] harming Germany with fairy tales about atrocities, while in the Middle Ages it was we who were supposed to have poisoned wells, etc. I felt like my own ghost wandering the streets. Were we dreaming, or was it real? Could people really do this to each other? And why, why? Did any of those in power really believe that these Jews were to blame for spreading this so-called atrocity propaganda?[10]

Fortunately, most Germans ignored the boycott and simply walked past the SA men posted outside businesses to discourage patronage. The boycott was canceled within two days because of this, as well as hostile reaction abroad. But from April to October, laws were enacted to exclude "non-Aryans" from the civil service, the legal profession, judgeships, the medical profession, teaching positions, cultural and entertainment enterprises, and the press. "Non-Aryans" were defined as persons with one or more Jewish parents or grandparents. Every civil servant was required to prove Aryan descent through birth certificates and parents' marriage certificates. Under pressure from President Hindenburg, Hitler agreed to exempt Jewish veterans of World War I from these laws. Additional acts limited the number of "non-Aryans" who could attend secondary schools and universities to 1.5 percent of the total number of students. The loss

---

[10]Quoted in Jürgen Matthäus and Mark Roseman, eds., *Jewish Responses to Persecution, Volume I, 1933–1938* (Lanham, Md., 2010), p. 22. By permission of AltaMira Press.

of one's occupation, and the personal connections associated with it, was devastating. Hanna Bergas recalled her last day as a school teacher in April 1933:

> When I arrived at the school building, . . . the principal, saying "good morning" in his customary, friendly way, stopped me, and asked me to come to his room . . . When we were seated, he said, in a serious, embarrassed tone of voice, he had orders to ask me not to go into my classroom. I probably knew, he said, that I was not permitted to teach anymore at a German school. I did know, but was it to happen so abruptly? . . . Mr. B. was extremely sorry . . . I collected myself [and] my belongings . . . There was nobody . . . to say goodbye to, because everybody else had gone to the classroom . . . In the afternoon . . . colleagues, pupils, their mothers came, some in a sad mood, others angry with their country, lovely bouquets of flowers, large and small, in their arms. In the evening, the little house was full of fragrance and colors, like for a funeral, I thought; and indeed, this was the funeral of my time teaching at a German public school.[11]

In 1933, over 500,000 Jews lived in Germany, making up 1 percent of the population. About 70 percent of them lived in large cities, 30 percent in Berlin alone. Sixty percent of the Jews worked in trade and commerce, another 20 percent in industry and manual trades, and 17 percent in public service and professions, especially law and medicine. The *Central-Verein* served as the largest representative organization of German Jewry. With 70,000 members, it emphasized the belief that German Jews belonged in Germany.

Initial response to the Nazi regime's anti-Jewish legislation was a combination of despair and a notable increase in suicides on the one hand and a stubborn will to resist on the other. The *Central-Verein's* newspaper editorialized that "no one will dare to violate our constitutional rights" and stressed the right of Jews to be Germans, to live in and love Germany.[12] For many Jews, the affirmation of the right to live in Germany was combined with a strong reaffirmation of their identity as Jews. For some this meant a stinging rejection of assimilation into German life. The newspaper *Jüdische Rundschau* proclaimed the need to "Wear the Yellow Badge with Pride!"

> The Jews refused to acknowledge that "the Jewish question exists." They thought the only important thing was not to be recognized as Jews. Today we are being reproached with having betrayed the German people; the National Socialist press calls us the "enemies of the nation" and there is nothing we can do about it. It is not true that the Jews have betrayed Germany. If they have betrayed anything, they have betrayed themselves and Judaism. Because the Jews did not display their Jewishness with pride, because they wanted to shirk the Jewish question, they must share the blame for the degradation of Jewry.[13]

Jews also reacted to their tribulations by returning to their religious practices and to the life of the Jewish community.

Jews soon realized they needed to forget their differences and form a single body that could protect their rights and possibly negotiate with the German authorities. This organization, entitled the Reich Representation of German Jews, was established on September 17, 1933, under Leo Baeck. Its initial policy was grounded in the belief that

---

[11]Quoted in Marion Kaplan, *Between Dignity and Despair: Jewish Life in Nazi Germany* (New York, 1998), p. 25.

[12]Dawidowicz, *The War Against the Jews*, p. 172.

[13]Ibid.

Jews had to hold out in the hope that the Nazis would moderate their policies against the Jewish community and allow Jews sufficient space for their continued existence. Although the attempts of the Reich Representation of German Jews to represent the Jewish community in negotiations with the Nazi government were ignored by the authorities, the organization did become increasingly important to the German Jewish community itself. In addition to aiding Jews' economic existence by retraining people for manual trades and agriculture, defending Jews against defamation, and establishing schools for Jewish children after they were expelled from "German" schools, the Reich Representation came to view its most important task and only viable response to Nazism as planning and organizing the emigration of Jews from Germany. The "Nuremberg laws" of 1935 made it especially clear to Jews that they had no future in Germany.

The "Nuremberg Laws"

The initial burst of anti-Jewish legislation from April to October 1933 was followed by a cessation in any overt anti-Semitic activity until 1935, when Hitler and the Nazis unleashed a new round of anti-Jewish activity. Acts of terror and boycotts of Jewish businesses began in March. During the summer Jews were forbidden to enter cinemas, theaters, swimming pools, and resorts. Jewish newspapers were coerced into suspending publication for several months. These actions socially isolated Jews, creating what has been termed a social death. As Rabbi Joachim Prinz of Berlin explained, a new kind of ghetto, a psychological one, was created:

> That we live in the ghetto now begins to penetrate our consciousness. This ghetto clearly differs in many ways, in terms of what is still to happen and what is reality, from what we understood up till now . . . The ghetto is no longer a geographically defined district, at least not in the medieval sense. The ghetto is the "world." It has no visible sign. The sign is: being neighborless. This is the fate of the Jews: to be neighborless. Perhaps this happens only once in the world, and who knows how long it must be endured: life without neighbors.[14]

However, these activities were halted rather quickly because of Hitler's dislike of authentic spontaneous mob violence, which could become ungovernable. There were also strenuous objections from economic leaders, such as Hjalmar Schacht, the Reichsbank's president, who lamented the economic difficulties created by such activities. Anti-Jewish activity was thereupon channeled into law by Hitler's announcement of the "Nuremberg laws" at the annual party rally in Nuremberg on September 15, 1935. The first law, the Reich Citizenship Law, differentiated between a "citizen of Germany or kindred blood," who was "the sole bearer of full political rights," and a "subject," who was anyone "who enjoys the protection of the German Reich and for this reason is specifically obligated to it."[15] A decree implementing this citizenship law provided the basic definition of a Jew—"anyone descended from at least three grandparents who are fully Jewish as regards race."[16] Those of mixed ethnic heritage, the *Mischlinge* (meaning of mixed blood, with a

---

[14]Quoted in Konrad Kwiet, "Without Neighbors: Daily Living in *Judenhäuser*," in Francis R. Nicosia and David Scrase, eds, *Jewish Life in Nazi Germany: Dilemmas and Responses* (New York, 2010), p. 118.

[15]Ibid., p. 45.

[16]Ibid., pp. 46–47.

negative connotation of being a mongrel or half-breed), found themselves in a precarious position. While not persecuted to the degree of so-called full Jews, they nonetheless faced discrimination, with limits placed on potential future marriage, education, and service to the state. The second "Nuremberg law," the Law for the Protection of German Blood and Honor, forbade marriages and extramarital relations between Jews and "subjects of German or kindred blood." Marriages already committed between Aryans and Jews became increasingly difficult, and the children of these unions, as *Mischlinge*, faced a difficult future in the new Germany. Erna Becker-Kohen, of Jewish ancestry and married to an Aryan, worried about both her husband and child: "We will be surrounded by . . . hatred and contempt because I am Jewish and my husband is a race defiler. Although he is loyal to me, because he loves me very much, he won't be able to change [the situation] that one scorns not just me, but also his child."[17] Jews were also forbidden to fly the "Reich and national flag" and to employ female "subjects of German or kindred blood" who were under forty-five years of age.

The "Nuremberg laws" effectively separated the Jews from the Germans politically, legally, and socially. They were the natural extension of Hitler's emphasis on the establishment of a pure Aryan race. In the National Socialist twenty-five-point program of 1920, points 4, 5, and 7 had stated:

> Only a member of the race can be a citizen. A member of the race can only be one who is of German blood, without consideration of creed. Consequently, no Jew can be a member of the race. Whoever has no citizenship is to be able to live in Germany only as a guest, and must be under the authority of legislation for foreigners. We demand that the state be charged first with providing the opportunity for a livelihood and way of life for the citizens. If it is impossible to sustain the total population of the State, then the members of foreign nations (noncitizens) are to be expelled from the Reich.[18]

By 1935, Hitler had taken major steps toward achieving one of his cherished racial goals, but in introducing the "Nuremberg laws" to the party congress he openly hinted at another step: "an attempt to regulate by law a problem that, in the event of repeated failure, would have to be transferred by law to the National Socialist party for final solution."[19]

Jewish Emigration from Germany

Emigration figures reflect the cycles of optimism and pessimism that Jews experienced in response to Nazi policy. After an initial rush to emigrate in 1933, when 37,000 Jews left, the number of emigrants dwindled to 23,000 in 1934 and 21,000 in 1935. For many Jews, the crushing of the SA in 1934 had led to the feeling that a greater sense of legality was being restored in Germany. After the "Nuremberg laws" another increase occurred, to 25,000 in 1936. But the calm atmosphere created in the year of the Olympic Games led to a decrease to 23,000 in 1937.

Uncertainty over whether to leave Germany or not was, however, only one factor inhibiting Jewish emigration. Other obstacles existed as well. There was a scarcity of visas from countries to which Jews might hope to move. The democratic states, such as the

---

[17]Kaplan, *Between Dignity and Despair*, p. 82.

[18]*Nazi Conspiracy and Aggression* (Washington, D.C., 1946), vol. 4, p. 209.

[19]Dawidowicz, ed., *A Holocaust Reader*, p. 37.

United States, Great Britain, and France, refused to alter their immigration quotas to permit more German Jews to enter their countries, a situation that the Nazis gleefully observed: "We are saying openly that we do not want the Jews, while the democracies keep on claiming that they are willing to receive them—and then leave the guests out in the cold! Aren't we savages better men after all?"[20] A conference of thirty-two nations was held in the French spa town of Évian from July 6 to 14 to address the emigration crisis of "political refugees" (the plight of Jews was not explicitly referenced in the invitations). As all nations involved were assured that they would not be forced to accept immigrants beyond already existing quotas, the conference was a failure before it even started. It is difficult to know what was more important in producing the inflexible attitude of the democracies, an undercurrent of anti-Semitism or a fear of swamping labor markets that already contained too many unemployed workers because of the depression of the 1930s.

The reluctance of other countries to take Jews often led to tragic scenes. In 1938, 900 Jewish refugee passengers on the *St. Louis* were refused entry to Cuba, although they possessed Cuban visas. The captain returned them to western Europe after the United States made it clear they were not wanted by sending out a coast guard ship to prevent the *St. Louis* from landing on the American coast. Visas were often made available by countries in Latin America that wanted hardy pioneers with agricultural skills, which the largely middle-age and middle-class urbanized German and Austrian Jews did not have. Another alternative, emigration to Palestine, was tightly controlled by the British and by the Zionist movement itself. Financial problems, including a lack of means or fear of major financial loss as a result of a "flight tax" and prohibitions against the removal of money from Germany, kept many Jews from leaving Germany.

After 1936, Jews experienced a steady deterioration in their position in Germany. Censorship of the Jewish press and constant Gestapo surveillance and harassment combined with growing economic need made the Jewish situation bleak. Even worse oppression, however, occurred with the *Kristallnacht* pogrom in November 1938. Jewish institutions were burned and the Jewish press completely suppressed. The Reich Representation of German Jews was replaced by a new organization known as the Reich Association, which was under complete Gestapo control and pushed a policy of forced emigration. Between 1933 and November 1938, 150,000 Jews left Germany. After the November pogrom, discussed later, another 150,000 hastily exited. But even this possibility of survival was halted when war began in September 1939. In 1940, the Nazi state began to deport German Jews to the Government General of Poland. After the police decree of 1941 requiring all Jews over six to wear an identifying Star of David, general deportations to the major ghettos of Lodz, Warsaw, and Lublin began. By the end of 1942, 150,000 had been deported. After additional deportations at the beginning of 1943, Berlin was declared free of Jews. Only 28,000 Jews survived in the "Greater German" state (Germany and Austria).

Kristallnacht *and Its Aftermath*

As in 1933, the outburst of anti-Jewish activity in 1935 was followed by a respite. The holding of the 1936 Olympic Games in Berlin made it especially important to create a good public image for the thousands of foreign visitors. Consequently, anti-Semitic

---

[20]Quoted in Arthur D. Morse, *While Six Million Died* (New York, 1968), p. 288.

Anti-Jewish Activity in Nazi Germany. This photograph shows smashed Jewish shop windows in Berlin the morning after *Kristallnacht*, "the night of shattered glass." *(Bettmann/Corbis)*

activity was downplayed and many of the anti-Semitic posters were removed. However, this pause was followed in 1938–1939 by a third and considerably more violent phase of anti-Semitic activity. This phase was intimately tied to Hitler's increasing preparations for war. Foreign and domestic policies were always closely intertwined in the Third Reich. Hitler's foreign policy meant war, especially for *Lebensraum* in the east at the expense of the Soviet Union. The achievement of this goal demanded a domestic policy of internal restoration that would create a dedicated and unified German people. The enemies at home (the Jews) must be removed.

Beginning on July 23, 1938, all Jews were required to carry special identification cards at all times, making police control of the Jews considerably easier. SA violence was heightened and mass arrests began late in May, with Jews being sent "temporarily" to concentration camps at Buchenwald, Dachau, and Sachsenhausen. Even more drastic action occurred on November 9 and 10, the so-called *Kristallnacht*, or night of glass. The ostensible excuse for this orgy of violence against the Jews was the assassination of a third secretary in the German embassy in Paris by a seventeen-year-old Polish Jewish student whose parents had recently been expelled from Germany and forced to live in a squalid refugee camp. The secretary's death was the signal for a destructive rampage initiated by Propaganda Minister Joseph Goebbels that led to the burning of synagogues, the destruction of Jewish businesses and homes, and the violent manhandling of Jews.

Seven thousand Jewish businesses were destroyed, one hundred Jews killed, and thousands more sadistically tormented. The Swiss consul reported that:

> Organized parties moved through Cologne from one Jewish apartment to another. The families were either ordered to leave the apartment or they had to stand in a corner of a room while the contents were hurled from the windows. Gramophones, sewing machines, and typewriters tumbled down into the streets. One of my colleagues even saw a piano being thrown out of a second-floor window.[21]

One American described an even worse scene in Leipzig:

> Jewish dwellings were smashed into and contents demolished or looted. In one of the Jewish sections, an eighteen-year-old boy was hurled from a three-story window to land with both legs broken on a street littered with burning beds and other household furniture . . . Jewish shop windows by the hundreds were systematically and wantonly smashed throughout the city at a loss estimated at several millions of marks . . . the main streets of the city were a positive litter of shattered plate glass . . . the debacle was executed by SS men and Storm Troopers, not in uniform, each group having been provided with hammers, axes, crowbars and incendiary bombs.[22]

In addition, 30,000 Jewish males were arrested and sent to concentration camps. One man recalled of his experience:

> It was no picnic in Sachsenhausen . . . We were made to stand for twenty four hours if not more, . . . our clothing was taken and carefully marked with names; then you were given a striped uniform and marched off to a block . . . There were two roll calls a day and in that cold weather you had to stand for ages. The guards also had inmates to take over certain duties. Jews had yellow triangles on our jackets; politicals, red; criminals, green; and homosexuals, pink. The foremen were either criminals or politicals, so within the camp there was a grading of the degrading of inmates—extraordinary!

He added, with some hindsight, "I think they were organizing us and learning lessons for future reference."[23]

Indeed, the Nazis used *Kristallnacht* as an opportunity to proceed with the total exclusion of the Jews and the removal of their remaining freedom. Drastic steps were now taken. On November 5, all Jewish children were barred from schools. On November 28, curfew restrictions were placed on the Jews and they were restrained from entering all public places. The elimination of the Jews from the German economy was accomplished by excluding Jews from owning, managing, or working in any retail or mail-order stores. Jews were forced to sell business concerns, such as large department stores, at a loss, and the businesses were subsequently taken over by "Aryan" owners. This "Aryanization" of Jewish-owned business, which began shortly after Hitler came to power, now was extended and accelerated. In addition to the loss of businesses, the Jews were forced to pay a penalty of 1 billion marks because "the hostility of the Jewry toward the German people and Reich, which does not even shrink back from committing cowardly murder, makes a decisive defense and a harsh penalty necessary."[24]

---

[21]Quoted in Friedländer, *Years of Persecution*, p. 277.

[22]Quoted in Nora Levin, *The Holocaust* (New York, 1968), p. 81.

[23]Quoted in Lyn Smith, *Remembering: Voices of the Holocaust* (New York, 2006), pp. 53–54. By permission of Perseus Books Group.

[24]*Nazi Conspiracy and Aggression*, vol. 4, p. 6.

In the aftermath of *Kristallnacht* the expulsion of Jews from Germany was accelerated. A Reich Central Office for Jewish Emigration was established under Reinhard Heydrich, head of the Security Service (SD) branch of the SS. Its object was to promote the "emigration" of Jews from Germany. The SS, whose racial policy favored complete expulsion of the Jews, vigorously pursued forced emigration. Even after the outbreak of war in September 1939, emigration was still the policy. The most ambitious project of 1940, after the defeat of France, was the Madagascar Plan, which aimed at the mass shipment of Jews to an island off the east coast of Africa. But this plan was never seriously considered, and the policy of emigration was soon replaced by a more gruesome one as the war severely radicalized the situation.

INSTRUMENT OF TERROR: THE SS POLICE STATE

To win Germans over to the sense of community embodied in their conception of the Volksgemeinschaft, and to justify and perpetrate its anti-Jewish policies, the Nazis expended considerable effort in propaganda and indoctrination. For many Germans, this was sufficient to make them willing participants in the new Nazi state. But Hitler and the Nazis did not rely only on verbal persuasion. From the beginning of the movement they counted on force and violence to achieve their goals. And so it was in their seizure of power. One party organization came to be the dominant symbol of the Nazi use of force and terror. The SS, with its black uniforms and death's head insignia and all its various police organizations, struck fear into the hearts of those who either opposed the regime or would not be allowed to live in the new pure German state.

Beginnings

The SS was established in 1925 with the formation of a small personal guards unit whose function was to protect Hitler and other party leaders. It was called the *Schutzstaffeln* (protection squads), or SS. SS members wore black caps with a skull and crossbones on them. From its beginning the SS was given the special purpose of intelligence gathering. By July 1926, the new organization had seventy-five members, including the man who would eventually build the SS in his own image—Heinrich Himmler. The early SS did not look particularly promising. Between 1927 and 1929 the organization actually declined in membership, from 1000 to 280. Its early leaders accepted completely the subordination of the SS to the leadership of the SA. But on January 20, 1929, Himmler, who had been second in command in the SS since 1927, was put in charge as Reichsführer-SS.

The Role of Himmler and Growth of the SS

Heinrich Himmler was the dominant force in the development of the SS. He, like Hitler, created a movement that reflected his own ideological foundations. Born in 1900, Heinrich Himmler was the product of a middle-class background. His father was a teacher. Himmler was educated at a secondary school near Munich. Although he hoped to see action in World War I, the war ended while he was still an officer cadet. He received a diploma in agronomy from a technical institute in Munich in 1922. While a student he joined the Nazi Party in 1921 and participated in the Beer Hall Putsch as a standard-bearer next to Ernst Röhm. In 1924, he became secretary to Gregor Strasser, and in the next year he became his business manager while Strasser served as *Gauleiter* of Lower Bavaria. He came to Munich in 1927 as Strasser's deputy for Nazi propaganda. After trying unsuccessfully to make a living as a chicken farmer, he achieved the leadership of the SS in 1929 and the opportunity to seek even greater vistas.

Himmler was a true believer in the racial ideology that Hitler had placed at the center of his National Socialist movement. From 1926 to 1928, Himmler had belonged to the Artamanen, a group that believed in the sacred role of the peasants in German culture and the need to reconquer and recolonize eastern Europe for Germany. Like Hitler, Himmler believed that the racial struggle between Aryans and Jews was the key to world history. The development of a healthy German race depended not only on the elimination of the Jewish influence but also on the furthering of the German peasants as the healthy stock of the German nation. "The peasant . . . is the backbone of the German people's strength and character." For the German race to grow, the Germans needed living space in the east (Soviet Russia), where German peasants would settle. As Himmler had written in his diary in 1922, "In the East we must fight and settle."[25]

Himmler's ideas dramatically influenced his vision of the SS, which he looked upon as the elite group of National Socialism. His models were twofold. Raised in a pious Catholic household, he was familiar with the Jesuits and their emphasis on absolute obedience to the pope and total dedication to the ideals and wishes of the church they served. Hitler used to refer to Himmler as "our Ignatius Loyola," a reference to the sixteenth-century founder of the Jesuit order. But Himmler's primary model was the medieval order of knights, especially the Order of Teutonic Knights, who had fought and carried their Christian ideology into eastern Europe. Like them, his new order would be an elite—not a Christian one but a racial elite—and would be based on the traditional values of honor, obedience, loyalty, and courage. Like them, his new order would conquer the East, on behalf not of Christian ideology but of a racial ideology that was the key to history. In a speech given in 1939 after the SS acquired the headquarters of the Teutonic Knights in Vienna, Himmler reflected on the history of the group. He noted its origins in the Crusades, where it was "led astray by the Christian church" and "bled to death" in the Middle East. According to Himmler, the Germanic knights then made the proper decision to conquer Eastern Europe:

> This order of knights then made the bold move to East Prussia and there became the order of Teutonic Knights. It founded the state, the order's own state of East Prussia, in accordance with its strict, soldierly code and Christian outlook. [. . .] It is my firm intention to appropriate from it all that was good about this order: bravery, extraordinary loyalty to a revered idea, sound organization, riding out into far countries, riding out to the east.[26]

Like Adolf Hitler, Heinrich Himmler was a fanatic whose visions would be translated into reality with a determination that would create nightmares for millions of innocent people.

But Heinrich Himmler was more than an ideologist. He was also a cold, calculating, rational, efficient bureaucrat whose ruthlessness made him an ideal head of the SS. Within a year the SS had returned to its 1927 level of 1000 members, by spring 1932 it had grown to 25,000, and by January 1933 it had reached 52,000. In theory, the SS recruited

---

[25]Quoted in Josef Ackermann, *Heinrich Himmler als Ideologe* (Göttingen, 1970), p. 198.
[26]Quoted in Peter Longerich, *Himmler* (New York, 2012), p. 273.

new members on the basis of racial purity. Although Himmler would later establish more rigid guidelines for selection, during this period the SS used only physical appearance, seeking to recruit pure Nordic types with blond hair, blue eyes, and good physique—traits conspicuously absent in the Nazi leaders themselves.

Like the SA, the early SS spent much time participating in street fights with Communists and Socialists. Himmler struggled, however, to maintain a certain degree of independence. He worked consciously to differentiate the SS from the SA. He instituted the all-black uniform with the death's head insignia. Since the SA was a mass organization recruiting anybody and was often unreliable, the SS deliberately sought to recruit members from the old German aristocracy and university graduates. Himmler molded the SS into an elite organization and emphasized its role as an elitist group by making it the police service of the NSDAP. Its police tasks included not only the personal defense of the Führer and other party leaders but also the service of preventing the rowdy SA and party personnel from threatening public order (SS men were often asked to search SA men for concealed firearms) and intelligence gathering.

Himmler systematized SS intelligence activities by founding a new unit called the *Sicherheitsdienst* (SD), or Security Service, in 1931. He chose as its leader Reinhard Heydrich, an ex-naval officer who was well educated and had a middle-class background. Heydrich fit the Aryan ideal. He was blond, blue-eyed, intelligent, and well built. Unlike Himmler, he was motivated not so much by ideology as by the desire for power. But Himmler liked him. He was ambitious, unscrupulous, and loyal. Heydrich set about to build up a rational system of intelligence gathering. The function of the SD was to gather information on opponents of the NSDAP and even on party members and leaders themselves. Heydrich was especially adept at recruiting young university graduates who were eager for power and an opportunity to use their skills. He developed a network that eventually covered Germany with thousands of informers.

Himmler had strong opinions about the SS officer corps, which was to be based on the principle of absolute obedience to Hitler and the voluntary subordination of leaders to their superiors in the interest of the higher good of the SS. Himmler insisted that SS officers have an indestructible esprit de corps and be thoroughly trained in all branches of SS discipline. SS superiority should be evident in everything the officers did, since the SS was the "best human material" in Germany after what Himmler saw as the "decline in human heredity" during the previous century.

Although the SA and the SS coordinated their functions and operated in parallel directions, Himmler soon began to separate the SS from the SA. While the membership of both SA and SS grew enormously from January to May 1933 (the SA from 300,000 to 500,000, the SS from 50,000 to 100,000), Himmler closed his membership in April to strengthen its elitist image, whereas Röhm went on to add an additional 1 million members to the SA from other paramilitary groups. The SS also emphasized its elite status by organizing specialized military units. These included the *Leibstandarte SS Adolf Hitler*, Hitler's personal bodyguard regiments under Sepp Dietrich; the Death's Head Formations, responsible for the concentration camps; and Special Duty troops.

In the winter of 1933–1934 a noticeable change took place that shaped the history of both the SA and the SS. The SA, by its calls for a second revolution and a new revolutionary army, began to move outside the National Socialist system while the SS positioned itself carefully in the front ranks as defenders of the new National Socialist order. When the Reichswehr began to suspect the SA's ambitions, Himmler and the SS cunningly contributed from behind the scenes to the belief that the SA was dangerous and was planning a putsch. In the blood purge of the SA at the end of June 1934, it was the "loyal" SS that was responsible, with the support of army trucks and weapons, for the arrests and execution of SA leaders. Its reward came on July 20, when the SS became independent of the SA. The SS could now continue its campaign to gain a complete monopoly over the police forces of Germany.

Toward the Police State

Both Himmler and Heydrich had perceived at the beginning of the Nazi seizure of power that control of the police offered a path to real power. Himmler began this quest in the relatively obscure post of police president of Munich. On April 1, 1933, however, he was promoted to political police commander of Bavaria with Heydrich as his deputy. During the winter of 1933–1934, Himmler managed to be appointed chief of the political police in all the states except Prussia, where Hermann Göring still held control over the secret state police known as the Gestapo. After a power struggle, Göring conceded defeat by appointing Himmler inspector of the Gestapo in April 1934. The SS completed its control of the police when Himmler was made chief of the German police in 1936. Theoretically he was subordinate to Minister of the Interior Wilhelm Frick. But, as Frick soon found out when he tried to challenge Himmler on a number of issues, it was Himmler who exercised the real authority over the police forces in Germany.

Heinrich Himmler was now Reichsführer-SS and chief of the German Police, an unusual combination of party and state leadership positions. The head of a party organization was now head of all the police. As leader of the SS, Himmler was subordinate only to Hitler. He was therefore free to operate independently, above both party and state, to enforce the will of Hitler. Himmler could act within the law as head of the police or outside the law as head of the SS, depending on his needs. In either case, there could be no legal redress for any of his actions, since members of the SS were not responsible to the state or party courts. The SS had truly established a total police state in which any act of terror could now be interpreted as legal.

The System of Terror

As master of the police, the SS was concerned primarily with the domestic enemies of the regime. A total system of terror, of course, thrives on enemies, and the SS had no difficulty in finding them everywhere. For Himmler the SS was a group of "political soldiers" who had the responsibility of destroying Germany's enemies. Initially those enemies were domestic, but eventually they would include Germany's foreign enemies. To deal with the latter, in the late 1930s the SS created the nucleus of a combat group called the Waffen-SS (armed SS). There were 20,000 Waffen-SS troops by the end of 1938, but during World War II it became a force of more than 600,000 men.

The role of the Waffen-SS lay in a future war with Germany's external enemies. In the 1930s the SS concerned itself with establishing a *Volksgemeinschaft* free of domestic enemies. Internal enemies were divided into three major groups: Jews, considered the most dangerous enemies to a *völkisch* state; ideological enemies of National Socialism, a category that included not only political enemies such as Communists and Socialists but also several Christian groups and the Freemasons; and moral enemies, the criminals, pornographers, homosexuals, and other "asocials" who contaminated the mores of the national community. The ideological and moral enemies, the SS thought, might be redeemed in concentration camps and made respectable citizens again. The Jews were enemies who would have to be eliminated from German life if the nation was to maintain its racial purity. It was no accident that the SS was eventually given responsibility for the "final solution" of the Jewish problem during the war.

Both party and state offices were responsible for dealing with these domestic enemies. The SD tended to be composed of members who were more ideologically oriented to the ideals of National Socialism. The intelligence network of the SD was used to ferret out opponents to the regime. The SD was interested not only in political opponents but also more subtle kinds of opposition in art, literature, and music. Comments disparaging or even mildly critical of National Socialism and its ideology could constitute treason. The work of arresting and dealing with opponents was left to the Security Police and especially the Gestapo.

The Gestapo as a state agency consisted of more professional police agents and was known for its efficiency in dealing with opponents. Although the Gestapo had its own agents, it made good use of block wardens, whose job was to keep close watch on tenants in their block. Block wardens visited every household at least once a week and made regular reports to the SD offices. The Gestapo felt bound by no legal restrictions. Even accused individuals found innocent by a regular court could be arrested by the Gestapo after their release by the court. Gestapo legality was rationalized by its lawyers on the basis that as long as the police carried out the will of the government it was acting legally, regardless of what it did.

As a means of systematizing the instruments of terror, the concentration camp came to play an important role. Concentration camps were spontaneously organized by both SA and SS units during the first months of the Nazi seizure of power. Initially they held Communists, Socialists, and labor leaders. The camp at Dachau, established in March 1933, came to have special significance. In June, Dachau received a new commandant, Theodor Eicke. He developed an efficient and rational system of terror in which guards were carefully trained in dehumanizing their prisoners so they could treat them not as fellow human beings but as animals. Of course, in destroying their prisoners' humanity they also destroyed their own. Eicke turned Dachau into the model camp that became a training school for later commandants. Rudolf Höss, later commandant of the camp at Auschwitz, was a product of Eicke's system.

By 1934, the SS had taken over all the concentration camps. Eicke was appointed inspector of all camps in July 1934 and proceeded to regularize them on the Dachau model. SS units guarding the camps were separated from the regular police and reorganized into the Death's Head Formations, which numbered 3500 by 1936. By 1937, the SS had reduced the numerous camps to three major ones—Dachau, Sachsenhausen, and Buchenwald—which covered the major regions of Germany. Life in the concentration camp for those taken into so-called protective custody was often described as hell.

SS Ideology

The SS was not only the primary Nazi instrument of terror but also the self-appointed carrier of its ideals, especially the racial ideals at the core of Hitler's National Socialism. The SS considered itself the racial elite of the nation, a new nobility that could be replenished only by the begetting of children between pure Aryan males and females. Already in 1931, Himmler had promulgated an SS marriage order whose purpose was to create a strictly Nordic German type. To get married, SS men were required to obtain a marriage certificate from the SS Race Office under Walter Darré. Prospective wives had to be guaranteed as racially pure and "hereditarily healthy." Himmler's emphasis on racial principles is also seen in his recruitment policies. The SS investigated the entire family of every SS candidate to be sure there was no evidence of hereditary disease or mental illness. Himmler even advocated tracing family trees back to 1650 to guarantee racial purity.

In a 1935 speech Himmler outlined the principles of selection for SS men. The first principle was "recognition of the values of blood and selection." Only those who came physically closest to the ideal of a Nordic man could be chosen. He highlighted the importance of loyalty and honor, especially loyalty to Hitler and the German race. Hitler had given the SS its motto—"Your honor is loyalty"—and for the SS loyalty meant absolute obedience to Hitler.

Himmler saw the elimination of Christianity and Christian ethics as another of his goals in achieving the pure Aryan state. He wished to foster a new morality based on National Socialist ideology and its ancient "Germanic heritage." His belief in these ideas was often combined with a fuzzy occultism that led even other Nazis to view Himmler as a crank. Himmler established a department in the SS known as the *Ahnenerbe*, the Ancestral Heritage Organization. Its task was to investigate all aspects of ancient German tradition. It conducted "research" into earth mysteries by studying the connection of race with house design; the occult properties of church bells; and runes, a form of ancient German script believed to possess magical properties.

Himmler also established SS rituals and symbols appropriate to an elite racial group. SS weddings and baptisms were performed in special services conducted before an SS altar containing the various "sacred" objects of the order. Himmler created his own special headquarters at Castle Wewelsburg in Westphalia, described by SS leaders as a sort of SS monastery where Himmler established a Round Table surrounded by thirteen chairs for Himmler and his twelve disciples (SS officers). Himmler also instituted special ceremonies for honoring the Saxon king Henry the Fowler, believing himself to be the reincarnation of that medieval German king who also had made conquests in the East.

To maintain his racial elite, Himmler promulgated a strict marriage law in 1931. In order not to lose any opportunity for the procreation of pure Aryan children, Himmler established the *Lebensborn* (Spring of Life), homes for wed and unwed mothers of children sired by SS men and other racially valuable Germans. These homes were well furnished and lavishly supplied, even in wartime. After the outbreak of war, Himmler issued his infamous procreation order of October 28, 1939, to the entire SS, in which he emphasized that it was the task of German women of "good blood" acting not frivolously but from a "profound moral seriousness" to become mothers to children of soldiers setting off to battle. In the SS, even a sexual revolution was justifiable if it meant the production of pure Aryans.

LEGAL AND JUDICIAL SYSTEMS

Hitler and Nazi leaders interpreted the law and the legal system in their own unique way. For them, law did not encompass a set of rules of conduct regulating a community in a reasonably predictable fashion, but was used simply as an instrument to secure the regime's goals. Hans Frank, head of the Reich Lawyers' Association, once said that in the Nazi state the law is only a means to maintain the *völkisch* community. For Hitler the traditional Western legal concern for equality before the law was only for those who backed the national interest and "do not fail to support the government." The traditional concern for the rights of the individual had to be subordinated to the interests of the national community. As Hitler said, "Not the individual but only the nation must be regarded as the center of legal concern."[27] And in the Führer state, the interests of the nation were really those of the Führer.

Unwilling to institute a new legal system, the Nazis largely maintained the old one. But they devised a multitude of ways to make the old system serve their needs. One procedure was to enact new laws that eliminated previous legal rights of Germans. Especially prominent were new laws dealing with political offenses, race, and the civil service. By having to implement these new Nazi laws, members of the old legal system became accomplices in the nazification of German society.

Given the significance of political crimes to the regime, the Nazis chose to handle them directly by creating two new kinds of courts. In March 1933, they established the Special Courts, whose function was to deal with political crimes except high treason. The judges were ardent Nazis. Their decisions could not be appealed. After 1935, these courts dealt mostly with violations of the Law Against Malicious Attacks on State and Party. Enacted in December 1934, this law stipulated that people who made base or "rabble-rousing remarks" against state or party officials would be jailed. In practice the law meant that any disparaging remark, even political jokes, would be punished. This inability of the regime to tolerate any critical comments, even innocuous ones, was based on the Nazi concept of the national community. Ideally, the national community was a single entity united behind its leadership and consisted only of friends or foes. No opposition could be tolerated without undermining the regime. Between 1933 and 1939, approximately 5400 people were brought before the Munich Special Court, of whom 5000 were supposed violators of the Law Against Malicious Attack. Almost 1900 of the accused were put on trial and 1500 were convicted and imprisoned, usually for one to six months. The criminals were people who had made "malicious" statements such as "In the Dachau concentration camp people get beaten," "The Hitler Youth is ruining children," and "Hitler is a scoundrel." Obviously the Nazi regime was not to be taken lightly.

A second new Nazi court was the People's Court, created in April 1933. This court took cases of high treason out of the hands of the regular Supreme Court. The five judges included two qualified judges and three Nazi Party officials. There was no appeal of decisions, which were made primarily for political reasons. This is the court that tried the participants in the July 20, 1944, attempt to assassinate Hitler.

Because many judges were already extremely conservative, the Nazis experienced little difficulty in controlling regular German courts. We have already seen, in the case of the Beer Hall Putsch, how lenient judges could be toward the far right. Since judges constituted a branch of the civil service, the Nazi civil service laws enabled Nazi leaders to dismiss judges for political reasons. Few judges were touched, however, because most had right-wing sentiments. The most important factor in the Nazi control of the courts was that the Nazis forced judges to follow the guidelines of the regime, which were defined by the government as National Socialist ideology, Führer decrees, and the "present sound feelings of the people." In accommodating themselves to these standards, judges often tried to outdo the Nazis. In the final analysis, however, judges knew that regardless of their verdicts, the SS police state would make the final decision.

---

[27]Max Domarus, ed., *Hitler: Reden und Proklamationen, 1932–1945*, vol. 1 (Munich, 1962), p. 233.

This last statement reminds us of the ultimate limitations on the old legal system that were created by the SS police state. The SS created its own legal system that operated independently of the state. In the concentration camp it had its own prisons. In its arrest of people who had been acquitted by the regular courts, the Gestapo demonstrated its freedom from the regular legal system. As in the administration of government, the Nazis developed a dualistic system of justice—the state system of courts and judges and the SS system, which acted ultimately on the basis of arbitrary Führer authority. The war years would show that the SS system was the only significant one.

THE CHURCHES

The churches of Germany proved to be a stubborn obstacle to the attempt of Hitler and the Nazis to establish total control over the German people. The organizations of the established churches had survived the *Gleichschaltung* that many other institutions suffered in the first six months of Nazi power. In part this was because the Nazis had no clear-cut policy on the churches when they came to power and because they feared alienating potentially large numbers of Germans. Point 24 of the party platform had promised freedom for all religious denominations as long as they were not a danger to the German race. The party claimed to stand for positive Christianity, which was ambiguous enough to be interpreted favorably if people wanted to. Hitler and some elite Nazis had personally rejected traditional forms of Christianity as an ideology ultimately opposed to their own "spiritual movement," but were reluctant to publicize or push these views. The churches tended to ignore serious differences because Hitler had avoided attacking the churches while campaigning for votes and had even tried to gain the support of Catholics and Protestants. He was remarkably successful, especially with the many Protestants who shared his beliefs in traditional nationalistic and conservative values. Although both Catholic clergy and laity were often critical of Nazism, the Nazis' nationalism and anticommunism had also attracted some Catholic support. Theoretically opposed to anti-Semitism, the churches' opposition to this Nazi belief was undermined by the number of lay people and clergy who shared it.

Once the Nazis were in power, both Protestants and Catholics overwhelmingly accepted the new regime. Hitler appeared to support traditional Christian values. Although anti-Christian Nazi radicals wanted to move against the churches, churchmen believed that Hitler was more moderate and held the extremists in check. Both Protestants and Catholics were sympathetic to Hitler's anticommunist crusade. The willingness of both Catholics and Protestants to support the state made it difficult for them later to create any real resistance movement against the Nazi state. Although there were similarities in Nazi activities against different Christian churches, the Nazis themselves realized the need to use certain tactics with the Catholics and certain tactics with the Protestants. The Catholic church was part of a vast international body with a firm doctrine and an ultimate ruling authority outside Germany. Protestantism had been closely tied to the German state since the Lutheran Reformation of the sixteenth century. Protestants were also divided doctrinally between Lutherans and Calvinists.

The Catholics

Before the Nazi seizure of power in 1933, the Catholic church had been a major opponent of Nazism. This position was dramatically reversed in July 1933, when the new

Nazi government concluded a concordat (agreement) with the Roman Catholic Church leadership. The church agreed to recognize the legitimacy of the Hitler regime and to eliminate all the political and social organizations of German Catholicism. In return, the German government guaranteed freedom of religion, protection of church institutions, the right to disseminate papal letters and encyclicals, and the preservation of Catholic schools. The concordat's recognition of the Hitler regime was a tremendous boost to the prestige of the regime. It soon became apparent, however, that the Nazis had no intention of keeping their promises.

Nazi attacks on Catholic organizations quickly evaporated hopes for cooperation with the new regime. Catholic teachers were dismissed from their jobs. Young people in Catholic youth groups were pressured to join the Hitler Youth. In the blood purge of June 1934 the leaders of Catholic Action and Catholic Youth Sports were among the murder victims, although both were officially listed as suicides.

The Protestants

The Protestant problem was initially approached differently. The Nazis had encouraged the formation in 1932 of a Protestant pro-Nazi organization called German Christians, who ardently supported the regime's racial doctrines. The German Christians wanted to establish the *Führerprinzip* in Protestantism by uniting all Protestant churches into a single Reich church under one bishop. Hitler approved and used state power to force the election of Ludwig Müller, a military chaplain from East Prussia who was an ardent Nazi. Müller was made Reich bishop, and German Christians took over church offices.

The victory of the German Christians proved to be short lived when the attempts to nazify the Protestant churches aroused opposition. In September 1933, a Pastors' Emergency League was set up under Martin Niemöller, pastor of a fashionable church in Berlin and an initial supporter of National Socialism. The Emergency League opposed nazification as contrary to church doctrine and especially objected to Nazi racial doctrines, which denied the power of conversion to save Jews. By the beginning of 1934, 4000 pastors had joined the league.

The Reich church under Müller reacted to this challenge by reprimanding pastors and even having the police arrest them. These pressures led in April 1934 to the formation of the Confessional church as a rival authority to the Reich Church. It was to be led by a Reich Council of Brethren under the theologian Karl Barth. Many of its members were from the Pastors' Emergency League. The Confessional church held a national synod at Barmen and produced a statement of principles known as the Barmen Confession in May 1934. The Barmen Confession rejected the views of the German Christians and denied the totalitarian claims of the state on the church. The Barmen Confession, however, did not represent a program of political protest. It was drafted not by politicians but by theologians who largely remained loyal to Hitler and maintained the traditional Lutheran respect for ruling authorities. Clerical opposition to Hitler rarely exceeded passive resistance to certain features of Nazi tyranny.

In the meantime, to the Nazis the Barmen Confession appeared to be an act of resistance. Their response was more persecution. The Gestapo's arrest of orthodox Lutheran bishops led to mass demonstrations in a number of cities and adverse reaction abroad. At this point Hitler intervened, disturbed by the dissension within the Protestant camp. It was clear that Müller and the German Christians had failed to produce Protestant unity and the Nazis temporarily backed off. Conservative orthodox bishops and officials replaced the German Christians, who now began to decline in significance. The Confessional church remained in existence, although its members were increasingly harassed by the authorities. Reich Bishop Müller remained in office, but was virtually stripped of any real power and became totally ineffective. Other Protestant theologians sympathetic to the Nazis were not deterred by these developments. In 1939 the Institute for the Study and Eradication of Jewish Influence on German Religious Life was founded to defame Judaism, "dejudaize" the New Testament by eliminating everything deemed Jewish, and to "prove" that Jesus was not a Jew himself, but in fact was an Aryan savior. This type of intellectual Christian anti-Judaism only served to complement, rather than combat, the racist policies of the Nazis at this time.

Nazi Policy, 1935–1939

From 1935 to 1939, Nazi policy toward the churches was conducted along three separate avenues simultaneously: an attempt to gain administrative control so that the Protestant and Catholic churches could be brought under the authority of the state; the waging of an ideological struggle to replace Christianity with a new cult in the hearts and minds of all Germans; and a campaign of terrorism and intimidation designed to gradually reduce the Christian churches to extinction.

By 1935, after the failure of Müller and the German Christians, Hitler had come to feel that more centralized leadership was needed to gain administrative control over the churches. In July 1935, a Ministry of Church Affairs was created under Hans Kerrl, a former minister of justice for Prussia. As was typical with Hitler, he gave no clear definition to Kerrl's position. Kerrl himself saw his office as an instrument for controlling the Protestant factions and ensuring that the Catholic church fulfilled its obligations to the Nazi regime. But Kerrl soon found he had little real power over church affairs because he was unable to prevent other Nazis from weakening his powers, and he became increasingly frustrated both by infighting within the Nazi Party and by his inability to achieve anything with the churches. He resorted more and more to force.

A second Nazi approach to church policy was grounded in ideological fervor. The high point of the ideological campaign came in 1936 and 1937, when the Nazis hoped that indoctrinating Germans with Nazi ideology would cause them to abandon their tainted Christian beliefs. Hitler had emphasized in *Mein Kampf* that one spiritual movement could be overcome only by another one. Thus, Rosenberg, Himmler, Bormann, and other strong anti-Christian Nazis pushed for increased Nazi indoctrination that stressed race and pure Aryan blood, German nationalism, and Hitler as a messiah figure.

The Nazis themselves were divided on the ideological campaign. Some Nazis, such as Kerrl, continued to believe that Nazism and Christianity could be compatible. A "positive Christianity" purged of theological bickering could be dedicated to national and racial purposes. The more ideologically extreme Nazis, such as Rosenberg, Bormann, and Himmler, believed they could achieve their ideological goals through quick destruction of Christianity by eliminating the role of the clergy. This tactic led in part to the "immorality" trials of Catholic priests and nuns in 1936 and 1937. Still another group of Nazis, including Hitler himself, believed not only that Nazi ideology was incompatible with Christianity but also that a more gradual approach was needed. These Nazis believed that the ultimate victory would be theirs, but the process should not be rushed. Hitler certainly realized that if he were to achieve his war plans in Europe, he would need the Christian population of Germany. There was no need to alienate them unnecessarily.

Nevertheless, the third avenue of Nazi church policy from 1935 to 1939 involved the use of terror and intimidation. Both Protestant and Catholic groups responded to these pressures. In 1936, the Confessional church directed a memorandum to Hitler in which it attacked the government's anti-Christian campaign, asked whether anti-Semitism was not contrary to the Christian commandment to love one's neighbor, and openly criticized the lawlessness of the Gestapo. Catholics also reacted to the regime's policies, but their tactics were different. An appeal for papal assistance brought Pius XI's encyclical *Mit Brennender Sorge* (With Burning Anxiety), which was read in Catholic churches in March 1937. This document denounced the Nazi persecution of the church and attacked the insidious cult of race, although it did not specifically mention the plight of German Jews. Nazi response to these criticisms was swift and deadly.

Nazi persecution of the churches in the second half of the 1930s involved a variety of tactics. Persecutions and arrests of individual clergymen were especially noticeable. Attacks on Catholic clergy focused on moral trials. Hundreds of priests, nuns, and monks were accused and convicted of illicit and perverse sexual practices. Public accounts were grossly exaggerated to make almost all the Catholic clergy appear to be sexual criminals.

In response to the 1936 Confessional church memorandum, Hitler ordered a crackdown on the Confessional church. One of its leaders, and a signer of the memorandum, Friedrich Weissler, was murdered in Sachsenhausen concentration camp. By 1937, over 700 pastors had been arrested and some of them sent to Buchenwald. Martin Niemöller was among those arrested. Although virtually acquitted by the courts, he was rearrested by the Gestapo and sent to Buchenwald and later to Dachau, where he was liberated at the end of the war. It should be noted that Nazi persecution of the clergy was sometimes restrained, undoubtedly for tactical reasons. Although numerous clergymen were imprisoned, their sentences were not lengthy. Of 17,000 pastors in the Protestant church, no more than fifty were sentenced to long terms of imprisonment.

Another special Gestapo target was the activities of smaller, less significant religious sects. These groups had little legal standing, received no state subsidies, and hence had few friends. Of these groups, the most visible opponents of Nazism were the Jehovah's Witnesses, who refused to cooperate with the Nazi state. They declined to join any Nazi organization or to be drafted into the military. But they, like Freemasons and other groups, were officially attacked because they were supposedly influenced by world Jewry and communism. The Jehovah's Witnesses did not shrink from confrontation with the Nazi state: 97 percent of them suffered persecution, a third of their number were killed.

By 1938 and 1939, there was a pervasive feeling in the German church community that the Nazi work of attrition had achieved much of its objective. Church members felt defeated, weary, and dispirited. Protestant visitation reports observed that although people were still faithful to their Christian beliefs, they felt they could do nothing against the new forces and did not dare to act as easily as they once had. These observers especially noted the ominous trend among the youth not to attend church regularly. Of course, the foreign policy successes of Hitler and the Nazis played an important role in the campaign against the church. The Anschluss with Austria in 1938 and the acquisition of the Sudetenland the same year brought increased glory to the regime. Even the clergy of both churches responded, sending congratulations to Hitler on these occasions. No doubt many parishioners felt the same way. As long as the clergy found redeeming values in German nationalism, it was impossible for them to mount any real resistance to Nazism. With the coming of war, the Nazis needed Christian support more than ever. Activities against the churches would again have to cease, giving the churches even less reason to resist.

THE MILITARY

The Nazi total state was never quite total. Nowhere were the limits to Nazi power more observable than in the military, which had not been coordinated in 1933 and 1934. The army, as in the Weimar Republic, continued to maintain a high degree of independence. At the end of World War I, the Reichswehr, Germany's military forces, were reduced to an army of 100,000 men and a navy of 15,000. An air force was completely outlawed. Although the Reichswehr initially supported the Weimar Republic, many officers came to hope for an authoritarian state that would rearm Germany. Some were sympathetic to Hitler for that reason.

In 1933, the leaders of the Reichswehr had accepted Hitler and his regime. Although claiming to be above party politics, General Blomberg, minister of defense, and his chief political adviser, General Reichenau, stood by benevolently and refused to intervene while the Nazis seized power. They strongly believed that Hitler would create a national revival that would mean a stronger army. Hitler had told the generals from his first day as chancellor that he intended to rearm Germany. These officers believed that by recognizing the political leadership of the party they could maintain the independence and privileged position of the army and play an important role in German life. Hitler's crushing of the SA as the army had demanded reassured Blomberg and Reichenau in their feelings about Hitler and the Nazi regime.

Hitler was undoubtedly suspicious of the military leaders. To him they were part of the old, conservative Germany. While Hindenburg was president, Hitler knew that the army was the one major force that could overthrow him. Just as he needed the industrial barons for economic recovery, he needed the generals to create a strong military to pursue his foreign policy goals. The military, consequently, was not nazified, and in the eyes of many it remained the last bastion against Nazi barbarism.

But some Nazi influences did creep in. After Hindenburg's death, soldiers and their leaders took an oath of allegiance to Hitler. There were Nazi supporters within the Reichswehr itself, especially among the younger officers. As the army expanded, especially after the establishment of military conscription in 1935, new recruits included many young people who had been indoctrinated in Nazi ideas. As early as 1935, Hitler began enforcing his own decisions without heeding the advice of the military.

By that time, Hitler had also taken major steps toward rearmament that pleased many military leaders. In 1934 and 1935, expenditures on armaments rose dramatically. Moreover, on March 8, 1935, Hitler announced that Germany already had an air force (Luftwaffe) consisting of almost 2000 aircraft and 20,000 officers and men. The Luftwaffe was intended to play a major role in the new concept of *Blitzkrieg*, or lightning war. Hitler and some of his military commanders wanted to avoid the trench warfare of World War I and conceived a lightning warfare that depended on mechanized columns and massive air power to cut quickly across battle lines and encircle and annihilate entire armies. *Blitzkrieg* meant the quick defeat of an enemy. Although Hermann Göring was put in charge of the new Luftwaffe, his subordinate, Erhard Milch, who had been director of Lufthansa airlines, played the chief role in enlarging and preparing the Luftwaffe for its new wartime role.

On March 16, 1935, Hitler introduced compulsory military service and at the same time changed the official name of the Reichswehr to Wehrmacht, which comprised the army, navy, and air force. The size of the army was now increased from 100,000 to 550,000 men. By the beginning of World War II in 1939, the Wehrmacht had 4.5 million men in uniform. Naval rearmament also proceeded in 1935 after the Anglo-German Naval Pact of June 18, 1935 (see Chapter 7).

PUBLIC OPINION IN THE THIRD REICH

The Nazi total state was theoretically built upon the Nazi ideal of a national community obedient to the wishes of its leaders. Of course, Hitler's ultimate reason for community was to make sure of national unity while pursuing war. He, like other right-wing politicians, had believed that the German failure in World War I was the result of lack of unity at home, not the performance of the German army abroad. The Nazis were obsessed with a dualistic scheme of reality. An ideal *Volksgemeinschaft* consisted of national racial comrades. Those who were not racially German were enemies who must be removed or eliminated. Those who opposed the regime in any way were also enemies. The SS police state and its system of terror were designed to deal with both kinds of enemies. But the Nazis were also concerned about generating popular enthusiasm for the *Volksgemeinschaft* through propaganda and indoctrination.

Consent

Historians have found it difficult to ascertain the degree of popular enthusiasm for the Nazi regime. Undoubtedly differences existed among social groups, and economic, political, and psychological factors would have affected public opinion. In addition, Germans were obviously reluctant to express their opinions, out of fear of the Law Against Malicious Attack and other elements of the terror system. Even the SD, a branch of the SS, did not find it easy to get an idea of public opinion. The SD used an extensive system of informers numbering some 3000 full-time agents and 50,000 part-time deputies to monitor casual conversations and assess the effects on morale of both domestic and foreign events.

Despite the use of terror, which of course would be most frightening to opponents of the regime, there seemed to exist considerable consent for the Nazi regime. One major source for this consent was Hitler's popularity as the German Führer. This was due in part to the need of many Germans for strong leadership, which had been traditional in imperial Germany but missing in the Weimar era. Economic depression added to the desire for an authoritarian leader, a knight on horseback, who would solve the nation's problems. And of course Hitler seemed to do so. He cleared up the unemployment problem and he regained national prestige. As one Socialist report put it, "He has created work. He has made Germany strong." Hitler was also viewed by a number of Germans as a messiah figure, as one sent by God to save Germany. The depth of Hitler's appeal is readily observable in the emotional crowd scenes that took place wherever he appeared in Germany.

Undoubtedly, popular consent for the Nazi regime was also based on the clever use of forces popular in Germany, especially nationalism and militarism. Even Christian ministers opposed to Nazi anti-Christian policies could still be fervently pro-Nazi in their support of a strong German state. Moreover, the regime's attacks on the modern art and sexual license associated with the large cities in the Weimar era undoubtedly brought the approval of many Germans, especially those in the rural areas. And the regime's crackdown on deviants, tramps, and habitual criminals produced a sense of security based on the return of law and order.

The Nazi regime tried to convince itself and the world of public approval by the use of plebiscites, a favorite technique of authoritarian regimes. Of course, the results were foreordained. Majorities of 98.9 percent could hardly be the result of free elections. Indoctrination of voters before the plebiscites, open voting, and falsified vote counts guaranteed such majorities.

To generate mass enthusiasm and create a feeling of community, the Nazis made use of well-planned mass rallies. Ceremony, ritual, flags, dramatic music, and party groups were all fused into emotional gatherings meant to inspire the Germans with National Socialist ideals. Hitler placed himself at the very center of these rallies.

The Atomization of Society

In his masterful study of the small town of Northeim, William S. Allen showed how the Nazis effectively atomized communities in order to solidify their own rule. Atomization involved the reorganization of all social units. We have already seen how the Nazis coordinated unions, artisans, and business associations either by creating new organizations such as the Labor Front or by taking over existing ones. Organizations controlled by the Nazis were also created for occupational groups. The National Socialist Physicians' League, the National Socialist Professional Dentists' Group, and the National Socialist Teachers' League were examples. Membership was mostly compulsory: If these professionals wanted to keep their jobs, they had to join. The Nazis also coordinated private clubs such as patriotic societies, choral groups, shooting societies, and sports clubs. Such groups had to have a Nazi majority on their executive committee and accept the leadership principle. Some groups simply dissolved instead.

Coordination of public and private organizations left no independent social groups. Nazis infiltrated every one. These organizations ensured that people were not left to themselves. There was no common ground; no voluntary combinations could form. Each individual became isolated; people related not to their fellow individuals but to a Nazi-directed social unit.

In our survey of the Nazis' attempt to establish a total state from 1933 to 1939, we have repeatedly witnessed the mixture of old and new that prevailed in the Nazi system, whether in the organization of the government, the judiciary, the military, or the economic sphere. The new Nazi structure was characterized by a dualism that often created considerable confusion about lines of authority. But Hitler and the Nazi leadership were clear about the underlying goal of establishing a national community that would be unified and mobilized for war so that Hitler could pursue his expansionary aims. In 1937 and 1938, Hitler made changes in the domestic sphere that corresponded to his more radical foreign policy shift to possible military adventures. Until then, the government had been based on cooperation with old-line conservatives such as Schacht in the Ministry of Economics and Neurath in the Ministry of Foreign Affairs. In November 1937, Schacht resigned over differences with Göring's handling of the war economy and was replaced by the ardent Nazi Walther Funk. Early in 1938 the conservative Neurath was replaced by Joachim von Ribbentrop, ill-qualified but totally dedicated to Hitler's grandiose plans. Military leadership was also shifted to give Hitler more control. One is left with the strong impression that the goal of these changes was to make it easier for Hitler to realize his dreams in the foreign-policy and military spheres. Before we examine these goals and their results, though, we need to look in more detail at the man whose ideas and actions have dominated this story.

SUGGESTIONS FOR FURTHER READING

The basic study of Nazi rule is Richard J. Evans, *The Third Reich in Power* (New York, 2005). The Nazi administration of the state is examined in Martin Broszat, *The Hitler State: The Foundations and Development of the Internal Structure of the Third Reich* (New York, 1981); and Ernst Fraenkel, *The Dual State* (New York, 1941). Other studies include Norbert Frei, *National Socialist Rule in Germany: The Führer State 1933–1945,* trans. Simon B. Steyne (Oxford, 1993); Edward N. Peterson, *The Limits of Hitler's Power* (Princeton, N.J., 1970); Peter Hoffmann, *Hitler's Personal Security* (London, 1979); and a collection of essays edited by Jeremy Noakes, *Government, Party and People in Nazi Germany* (Exeter, 1980). Jane Caplan's *Government without Administration. State and Civil Service in Weimar and Nazi Germany* (Oxford, 1988) analyzes the effect of the Nazis on the bureaucracy. The charismatic base of Hitler's power is examined in Ian Kershaw, *Hitler* (London and New York, 1991); and Martin Kitchen, *The Third Reich: Charisma and Community* (New York, 2008).

The most complete work on Nazi economics is Adam Tooze, *The Wages of Destruction: The Making and Breaking of the Nazi Economy* (New York, 2007). A brief perspective on Germany's economic recovery can be found in Richard J. Overy, *The Nazi Economic Recovery, 1932–1938,* 2nd ed. (Cambridge, Mass., 1996), but also see Dan P. Silverman, *Hitler's Economy: Nazi Work Creation Programs, 1933–1936* (Cambridge, Mass., 1998); and Avraham Barkai, *Nazi Economics: Ideology, Theory, and Policy,* trans. Ruth Hadass-Vashitz (New Haven, Conn., 1990). On big business, see Arthur Schweitzer, *Big Business in the Third Reich* (London, 1964). Economic preparations for war are covered in Berenice Carroll, *Design for Total War: Arms and Economics in the Third Reich* (The Hague, 1968); Wilhelm Deist, *The Wehrmacht and German Rearmament* (Toronto, 1981); Edward L. Homze, *Arming the Luftwaffe* (Lincoln, Nebr., 1976); and Richard J. Overy, *War and Economy in the Third Reich* (Oxford, 1994). The relationship between the Nazi state and German industry is examined in Peter Hayes, *Industry and Ideology: IG Farben in the Nazi Era* (Cambridge, Mass., 1987); Diarmuid Jeffreys, *Hell's Cartel: IG Farben and the Making of Hitler's War Machine* (New York, 2008); John Gillingham, *Industry and Politics in the Third Reich* (London, 1985); Neil Gregor, *Daimler-Benz in the Third Reich* (New Haven, Conn., 1998); Alfred C. Mierzejewski, *The Most Valuable Asset of the Reich: A History of the German National Railway,* 2 vols. (Chapel Hill, N.C., 1999–2000); Gerald D. Feldman, *Allianz and the German Insurance Business, 1933–1945* (Cambridge, Mass., 2001); and Harold James, *The Nazi Dictatorship and the Deutsche Bank* (Cambridge, Mass., 2004). Nazi agricultural policies and attitudes are examined in John Farquharson, *The Plough and the Swastika: The NSDAP and Agriculture in Germany, 1928–1945* (London, 1976); Timothy Tilton, *Nazism, Neo-Nazism and the Peasantry* (Bloomington, Ind., 1975); and Gustavo Corni, *Hitler and the Peasants: Agrarian Policy in the Third Reich* (New York, 1990). On the working class in the Nazi regime, see F. L. Carsten, *The German Workers and the Nazis* (Aldershot, Great Britain, 1995). On the KdF see Shelley Baranowski, *Strength Through Joy: Consumerism and Mass Tourism in the Third Reich* (Cambridge, Mass., 2004); and Kristin Semmens, *Seeing Hitler's Germany: Tourism in the Third Reich* (New York, 2005). On the importance of consumer satisfaction and the manufacturing of consent, see Jonathan S. Wiesen, *Creating the Nazi Marketplace: Commerce and Consumption* (New York, 2011); and the essays in Pamela E. Swett, Corey Ross, and Fabrice d'Almeida, eds., *Pleasure and Power in Nazi Germany* (New York, 2011).

On anti-Semitism in Germany prior to the Holocaust, see Hermann Graml, *Antisemitism in the Third Reich,* trans. Tim Kirk (Cambridge, Mass., 1992); Philipe Burrin, *Nazi Anti-Semitism: From Prejudice to the Holocaust,* trans. Janet Llyod (New York, 2005); Saul

Friedländer, *Nazi Germany and the Jews: The Years of Persecution, 1933–1939* (New York, 1997); Karl A. Schleunes, *The Twisted Road to Auschwitz: Nazi Policy Towards German Jews, 1933–1939* (Chicago, 1970); Sarah Gordon, *Hitler, Germans and the "Jewish Question"* (Princeton, N.J., 1984); and the useful collection of essays found in David Bankier, ed., *Probing the Depths of German Antisemitism: German Society and the Persecution of the Jews* (New York, 2000).

On the Jewish experience of Nazi anti-Jewish policy see Marion A. Kaplan, *Between Dignity and Despair: Jewish Life in Nazi Germany* (New York, 1998); and the essays found in Francis R. Nicosia and David Scrase, eds., *Jewish Life in Nazi Germany: Dilemmas and Responses* (New York, 2010). Valuable documentary accounts can be found in Margarete Limberg and Hubert Rübsaat, eds., *Germans No More: Accounts of Jewish Everyday Life, 1933–1938* (New York, 2006); Jürgen Matthäus and Mark Roseman, eds., *Jewish Responses to Persecution, vol. I, 1933–1938* (Lanham, Md., 2010); and Alexandra Garbarini, ed., *Jewish Responses to Persecution, vol. II, 1938–1940* (Lanham, Md., 2011). The German Zionist response to anti-Semitism is discussed in Francis R. Nicosia, *Zionism and Anti-Semitism in Nazi Germany* (New York, 2008); On suicide as a response to Nazi policy, see Christian Goeschel, *Suicide in Nazi Germany* (New York, 2009); and The problem of emigration is discussed in Deborah Dwork and Robert J. van Pelt, *Flight from the Reich: Refugee Jews, 1933–1946* (New York, 2009). On the Aryanization of Jewish businesses see Martin Dean, *Robbing the Jews: The Confiscation of Jewish Property in the Holocaust, 1933–1945* (New York: 2008).

The idea of a genuine social revolution in Nazi Germany is explored in David Schoenbaum, *Hitler's Social Revolution* (London, 1967). The problems of popular opinion in Nazi Germany and popular support for Hitler have been discussed in two books by Ian Kershaw, *Popular Opinion and Political Dissent in the Third Reich*, 2nd ed. (Oxford, 2002) and *The "Hitler Myth." Image and Reality in the Third Reich* (Oxford, 1987). See also Robert Gellately, *Backing Hitler: Consent and Coercion in Nazi Germany* (New York, 2001), which argues that the majority of Germans were well aware of Nazi atrocities and yet continued to the support the regime. Domestic resistance to the Nazi regime is examined in David Clay Large, ed., *Contending with Hitler: Varieties of German Resistance in the Third Reich* (Cambridge, Mass., 1991).

Works on other Nazi leaders include Joachim Fest, *The Faces of the Third Reich: Portraits of the Nazi Leadership* (New York, 1970); Ronald Smelser and Rainer Zitelmann, eds., *The Nazi Elite* (New York, 1993); Louis L. Snyder, *Hitler's Elite* (New York, 1989); Richard J. Overy, *Goering, the Iron Man* (London, 1984); Jochen von Lang, *The Secretary Martin Bormann: The Man Who Manipulated Hitler* (New York, 1979); Randal L. Bytwerk, *Julius Streicher* (New York, 1983); Helmut Heiber, *Goebbels* (New York, 1972); Ralf Reuth, *Goebbels* (New York, 1993); Ronald Smelser, *Robert Ley: Hitler's Labor Front Leader* (New York, 1988); Gitta Sereny, *Albert Speer: His Battle with Truth* (New York, 1995); Joachim Fest, *Speer: The Final Verdict*, trans. Ewald Osers and Alexandra Dring (New York, 2001); and Peter Padfield, *Dönitz, the Last Führer* (New York, 1984).

Basic studies of the SS include Robert Koehl, *The Black Corps: The Structure and Power Struggles of the Nazi SS* (Madison, Wisc., 1983); Heinz Höhne, *The Order of the Death's Head* (New York, 1971); Helmut Krausnick and Martin Broszat, *Anatomy of the SS State* (London, 1970); and Gerald Reitlinger, *The SS: Alibi of a Nation, 1922–1945* (New York, 1957). The leadership of the SS is examined in Herbert F. Ziegler, *Nazi Germany's New Aristocracy, the SS Leadership, 1925–1939* (Princeton, N.J., 1989). On Himmler, see Peter Longerich, *Himmler* (New York, 2012); Bradley Smith, *Heinrich Himmler: A Nazi in the Making, 1900–1926* (Stanford, Calif., 1971); Peter Padfield, *Himmler, Reichsführer-SS* (New York, 1990). On Himmler's research interests and the role of the Ahnenerbe, see Heather Pringle, *The Master Plan: Himmler's Scholars and the Holocaust* (New York, 2006);

and Christopher Hale, *Himmler's Crusade: the True Story of the 1938 Expedition into Tibet* (London, 2003). On other SS leaders, see Robert Gerwarth, *Hitler's Hangman: The Life of Heydrich* (New Haven, 2011); Günther Deschner, *Reinhard Heydrich* (New York, 1981); David Cesarani, *Becoming Eichmann: Rethinking the Life, Crimes, and Trial of a "Desk Murderer"* (Cambridge, Mass., 2006); and Peter B. Black, *Ernst Kaltenbrunner, Ideological Soldier of the Third Reich* (Princeton, N.J., 1984). George Stein, *The Waffen SS: Hitler's Elite Guard at War, 1939–1945* (Ithaca, N.Y., 1966); Bernd Wegner, *The Waffen-SS*, trans. Ronald Webster (Oxford, 1990); and Charles Sydnor, Jr., *Soldiers of Destruction. The SS Death's Head Division, 1933–1945* (Princeton, N.J., 1977) are studies of SS armed forces. On *Das Schwarze Korps*, see William L. Combs, *Voice of the SS: A History of the SS Journal Das Schwarze Korps* (New York, 1986). An important study on the machinery of the Nazi police state can be found in George C. Browder, *Foundations of the Nazi Police State, The Formation of Sipo and SD* (Lexington, Ky., 1990). The role of the Gestapo is examined in Robert Gellately, *The Gestapo and German Society* (Oxford, 1990). On the involvement of ordinary Germans in the terror system, see Eric A. Johnson, *Nazi Terror: The Gestapo, Jews, and Ordinary Germans* (New York, 1999); and Vandana Joshi, *Gender and Power in the Third Reich: Female Denouncers and the Gestapo, 1933–1945* (New York, 2003).

On the legal and judicial systems, see Ingo Müller, *Hitler's Justice: The Courts of the Third Reich*, trans. Deborah Schneider (Cambridge, Mass., 1991); H. W. Koch, *In the Name of the Volk: Political Justice in Hitler's Germany* (New York, 1989); Nikolaus Wachsmann, *Hitler's Prisons: Legal Terror in Nazi Germany* (New Haven, Conn., 2004); and Michael Stolleis, *The Law under the Swastika* (Chicago, 1998). On the relationship of the churches to the Nazi regime, see Doris L. Bergen, *Twisted Cross: The German Christian Movement in the Third Reich* (Chapel Hill, N.C., 1996); Ernst Helmreich, *The German Churches under Hitler* (Detroit, 1979); John S. Conway, *The Nazi Persecution of the Churches, 1933–1945* (New York, 1968); Klaus Scholder, *The Churches and the Third Reich*, 2 vols. (London, 1987–1988); and Susannah Heschel and Robert Ericksen, eds., *Betrayal: German Churches and the Holocaust* (Philadelphia, 1999). On the Catholic church, see Emma Fattorini, *Hitler, Mussolini, and the Vatican: Pope Pius XI and the Speech That Was Never Made*, trans. Carl Ipsen (Malden, Mass., 2011); Guenter Lewy, *The Catholic Church and Nazi Germany* (New York, 1964); Beth Griech-Polelle, *Bishop von Galen: German Catholicism and National Socialism* (New Haven, Conn., 2002); Michael Phayer, *The Catholic Church and the Holocaust, 1930–1965* (Bloomington, Ind., 2000) and *Pius XII, the Holocaust, and the Cold War* (Bloomington, Ind., 2008); Kevin Spicer, *Resisting the Third Reich: The Catholic Clergy in Hitler's Berlin* (Dekalb, 2004) and *Hitler's Priests: Catholic Clergy and National Socialism* (Dekalb, 2008); Carol Rittner and John K. Roth, eds, *Pope Pius XII and the Holocaust* (New York, 2002); and Gerhard Besier, *The Holy See and Hitler's Germany* (New York, 2007). Also of value are James Bentley, *Martin Niemöller* (New York, 1984); and Robert P. Ericksen, *Theologians under Hitler* (New Haven, Conn., 1985). On the Confessing Church, see Shelley Baranowski, *The Confessing Church, Conservative Elites, and the Nazi State* (Lewiston, 1986); and Victoria Barnett, *For the Soul of the People: Protestant Protest Against Hitler* (New York, 1992). On Nazi attitudes toward Christianity, see Richard Steigman-Hall, *The Holy Reich: Nazi Conceptions of Christianity, 1919–1945* (New York, 2003). The importance of new religious movements supporting National Socialism is discussed in Karla Poewe, *New Religions and the Nazis* (New York, 2005). On women and religion during the Third Reich see Michael Phayer, *Protestant and Catholic Women in Nazi Germany* (Detroit, 1990). On the Institute for the Study and Eradication of Jewish Influence on German Religious Life see Susannah Heschel, *Aryan Jesus: Christian Theologians and the Bible in Nazi Germany* (Princeton, 2008).

MySearchLab™ Connections

Study and Review

After the defeat of the Weimar parliamentary system, the Nazi Party was able to form a totalitarian dictatorship. The Nazis pushed Germany toward increasing radicalization by seeking the elimination of individual political will, the omnipresence of the Nazi state in the average German's life, and the creation of the "new total state" in Germany.

Read the Document

1. **Speech to Spaniards (1936) Francisco Franco**
   This document presents a call to the Spanish people by Francisco Franco to revolt against the Spanish republican government in the name of a virulent patriotic nationalism.

Read the Document

2. **Gertrud Scholtz-Klink, "Speech to the Nazi Women's Organization" (Germany), 1935**
   This document illustrates one result of the Nazi assertion that Germany did not have enough new births to sustain the population. In response to this perceived need, the Nazis established the Reichs Maternity Service.

Read the Document

3. **Neville Chamberlain, In Search of Peace**
   This document recounts British Prime Minister's Neville Chamberlain's alarm at Hitler's demands for German territorial expansion. Chamberlain sought the prevention of world war through a policy now known as appeasement.

RESEARCH AND EXPLORE

The Nazi regime had to deal with the economic turmoil, high unemployment, and the war reparations with which Germany had been burdened. Without a consistent economic program, the majority of Germany's economic improvements came from massive public works and armaments programs.

1. How did the Reinhardt Plan affect the national esteem of Germany? Were the economic gains made under the Reinhardt Plan permanent or simply a stopgap measure?

2. In what way did the New Plan predicate the economic crisis of 1935 in Germany? Was Schacht's recommendation to resolve the balance-of-payments crisis the best approach to the problem?

3. In what way did Hermann Göring's Four-Year Plan drive Germany's foreign policies? Can it be argued that the Four-Year Plan was the rationale for going to war?

ADDITIONAL RESOURCES

The Nazi Party Rally

Hitler

The Dictator

One of the frequent debates in history is whether it is individuals, by the sheer strength of their personalities, or impersonal forces, be they economic, social, or political, that determine the course of history. In the last three chapters we have seen the important role of economic, social, and political factors in the rise of Adolf Hitler in Germany. But we have also witnessed the crucial role played by Hitler himself. The unknown soldier of World War I came to power in 1933 in a country in despair because of its political and social problems. Within five years Hitler had given many Germans new hope. They saluted him as their Führer, as a messiah who had lifted them out of the depression and renewed their prosperity. He had built magnificent highways and pledged that every laborer would own an automobile. He had provided a Strength Through Joy movement that became the symbol of a progressive social policy designed to benefit the workers. Moreover, as we will see in subsequent chapters, Hitler reversed the shame of the Treaty of Versailles, rearmed the nation, remilitarized the Rhineland, and created Greater Germany by annexing Austria and parts of Czechoslovakia. If he had died in 1938, as one German historian has suggested, he might then have been viewed as "Adolf Hitler the Great, one of the outstanding figures in German history."[1]

Nazi Germany is inexplicable without Adolf Hitler. What was the source of this man's power to sway millions of people to follow him with passionate commitment, even to death? How could one man mobilize a nation raised on Luther, Bach, and Beethoven to conquer Europe and methodically eliminate its avowed enemies in gas chambers? An examination of Hitler's personality, his messianic complex, his flair for oratory, his ideology, and his attempt to translate that ideology into reality through propaganda and mass spectacles should help answer these questions.

HITLER'S PERSONALITY

Many who examine photos of Hitler today wonder how such a commonplace and in some ways comical-looking figure could have become the object of such mass hysterical adulation. Females especially swooned in his presence. Except for his pale blue eyes,

---

[1]Helmut Heiber, *Adolf Hitler: A Short Biography* (London, 1961), p. 14.

which seemed to many to have a hypnotic effect, Hitler's physical characteristics were in fact quite undistinguished.

Mind

Hitler's mind was considerably more important than his physical appearance in his rise to power. Those who see Hitler only as a diabolical adventurer motivated solely by a lust for personal power misunderstand his mental capabilities. He possessed an unusually retentive memory. He remembered minute details from his early life, the industrial production figures of European countries, and precise statistics on ships and military armaments. One secretary recounted, "I often ask myself how one human brain could preserve so many facts."[2] Hitler used this wealth of detailed knowledge to convince others that he had a superior intellect. However, he was not interested in grappling seriously with profound intellectual problems. Instead, he portrayed himself as a "great simplifier" who could take complex ideas and problems and reduce them to elementary slogans and solutions. He described this ability, which he believed stemmed from a higher intellectual capacity, in an interview with a French correspondent.

> People have said that I owe my success to the fact that I have created a mystique . . . or more simply that I have been lucky. Well, I will tell you what has carried me to where I am. Our political problems appeared complicated. The German people did not comprehend them. In these conditions they preferred to leave it to the professional politicians to get them out of this confused mess. I, on the other hand, simplified the problems. I reduced them to the simplest terms. The masses realized this and they have followed me.[3]

His success in pulling Germany out of the depression and virtually eliminating unemployment reinforced this view of himself as a great simplifier. Hitler's nightly monologues to his postdinner guests demonstrate that he saw himself as an expert on everything. He expressed decided opinions on art, history, philosophy, theology, linguistics, medicine, and science. These views became the basis for policies affecting millions of people.

Character Traits

Specific character traits predominated in Hitler's personality. His rigidity, due to his inability or refusal to change in any significant way, was one feature of his life. He described this quality in *Mein Kampf*, maintaining that he had developed all his basic ideas in Vienna early in his adult life: "In this period there took shape within me a world picture and a philosophy which became the granite foundation of all my acts . . . I have had to alter nothing."[4] While this is certainly an overstatement, as his postwar tutelage under Dietrich Eckart and Alfred Rosenberg dramatically shaped his later thought, it

---

[2]Quoted in Robert G. L. Waite, *The Psychopathic God: Adolf Hitler* (New York, 1977), p. 56.

[3]Norman H. Baynes, ed., *The Speeches of Adolf Hitler, 1922–1939*, vol. 2 (Oxford, 1942), p. 1268.

[4]Excerpts from *Mein Kampf* by Adolf Hitler, translated by Ralph Manheim, p. 22. Copyright © 1943, renewed 1971 by Houghton Mifflin Harcourt Publishing Company. Reprinted by permission of Houghton Mifflin Harcourt Publishing Company. All rights reserved.

does reflect an essential character trait. His boyhood friend and Viennese companion August Kubizek also singled out rigidity as Hitler's most notable trait.

> The most outstanding trait in my friend's character was, as I had experienced myself, the unparalleled consistency in everything that he said and did. There was in his nature something firm, inflexible, immovable, obstinately rigid, which manifested itself in his profound seriousness and was at the bottom of all his other characteristics. Adolf simply could not change his mind or his nature.[5]

This inflexibility was expressed throughout Hitler's life. He continued to make the same grammatical and spelling errors in his adult years that he had made as a youth. His daily routine was maintained intact, down to the smallest detail. His daily walks when he was chancellor followed the same path. He insisted on a fixed seating order for meals, and any deviation resulted in an outburst of anger. Postdinner routine, consisting of motion pictures and multihour Hitler monologues, quickly became monotonous for regular guests.

Hitler's unwillingness to change was the result of his personal insecurity and anxiety. He was tormented by the fear of appearing ridiculous. He would not allow himself to be photographed doing anything insignificant lest it detract from his dignity. He was disgusted with Mussolini for permitting himself to be photographed in a bathing suit, something a "great statesman" would never do. Hitler constantly blamed others for his own failures and could not bear the thought of making a mistake. When a secretary corrected him while he was humming a classical melody, he went into a rage and insisted that it was not he but the composer who was wrong in that passage. Unable to tolerate having others around him who might be considered superior, he often surrounded himself with people of inferior intelligence. One exception was Albert Speer, whose architectural talents were congenial to Hitler's own image of himself as a great architect. Hitler also liked to have men with physical or emotional deficiencies in his presence so that he could ridicule them.

Hitler did not permit others to know his feelings and desires and carefully guarded his private life. To maintain his privacy, Hitler disciplined his life in a highly unnatural way. Even his outbursts of rage, giving the impression of a man governed by his emotions, were often calculated to produce certain effects. Such a guarded life left no opening for any real relationships. People did not really interest Hitler. He was incapable of normal conversation based on a genuine exchange of ideas. Conversations were simply monologues. Even with foreign guests, such as Mussolini, Hitler would talk uninterrupted for one and a half hours after dinner. When forced to listen to others he paid little attention and withdrew into his own world. Magda Goebbels, the wife of the propaganda minister and a fervent admirer of the Führer, remarked that "in a sense, Hitler is not human— unreachable and untouchable."[6]

Hitler's impersonality is unmistakable even in his relationship with his long-time companion and mistress, Eva Braun. He met her in the late 1920s when she was an assistant in the studio of Hitler's photographer, Heinrich Hoffmann. Eva became Hitler's mistress after the suicide of his niece Geli Raubal in 1931. The latter is spoken of as the only other

---

[5]August Kubizek, *The Young Hitler I Knew,* translated by Geoffrey Brooks (St. Paul, Minn., 2006), p. 49.

[6]Quoted in Joachim Fest, *Hitler,* translated by Richard and Clara Winston (New York, 1974), p. 523.

woman besides his mother whom Hitler might have loved. Eva was a rather attractive girl who cared little about politics and ideas. Her interests were fashion clothes, movies, parties, and gossip. Hitler could be intensely jealous of her and yet also cruel. He once remarked to Albert Speer in Eva's presence, "A highly intelligent man should take a primitive and stupid woman. Imagine if on top of everything else I had a woman who interfered with my work! In my leisure time I want to have peace."[7] Hitler's tendency to take Eva for granted led to her two suicide attempts, one in 1932 and the other in 1935. After the latter, Eva was permanently installed in the Berghof, Hitler's mountain retreat in the southern Bavarian Alps. Even then, she was not allowed to appear publicly when Hitler had important guests. Gradually she was brought into the innermost circle of persons in the Berghof who shared Hitler's teatime and evening pleasures. Eva's color films of life at the Berghof give some of the best glimpses of Hitler's private life. They clearly show how he was always on guard, protecting his image even in this supposedly relaxed atmosphere.

Contemporaries identified Hitler's lack of humor as another personality trait. His friend August Kubizek observed this quality in Hitler in his teenage years.

> I have often been asked . . . whether Adolf, when I knew him, had any sense of humor . . . Certainly one's impression of Hitler, especially after a short and superficial acquaintance, was that of a deeply serious man. This enormous seriousness seemed to overshadow everything else. It was the same when he was young. He approached the problems with which he was concerned with a deadly earnestness which ill suited his sixteen or seventeen years.[8]

Hitler maintained this humorlessness throughout his life. Although he was capable of laughing, he seldom did so in public and certainly never at himself.

In his work *Three Faces of Fascism,* the German historian Ernst Nolte wrote at length about Hitler's infantilism, which he considered "the dominant trait in Hitler's personality."[9] He defined this infantilism as a persistence in remaining in the child's world of being aware of no one or nothing except himself and his mental images. As he grew older, Hitler refused to enter the adult world of compromise and moderation. His fits of rage, when not calculated, were those of the spoiled boy who wants his own way. His compulsion to fulfill his dreams, regardless of their impracticability, was apparent in the purchase of his dream car, a Mercedes, for an extraordinary 26,000 marks after his release from Landsberg prison in late 1924.

Hitler's obsession with size was another aspect of his infantilism. Hitler had a mania for record sizes, speed, and numbers. Already at sixteen he dreamed of lengthening the 360-foot-long frieze on the museum in Linz by another 360 feet so that the city would have "the biggest relief frieze on the Continent."[10] He boasted of how his Mercedes was able to pass every car on the highway. He planned and had built the largest lowerable window in the world at his mountain retreat in Obersalzberg. The Berghof was also home to the largest marble tabletop made of one piece (eighteen feet long). His plans for the architectural reconstruction of Germany revolved around the largest domes, the most grandiose triumphal arches, the biggest buildings, and stadiums.

[7]Quoted in Albert Speer, *Inside the Third Reich,* translated by Richard and Clara Winston (New York, 1970), p. 92.

[8]Kubizek, *The Young Hitler I Knew,* p. 42.

[9]Ernst Nolte, *Three Faces of Fascism* (New York, 1966), p. 289.

[10]Kubizek, *The Young Hitler I Knew,* p. 108.

Further examination of Hitler's personality reveals a man governed by dualities. He saw everything in terms of extreme opposites. People were either his followers or his enemies. War for Germany meant either *Weltmacht*—world power—or *Niedergang*—defeat. French ambassador to Germany André François-Poncet, who had numerous opportunities to observe Hitler at close range, was especially bewildered by these dualities.

> The same man, good-natured in appearance and sensitive to the beauties of nature, who across a tea table expressed reasonable opinions on European politics, was capable of the wildest frenzies, the most savage exaltation, and the most delirious ambition. There were days when, bending over a map of the world, he upset nations and continents, geography and history, like some demiurge in his madness. At other times he dreamed of being the hero of an eternal peace within whose framework he would raise the loftiest of monuments.[11]

Other dualities inherent in Hitler were honesty and duplicity, kindness and viciousness, and charm and rage. He occasionally portrayed himself as a man of complete honesty. Hence his reaction when told that the British did not believe his promise not to invade Poland: "Idiots! Have I ever in my entire life ever told a lie?"[12] But to one of his generals he remarked: "You will never learn what I am thinking. And those who boast most loudly that they know my thought, to such people I lie even more."[13] Hitler was capable of displaying kindness, especially toward children and animals. During his first few months as chancellor, Hitler had the Reichstag enact laws for the protection of animals, and in 1936 he decreed regulations for the humane killing of lobsters and crabs.

Any assessment of Hitler's personality traits must also focus on his intuition, opportunism, and capacity for hatred. Hitler believed that he possessed a special sense of right timing that was a product of his intuitive abilities. According to Hitler, his intuitive abilities guaranteed him invincibility and absolute success. After his triumphant reoccupation of the Rhineland, Hitler felt that his power of intuition had been vindicated against the advice of experts who had encouraged him not to act. He exclaimed in a speech on March 15, 1936, "I go with the assurance of a sleepwalker on the way which Providence dictates."[14] Hitler saw a similar vindication of his intuitive powers when he waited patiently for the chancellorship to be offered to him while others in the party were urging him to compromise and take a lesser position.

Although Hitler was an ideologist who cared deeply about translating ideas into reality, he was also a shrewd opportunist who knew how to take advantage of changing conditions. He had no scruples about using people for his own profit and was uninhibited about fostering his own power. His utter ruthlessness placed people who had some sensitivity at a distinct disadvantage. This is one reason his political opponents in Germany, such as Alfred Hugenberg and Franz von Papen, were so easily outmaneuvered by Hitler. Neville Chamberlain, prime minister of Great Britain, whose political world assumed that leaders observed common decencies, was shattered by his experiences with Hitler, unable to believe that a leader of a major state would lie and deceive him as Hitler had. But Hitler understood Chamberlain's world and perceived it as a weakness to be manipulated.

[11]André François-Poncet, *The Fateful Years: Memoirs of a French Ambassador in Berlin, 1931–38*, translated by Jacques LeClercq (New York, 1949), p. 286.

[12]Quoted in Waite, *The Psychopathic God*, p. 97.

[13]Ibid., p. xi.

[14]Baynes, ed., *The Speeches of Adolf Hitler*, vol. 2, p. 1307.

German politicians and European leaders were also initially incapable of perceiving the depth of Hitler's hatred. The list of people he despised at one time or another was endless: Jews above all, Marxists, Czechs, Poles, French, intellectuals, and the middle class. Hitler's hatred was often coupled with revenge and the desire to destroy those he loathed. To the very end of his life, as witnessed in his last political testament, written in the Bunker shortly before his death, Hitler continued to spew forth abominations upon his world.

HITLER AS MESSIANIC LEADER

Adolf Hitler came to regard himself as a man singled out by Providence for a special mission, and he clothed himself in the mantle of a messiah. He claimed that his awareness of his special position dated from 1919, when he lay temporarily blinded in a military hospital. He contended that he had received a "divine mandate" to "liberate the German people and make Germany great."[15] Subsequent speeches reinforced this sense of mission. At his trial in 1924 after the abortive Beer Hall Putsch, Hitler said: "The man who is born to be a dictator is not compelled, he wills it. He is not driven forward, but drives himself."[16] In the early days of his movement Hitler likened himself to Jesus: "Just like Christ, I have a duty to my own people."[17] After his accession to the chancellorship in 1933, Hitler's sense of mission grew with every increase in his power. At Würzburg in 1937, he exclaimed to his audience:

> I see clearly what man can do and where his limitations lie, but I am convinced that men who are created by God should live in accordance with the will of the Almighty. However weak the individual may be in the last resort in his whole being and action when compared with the omnipotence and will of Providence, yet at the moment when he acts as this Providence would have him act he becomes immeasurably strong. Then there streams down upon him that force which has marked all greatness in the world's history. And when I look back only on the five years which lie behind us then I feel that I am justified in saying: That has not been the achievement of men alone! If Providence had not guided us I could often never have found these dizzy paths. And that should be recognized especially by our critics! Thus it is that we National Socialists, too, have in the depths of our hearts our faith. We cannot do otherwise: no man can fashion world-history or the history of peoples unless upon his purpose and his powers there rests the blessing of this Providence.[18]

The failure of the attempts on his life reinforced Hitler's conviction of his "divine mission." After the abortive attempt of July 20, 1944, to kill him with a bomb, Hitler remarked to an aide: "Now the almighty has stayed their [the assassins'] hands once more. Don't you agree I should consider it as a nod of Fate that it intends to preserve me for my assigned task?" And to his valet: "That is new proof that I have been selected from among other men by Providence to lead greater Germany to victory."[19]

---

[15]Rudolph Binion, *Hitler Among the Germans* (New York, 1976), p. 136.

[16]Quoted in Alan Bullock, *Hitler, A Study in Tyranny* (New York, 1962), p. 117.

[17]Quoted in Waite, *The Psychopathic God*, p. 27.

[18]Baynes, ed., *The Speeches of Adolf Hitler*, vol. 1, p. 411. By permission of the Royal Institute of International Affairs.

[19]Quoted in Waite, *The Psychopathic God*, p. 28.

Further, Hitler saw National Socialism not so much as a political movement but rather as a religious one. The use of sacred oaths of allegiance, the Blood Flag ceremony as a religious ritual, the Nazi holy days as substitutes for traditional religious holidays, and the call for miracles of faith were all manifestations of Nazism's quasi-religious character. It was effective. Kurt Lüdecke, an early supporter of Hitler, recalled that after hearing him speak for the first time, "I experienced something like a secular conversion. The sincerity of his conviction redoubled my loyalty. In the face of every difficulty this man would lead us forward, because in his soul he believed that circumstance had laid upon his shoulders the burden of Germany's salvation." When Lüdecke later told Hitler of his experience, the Führer replied, "Yes, National Socialism is a form of conversion, a new faith, but we don't need to raise that issue—it will come of itself."[20]

Many Germans shared Hitler's vision of himself as their messiah. The American journalist William Shirer, an observer of Hitler's triumphant entry into Nuremberg for a party rally, grasped this aspect of Nazism in Germany.

> About ten o'clock tonight I got caught in a mob of ten thousand hysterics who jammed the moat in front of Hitler's hotel, shouting: "We want our Führer." I was a little shocked at the faces, especially those of the women when Hitler finally appeared on the balcony for a moment. They reminded me of the crazed expressions I saw once in the back country of Louisiana on the faces of some Holy Rollers who were about to hit the trail. They looked up at him as if he were a Messiah, their faces transformed into something positively inhuman. If he had remained in sight for more than a few moments, I think many of the women would have swooned from excitement.[21]

Nazi leaders encouraged this messianic view of Hitler in the German schools. Children were required after 1934 to write out compositions comparing Hitler to Jesus. The Hitler *Jungvolk,* one of the youth organizations for boys, used the following song:

> Adolf Hitler is our Saviour, our hero
> He is the noblest being in the whole wide world.
> For Hitler we live,
> For Hitler we die.
> Our Hitler is our Lord
> Who rules a brave new world.[22]

Such adoration inspired a cult of Hitler as the new messiah of a reborn Germany.

HITLER THE ORATOR

Hitler's ability as an orator was a major reason for his success. His oratorical triumphs emerged out of two contrasting elements—his natural capacity to arouse deep and passionate emotions in his listeners and his careful preparation of his speeches and their setting. Hitler did possess an unusual ability to sense the mood of his audience. The importance of

---

[20]Kurt Lüdecke, *I Knew Hitler* (New York, 1937), pp. 128, 137.
[21]William Shirer, *Berlin Diary* (New York, 1941), pp. 17–18.
[22]Gregor Ziemer, *Education for Death: The Making of the Nazi* (Oxford, 1941), p. 120.

this sensitivity to assembled crowds was stressed in *Mein Kampf*: "He [the orator] will always let himself be borne along by the great masses in such a way that instinctively the very words come to his lips that he needs to speak to the hearts of his audience."[23] Although his speeches were carefully structured and he used notes in delivering them, he was not restricted by these preparations. It took him ten to fifteen minutes "to inhale the feelings of his audience," as he stated it. Having done this, he expressed to his listeners their deepest dreams and desires. As one-time associate Ernst "Putzi" Hanfstaengl remarked: "Where other national orators gave the painful impression of talking down to their audience, he had the priceless gift of expressing exactly their own thoughts."[24] The content of Hitler's speeches and his own messianic pretensions also played on the emotions and desires of his audience. As Hanfstaengl explained: "Far beyond his electrifying rhetoric, this man seemed to possess the uncanny gift of coupling the Gnostic yearning of the era for a strong leader-figure with his own missionary claim and to suggest in this merging that every conceivable hope and expectation was capable of fulfillment—an astonishing spectacle of suggestive influence of the mass psyche."[25]

It was not unusual for people to describe their reactions to Hitler's speeches in sexual and religious overtones. One writer spoke of Hitler's speeches as "sex murders"; and others used the vocabulary of sexual experience, including such words as *climax, discharge,* and *mass orgasm,* to describe the interaction of Hitler and the crowds during his speeches. Some used religious terminology. Consider this description by businessman Kurt Lüdecke.

> Presently my critical faculty was swept away . . . I do not know how to describe the emotions that swept over me as I heard this man. His words were like a scourge. When he spoke of the disgrace of Germany, I felt ready to spring on any enemy. His appeal to German manhood was like a call to arms, the gospel he preached a sacred truth. He seemed another Luther. I forgot everything but the man; then, glancing around, I saw that his magnetism was holding these thousands as one. Of course, I was ripe for this experience. I was a man of thirty-one, weary of disgust and disillusionment, a wanderer seeking a cause; a patriot without a channel for his patriotism, a yearner after the heroic without a hero. The intense will of the man, the passion of his sincerity seemed to flow from him into me. I experienced an exaltation that could be likened only to religious conversion. I felt sure that no one who had heard Hitler that afternoon could doubt that he was a man of destiny, the vitalizing force in the future of Germany.[26]

Generating such an emotional response from his audience required an intensity of effort that left Hitler drenched in sweat and totally drained at the end of a speech. He sometimes lost five pounds in the process. His associates always described him as unable to function in any normal fashion after speaking.

Hitler has often been compared to a medium or a shaman in his uncanny abilities with an audience, but there was also deliberation behind most aspects of his public speeches. The man who created emotional reactions by gesticulating wildly as if out of

[23]Excerpts from *Mein Kampf* by Adolf Hitler, translated by Ralph Manheim, p. 470. Copyright © 1943, renewed 1971 by Houghton Mifflin Harcourt Publishing Company. Reprinted by permission of Houghton Mifflin Harcourt Publishing Company. All rights reserved.

[24]Ernst Hanfstaengl, *Hitler: The Memoir of a Nazi Insider Who Turned Against the Führer* (New York, 2011), pp. 67–68.

[25]Quoted in Ian Kershaw, *Hitler 1889–1936: Hubris* (New York, 1998), p. 187.

[26]Kurt Lüdecke, *I Knew Hitler* (New York, 1937), pp. 13–14.

control was the same man who worked constantly to be in control—a feat he accomplished, first of all, by improving his techniques of public speaking. Supposedly, Hitler studied the example of a Munich entertainer for gaining the attention of rowdy beer-cellar crowds. One of Hitler's early biographers recounts that Hitler often practiced gesturing in front of a mirror in his Munich room on the Thierschstrasse. He spent hours in a studio being photographed by the party photographer, Heinrich Hoffmann, in a variety of posed gestures. After examining the photos, he used the gestures that looked attractive to him in his speaking engagements.

To augment his effectiveness as a speaker, Hitler paid equal attention to the physical environment in which his speeches were given. Early in his career, he checked the acoustics of the major beer halls in Munich so that he could adjust the loudness of his voice to each one. He also examined the ventilation and physical arrangement of the rooms. As the party grew and Hitler's oratory became more important he continued to busy himself with the trappings of his gatherings. The theatrical element became paramount. Official party guidelines were established for every meeting: Halls should always be too small rather than too large to create the effect of being overwhelmed by supporters; at least one-third of the audience should be party followers; nighttime was better than daytime because the emotional effect on the listeners would be greater in the evening; people were to be kept waiting for Hitler in order to increase the air of expectation and the joy when he arrived; and Hitler would enter triumphantly without introductory speeches so that all interest would be focused on the leader. All these effects were calculated to heighten Hitler's emotional impact on the audience.

The content of Hitler's speeches remained remarkably consistent. Before coming to power, Hitler did present his favorite ideological concerns, especially anti-Semitism and *Lebensraum*, but he emphasized general subjects as well. He condemned the present and pointed to all the signs of Germany's disintegration and ruin—the danger of Marxism, the weaknesses of the government, the humiliation of Germany in the dictated peace of Versailles, corruption in everyday affairs, the large number of unemployed, wretched, and hungry (Germany is starving on democracy), and the decadence of the West from which the Weimar Republic stemmed. In a speech in 1932, Hitler said:

> Starting with the day of the Revolution up to the epoch of subjugation and enslavement, up to the time of treaties and emergency decrees, we see failure upon failure, collapse upon collapse, misery upon misery. Timidity, lethargy and hopelessness are everywhere the milestones of these disasters . . . The peasantry today is ground down, industry is collapsing, millions have lost their saved pennies, millions of others are unemployed. Everything that formerly stood firm has changed, everything that formerly seemed great has been overthrown. Only one thing has remained preserved for us: the men and the parties who are responsible for the misfortunes. They are still here to this day.[27]

Hitler's speeches contained negative themes: "There is only defiance and hate, hate and again hate." "No, we forgive nothing; we demand revenge."[28] But there was a very positive element in Hitler's speeches as well: His visionary images for the future. Germany could be great again if it were unified with a strong government led by a party that would have a free hand in domestic and foreign policy. Nazism was portrayed as the movement

---

[27]Quoted in Fest, *Hitler*, p. 330.
[28]Ibid., p. 151.

that could unify the nation, create racial and national rebirth, and lead Germany back to greatness. *Fatherland, honor, greatness,* and *power* were key words in Hitler's appeal.

HITLER AS AN IDEOLOGIST

Many biographers portray Adolf Hitler as an opportunist whose primary goal was the acquisition of power for himself. There are some elements of truth in this depiction. As we have seen, Hitler cleverly manipulated the weaknesses of others for his own ends. He was also obsessed with obtaining power. But his opportunism and quest for power were not ends in themselves. Hitler possessed a set of ideas that were internally consistent and provided a blueprint for his actions. The acquisition of power was the prerequisite for the implementation of this master plan, for Hitler was a fantast who believed that his creative fantasies could be converted into external realities.

Hitler's ideological blueprint was substantially complete when he wrote *Mein Kampf* in the mid-1920s. Some historians maintain that the principal components of this ideology were already decided during his years in Vienna (1909–1913), while others argue the years immediately following the cessation of World War I were key. Regardless of when it first took root, Hitler's ideology was complete by 1925, and he never deviated from it thereafter. Once he gained power, it became the guiding thread of both his domestic and his foreign policy.

Three theses constituted the core of Hitler's ideology: the idea of struggle, racial conflict as the key to historical development, and the role of leadership. His writing and speeches contain numerous references to these ideas. At Chemnitz on April 2, 1928, he summarized the essence of his thought:

> The first fundamental of any rational Weltanschauung is the fact that on earth and in the universe force alone is decisive. Whatever goal man has reached is due to his originality plus his brutality. Whatever man possesses today in the field of culture is the culture of the Aryan race. The Aryan has stamped his character on the whole world. The basis for all development is the creative urge of the individual, not the vote of majorities. The genius of the individual is decisive, not the spirit of the masses. All life is bound up in three theses: struggle is the father of all things, virtue lies in blood, leadership is primary and decisive.[29]

The Idea of Struggle

"Struggle is the father of all things." Hitler perceived struggle not only as the essence of all nature, thus postulating a crude Darwinism, but also as the central principle for both individuals and nations, thus exalting a crass Social Darwinism. In a 1928 speech at Kulmbach, he stated:

> The idea of struggle is as old as life itself, for life is only preserved because other living things perish through struggle . . . In this struggle, the stronger, the more able win, while the less able, the weak lose. Struggle is the father of all things . . . As it is with the individual so it is in the destiny of nations. Only by struggle are the strong able to raise themselves above the weak. And every people that loses out in this eternally shifting struggle has, according to the laws of nature, received its just dessert. A Weltanschauung that denies the idea of struggle is contrary to nature and will lead a people that is guided by it to destruction.[30]

[29]Gordon W. Prange, ed., *Hitler's Words* (Washington, D.C., 1944), p. 8.
[30]Ibid., p. 8.

"Only force rules," as Hitler liked to say, and the only correct way to deal with any problem was to use force. In a 1937 discussion with the English diplomat Lord Halifax on India, Hitler explained how he would solve the problem of Gandhi:

> Shoot Gandhi and if that does not suffice to reduce them to submission, shoot a dozen leading members of Congress; and if that does not suffice, shoot 200 and so on until order is established. You will see how quickly they will collapse as soon as you make it clear that you mean business.[31]

The rightness of any policy was predicated on force: "Always before God and the world, the stronger has the right to carry through what he wills."[32]

Hitler's emphasis on struggle influenced both his domestic and his foreign policy. Hitler infused German society with military terminology and values. The "battle for culture," "the battle for population," "the battle for the cradle" became regular slogans of social life after 1933. Likewise, battle and conflict meant that the logical outcome of Hitler's foreign policy would be war. "The battlefield is the final test of the foreign policy of a people . . ."[33] World War II was clearly Hitler's war: "Basically I did not organize the armed forces in order not to strike. The decision to strike was always in me."[34]

Racial Conflict: Aryan Versus Jew

Whereas Karl Marx had found the heart of human development to be in class struggle, Hitler found it in race. "The racial question gives the key not only to world history, but to all human culture."[35] Race was not simply a political issue to be used to curry the favor of the masses, but the "granite foundation" of Hitler's ideology.

Hitler's racial ideology stemmed from what he called "the basic principle of the blood." This meant that the blood of every person and every race contained the soul of a person and likewise the soul of his or her race, the *Volk*. Hitler believed that the Aryan race, to which all "true" Germans belonged, was the race whose blood (soul) was of the highest degree. The Almighty Himself had, in fact, created the Aryans as the most perfect people, both physically and spiritually.

Since the blood of the Aryans contained specific spiritual energies—the "cultural energies" or "racial primal elements," Hitler often called them—the Aryans supplied the culture that created the beauty and dignity of higher humanity. In Hitler's words:

> All the human culture, all the results of art, science, and technology that we see before us today, are almost exclusively the creative product of the Aryan. This very fact admits of the not unfounded inference that he alone was the founder of all higher humanity, therefore representing the prototype of all that we understand by the word "man." He is the Prometheus of mankind from whose bright forehead the divine spark of genius has sprung at all times . . . Exclude him and perhaps after a few thousand years darkness will again descend on the earth, human culture will pass, and the world turn to a desert . . . Human culture and civilization on this continent are inseparably bound up with the presence of the Aryan.[36]

[31]Quoted in Ivone Kirkpatrick, *The Inner Circle* (London, 1959), p. 97.

[32]Quoted in Bullock, *Hitler*, p. 399.

[33]Quoted in Waite, *The Psychopathic God*, p. 77.

[34]*Documents on German Foreign Policy*, Series D, vol. 8, p. 441.

[35]Excerpts from *Mein Kampf* by Adolf Hitler, translated by Ralph Manheim, p. 339. Copyright © 1943, renewed 1971 by Houghton Mifflin Harcourt Publishing Company. Reprinted by permission of Houghton Mifflin Harcourt Publishing Company. All rights reserved.

[36]Ibid., pp. 290, 383.

Indeed, this dying off of the Aryans, this racial apocalypse, was what Adolf Hitler perceived to be happening around him. This decline occurred because of the original sin of blood poisoning—the contamination of the Aryan blood by an inferior race.

> The Aryan gave up the purity of his blood and, therefore, lost his sojourn in paradise which he had made for himself. He became submerged in the racial mixture, and gradually, more and more, lost his cultural capacity, until at last, not only mentally but also physically, he began to resemble the subjected aborigines more than his own ancestors . . . Thus cultures and empires collapsed to make place for new formations. Blood mixture and the resultant drop in the racial level is the sole cause of the dying out of all cultures; for men do not perish as a result of lost wars, but by the loss of that force of resistance which is contained only in pure blood. All who are not of good race in this world are chaff.[37]

The "serpent" that brought about the contamination of pure Aryan blood was, of course, the Jew. "The mightiest counterpart to the Aryan is represented by the Jew."[38] Anti-Semitism is the cement that binds all of Hitler's ideology. From Hitler's perspective the Jewish race was not created by God as one of the original root races of humankind and thus was ungodly, inhuman, and the embodiment of all that was evil. Hence, the Jew "stops at nothing and in his vileness he becomes so gigantic that no one need be surprised if among our people the personification of the devil as the symbol for all evil assumes the living shape of the Jew."[39] The goal of the Jews was the domination of the world, a task that could be achieved by the poisoning of Aryan blood. Hitler contended that the Jews used a variety of methods to accomplish this task. The most blatant was miscegenation, accomplished by Jewish "rape" of Aryan girls and Jewish importation of blacks into Germany. Thus did the Jew destroy Aryan purity and carry out "disarmament of the spiritually leading class of his racial adversaries."

To Hitler, the Jewish race was also attempting to poison the Aryan blood (soul) through cultural and political means. The Jew was the fundamental cause of the decadence that Hitler saw in modern art and literature. Jewish modern art was a deliberate attempt to infect the unconsciousness of the Aryan people. "Culturally [the Jew] contaminates art, literature, the theater, makes a mockery of natural feeling, overthrows all concepts of beauty and sublimity, of the noble and the good, and instead drags men down into the sphere of his own base nature."[40]

But it is in the area of politics that Hitler perceived the greatest Jewish threat to the Aryan race. Jewish infiltration of the bourgeoisie had made the latter puppets for the execution of the Jewish plan for world domination. Thus, the bourgeois economic institution of capitalism and the political institutions of liberalism, democracy, parliamentarianism, freedom of the press, and internationalism were all Jewish stepping-stones to domination; all were instruments creating disorder in the world. By far the most powerful political tool of the Jewish race, however, was Marxism. Marxism was a rival *Weltanschauung*, a "view of life" directly hostile to everything Hitler believed. Marxists maintained that the state had in itself the "creative culture-forming force," meaning that the state created a nation's culture out of economic necessities. In Hitler's view, the state could not create a nation's

[37]Ibid., p. 296.
[38]Ibid., p. 300.
[39]Ibid., p. 324.
[40]Ibid., p. 326.

culture. Since the nation was the manifestation of a race's (*Volk*'s) soul, the state could only be the instrument by which a race expresses its cultural energies.

Hitler also deplored Marxism for its principle of racial equality and denounced its egalitarianism, which he felt destroyed the natural principle of inequality and the consequent domination of some individuals (an elite) over others. Hitler saw the Marxist threat to Aryan culture not as coincidental but as a deliberate plan to destroy culture, bring civilization into chaos, and enable the Jews to achieve their goal of world domination. To Hitler, "the Jew Karl Marx" knew precisely which policies would lead to world chaos.

> Actually Karl Marx was only the one among millions who, with the sure eye of the prophet, recognized in the morass of a slowly decomposing world the most essential poisons, extracted them, and, like a wizard, prepared them into a concentrated solution for the swifter annihilation of the independent existence of free nations on this earth. And all this in service of his race.[41]

In conjunction with his racial ideology and anti-Semitism, Hitler often spoke of a "historic mission" or "higher mission" of the Aryan race and its elite core, the German people. The Aryans, according to Hitler, were once rulers of the earth, the highest race of humankind, the only one capable of producing a higher civilization. Through blood poisoning the Aryans had lost their ruling position. But as their "higher mission" the German people were destined to regain this position for the Aryan race. For them to do so, Germany had to restructure its political and social foundations and create a state whose function was to promote the Aryan culture-creating "spiritual elements" that existed in the blood of the German race. If this were done, racially and thus spiritually pure human beings could be produced, ensuring Aryan world domination.

> Anyone who speaks of a mission of the German people on earth must know that it can exist only in the formation of a state which sees its highest task in the preservation and promotion of the most noble elements of our nationality, indeed of all mankind, which still remain intact. Thus, for the first time the state achieves a lofty inner goal . . . the task of preserving and advancing the highest humanity, given to this earth by the benevolence of the Almighty, seems a truly high mission . . . The German Reich as a state must embrace all Germans and has the task, not only of assembling and preserving the most valuable stocks of basic racial elements in this people, but slowly and surely of raising them to a dominant position.[42]

But if this Aryan destiny were to be fulfilled, Hitler believed, one major obstacle would have to be dealt with—the Jews. The Jews were the poisoners of the blood of the Aryan race, and thus their elimination became Hitler's special "higher" mission. The Nazi Party was conceived by Hitler as a "spiritual movement"—not just a political movement—whose purpose would be to achieve power in order to create a state that would foster the historic destiny of the Aryan race. The first task of this Aryan state would be to eliminate the Jewish threat. This is why Hitler's political career both began and ended with a warning against the Jewish threat. In a letter dated September 16, 1919, called "the first piece of writing of Hitler's political career," Hitler was quite clear about his motives: "A rational anti-Semitism . . . must lead to the systematic legal fight . . . Its ultimate goal must unalterably be the elimination

[41]Ibid., p. 382.
[42]Ibid., pp. 397–398.

of the Jews altogether."[43] At the very end of his career, when he wrote his political testament to the German people, his preoccupation with the Jewish threat was still uppermost in his mind: "Above all I charge the leaders of the nation and those under them to scrupulous observance of the laws of race and to merciless opposition to the universal poisoner of all peoples, international Jewry."[44] It is obvious that the final solution of the Jewish question, manifested in the Holocaust, was a logical consequence of Hitler's racial ideology and obsessive anti-Semitism.

The Role of Leadership

The third essential element of Hitler's ideology is the role of leadership. "Leadership," Hitler said, "is primary and decisive." The *Führerprinzip*, or leadership principle, was directly related to Hitler's concept of the *völkisch* state. To win the racial struggle, Germany must be molded into a *völkisch* community. This community took priority over any individual concern. Hitler once declared:

> National Socialism takes as the starting point of its view and its decisions neither the individual nor humanity. It puts consciously into the central point of its whole thinking the *Volk*. This *Volk* is for it a blood-conditioned entity in which it sees the God-willed building-stone of human society. The individual is transitory, the *Volk* is permanent. If the liberal Weltanschauung in its deification of the single individual must lead to the destruction of the *Volk*, National Socialism, on the other hand, desires to safeguard the *Volk*, if necessary even at the expense of the individual. It is essential that the individual should slowly come to realize that his own ego is unimportant when compared with the existence of the whole people . . . above all he must realize that the freedom of the mind and will of a nation are to be valued more highly than the individual's freedom of mind and will.[45]

Citizenship in this *völkisch* community would be based upon blood. The result would be a *Volksstaat* (racial state) whose responsibility would be the preservation and advancement of the Aryan race.

The goals of this racial state could never be realized through a system of majority rule in which the masses count for more than the individual. For just as Hitler believed in the inequality of races, he also took for granted the inequality of individuals. He made this clear in a speech to the Düsseldorf Industry Club in 1932.

> There are indeed in especial two other closely related factors which we can time and again trace in periods of national decline: the one is that for the conception of the value of personality there is substituted a leveling idea of the supremacy of mere numbers—democracy—and the other is the negation of the value of a people, the denial of any difference in the inborn capacity, the achievement of individual peoples. Thus both factors condition one another or at least influence each other in the course of their development. Internationalism and democracy are inseparable conceptions.[46]

[43]Eberhard Jäckel, *Hitler's Weltanschauung*, translated by Herbert Arnold (Middletown, Conn., 1972), p. 48.

[44]Quoted in *Nazi Conspiracy and Aggression*, vol. 6 (Washington, D.C., 1946), p. 263.

[45]Baynes, ed., *The Speeches of Adolf Hitler*, vol. 1, pp. 871–872. By permission of the Royal Institute of International Affairs.

[46]Ibid., pp. 871–872.

Ein Volk, ein Reich, ein Führer

Hitler and the Power of Community. The Nazis claimed to have replaced the social fragmentation and class antagonism of the Weimar period with a unified community of racial equals, the *Volksgemeinschaft* (National or People's Community). Hitler is presented here as the embodiment of that unity, represented in the phrase "One People, One Empire, One Leader." (Pictorial Press Ltd/Alamy Limited)

Thus, Hitler's principle of evaluation: "I must evaluate people differently on the basis of the race they belong to, and the same applies to the individual men within a national community." Even in the Aryan racial community, then, superior individuals would emerge from the struggles of daily life. "This sifting according to capacity and ability cannot be undertaken mechanically; it is a task which the struggle of daily life unceasingly performs."[47] The result would be the emergence of the leaders of the racial state—the Nazi elite.

> A philosophy of life which endeavors to reject the domestic mass idea and give this earth to the best people—that is, the highest humanity—must logically obey the same aristocratic principles within this people and make sure that the leadership and the highest influence in this people fall to the best minds. Thus, it builds, not upon the idea of the majority, but upon the idea of personality.[48]

To Hitler, then, the best people would lead the *Volksstaat*, and at the very top would stand the Führer, the supreme leader who seeks to embody and actualize the will of the *Volk*. In accepting the responsibility of power, this leader alone would possess the "right to command." After coming to power, Hitler lost no time in putting his leadership principle into action, establishing the *Volksstaat* with himself as absolute ruler. In a speech to the Hitler Youth on September 2, 1933, Hitler expounded on the continuity of his vision: "We have to learn our lesson: one will must dominate us, we must form a single unity; one discipline must weld us together; one obedience, one subordination must fill us all, for above us stands the nation."[49] The German youth responded with the chant of *"Ein Volk, ein Reich, ein Führer"*—one people, one empire, one leader.

PROPAGANDA AND MASS MEETINGS

Adolf Hitler was a man obsessed by a set of ideas that he wished to translate into reality. This ideal necessitated molding the German people into a unit that would follow him under any circumstances. Propaganda and mass rallies were the instruments by which the Germans could be prepared for the tremendous tasks that lay before them.

Hitler had taken an acute interest in the use of propaganda when he first began to study political events, presumably in Vienna. World War I, however, convinced him of the enormous significance of a well-developed propaganda campaign. In *Mein Kampf*, Hitler elaborated his basic principles for effective propaganda. Propaganda must be addressed not to the intellectuals of society but only to the masses. "The function of propaganda does not lie in the scientific training of the individual, but in calling the masses' attention to certain facts." Since its appeal was directed to the masses, it must be "aimed at the emotions and only to a very limited degree to the so-called intellect." Its intellectual level needs to be adjusted to "the most limited intelligence among those it is addressed to."

---

[47]Excerpts from *Mein Kampf* by Adolf Hitler, translated by Ralph Manheim, p. 443. Copyright © 1943, renewed 1971 by Houghton Mifflin Harcourt Publishing Company. Reprinted by permission of Houghton Mifflin Harcourt Publishing Company. All rights reserved.

[48]Ibid.

[49]Baynes, ed., *The Speeches of Adolf Hitler*, vol. 1, p. 538.

For Hitler, this "limited intelligence" of the masses meant that effective propaganda had to rely on constant repetition of a few basic points, since "only after the simplest ideas are repeated thousands of times will the masses finally remember them."[50]

Hitler perceived the psychological importance of mass meetings in creating support for a movement. They offered a sense of community that satisfied the need to belong to a larger group, and subsequently gave greater meaning to life. In the mass meeting "the individual, who at first, while becoming a supporter of a young movement, feels lonely and easily succumbs to the fear of being alone, for the first time gets the picture of a larger community, which in most people has a strengthening, encouraging effect."[51] Hitler realized that mass meetings had such emotional effects that people came away from them with stronger convictions than ever before.

> When from his little workshop or big factory, in which he [a representative of a new doctrine] feels very small, he steps for the first time into a mass meeting and has thousands and thousands of people of the same opinions around him, when, as a seeker, he is swept away by three or four thousand others into the mighty effect of suggestive intoxication and enthusiasm, when the visible success and agreement of thousands confirm to him the rightness of the new doctrine and for the first time arouse doubt in the truth of his previous conviction—then he himself has succumbed to the magic influence of what we designate as "mass suggestion." The will, the longing, and also the power of thousands are accumulated in every individual. The man who enters such a meeting doubting and wavering leaves it inwardly reinforced: he has become a link in the community.[52]

Hitler's convictions about propaganda and mass spectacles quickly became public policy in the Third Reich. His willingness to establish a Ministry for Public Enlightenment and Propaganda under Joseph Goebbels demonstrated his admiration for propaganda. It was, after all, the means to manipulate the German people to any end, as Hitler revealed in a secret speech to the editors of the domestic press in 1938.

> Circumstances have forced me to talk almost exclusively of peace for decades . . . It has now become necessary to psychologically change the German people's course in a gradual way and slowly make it realize that there are things that must . . . be carried through by the methods of force and violence . . . This work has required months, it was begun systematically; it is being continued and reinforced.[53]

Mass Spectacles

Mass spectacles were employed to integrate the German nation and to mobilize it as a useful instrument in the hands of Adolf Hitler and the Nazis. Hitler, realizing their importance, actively participated in their general conception and specific planning. The German people were subjected to a variety of mass spectacles.

---

[50]Excerpts from *Mein Kampf* by Adolf Hitler, translated by Ralph Manheim, pp. 179–180, 185. Copyright © 1943, renewed 1971 by Houghton Mifflin Harcourt Publishing Company. Reprinted by permission of Houghton Mifflin Harcourt Publishing Company. All rights reserved.

[51]Ibid., p. 478.

[52]Ibid., pp. 478–479.

[53]Quoted in Fest, *Hitler*, pp. 536–537.

The mass meetings of the election campaigns before Hitler came to power were, as Joseph Goebbels explained, "organized down to the least item." Travel routes were carefully chosen, SA and party units strategically placed, the size of meetings carefully determined, and suspense created through the use of marching bands and processions with swarms of fluttering flags and shouts of "*Heil.*" Hitler's appearance at these rallies was delayed in order to heighten expectations, so that when he finally did appear, highlighted by a blaze of spotlights and surrounded by mobs of shouting people in the darkness, the crowd was thrown into a frenzy. Hitler would enter the meeting hall from the rear, increasing the tension with a long procession. The first notes of his special music, the Badenweiler march, alerted the audience to his entry. After his flood of impassioned oratory, the meetings were concluded with the playing of "Deutschland, Deutschland über Alles" or a party anthem while Hitler made his exit. The overall impression generated by these mass rallies was one of strength, conviction, unity, and purpose. Hitler understood the psychological impact created by proper timing, march music, and the play of lights. He was also flexible in using new techniques that could catch the imagination of the German people. He made spectacular use of his illuminated plane circling over the crowds waiting below.

After coming to power, Hitler ritualized mass meetings in order to reach large crowds. He used every opportunity to provide a grand spectacle. Parades, drills, torchlight processions, dedications, bonfires, and demonstrations became integral parts of harvest festivals, memorial days, and state visits. These mass spectacles, whose grand scenes were aimed at conquering the hearts of the masses, had a hypnotic quality that can be seen in the documentary films of the period. Here again Hitler paid close attention to the details of these events, even overseeing trivial items. He was especially good at creating impressive effects for funeral celebrations, as evidenced in the memorial celebrations on November 9 of each year honoring the dead from the Beer Hall Putsch march in Munich in 1923. These memorial celebrations, as so many others of Hitler's mass rallies, were staged in the evening because Hitler believed people were more emotionally vulnerable then. Hitler even established a special Bureau for Organization of Festivals, Leisure and Celebrations, whose purpose was to create "model programs for celebrations" of the National Socialist movement.

To foster reverence for the National Socialist Party and create substitutes for religious holy days, Hitler and the National Socialists established a cycle of important days: January 30, the date of Hitler's accession to the chancellorship of Germany; February 24, Foundation Day of the National Socialist Party (the day on which the party program had been published in 1920); March 16, National Day of Mourning, or Heroes' Remembrance Day; April 20, Hitler's birthday, celebrated by torchlight parades and mass choruses; May 1, National Labor Day, celebrated by maypole dances, parades, and huge bonfires; the second Sunday in May, Mother's Day, when crosses of honor were awarded to prolific mothers at public ceremonies; the Nuremberg party rallies in September; and the Harvest Thanksgiving Festival, which honored German farmers and was celebrated throughout Germany with speeches, concerts, parades, and picnics. A special gathering of half a million to a million farmers was held yearly at the Bückeberg near Hameln. It featured music, parades, military maneuvers, and appearances by Hitler and other leading Nazis. Here Hitler praised the peasantry as the source of all racial strength and wisdom. The remaining holidays were November 9, anniversary of the Beer Hall Putsch, the holiest day of the Nazi regime, when the

The Nazi Mass Spectacle. Nazi mass spectacles evoked intense enthusiasm, as is evident in this photograph of Hitler arriving at the Bückeberg near Hamelin for the Harvest Festival in 1937. Nearly 1 million people attended the celebration. *(Hugo Jaeger/Timepix/Time Life Pictures/Getty Images)*

survivors of the putsch reenacted their march through the streets of Munich; and the Day of the Winter Solstice, which failed to supplant Christmas as it was designed to do.

The Nuremberg Party Rallies

Of all the mass gatherings staged in Nazi Germany, the Nuremberg rallies, known as the *Parteitage*, or party days, became the most spectacular. The first party day had been held in Munich in 1923. Its purpose was to bring together party members in order to show the strength of the organization and to attract popular support, including that of other right-wing political groups. Beginning in 1927, the *Parteitag* was held every September in Nuremberg; the last one took place there in 1938. From 1934 on, the rallies lasted for a week. Nuremberg was chosen because of its historical symbolism. It had been one of the leading German cities of the Holy Roman Empire in the late Middle Ages and the Reformation Period and became the embodiment of national ideals in the nineteenth century. By holding modern rallies in historic "Old German" settings, Hitler hoped to fuse past and present into a new cultural unity.

Practices introduced during the party days of the 1920s were used in the gigantic rallies of the 1930s. In the *Fahnenweihe* (consecration of the flags) ceremony, the original flag of the party, which had been carried by the SA during the Beer Hall Putsch and was stained with the blood of Nazis wounded in the street fighting, was touched to new flags, initiating them for use as party banners. Richard Wagner's music and Wagnerian stage effects were also introduced in the 1920s. What was significantly different about the rallies of that decade from the later ones was Hitler's blatant proclamation of the real aims of the Nazi program—anti-Semitism, the annexation of German-speaking territories in Europe, stringent nationalism, and ruthless destruction of the enemies of National Socialism. The latter included Marxism, the Jews, pacifism, the Weimar Republic, the parliamentary system, and international capitalism. In these early rallies, Hitler appeared as the revolutionary visionary.

Once in power, Hitler changed the function of the party rallies. Before 1933, they were the isolated project of a single party; in 1933 they became a major national undertaking. The *Parteitage* employed all the mass media of Germany in order to propagandize to the nation and the world. Hitler studied the blueprints for the rallies and usually visited Nuremberg one month early to inspect the construction work and to discuss the particulars of the party day with the leaders of the rally's organization committee.

To fulfill the new function of the party days, Hitler emphasized the construction of permanent installations for the rallies. He saw the need for an enormous stage outside of Nuremberg for gigantic rallies full of ceremony and pageantry that would ritually demonstrate the greatness of Nazi Germany. Large-scale construction began in 1934, and by 1937 three major facilities had been built. The Luitpold Arena, consisting of five square miles of parade ground, could accommodate 150,000 participants and 50,000 spectators. Since this arena was considered too small for really large rallies, an adjacent field known as the Zeppelinwiese was turned into a parade ground that could accommodate 400,000 participants watched over by a grandstand with a speaker's platform in the center. Completed in 1936, it was the principal parade ground for the 1930s rallies. Operatic effects, copied from Hitler's favorite Wagnerian operas, were created for night ceremonies through the use of hundreds of spotlights illuminating flagpoles, columns, the speaker's platform, and the field itself. A third center for activities was Congress Hall, which seated 20,000 people and was used for all indoor meetings. The construction of a new Congress Hall that would seat 40,000 people was initiated in 1935 but never completed because of war. Plans for two more large areas were likewise never finished. Hitler, in his usual megalomaniacal fashion, announced plans in 1938 to construct a completely new congress city that would be tied to the old Nuremberg by a wide avenue.

In these settings, Hitler and the Nazis mesmerized a nation with displays of the unity and strength of a reawakened Germany. The structure of these rallies was laid down in the 1934 *Parteitag*—the party day of unity. The weeklong activities consisted primarily of massive rallies and marches of prominent groups in the new Nazi state. There were organized demonstrations and marches by the Nazi political leaders, the SA, the SS, the Hitler Youth, the Labor Service men, and the army, including actual military exercises. Hitler was the featured speaker at each gathering. In the rallies of the 1930s, unlike those of the 1920s, Hitler spoke of German unity and honor and, especially for diplomatic purposes, emphasized his desire for peace. Additional activities included meetings of the National Socialist Women's Association, the consecration of flags, gymnastic exercises by male and female youth groups, fireworks, memorial celebrations for veterans of World War I and Nazis killed in the struggle for power, and a torchlight serenade for Hitler at his hotel on the last evening of the rallies. Special effects, such as timing Hitler's

The Nuremberg Party Rally. The Nuremberg Party rallies were the most spectacular of the Nazi mass spectacles. Shown here at the 1937 rally are Labor Service men marching past the Führer. *(National Archives and Records Administration[242-HB-8199a 43])*

closing remarks to coincide with the arrival of darkness and the lighting of bonfires on the horizon and turning on of searchlights, were designed to have an emotional impact on the spectators. Besides the obvious use of Wagnerian theatrical motifs, a conscious imitation of Catholic church ritual was increasingly incorporated into Nazi ceremonies upon Hitler's recommendation.

One of the reasons for the emphasis on precise organization of the rallies was that the *Parteitage* events were being filmed for propaganda purposes. The most famous of these was the *Triumph of the Will*, the official propaganda film of the 1934 party day directed by Leni Riefenstahl. Even to this day, *Triumph of the Will* captures the excitement as well as the disturbing quality of these Nazi rallies.

The Nuremberg rallies had an enormous impact on all who participated in them, including Hitler. The adulation and deification of Hitler at Nuremberg fed his own messianic image of himself and increased his megalomaniacal tendencies. At the 1936 party day, he expressed his feeling of deep mystical communion with the crowds at Nuremberg:

> Do we not feel once again in this hour the miracle that brought us together? Once you heard the voice of a man, and it struck deep into your hearts; it awakened you, and you followed this voice. Year after year you went after it, though him who had spoken you never even saw. You heard only a voice, and you followed it. When we meet each other here, the wonder of our coming together fills us all. Not everyone of you sees me, and I do not see everyone of you. But I feel you, and you feel me. It is the belief in our people that has made us small men great, that has made us poor men rich, that has made brave and courageous men out of us wavering, spiritless, timid folk; this belief made us see our road when we were astray; it joined us together into one whole! . . . You come, that . . . you may, once in a while, gain the feeling that now we are together; we are with him and he with us, and we are now Germany![54]

The Germans present at Nuremberg reciprocated his sentiments, reflected for all of them in the chants of the Labor Service Corps: "We want one leader! Nothing for us! Everything for Germany! *Heil* Hitler!" Even foreigners seem to have been affected by the passions engendered by these rallies. Thus these observations by French ambassador François-Poncet:

> Seven years yearly Nuremberg was a city devoted to revelry and madness; almost a city of convulsionaries, Holy Rollers and the like. The surroundings, the beauty of the spectacles presented, and the luxury of the hospitality offered exerted a strong influence upon the foreigners whom the Nazi Government was careful to invite annually. Many visitors, dazzled by Nazi display, were infected by the virus of Nazism. They returned home convinced by the doctrine and filled with admiration for the performance.[55]

It was reported that at the 1937 rally, a group of foreign correspondents were so overcome by emotion that they rose to their feet with arms raised in the Nazi salute and

---

[54]Baynes, ed., *The Speeches of Adolf Hitler,* vol. 1, pp. 206–207. By permission of the Royal Institute of International Affairs.

[55]François-Poncet, *The Fateful Years,* p. 209.

joined in the singing of "Deutschland, Deutschland über Alles." In his book on the Nuremberg rallies, Hamilton Burden concluded that they

> will probably remain one of the most startling chapters of twentieth-century history. They are a frightening example of the awesome power of modern propaganda techniques. Borrowing from pagan cults, church rituals, and Wagnerian theater, and other ways of reaching the thoughts and dreams of the masses, the absolute state perfected, in Nuremberg, its ability to dominate man's mind.[56]

What Burden says about the Nuremberg party days can be said equally about the other mass rallies set up by Hitler and the Nazis. If the mass meetings before 1933 were aimed at creating the kind of emotional upheaval that would lead millions to vote Hitler into power, then the mass spectacles after Hitler came to power were directed at creating an atmosphere in which Germans would become fanatically dedicated to Hitler and to their unity in a truly Germanic *Volksgemeinschaft*. Hitler repeatedly expressed the need for unity, harmony, discipline, willpower, and obedience, and many Germans clearly became enthusiastically committed to those ideas in response.

To Hitler, the successful realization of his ideology called for an active foreign policy based ultimately on expansion achieved by war. The German people had to be made willing and able tools for executing that foreign policy. To Hitler that could be achieved only if the German race could be purified of the Jews and made into such a unified whole that Germans would consciously renounce their individuality and submerge their wills with that of Germany and the Führer. The mass spectacles, with their "awesome power of modern propaganda techniques," became a major instrument in achieving Hitler's goal of educating the German people to his new state and its ideals. That Hitler conquered as much of Europe as he did and convinced the German people to assist him in annihilating the Jews and to hold out against the Allies as long as they did certainly proves that he came frighteningly close to accomplishing that goal.

SUGGESTIONS FOR FURTHER READING

In addition to the material in the Hitler biographies listed at the end of Chapter 2, specific works dealing with Hitler's personality include William Carr, *Hitler: A Study in Personality and Politics* (New York, 1979); Horst von Maltitz, *The Evolution of Hitler's Germany: The Ideology, the Personality, the Movement* (New York, 1973); and Bradley Smith, *Adolf Hitler: His Family, Childhood and Youth* (Stanford, Calif., 1967), which discusses the influences in his early years that left a mark on Hitler's personality. The work by Fritz Redlich, *Hitler: Diagnosis of a Destructive Prophet* (New York, 1999), is a biography that focuses on Hitler's mental and medical history and its influence on his behavior. Ronald Hayman, *Hitler and Geli* (New York, 1997) is an interesting examination of Hitler's relationship with his niece.

Some insights into Hitler's personality can be gleaned from the memoirs of men and women around him. However, these memoirs are not always reliable and

---

[56]Hamilton Burden, *The Nuremberg Party Rallies, 1923–1939* (New York, 1967), p. 166.

must be used cautiously. The most famous is Albert Speer, *Inside the Third Reich*, trans. Richard and Clara Winston (New York, 1970). Others include Henry A. Turner, *Hitler: Memoirs of a Confidant* (New Haven, Conn., 1985), which contains selections from the memoirs of Otto Wagener; Ernst Hanfstaengl, *Hitler: The Memoirs of a Nazi Insider Who Turned Against the Führer* (New York, 2011); and Otto Strasser, *Hitler and I* (Boston, 1940). Interesting details are included in the account by his childhood friend August Kubizek, *The Young Hitler I Knew*, trans. Geoffrey Brooks (St. Paul, Minn., 2006). See also the recent English translations and reprints of Heinz Linge, *With Hitler to the End: The Memoirs of Adolf Hitler's Valet*, trans. Geoffrey Brooks (New York, 2009); Christa Schroeder, *He Was My Chief: The Memoirs of Adolf Hitler's Secretary*, trans. Geoffrey Brooks (New York, 2009); Otto Dietrich, *The Hitler I Knew: Memoirs of the Third Reich's Press Chief* (New York, 2010); and Heinrich Hoffmann, *Hitler Was My Friend* (Barnsley, 2011). A record of Hitler's nightly monologues, *Hitler's Secret Conversations*, trans. Norman Cameron and Richard H. Stevens (New York, 1961), provides much insight into Hitler's personality. For the crucial war years, see Hugh R. Trevor-Roper, ed., *Hitler's Table Talk, 1941–1944* (New York, 2008).

There is no single volume in English dedicated to Hitler as a messianic leader. However, James Rhodes, *The Hitler Movement* (Stanford, Calif., 1980), treats the entire Nazi movement as a modern messianic movement. See also Chapters 4 and 5 of David Redles, *Hitler's Millennial Reich: Apocalyptic Belief and the Search for Salvation* (New York, 2005). On Hitler's religious beliefs, see Rainer Bucher, *Hitler's Theology: A Study in Political Religion* (New York, 2011).

Hitler's oratorical skills can be examined in the Hitler biographies, as well as in some of the speeches in Norman Baynes, ed., *The Speeches of Adolf Hitler, 1922–1939*, 2 vols. (Oxford, 1942); Max Domarus, ed., *Hitler: Speeches and Proclamations*, 4 vols. (London, 1990–1997); and Gordon W. Prange, ed., *Hitler's Words* (Washington, D.C., 1944).

The most important study of Hitler's ideology is Eberhard Jäckel, *Hitler's Weltanschauung*, trans. Herbert Arnold (Middletown, Conn., 1972). Older, but still useful works dealing with Nazi ideology are George Mosse, *The Crisis of German Ideology: Intellectual Origins of the Third Reich* (New York, 1964); Peter Viereck, *Metapolitics: The Roots of the Nazi Mind* (New York, 1965); and Fritz Stern, *The Politics of Cultural Despair: A Study in the Rise of Germanic Ideology* (Berkeley, Calif., 1961). Also of value is Hermann Glaser, *The Cultural Roots of National Socialism*, trans. Ernest A. Menze (Austin, Tex., 1978). Hitler's ideology is best studied by reading *Mein Kampf*, trans. Ralph Mannheim (Boston, 2001). Analysis of this work can be found in Felicity Rash, *The Language of Violence: Adolf Hitler's Mein Kampf* (New York, 2006) and Neil Gregor, *How to Read Hitler* (New York, 2005). Also insightful is Hitler's unpublished sequel to *Mein Kampf*, now available as *Hitler's Second Book*, trans. Krista Smith (New York, 2006). The intellectual world that informed Hitler's ideology can be found in Timothy W. Ryback, *Hitler's Private Library: The Books that Shaped His Life* (New York, 2008). On the importance of German occultism in the development of Nazi racial ideology, see Jackson Spielvogel and David Redles, "Hitler's Racial Ideology: Content and Occult Sources," *Simon Wiesenthal Center Annual*, vol. 3, Henry Friedlander and Sybil Milton, eds. (White Plains, N.Y., 1986), pp. 227–246; and Nicholas Goodrick-Clarke, *The Occult Roots of Nazism: Secret Aryan Cults and Their Influence on Nazi Ideology* (New York, 1992). Other aspects of Nazi ideology, with key supporting documents, are covered in Barbara M. Lane and Leila J. Rupp, eds., *Nazi Ideology Before 1933* (Manchester, 1978); and Robert Cecil's work on Alfred Rosenberg, *The Myth of the Master Race: Alfred Rosenberg and Nazi Ideology* (London, 1972). The myth of 'Jewish-Bolshevism' is covered in Lorna Louise Waddington, *Hitler's Crusade: Bolshevism and the Myth of the International Jewish Conspiracy* (New York, 2007). The importance of racial ideology in Nazi Germany is examined in Michael Burleigh and Wolfgang Wippermann, *The Racial State: Germany 1933–1945* (Cambridge, Mass., 1991).

The best-known psychoanalytical studies of Hitler are Rudolph Binion, *Hitler Among the Germans* (New York, 1976); Robert G. L. Waite, *The Psychopathic God: Adolf Hitler* (New York, 1977); Walter Langer, *The Mind of Adolf Hitler* (New York, 1972); Helm Stierlin, *Adolf Hitler: A Family Perspective* (New York, 1976); Edleff H. Schwab, *Hitler's Mind: A Plunge into Madness* (New York, 1992); Norbert Bromberg and Verna Small, *Hitler's Psychopathology* (New York, 1983); Theodore L. Dorpat, *Wounded Monster: Hitler's Path from Trauma to Malevolence* (Lanham, Md., 2002); and George Victor, *Hitler: the Pathology of Evil* (Washington, D.C., 1998).

For a succinct summary of propaganda, see Z. A. B. Zeman, *Nazi Propaganda* (London, 1973). A highly popularized account with many illustrations is Ward Rutherford, *Hitler's Propaganda Machine* (New York, 1978). See also the USHMM exhibit publication, *State of Deception: The Power of Nazi of Propaganda*, eds., Susan Bachrach and Steven Auckert (Washington, D.C., 2009). More specialized works are Ernest K. Bramsted, *Goebbels and National Socialist Propaganda* (East Lansing, Mich., 1965) and Russel Lemmons, *Goebbels and Der Angriff* (Lexington, Ky., 1994). There is a valuable collection of essays in David Welch, ed., *Nazi Propaganda, The Power and the Limitations* (London, 1983). For a good survey of the role and importance of propaganda, see David Welch, *The Third Reich: Politics and Propaganda*, 2nd ed. (London, 2002). Hamilton Burden discusses the Nuremberg mass rallies in *The Nuremberg Party Rallies, 1923–1939* (New York, 1967).

MySearchLab™ Connections

Study and Review

Adolf Hitler became the central symbol of the Nazi Party. Though contemporary accounts indicate Hitler was insecure, physically unimpressive, and impersonal, he developed a cult of personality few others in modern history have been able to attain. It was by the sheer force of this personal charisma that he remolded the Nazi Party to his own ideology, conquered Germany with popular support, and waged military aggression.

Read the Document

1. **Adolf Hitler, The Obersalzberg Speech, 1939**
    This document presents Hitler's speech to his commanders at his Obersalzberg headquarters. The speech illustrates his typical references to history, his rhetorical style, and his ability to persuade and convince through his personality and iron will.

View the Image

2. **German Painting Idolizing Hitler**
    This image presents Adolf Hitler as a white knight. Millions of Germans idolized Adolf Hitler as a heroic figure, like a knight from a German medieval saga.

View the Map

3. **German Expansion under the Third Reich**
    This map shows Hitler's drive for more territory for the German people. Hitler's beliefs that the German people did not have enough children and enough living space were key components of his ideology.

RESEARCH AND EXPLORE

Hitler's duality as a charismatic leader and as an insecure, self-conscious doubter influenced his actions and abilities as leader of Nazi Germany. While Hitler projected a powerful, charismatic image (heavily fueled by propaganda), he was also arrogant and unable to admit when he was wrong. He surrounded himself with people who were physically or mentally inferior, and he was ideologically rigid, seeing as enemies anyone who disagreed with his plans or worldview.

1. What was Hitler's opinion of Karl Marx? How did Hitler contrast Marxism with the tenets of Aryanism?
2. How did Hitler define his role as leader of the German people? Did he see it as a moral or political responsibility?
3. To what extent did propaganda influence the German people's view of Hitler?

ADDITIONAL RESOURCES

Hitler and Mussolini in Munich, 1940

Hitler at Nuremberg Rally, ca. 1928

6

Culture and Society in Nazi Germany

I n Hitler's mind, the acquisition of political power was only the first prerequisite toward the fulfillment of his real mission—the revival of German strength, the acquisition of "living space," and the foundation of a pure racial state and empire that would dominate Europe and possibly even the world. The achievement of these goals required a single *Volksgemeinschaft*, a national community unified in mind, will, and purpose. The Nazi ideal of the "total state" was a crucial element in the attainment of that community. This required not only that political and economic life be coordinated but that every facet of cultural and social life be controlled and used to inculcate Nazi ideological ideals. To Joseph Goebbels, leader of the regime's propaganda efforts, all cultural activities were public exercises that required guidance and police supervision. But as usual in Nazi Germany, ideals and practices were often at odds. While busy indoctrinating, the regime was also concerned, for the sake of its popularity, with providing popular entertainment that would amuse and relax people. The needs of ideological purity were often subordinated to very practical considerations and party infighting.

CULTURE

The Nazi approach to culture was anti-intellectual. In an interview with foreign correspondents, Hitler had bluntly commented on intellectuals: "Unfortunately, one needs them. Otherwise, one might—I don't know—wipe them out or something. But, unfortunately one needs them."[1] Other Nazis were equally blunt in degrading intellectuals. "We think with our blood" was a common Nazi epithet. Early on, the regime began purging Jewish, Communist, Socialist, and liberal artists and intellectuals. Numerous luminaries chose to emigrate—the writers Thomas and Heinrich Mann, the playwright Bertolt Brecht, the artists Max Beckmann and Oscar Kokoschka, the architect Walter Gropius, the musician Bruno Walter, and the filmmaker Fritz Lang, to name a few. Others chose silence, or "inner emigration," as it was called.

[1]Wilhelm Treue, "Rede Hitlers vor der Deutschen Presse," *Vierteljahrshefte für Zeitgeschichte,* 6 (1958), 188.

A number of leading intellectual and artistic figures chose to support National Socialism, however, some more publicly than others. The playwright Gerhart Hauptmann, the writer Gottfried Benn, the philosopher Martin Heidegger, and Carl Schmitt, one of the most respected political scientists of his day, all chose at some point to speak or write favorably about the regime. The Nazis enthusiastically welcomed this support as proof of the regime's legitimacy, especially to impress foreigners. The intellectuals who supported the Nazi government embraced Hitler's national community, believing sincerely that Weimar culture had been too international. Moreover, some intellectuals even approved of the Nazis' use of violence. Perhaps most simply feared the consequences for their careers if they did not accept the regime.

There was no more visible symbol of Nazi anti-intellectualism than the infamous book burnings, especially since these activities were organized by German student groups. They were intended as symbolic acts against the "un-German spirit" and featured, especially on May 10, 1933, the burning of books in Berlin and other important university towns. The "undesirable and pernicious" writers whose books went up in flames included Karl Marx, Sigmund Freud, and Erich Maria Remarque, among others. Goebbels gave a speech in which he said, "the age of extreme intellectualism is over . . . the past is lying in flames . . . the future will rise from the flames within our hearts . . . Brightened by these flames our vow shall be: the Reich and the Nation and our Führer Adolf Hitler: Heil! Heil! Heil!"[2]

Institutional Controls

The institutional control of Nazi cultural policy was heavily contested between two prominent Nazi leaders, Joseph Goebbels and Alfred Rosenberg. Already on March 13, 1933, Hitler had authorized the establishment of a Reich Ministry for Public Enlightenment and Propaganda. Naturally, the chief of Nazi Party propaganda activities, Goebbels, was given control of the new ministry. Goebbels said to the press two days later: "It is not enough to reconcile people more or less to our regime, to move them towards a position of neutrality towards us, we would rather work on people until they are addicted to us."[3] The aim of the ministry was to unite the nation behind the "ideal of the national revolution," and propaganda was the means to that end. Of course, Goebbels felt that his office should logically dominate the field of culture in the new Third Reich.

But as usual in the backbiting politics of Nazi Germany, Goebbels had a fanatical rival in the person of Alfred Rosenberg. Even before the Nazi seizure of power, Rosenberg had established a party organization known as the Combat League for German Culture, whose purpose was to combat "modernism" in art and protect the "German" tradition. In addition, after the Nazis had seized control, Rosenberg was put in charge of the party's Office for the Supervision of Ideological Training and Education. Rosenberg was a hardliner on ideological principles. Goebbels was not; his cynical attitude included a belief in the need to compromise even ideological principles for propaganda purposes. Goebbels won the fight for control of cultural policy, largely because he held both party and state positions and thus additional levers of power.

---

[2]Quoted in David Welch, *The Third Reich: Politics and Propaganda* (London and New York, 1993), p. 28.
[3]Ibid., p. 24.

The victory of the propaganda minister was made evident on September 22, 1933, when Goebbels was put in charge of a new Reich Chamber of Culture. This chamber consisted of seven divisions: music, theater, literature, radio broadcasting, the press, visual arts, and film. Anyone working in one of these fields had to belong to the chamber for his or her group. As president of the Reich Chamber of Culture, Goebbels appointed the presidents and advisory councils for each chamber. He could also annul any decisions made by individual chambers. Each chamber decided who would belong. People who lacked "the reliability or suitability" necessary for the exercise of their profession were rejected. The unsuitable were usually Jews, the unreliable those who were not pro-Nazi enough. Those rejected for membership basically could not practice their profession. The Reich Chamber could thus get around direct censorship by means of the self-censorship that occurs when people wish to keep their jobs. Jewish artists were, however, able to found their own separate cultural organizations. For instance, the Jewish Culture League, originally called the Culture League of German Jews, was able to provide work and performance opportunities that otherwise would have been impossible. In this way Jewish cultural life could continue, albeit in a segregated and limited fashion.

The Press

The press proved difficult to control because there were almost 5000 daily newspapers owned by a variety of individuals, political parties, and religious organizations. Consequently, the Nazis pursued three different approaches to gain control of the press.

As they did with other groups in Germany, the Nazis coordinated the associations of publishers and journalists. The Reich Association of German Newspaper Publishers came under the control of Max Amann, director of the Nazi Party's publishing house, the Eher Verlag. Amann was also made president of the Reich Press Chamber of the new Chamber of Culture. Since membership was compulsory for all involved in publishing (assuming, of course, that they met the racial and ideological standards), Amann acquired considerable power over the press.

But Amann had competition for control of the press from Goebbels and Otto Dietrich. The latter had been the Nazi Party press chief and was made head of the Reich Association of the German Press, the basic organization for German journalists. This position gave Dietrich considerable control over editors and journalists. Goebbels had also assumed some power over the press by issuing guidelines from the Propaganda Ministry for newspaper editors. Editors who failed to follow the guidelines were fired "for the public good."

Amann and his associate Rolf Rienhardt pursued a second strategy for controlling the press that was extremely lucrative for Amann personally. Together the two men produced a major reorganization of German newspapers, either eliminating them or bringing them under the ownership of the Eher Verlag. Of the 4700 dailies in 1932, less than 1000 existed 10 years later. The Eher Verlag controlled almost 70 percent of them. The Nazis' own newspaper, the *Völkischer Beobachter*, became the first national newspaper and the first German daily to exceed 1 million in daily circulation. One can hardly ascribe this figure to quality, since members of the Nazi Party were expected to subscribe to the party newspaper.

Finally, the Nazis sought to control the press by direct supervision of content. Simply put, the Nazi regime exercised a total monopoly on the news, using two instruments to achieve this goal. All newspapers received their foreign news from the German Press Agency, which was controlled by the minister of propaganda. The Propaganda Ministry also supervised the daily press conferences of the Reich government, determined which journalists could attend, and provided detailed directives on what could be printed. For important news, the ministry even provided complete articles for the newspapers to use. Moreover, the ministry specified what could not be printed, such as press photographs showing government officials at banquets where bottles of alcohol were visible.

In the ministry's numerous directives, Goebbels made it clear that the press was to convey the government's view to the German people. The press had no choice but to cooperate with the government. Even Goebbels commented: "No decent journalist with any feeling of honor in his bones can stand the way he is handled by the press department of the Reich Government."[4]

Government control of the press in Nazi Germany was successful in giving the Nazi version of the news. Such detailed regulation, however, often resulted in dreadfully boring newspapers. One could know what to expect with deadening regularity. Readers lost interest, and there was a 10 percent decline in newspaper circulation from 1933 to 1939. The Nazis tried to compensate with illustrated papers and magazines, which did tend to become very popular in both peacetime and wartime.

The Visual Arts

Hitler and the Nazis appeared to place a high value on the visual arts. They certainly gave them a noticeable place in public ceremonies. Hitler had stated that "art is the only truly enduring investment of human labor." Of course, the Führer portrayed himself as an artist by temperament, the frustrated architect who would have achieved great success if his talent had been recognized early on. The first public building dedicated by the Third Reich was an art museum, the House of German Art in Munich. As usual, however, as with all aspects of Nazi culture and society, Nazi interest in art also served political purposes.

After coming to power the Nazi leadership made changes in the art world. Art was now viewed in ideological terms. Hitler said, "Art has at all times been the expression of an ideological and religious experience and at the same time the expression of a political will."[5] Since the Aryans were the bearers of true culture, only they could produce true art. "Racial decline" had caused military defeat in war and resulted in the Weimar democracy, which fostered modern "degenerate" art. Now, as Hitler pointed out, the Nazis had laid the foundations for a "new and genuine German art." The foundation for this new art was the favorable environment created by the Nazis' own racial and ideological renewal of the German people. This art would glorify the strong, the healthy, the heroic—all of which were attributes of the Aryans.

Hitler and the Nazis rejected modern art, which they labeled "degenerate art" or "Jewish art." Such art was the result of "cultural Bolshevism," which was also seen as a Jewish creation. In his address at the premiere of the Great German Art Exhibition in the newly opened House of German Art in July 1937, Hitler proclaimed:

> The people regarded this art [modern art] as the outcome of an impudent and shameless arrogance or of a simply shocking lack of skill; it felt that . . . these achievements which might have been produced by untalented children of from eight to ten years old—could never be valued as an expression of our own times or of the German future.[6]

[4]Ibid., p. 39.
[5]Quoted in Peter Adam, *Art of the Third Reich* (New York, 1992), p. 9.
[6]Norman H. Baynes, ed., *The Speeches of Adolf Hitler, 1922–1939,* vol. 1 (Oxford, 1942), p. 591.

One day after this speech, a separate exhibition of "degenerate art" was put on display in Munich. These works, culled from museums and galleries all over Germany, contained some of Weimar Germany's greatest contributions to modern art—the works of cubists, futurists, expressionists, and dadaists. After this final showing, these and thousands of other modern works disappeared from public view. Many were sold; some went into the hands of collectors such as Göring, and a large number were simply burned. The removal of the "degenerate art" of the Weimar era from public display was a visible symbol to the German people that the hated Weimar system, in culture as well as politics, had indeed been overthrown.

The Reich Chamber of Culture, with its constituent Reich Chamber of Visual Arts, became the chief organizational agency for change on the art scene. It purged the German art world of racial and political undesirables. Jewish, Socialist, and Communist art museum directors and art academy professors were dismissed. Some artists wound up in concentration camps. Thousands simply left Germany. The dismissals made it possible for representatives of the "new German art" to move into teaching and administrative positions and form a new art bureaucracy.

By the mid-1930s, the Reich Chamber of Visual Arts had 42,000 members including painters, architects, landscape architects, illustrators, designers, and art and antique dealers. It regulated every facet of the German art world, from fees charged by textile designers to the opening times for antique dealers' showrooms. Aryan descent was a prerequisite for membership. The chamber provided the basic instrument for control and intimidation of the art world.

The Nazi "battle for art" was a campaign to discredit and eliminate modern "degenerate art" in favor of the "new German art." However, the Third Reich did not create a new art of its own but built upon existing traditions and revived trends established long before the Nazis took over. The Third Reich simply restored those artists and their traditions that had been left behind by the development of modern art. The Nazis revived genre painting, which had flourished in the nineteenth century, especially in the hands of numerous local and provincial artists. Genre painting was content oriented. It focused on the presentation of animals, landscapes, and scenes from everyday life that would increase appreciation of ordinary things. Genre artists had no inherent style. Their common thread was to portray things realistically or naturally.

The mere rendering of numerous details from everyday life, however, was insufficient to meet the National Socialist ideological goals. Rather, those details had to convey a deeper National Socialist message. Portraits of farmers, hunters, and woodcutters were supposed to convey figures close to nature, examples of a healthy and pure race. Artisans symbolized the importance of work. Representations of mother and child, children, and family circles were supposed to present the sacred, eternal values important to the Aryan race. Landscape paintings were intended to portray the sacredness of German soil and the German fatherland. Female nudes were to be vibrant beings demonstrating the biological value of the individual as a precondition for racial rebirth.

To transform genre scenes into works conveying fundamental messages, artists resorted to two techniques. One was to paint the same things the genre artists had done, but to give cosmic sounding titles to their works. Hence, ordinary landscapes became *Cloud of Doom* or *Heaven and Earth*; a farm scene became *German Earth*; and factories became *Fortresses of Our Time*. Hermann Hoyer's portrait of Hitler and his supporters in the Beer Hall Putsch received the biblically inspired title *In the Beginning Was the Word*. Female nudes, a favorite subject in the Third Reich, became primal images of women and life. In the *Four Elements* by Adolf Ziegler, president of the Reich Chamber of Visual Arts, female nudes became elemental forces personified. This particular work adorned a living room of the Führer's house in Munich. A second technique for lending greater substance and significance to genre subjects was to create monumental figures. Paul Harnisch's *Cowherd* is dominated by a giant cow, symbolizing the superiority of German livestock.

An interesting feature of Nazi genre painting was its lack of realism. Although the objects (cows, farmers, trees, etc.) were always natural and realistic, the scenes themselves were not realistic portrayals of contemporary German life. For example, the theme of work was often illustrated by farmers plowing with a team of horses. Noticeably missing were the tractors that were transforming German agriculture along modern lines. This is, of course, a reflection of the basic conflict we have seen in National Socialism. On one hand, it was an ideology based on a return to peasant values, the ideal of "blood and soil," and a rejection of modern, urban industrial society. On the other hand, Nazi reality dictated a flourishing modern industrial economy that would produce the armaments for a military state bent on territorial expansion.

The Nazi emphasis on military values produced an enormous number of works portraying SA and SS men and regular military troops. After 1939, battle scenes of the present war or historical scenes glorifying war and the heroic death of soldiers were common. A work by Hans Schmitz-Wiedenbrück entitled *Workers, Farmers, and Soldiers* portrayed these

In the Beginning Was the Word. This painting by Hermann Hoyer is a good example of the realistic style of genre painting favored by Hitler and the Nazi regime. A straightforward portrait of Hitler addressing his followers has been given a dramatic, biblically inspired title. *(© The U.S. Army Center of Military History)*

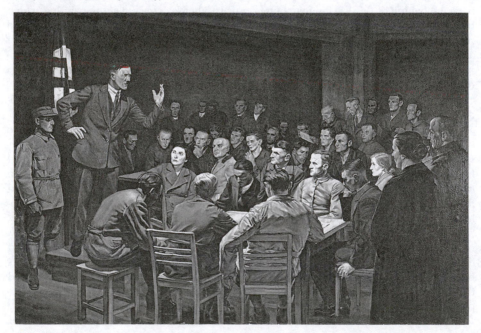

three groups as equal contributors to the common tasks of the new German national community. The dominance of the central panel, that of the soldiers, leaves no doubt that it was the soldiers who represented the highest ideals of the pure German race—a clear reflection of National Socialist ideology.

Sculpture in the Third Reich focused on the use of monumental figures. The official sculptors of the regime, Arno Breker and Joseph Thorak, were neoclassical realists. According to Nazi racial theory, the ancient Greeks were Nordic forerunners of present-day Germans, making classicism an appropriate form for the "new German art." The massive, heavily muscled figures produced by Breker and Thorak were displayed in new public buildings and on autobahn bridges. Like genre paintings, these realistically portrayed groups of supermen were given pretentious titles, such as *Sacrifice, Labor, Readiness,* and *Comradeship.*

To Hitler, architecture was the most appropriate art form for expressing national greatness. He believed that great buildings could awaken national consciousness and bring Germans together. He promised that "out of our new ideology and our political will we will create stone documents." Architecture was "the word in stone." Like the other arts, it would be used to indoctrinate people with the regime's ideology.

Nazi Germany experienced considerable difficulty in specifying what constituted a National Socialist style of architecture. It was relatively easy to denounce the modern architecture of the Weimar era. The Bauhaus school was castigated by the Nazis before their seizure of power and shut down after it by the summer of 1933. Building societies were coordinated and professional architectural organizations were reorganized. But the Nazis could still find no agreement on Nazi architectural principles. Rosenberg and his Combat League emphasized the need to impose a rigid, German, traditionally oriented style, but Goebbels opposed this. With his control of the Reich Chamber of Culture, Goebbels ensured there would be some variety in architecture.

The Nazis did try to emphasize the ideological significance of Nazi architecture. All Nazi buildings were to stress the new community spirit of Germany and be a living demonstration of the importance to Germans of their racial community. To the outside world those buildings should also speak of the power of that race. Although Hitler and the Nazi leaders agreed that a Nazi architecture should reveal their ideology, the actual building program of the Third Reich showed no uniformity in how that could be done. It contained a variety of styles and was basically decentralized with commissions coming from a variety of sources.

Hitler emphasized that Nazi architecture must be heroic, which meant building on a monumental scale. To build large was to build for eternity. Hitler's building projects thus included gigantic monuments, massive domed temples, and large-scale urban planning. He personally commissioned a number of buildings. His first was the House of German Art, commissioned in 1933 and completed by 1937. His personal architect for this museum was Paul Ludwig Troost. The building was done in a neoclassical style that evoked the Greek spirit. Hitler believed that the Greeks were Nordic or Aryan peoples and that their classical style was consistent with Germanness. But Troost's work also reflected the 1920s in its lack of ornamentation. This "modernized neoclassicism" was also used by Troost's successor as Hitler's personal architect, the young Albert Speer. Hitler commissioned Speer to design the new Chancellery building as well as buildings for party rallies in Nuremberg. Speer's massive neoclassical buildings were meant to convey a sense of the overwhelming power of Hitler and the National Socialist system. They were intended to awe people. These monumental buildings were elaborately publicized, and one could certainly get the impression that they constituted the essence of Nazi architecture.

House of German Art. The House of German Art was the first building commissioned by Hitler. Designed by Paul Ludwig Troost, it was built in the neoclassical and monumental styles that the Führer favored. *(SZ Photo/DIZ Muenchen GmbH, Sueddeutsche Zeitung Photo/Alamy Limited)*

But Germany was not alone in pursuing a variety of architectural styles. The 1930s also saw a resurgence of monumental styles using neoclassical forms, folk revivals, and modern Weimar styles elsewhere in Europe and in the United States. What stands out, however, is how the Nazis emphasized the ideological significance of their supposedly National Socialist, true German architecture. The Nazis constantly publicized their building programs and their significance, creating an impression of a far greater volume of construction than ever really took place.

Theater

The Nazis made a drastic impact on the world of theater. Almost all the famous directors and playwrights of the Weimar era, many of them Jewish, were blacklisted after the Nazi seizure of power. As a result, theater in Nazi Germany tended toward mediocrity. New plays carried Nazi political and ideological messages. "Blood and soil" was a frequent theme, and emphasis on the heroic became routine. A popular example was Hans Johst's *Schlageter*, a rather dreadful play glorifying an early proto-Nazi martyr of the French occupation of the Ruhr in 1923. A line from his play was often quoted in Nazi Germany: "When I hear the word Culture, I loosen the safety catch of my revolver." Goebbels felt that theater, like radio and cinema, needed to serve escapist functions. Consequently, comedy became king on the stage, especially so-called peasant comedies. The big hit of the 1934–1935 Berlin theater season was a play featuring two landholders fighting over custody of a pig. Coarse jokes were the mainstay of these peasant comedies.

The Nazis tried to create a new people's culture by means of the *Thingspiel*, or *Thing* theater. *Thing* plays were ceremonies with dramatic plots, individual speakers, and choruses. They included processions and audience participation in the singing of national songs. These spectacles were performed in *Thing* places, specially built open-air theaters based on the Greek amphitheater and thereby reinforcing Nazi belief in the kinship between modern Germans and ancient Greeks. These amphitheaters were built into the hills of the landscape and frequently incorporated ancient ruins or historic battlefields that were thought to have special significance for the German people. The *Thing* places were supposed to grow out of the German landscape to emphasize the Nazi reverence for nature. As one Nazi theorist put it, through the *Thing* place a new kind of German would develop who loved nature, sunshine, physical activity, community, and comradeship. Eventually 40 of the projected 1200 were built, basically using monumental and neoclassical architecture. But after an initial rush of enthusiasm, the *Thing* movement failed. Whether uncomfortable in the outdoor setting or bored by the spectacles themselves, Germans simply refused to attend the *Thingspiele*, bringing an end to the only Nazi cultural innovation.

Music

Nazi music policy was supposedly guided by the biological theory that each race had its own musical expression. Unique Nordic racial traits had produced the Germanic musical genius seen in such composers as Haydn, Mozart, and Wagner. Consequently, Jewish origin was attributed to all forms of modern music officially rejected by the regime. Atonal music contradicted the rhythm of the "blood and soul of the German people." Jazz was the result of race mixing in America, a "barbarian invasion supported by Jews," and was rejected. However, the conflict between Goebbels and Rosenberg for cultural domination led to considerable confusion in Nazi musical attitudes. Despite being condemned, jazz, for example, managed to survive the purge and was still being played in wartime Germany. Overall, Goebbels's victory over Rosenberg for control of music policy meant that ideological principles tended to be subordinated to the political requirements of propaganda.

Of course, it was virtually impossible to agree ideologically on what should constitute National Socialist music. Hitler himself said there was no such thing. But Nazi leaders did encourage the revival of German folk music by sponsoring contests for the best folk songs. The party also fostered the writing of popular songs that honored the heroes of the movement. The Horst Wessel song that became the party anthem is probably the most famous example of Nazi songs. Its lyrics were meant to rouse the fighting spirit of the Nazi Brown Shirts. The Nazi regime's revival of the military spirit resulted in considerable playing of military march music.

Of all the German composers, the nineteenth-century musical genius Richard Wagner became the center of the most popular music cult of the Third Reich. The city of Bayreuth, in which the annual Wagner festival took place, became virtually a national shrine. Hitler, a devotee of Wagner since his teens, contributed an annual subsidy to the festival. Wagner was honored not only as an ideal artist and musician but also as a spiritual and political pioneer of National Socialism. His compositions were used at Nazi cultural events, especially the Nuremberg party rallies.

Literature

After the Nazi seizure of power, an estimated 2500 writers, denounced as degenerates and racial undesirables, left Germany to escape the Nazi regime. Nazi ideologists viewed literature as a means to the political goals of the state. There were, of course, no clear artistic or aesthetic criteria for determining the acceptability of literature. Since the standards were political, it was content and not form that counted. Nazi literature, which was at best second-rate, focused on four major themes: the war or front experience, which emphasized the creation of a true community in wartime; race, which celebrated uniquely endowed Germans and their special mission; the return to the soil, exalted as Germany's salvation; and the Nazi movement, which exalted Hitler and his followers and reflected Nazi ideology.

The Propaganda Ministry had a special department that oversaw publishers, authors, and bookshops and had the right to approve every book manuscript before publication. The ministry promoted *Mein Kampf* as the highest form of German literary art. Hitler's book became Germany's best seller, selling 6 million copies by 1940.

The Reich Chamber of Literature, one of the branches of the Reich Chamber of Culture, was given supreme authority of censorship. It drew up a list of "damaging and undesirable" literature that endangered "National Socialist cultural aspirations." The circulation of these books, either in bookshops or libraries, was forbidden. The list was regularly updated. Two SS agencies, the Gestapo and the Security Service (SD), purged bookstores and libraries. Banned books were arranged according to two major categories. The entire works of Marxist and émigré authors were banned completely. Also prohibited were books on certain topics, such as pacifism; works critical of National Socialism or foreign policy; books harmful to the racial struggle (this included pro–birth control literature); pornography of all kinds; occult literature; and of course Jewish works.

Popular Culture

Joseph Goebbels and his Propaganda Ministry realized the potential and value of popular culture, especially film, radio, and sport. It was in the realm of film that the Third Reich made its most creative cultural contributions. Goebbels believed that films constituted one of the "most modern and scientific means of influencing the masses." In addition to a Reich Chamber of Film, a special film section was established in the Propaganda Ministry. Four of the major film studios were brought under government control.

Goebbels pursued a flexible film policy. Continuous Nazi propaganda films, he realized, would be box-office disasters. People wanted film experiences different from their everyday experiences in the outside world. Films, therefore, should serve as a form of escapism. To encourage the production of entertaining films, Goebbels allowed considerable freedom to film companies. He even protected movie stars from racial or political attack by zealous party leaders. The attractiveness of German films is evident in the quadrupling of cinema attendance between 1933 and 1942.

The German film industry produced about 1100 films between 1933 and 1944. Half were love stories or comedies—an indication of the escapist value of Nazi films. Of the 1100, only 96 were initiated by Goebbels's Propaganda Ministry, but these 96 had an advantage over the others in that extraordinary amounts of money, talent, and publicity were spent on them. Some of them, such as the epics about the SA, failed to attract wide audiences. Nevertheless, the regime-sponsored films dealt with themes dear to Nazi hearts. *Jud Süss* was a strongly anti-Semitic film. *Ich Klage an* (*I Accuse*) presented positive arguments for euthanasia. *Hitlerjunge Quex* stressed the heroism of a young Nazi martyr. A number of films on the Prussian Frederick the Great emphasized parallels between that monarch and Hitler.

Among the films of the Third Reich, perhaps the best known today are the documentaries, in particular those of Leni Riefenstahl. Riefenstahl was an actress who turned to directing in 1932. Hitler liked her work and invited her to make a film about the 1934 Nuremberg party rally. In filming this party day of unity—as it was called—Hitler was trying to demonstrate, in the wake of the purge of the SA on June 30, that the Nazi Party was strongly united behind its leader. Hitler provided the film's title, *Triumph des Willens* (*Triumph of the Will*).

Much of the success of this film was due to careful preparation. Good camera work was coordinated with the physical arrangements for the rally to produce a spectacle that was manipulated for cinematic purposes from beginning to end. The city of Nuremberg, the marching columns, the Hitler Youth camps, the swastika flags—all were subordinated to Riefenstahl's propaganda purpose. As a result, she produced a film not only renowned for its technical qualities but also forceful and dramatic in conveying to viewers the power of National Socialism.

Hitler had said "without motor-cars, sound films, and wireless, no victory of National Socialism." Of all the mass media, radio perhaps offered the greatest opportunity for reaching the masses. In *Mein Kampf*, Hitler had emphasized the importance of the spoken word over the written word. His master propagandist Goebbels realized completely the power of the new medium. In Weimar Germany control of the radio was the responsibility of the individual federal states. As part of the Nazi seizure of power, Hitler gained control of the radio system throughout Germany in the summer of 1933 by establishing the Reich Radio Company under his own Propaganda Ministry. But Goebbels also established close cooperation with the Reich director of broadcasting, Eugen Hadamovsky. News broadcasts, however, were the sole responsibility of the press department of the Reich Propaganda Ministry. During the Nazi seizure of power, a purge was made of the broadcasting staff, especially the top leadership.

The Nazi regime encouraged radio listening by fostering the purchase of radios. Manufacturers were urged to produce cheap radios (the "People's Receiver") that could be bought on installment. By 1939, 70 percent of German households (80 percent in cities) possessed a radio. This was three times the rate of ownership in Germany in 1932 and was the highest ownership rate in the world. Moreover, the Nazis encouraged communal radio listening, especially in factories, restaurants, cafes, and offices. Loudspeaker pillars were even erected in the streets. The Nazis believed that radio broadcasts of mass meetings and speeches made more of an impact if listened to by groups of people rather than individually at home. Radio wardens in each block encouraged people to listen to party programs and reported audience reactions and preferences to the authorities.

Sport was also used for propaganda purposes in the Third Reich. In *Mein Kampf*, Hitler had viewed sport as important for a healthy race and something to be promoted by the state. The *völkisch* state must be concerned not only with knowledge but also with "breeding absolutely healthy bodies." Sport and physical education were coordinated through the creation of the National Physical Education Union under Reich sport leader Hans von Tschammer und Osten. The Reich sport leader reorganized German physical education and sport in May 1933. All physical education programs had to include activities that fostered the *völkisch* characteristics of group attitude ("the age of individualism in sports is over"), soldierly qualities ("the spirit of attack"), and the heroic nature of the Aryan.

The presence of the Eleventh Olympic Games in Berlin in 1936 was used by the Nazi regime as an opportunity to show to the world Germany's physical prowess and new-found prestige. Goebbels was determined to put on a show for the world. The anti-Jewish campaign of the Nazis was suspended and a magnificent new Olympic Stadium was built in Berlin. Despite the propaganda successes, the Nazis were greatly perturbed by the victories of Jesse Owens, a black American, especially devastating to a regime that believed in the superiority of whites over blacks and other races.

THE MANIPULATION OF YOUTH

In their desire to establish a total state, the Nazis understood the importance of winning over the youth to their ideology. The future was theirs if they succeeded.

The Hitler Youth

The Weimar Republic had witnessed a striking variety of youth groups. Five million young people belonged to independent youth organizations as well as those sponsored by religious groups, political parties, and sporting associations. In no other country was there a youth movement of such numbers and vitality. The Nazi seizure of power dramatically changed the youth scene.

The first Nazi youth league was established in 1922 and came to a quick end with the failure of Hitler's Beer Hall Putsch in 1923. A new organization entitled the *Hitlerjugend* (the Hitler Youth) was founded in 1926 with Kurt Gruber as its leader, although control of the organization eventually passed to the young and dynamic Baldur von Schirach. The son of an aristocratic family, Schirach had joined the Nazi Party in 1925 at the age of eighteen. In 1931, Hitler appointed him Reich youth leader of the NSDAP and head of the Hitler Youth. At that time the organization and Schirach were subordinate to Ernst Röhm's SA. By the end of 1932, the Hitler Youth membership was still under 100,000, constituting a small percentage of youth-group membership. The members of the Hitler Youth were primarily from the lower-middle and working classes. In the summer of 1932, the organization was freed from the SA and given an independent status within the party.

After the Nazi seizure of power, Schirach's Hitler Youth consolidated its position among the youth of Germany. Under Schirach's leadership a group of Hitler Youth occupied the offices of the Reich Committee of German Youth Associations, the umbrella organization for all German youth groups. This action served to coordinate all youth groups except the Catholic organizations, which were protected by the concordat made with the Catholic church. Young people from the various groups were pressured to join the Hitler Youth. By the end of 1933, membership had increased dramatically to three and a half million. Although even schoolteachers were used to enlist new Hitler Youth, it is apparent from the testimony of a former member from the small town of Northeim that other motives were also at work.

> There was no pressure put on me by my father or anyone else to join the Hitler Youth—I decided to join it independently simply because I wanted to be in a boys club where I could strive towards a nationalistic ideal. The Hitler Youth had camping, hikes, and group meetings. I was number 9 in the Northeim group when I joined in 1930. There were boys from

The Hitler Youth. This photograph shows Hitler, accompanied by the Reich youth leader, Baldur von Schirach, reviewing the Hitler Youth at the 1934 Nuremberg party rally. *(National Archives and Records Administration[242-HB-8199a 152])*

all classes of families though mainly middle class and workers. There were no social or class distinctions, which I approved of very much. There was no direct or obvious political indoctrination until later—after Hitler came to power. Without really trying to get new members, the Northeim Hitler Youth grew rapidly. I think most of the other boys joined for the same reason I did. They were looking for a place where they could get together with other boys in exciting activities. It was also a depression time and there were many evil influences abroad from which decent boys wished to escape. In any event, I don't think the political factor was the main reason boys joined. We did march in parades and hated the SPD, but that was all general, not specific—it was all a part of it. We weren't fully conscious of what we were doing, but we enjoyed ourselves and also felt important.[7]

Apparently, there are no simplistic explanations for the attraction of the Hitler Youth to young people.

On June 17, 1933, Hitler named Schirach youth leader of the German Reich with control over all youth activities in Germany. In this same year Schirach introduced a structure based on age groups, which remained in force until 1945. The Hitler Youth was divided into two groups—the *Jungvolk* (Young People), ten to fourteen years of age,

[7]Quoted in William Sheridan Allen, *The Nazi Seizure of Power*, rev. ed. (New York, 1984), pp. 76–77. All rights reserved. Reprinted by permission of Franklin Watts, an imprint of Scholastic Library Publishing, Inc.

and the *Hitlerjugend* (Hitler Youth), fourteen to eighteen years of age. In 1936, Hitler freed the Hitler Youth from its subordination to the Ministry of the Interior and made the Hitler Youth an independent "Supreme Governmental Authority" subject only to the Führer. All other youth groups, including the remaining Catholic ones, were outlawed. The Hitler Youth was to be recognized as an educational institution equal to "being educated at home and at school." German parents and schoolteachers would soon learn that this would eventually threaten their own authority over children.

By 1936, about 63 percent of ten- to eighteen-year-olds belonged to the Hitler Youth. It was not until 1939 that the Hitler Youth was made compulsory for all young people. Upon entering the *Jungvolk*, each new member was required to take an oath to the Führer: "In the presence of this blood banner, which represents our Führer, I swear to devote all my energies and my strength to the savior of our country, Adolf Hitler. I am willing and ready to give up my life for him, so help me God." The motto of the Hitler Youth was "Führer, command—we follow!"

Hitler had clear-cut ideas about the education of the Hitler Youth. In his speech to the Hitler Youth at the 1935 Nuremberg party rally, Hitler emphasized his new image of German youth. The new National Socialist youth of the future must be "slim and slender, swift as the greyhound, tough as leather, and hard as Krupp steel." In a later speech Hitler stressed that all young people would join a Nazi organization at age ten and "not be free again for the rest of their lives."

Hitler's ideals were inculcated through the activities of the Hitler Youth. Young people anywhere would enjoy many of these activities such as arts and crafts, the building of model planes, group singing, storytelling, camping and hiking trips, sports activities, and evenings together in special youth "homes." The Hitler Youth were also required to engage in activities that are resisted by children everywhere, such as collecting charity contributions and performing land service, which required them to bring in harvests for farmers. Camping trips proved monotonous after the initial thrills. A typical day included twelve hours of programmed activities, four hours of free time, and eight hours of sleep.

Underlying all of these activities, whether enjoyable or not, was the Nazi reliance on competition and achievement. Almost all activities were made competitive. This was certainly true in sports, but also prominent in music, where choirs and instrumentalists competed for the designation of best performance, and in storytelling. Much of the competition was collective, since National Socialists worked hard to cultivate the idea that community interests were superior to individual needs and interests, as reinforced in another motto of the Hitler Youth: "We are born to die for Germany." Each group wanted to have the best "home" or the most interesting account of a hiking trip or the biggest collection for the Winter Relief Fund (see p. 171). Since competition glorified the fighter and the heroic, Hitler youth manifested a constant, restless, compulsive activity, a characteristic of the Hitler Youth that was at the heart of Nazism itself. This dynamic element explains the Nazi movement's success and its failure, for it was the kind of compulsive energy that could not stop until other forces destroyed it.

The Hitler Youth organization strove to indoctrinate the youth of Germany with the ideological values of National Socialism. Using all available opportunities, Hitler Youth leaders inculcated fervent patriotism, the need to serve Germany selflessly, and utter devotion to Adolf Hitler. Emphasis was also placed on the building of a true national community, where class differences and barriers should no longer exist. To Schirach the use of common uniforms was a symbol of the preliminary consummation of this single national community. On excursions, all lunches were placed in a common pool from which each member was given an equal share. But it is doubtful that the Hitler Youth created a real *Volksgemeinschaft*, since friendships still tended to be made along class lines. At least the official system did make it possible for underprivileged youngsters to advance into leadership positions.

Above all, the Hitler Youth fostered military values and virtues such as duty, obedience, honor, courage, strength, and ruthlessness. The uniforms and the constant drilling were supplemented by the honoring of the war dead, the exaltation of German military heroes, and constant stress on the need to become fighters, manly and heroic. The inculcation of military values was matched by systematic training in the military arts, which was being increasingly emphasized by 1938. Even the *Jungvolk* (the ten- to fourteen-year-olds) were given small-arms drill and practice with dummy hand grenades and small-bore rifles. The Hitler Youth (the fourteen- to eighteen-year-olds) actually shouldered army packs and rifles while practicing army maneuvers. A Hitler Youth rifle school provided training in shooting. The paramilitary training was encouraged by military authorities, for all Hitler Youth after the age of eighteen served six months in the Labor Front and two years in the armed forces.

What impact did the Hitler Youth have on German youth? A number of their activities had much appeal to young people. Camping trips, fireside gatherings, sporting events, comradeship—all of these were frequently mentioned after the war by Hitler Youth members as positive experiences. In rural areas in particular, youths were given a chance to participate in activities they had not experienced before. However, there were young people who objected to the organization's emphasis on obedience and its military aspects, especially drill.

The Hitler Youth organization did create serious problems for the parents and teachers of its members. Wearing Hitler Youth uniforms and participating in activities away from home and school intensified the natural rebelliousness against these authorities that is part of the teen years. Parents were alarmed at what they considered the brutalization of their offspring and the amount of time they were spending away from home. Teachers were disturbed by the Hitler Youth's lack of respect for intellectual activity. It was difficult for Hitler Youth members to be leaders in Hitler Youth activities outside of school and then subordinate in school. Hitler Youth leaders rejoiced in their contempt for school authority and school learning. Teachers were appalled by their students' lack of commitment and lack of learning, but because they feared the political authorities' support of the Hitler Youth, they were unable to impose traditional school discipline. This had a deleterious effect on the traditionally excellent German educational system.

The League of German Girls

The Hitler Youth had a female counterpart known as the *Bund Deutscher Mädel* (BDM, League of German Girls). This girls' section of the Hitler Youth had been formed in 1927, but was not formally integrated into the Hitler Youth until 1932. It had only 15,000 members by the end of that year, but like the Hitler Youth it grew considerably after the Nazis eliminated all other such organizations. By 1937, it had risen to 3 million members. In 1933, the BDM was divided into two groups. The *Jungmädel* (Young Girls) consisted of ten- to fourteen-year-olds; the BDM was reserved for girls fourteen to eighteen.

Hitler Youth girls were indoctrinated in the principles of service, regimentation, obedience, and discipline. For boys, these were meant to lead to the warrior personality. For girls, they were to shape dutiful wives and mothers. *Jungmädel* girls participated in a variety of activities similar to the *Jungvolk* activities such as attendance at youth "homes," learning of Nazi songs and facts, sports meetings, camping and hiking, and numerous other physical activities. They too had a uniform: white blouses, blue ankle-length skirts, and sturdy marching shoes. The activities of the older group, the BDM, increasingly emphasized skills that would be needed for domestic chores, nursing, and hygiene and information on how to be healthy mothers of robust children. After all, the woman's place was in the home as faithful wife and dutiful mother (see the section on women in this chapter, "Women in the Third Reich").

Since BDM service ended at eighteen and women were required to enter the National Socialist Women's Association at age twenty-one, a new party organization called Faith and Beauty was created in 1938 for young women seventeen to twenty-one years old. Supposedly voluntary, Faith and Beauty included sports, gymnastics, and body care. But it also emphasized female social graces, encouraging dancing and even fashion consciousness. The goal was to create "the ideal of the lovely, beautiful and proud girl" who, when she reached the age of twenty-eight, would take the title *Hohe Frau* (High Woman), which Himmler envisioned as appropriate for the racially pure and physically fit Aryan women he hoped Nazi family policy would create.[8] BDM members and women over the age of eighteen in general were also subject to labor service for six months. Ninety percent of Labor Service girls were employed as farmworkers. They helped both in the fields and in the house. This use of young women gave rise to considerable scandal when some of them returned home pregnant.

EDUCATION

In addition to the special organizations for youth, education in the schools was intended to capture the youth, "the repository of the national future," for the National Socialist state. The ideals were not too exacting: Boys would become efficient soldiers, girls diligent mothers for the sake of Hitler and Germany. Hitler had made no secret of his contempt for the intellectual instruction offered by the schools—a natural result of his own miserable school experience. Consequently, the Führer worked to submit the youth of Germany to strict National Socialist schooling. This goal involved a number of approaches to controlling the schools.

Control of the Schools

Coordination of the teaching profession was undertaken at an early date to ensure political reliability and commitment to National Socialist ideology. Many teachers had been extremely nationalistic and hostile to the Weimar Republic and were already sympathetic to the Nazis. Teachers were, in fact, overrepresented in the party. By 1936, 32 percent of teachers belonged to the Nazi Party, compared with less than 10 percent of the entire population. In 1933, the Nazis purged Communist, Socialist, and Jewish teachers.

The National Socialist Teachers' Association (NSLB), established in 1929, also assumed responsibility for the ideological indoctrination of teachers. In January 1933, the NSLB had 6000 members, but it had increased dramatically to 220,000 by the end of 1933

---

[8]Quoted in Lisa Pine, *Education in Nazi Germany* (New York, 2010), p. 129.

and to 320,000, or 97 percent of all teachers, by 1937. One of its primary duties was the ideological instruction of teachers "in the spirit of National Socialism" in training centers established for that purpose. By 1939, the NSLB had organized forty-one of these centers for 215,000 teachers that supplied special courses on German prehistory, the racial study of history, and folk art. Physical training and field sports were also emphasized in these special camps, which lasted two weeks.

The reorganization and centralization of the school system provided another means for achieving control over education. While education in the Weimar Republic had been in the hands of individual states, the Nazis placed responsibility for the schools in the Reich Ministry of Education under Bernhard Rust. Rust had been dismissed as a teacher in 1930 for molesting a schoolgirl. Neither this activity nor his mental instability resulting from a severe head wound in World War I prevented him from being appointed Reich minister of education by Hitler in 1934. In this position he was responsible for both the public schools and the universities. Rust's office actively reorganized the schools and introduced the leadership principle. Staff decisions were eliminated and the head teacher now served as a real leader.

The Nazi regime exercised further control over the schools by determining the content of the curriculum. In the late 1930s and early 1940s, the regime issued new guidelines and new textbooks based on Hitler's general ideas on education, according to which the "rearing of healthy bodies" was more important than the learning of "pure knowledge." It was in keeping with Hitler's ideas that the new school policies stressed physical education. Physical education was expanded to five hours per week, or 15 percent of school time. In the upper schools boxing became a required subject. Physical education was considered so important that pupils with physical disabilities or consistent records of failure in physical education classes were denied school-leaving certificates and hence barred from higher education. Physical education was intended to instill a corporate spirit, discipline, and bodily vigor.

The main impact of the changes in curriculum was seen in three subjects—German, history, and biology. Instruction in German was intended to inculcate racial ideology or "German awareness" and used literary works stressing the idea of folk, blood and soil, and national and military values, and praise for the Führer. In one reader, for example, the story is told of a young boy named Klaus who is waiting for the Führer's visit to his town:

> Today Klaus' mother does not need to wake him. He springs from bed on his own. Today is an important holiday . . . In the shop windows stand pictures of the Führer . . . The boys climb up trees . . . When a flag-bearer passes, Klaus raises his right arm in salute. All at once, Klaus sees the Führer. He stands in the car and waves in a friendly manner. Heil! Heil! calls Klaus as loud as he can. What a pity, the Führer is already past! But Klaus continually calls: Heil Hitler! Heil Hitler![9]

History classes focused on the Nazi revolution and Hitler's role in it. The whole of history was reinterpreted in the light of racial principles, especially the significance to world history of the Aryan race. Biology, especially important because of Nazi racial doctrine, centered in the laws of heredity and racial breeding and the need for racial purity.

---

[9]Quoted in Gilmer W. Blackburn, *Education in the Third Reich: A Study of Race and History in the Nazi Textbooks* (Albany, 1985), p. 41.

Children learned to measure skulls and to classify racial types accordingly. Biology classes underscored the necessity of cultivating racial health by the correct choice of Aryan spouses and the bearing of large families. To a lesser extent, the subject of geography also lent itself to National Socialist ideology, in the form of geopolitical and racial theories that justified expansion and the need for *Lebensraum* (living space). Foreign languages and mathematics were exempt from ideological reinterpretation because of the need for well-trained technicians, but even they could be used to inculcate militarism. Math problems, for example, focused on numbers of guns, planes, and other military instruments.

The quality of education suffered greatly during the Third Reich. Teachers' energies were overtaxed by extracurricular responsibilities and a noticeable increase in the pupil–teacher ratio. However, the most difficult problem came from the Hitler Youth. Their activities, such as marches and competitive games, were both physically exhausting and stimulating and made settling into a regular school routine difficult. Hitler Youth leaders resented being subordinated to the authority of teachers in school while exercising authority themselves out of school. Because of political pressure, Hitler Youth members were granted leaves of absence to attend Hitler Youth activities. Ultimately, the quality of education was affected. There was a noticeable decline in pupils' performance. Army reports stated that many of the candidates for officers' commissions displayed a "simply inconceivable lack of elementary knowledge." University professors complained about the lack of knowledge and skills of entering students.

Universities

The German university system had a proud tradition and was the model for higher education throughout the world. But German universities were also strongholds of nationalism and had been hostile or indifferent to the democratic Weimar government. The Nazis found it relatively easy to coordinate the university system.

After their accession to power, the Nazis dismissed around 1200 faculty members, or almost 15 percent of the teaching force. These dismissals included primarily Jews and Social Democrats. Among the dismissed were the Göttingen circle of quantum physicists and the theologian Karl Barth. Others resigned and emigrated. Numbers varied from university to university. While 32 percent of the staff was removed from Berlin, only 1.6 percent was dismissed at Tübingen. Some fields were hit harder than others. Eighteen percent of academics in the natural sciences were dismissed, including the physicist Albert Einstein and nineteen other past or future Nobel Prize winners. These dismissals help to explain Germany's loss of preeminence in the field of science. Many academicians strongly supported the new regime. Seven hundred professors signed a declaration of support for Hitler and the National Socialist state in November 1933. At Göttingen, thirty-three professors condemned one of their colleagues as a saboteur of the new Germany for resigning in protest against the regime's anti-Semitism.

The universities were reorganized as well. The traditional system of representatives and self-government was scrapped in favor of absolute leadership by the rector, the head of the university. New rectors were often reliable Nazis. The new rector of the university at Berlin had been an SA member. After nominations by the faculty and recommendations by the rectors, all academic appointments had to be approved by Reich Minister of Education Rust.

All professors were expected to adjust their teaching to National Socialist ideology. All new academics were required to complete a six-week course in Nazi ideology at camps run by the National Socialist Lecturers' Association. For most academics, adjustment to the new reality meant outward conformity to the regime. In some areas this required the introduction of courses in racial studies and eugenics. Other fields, such as biology, medicine, or Germanics, felt the impact of Nazi racial ideas. Anthropology became a favored discipline during the Third Reich as it was seen as exemplifying the study of human racial difference. It therefore could be used to validate and justify Nazi racial policies within Germany and, once the war started, in conquered territories. Some academicians managed, however, to maintain their traditional scholarship as well. Work in theoretical physics continued despite the Nazis' denunciation of modern physics as an instrument of world Jewry and their attempt to develop an "Aryan science."

Some historians were willing to provide historical rationalizations for Nazi ideology. This is especially true of historians who had been right-wing nationalists, antidemocratic and anti-Weimar Republic. The most notable of these historians was Walter Frank, who founded the Institute for the History of the New Germany. This was an attempt to create a "fighting science," a history subordinate to Nazi ideology. Many historians, however, like other German academicians, buried themselves in esoteric research that enabled them to remain apolitical and escape Nazi pressures.

The coordination of faculty was paralleled by the coordination of students. University students had been early supporters of Nazism, which had been especially attractive to them because of its nationalism. Moreover, National Socialism seemed to offer an egalitarianism that was engaging to idealistic students. Undoubtedly students also believed that this avenue would offer them better employment possibilities in the midst of a depression that had noticeably affected them. Already in 1931, about 60 percent of all undergraduates supported the Nazi Student League, a figure almost twice as high as the percentage of support for Nazism among the general public.

Coordination of students meant the creation of a new kind of student. The number of Jewish students was cut to 1.5 percent of the total, which was also the percentage of Jews in the entire population. Students were now required to spend several months in Labor Service and SA camps. Three hours of physical education became mandatory. The Nazis wished to inculcate an ideological orientation that downplayed the role of "pure intellect" and the "powers of critical analysis" and strengthened the ability to "feel" through experience. Students could then gain entrance to the profound truths of Nazism, which were basically grounded in "blood" or "racial instinct." This experience of Nazi truth could come only through comradeship in labor camps, where students would mingle with all classes of the new German national community. Students could then develop real character as true German citizens from this "great practical school." The university student body experienced a decline from 128,000 in 1933 to 58,000 in 1939. By that time, student complaints about the regime seemed to be on the increase.

WOMEN IN THE THIRD REICH

Ideological considerations largely determined the Nazi attitude toward women. Racial preservation meant that women had a crucial role to play as mothers—the bearers of the children who would make the strength of the Aryan race possible. The Nazis viewed the differences between men and women as natural. Men were meant to be warriors and political leaders. Women were designed to be wives and mothers. By observing this clear distinction, each could best perform his or her natural function "to maintain the whole community." Men were productive and creative; women were reproductive and imitative. Men used their intellect, competing and struggling to rule; women used their intuition and sacrificed for the sake of nurturing others. Women should not work, but stay at home. They needed little education beyond domestic science. Their efforts made possible men's ability to act for the nation. To Hitler, men and women must "mutually value and respect each other" since each performs the task that "nature and Providence have ordained."

The Weimar constitution had given women the right to vote. It had also called for the equality of females with males, but laws had never been passed to make that promise a reality. The Civil Code, stemming from the imperial days of the early twentieth century, was still in effect and essentially kept women in subordinate roles. Nazi policy, due to its ideological foundations, opposed the liberal and Socialist demands for female emancipation. But it should be remembered that radical feminism in the 1920s was an extremist view, and various traditional groups, such as the churches, the conservative and Catholic political parties, and the farmers, shared the Nazi position. The Nazi appeal to restrict women to their "natural" occupations was not a new one, and the Nazis won support not in spite of their antifeminist stance but because of it. We might also note that the Nazis were not alone in Europe. The progressive measures for women that they opposed were in fact not yet in effect in many other countries.

Nazi Organizations for Women

Nazi coordination in 1933 and 1934 included the dissolution of virtually all women's organizations, whether political, social, professional, charitable, or religious. The Nazis, of course, had never allowed women to play leadership roles in their party. A separate organization for women had existed, but was always subordinated to the needs of the male leadership of the NSDAP. A new national organization of women's cultural and social groups called the German Women's Bureau was established in 1933 to include all the women's organizations coordinated after the seizure of power.

Gertrud Scholtz-Klink was made head of the German Women's Bureau. She was an ideal choice for the job. She had four children from her first marriage, and with her blond hair and blue eyes, she fit the ideal Aryan image. She accepted the subservience of women to male leadership and at the same time was a strong leader of other women. Scholtz-Klink also headed the National Socialist Women's Association and was rewarded by Hitler with the title of Reich women's leader in November 1934.

Although Scholtz-Klink and other women were given leadership roles in women's organizations, they had absolutely no power and no influence over policy making in the Third Reich, including policies toward women. Indeed, even Scholtz-Klink complained that although she had frequently shared a public stage with Adolf Hitler, she had not once been able to discuss Nazi policy with him. Women were never promoted from women's organizations to other offices.

The German Women's Bureau had enrolled 1.6 million members by 1938. Staff positions within the organization did create employment possibilities for a number of women, although thousands of volunteer workers carried out many of the organization's activities. As one of its major functions, the Women's Bureau created a Reich Mother's Service, which provided both instruction and welfare for mothers. The service established classes in household management, child care, nutrition, housecleaning methods, and sewing. The courses also managed to include a fair dose of Nazi ideology. An average annual rate of 500,000 women attended 30,000 courses throughout Germany.

The Women's Bureau was supposed to influence women as consumers. Its most effective consumer campaign was the weekly "stew meal": all families were urged to consume a "one-pot, one-course" main meal and to donate to Nazi charities the money saved from not having a larger dinner. At a Nuremberg rally, Scholtz-Klink proclaimed that the soup ladle was women's weapon to help the Third Reich. The Women's Bureau was also responsible for charity work. Women, as well as boys and girls, were used as volunteers to collect money for relief funds. The biggest of these funds was the Winter Relief program for poor families in the cold winter season. By collecting money door to door, women financed a welfare program that helped almost 20 percent of the population annually. Only 2 percent of the money collected went to overhead—a direct result of the use of volunteers.

Whereas the Women's Bureau was a mass organization, the National Socialist Women's Association (NSF) was meant to be an elite group. Created in 1931, it originally served as a campaigning organization, but after the seizure of power its function was to direct the affairs of German women—under party control, of course. By 1938, with a membership of 2 million, it had lost its elite status and become a mass organization. The main function of the NSF was the "cultural, spiritual, and political education of German women." Consequently, the female leaders of the organization were indoctrinated in Nazi ideas of race, nationalism, and the need for large families. The NSF maintained control over the activities of the German Women's Bureau.

Employment

Women had been employed in ever larger numbers in Weimar Germany and were especially visible in white-collar jobs such as clerks, typists, and shop assistants, of whom they made up one-third of the total. Women were also employed in industries, especially textiles and clothing and food and drink. It has been estimated that 11.5 million women were employed in 1925, or 35 percent of the German labor force. However, that figure included assistants on farms or in family businesses. Women were paid considerably less than males. Skilled women earned 63 percent of a skilled man's wage, unskilled women only 52 percent of an unskilled laborer's wage. During the Great Depression, a variety of people began to complain that women were keeping men out of work. The "double earners," married women who worked in addition to their husbands, were especially attacked. The Nazis joined this rising chorus of criticism.

To the Nazis, men were the guardians and providers of home and family. Employment of males should take priority over that of females. The Nazis did not intend to drive women completely from the labor market. They wanted married women to pursue their families and even to have more children. Single women could work, but in appropriate jobs such as social work, nursing, primary school teaching, and welfare services. The Nazis wanted to take women out of heavy industry and other jobs that might prevent them from bearing healthy children. The regime promoted the employment of women in farm work and domestic service to provide cheap labor in these areas, even though they were unpopular with German working women.

After seizing power, the Nazis began to implement their ideas on the employment of females. On June 1, 1933, the regime issued its Law for the Reduction of Unemployment, which created a marriage loan scheme providing loans to newly married couples if the bride-to-be gave up her job before marriage (see p. 174). The major emphasis of the law was to encourage married women to give up work. Women were banned from heavy work in such places as mines and foundries. The regime also pushed its campaign against work-ing women with slogans on posters: "Get a hold of pots and pans and broom and you'll sooner find a groom!" "Not for you the business life; rather learn to be a wife!" Although Nazi policies seemed successful, since the percentage of employed women declined, in absolute terms this was not really the case. The actual number of women employed rose by 300,000 because of the increasing number of jobs. Nevertheless, most new jobs created from 1933 to 1936 went to men.

By 1936 and 1937, however, the Nazi regime made a major turnaround on female employment. The rearmament boom and the introduction of the compulsory Labor Service and the draft for males were producing a labor shortage. By 1937, the government was trying to persuade as many women as possible to work, especially in areas previously dominated by males. Hence, women now appeared in transport jobs such as ticket collec-tors and even streetcar conductresses. The need for married women to work as a service to the nation was increasingly emphasized. In 1937, the requirement that a woman give up her job to receive a marriage loan was dropped. Women seemed, however, to resist the regime's wish for more female employment. More women actually followed the gov-ernment's earlier advice to get married and have children. Low wages and poor working conditions undoubtedly discouraged some women from working. Middle-class women, in particular, refused to work once they were married.

Although the number of women employed rose from 11.5 million in 1933 to 12.7 million in May 1939, the increases were not sufficient for the needs of the German economy. Nevertheless, the Nazis seemed reluctant to force women, especially married women, to work. Compulsion was attempted, though, for one group of females. The Labor Service, in which all young Germans had to work for six months, had not been required for females. In its need for labor, however, the government announced in 1938 that it reserved the right to make all unmarried women under age twenty-five work for a year in agriculture or domestic service. Numerous exemptions were made and various techniques found to circumvent the law, so that shortages continued in agriculture and domestic service. Consequently, when war began in September 1939, the Labor Service for girls was made compulsory.

Once the war started, an attempt was made to push women into men's jobs, especially in munitions. But long hours, low pay, and hard work led to a decline in pro-ductivity by women and a noticeable lack of female volunteers. Since women who were married to soldiers were given an allowance, they had less incentive to work. Although the regime had created a law in 1938 for labor conscription in the event of a war, it did not implement it. Hitler refused to allow the conscription of married women in 1940 and 1941, apparently still hoping it would not be necessary. In fact, compulsory women's labor would not be introduced until 1943, and by that time it was too late to meet Germany's needs.

Education

In the Weimar period, new opportunities had opened up for young women in higher schooling and universities. The Nazis denounced this development, believing that females were not prepared for the masculine elements of education. After all, according to the Nazis, men were intellectual but women were emotional and fit primarily for their "natural" calling of being wives and mothers. The Nazis advocated giving all girls, even those in school, a better grounding in domestic service.

A school reform instituted in 1938 stressed that girls should be trained for different things because of the "natural difference between the sexes." Consequently, girls' secondary schooling differed somewhat from boys', with emphasis on needlework and homecraft at the expense of Latin and science. Despite its rhetoric, however, the regime allowed girls to pursue secondary education because of the need for trained people. In the 1930s, the percentage of girls in secondary schools dropped only slightly from 37 percent to 34.5 percent.

The Nazis did attempt to restrict female attendance at universities. When quotas were established in December 1933 on the number of new students that could be admitted into universities, an additional restriction was placed on women's numbers. Indeed new female students could not exceed 10 percent of the quota for each German federal state. But the quota system was not followed strictly. There was a noticeable drop in the proportion of female students from 16.7 percent in 1933 to 12.5 percent in 1934, but already by 1935 it had risen to 17 percent. As more males entered the military, the need for technically trained university graduates led the Nazis to officially encourage females to pursue a university education. The percentage of female students rose to 20 percent in 1939 and even 30 percent in 1940.

Women as Professionals

After World War I women had been admitted in increasing numbers into the professions. By 1930 they constituted 5.6 percent of the doctors, 25 percent of the elementary teachers, 50 percent of the middle school teachers, but only 0.6 percent of the university lecturers. There were few female lawyers, and they remained at the lower levels of the legal profession. Believers in the tradition of male dominance continued to resist the presence of women in the professions, especially married women. Already in the Brüning years, in the midst of economic crisis, legislation had been passed to retire married women from positions in the civil service.

The Nazis continued the policy of dismissing women from the civil service and teaching positions, although oftentimes for political reasons. All professional organizations were coordinated or dissolved by the regime, and separate Nazi organizations for teachers, doctors, university lecturers, lawyers, and civil service personnel were established. These professional organizations established women's sections. Women could serve in leadership positions only in their own sections, not in the whole organization. Although the Nazis believed that the best professional occupations for women were those that had direct practical applications, such as social work and nursing, they did not stop women from pursuing all the professions. In some professions, the percentage of women actually increased. For example, women doctors increased from 5.6 percent in 1930 to 7.6 percent in 1939. There was also a slight increase in teachers. But less favorable conditions existed in universities and especially in the legal profession. Women were largely excluded from the practice of law after Hitler decided in 1936 that they could not become lawyers or judges. As in industry, however, the Nazis' need for professionals led them to actually appeal for female recruits—another pragmatic reversal of Nazi policy.

In general, Nazi policy toward women emphasized their role as mothers and wives. Although the Nazis remained ideologically committed to that ideal, the practical economic consequences of rearmament led them to increase the number of women in the marketplace. The war, of course, further necessitated the contribution of women. The Nazis would almost certainly have insisted on returning women to their "natural" occupations if they had won the war. It would appear that most women in Nazi Germany were not unhappy with the regime's emphasis on female domesticity. Certainly the status of mother and housewife was elevated by the Nazis, and German women could rest assured that they were following honorable paths in filling these roles. At the same time, economic needs by 1936 and especially with the war meant that women still had numerous opportunities for employment and advanced education. Of course, those opportunities were intended not to improve the position of women individually, but only to serve the temporary needs of the Nazi regime. The same could be said for women's gains in health and welfare. The regime showed considerable concern for the health and welfare of women, which helps to account for women's acceptance of the regime. As we shall see, however, this concern derived primarily from the Nazis' racial policy and their desire to ensure that healthy women would have healthy children.

FAMILY AND POPULATION POLICY

The Nazis had emphasized that marriage and motherhood should constitute women's highest ideals. The institution of marriage served one primary purpose—the production of offspring. Children were to be produced not simply for the satisfaction of mothers and fathers but to maintain the race and the nation. Parents, then, were seen by Nazi ideologists as agents of the state, and it was their duty to raise children under the supervision of the state to become "hard-working national comrades."

There were two aspects to this central Nazi concern with the production of children. Some Nazis, especially the strict ideologists, Walter Darré and Heinrich Himmler, and in part Hitler himself, were interested in breeding a pure Germanic race. But the Nazis confronted a problem of quantity as well. When they came to power, the Nazis were faced with the basic fact that European states had experienced falling birthrates in the 1920s with Germany sustaining the most acute decline of them all. Undoubtedly, depressed economic conditions and the availability of contraception, which enabled parents to have fewer children and thereby raise their standard of living, had been the major causes. Hence, compared with 2,000,000 live births in 1900, the Germans had 1,300,000 in 1925 and only 971,000 in 1933. The Nazis were determined to undo these trends, for Hitler's ultimate goals of expansion and acquisition of *Lebensraum* required a large population.

Increasing Population Growth

The Nazis pursued a variety of policies to combat the falling birthrate and foster population growth. Financial incentives for having more children were begun in June 1933, when the Nazis introduced a rather original plan for marriage loans. Interest-free loans of 1000 Reichsmarks (150 Reichsmarks was the average industrial monthly wage) were granted to newly married couples providing that the bride agreed to give up her job at marriage. In addition, for every child born to the couple, 250 Reichsmarks of the loan were remitted. If the couple produced four children, the loan was essentially canceled. The demand for the loans became so heavy that the loan was eventually cut to 500 RM and the remittance for each child to 125 RM. The marriage loan scheme was a questionable success. The number of marriages rose, but there was no dramatic increase in the number of children per family. Many families perceived that it was cheaper in the long run to pay back the rest of the loan after having two children.

The government attempted to provide various forms of material relief for mothers. The Mother and Child auxiliary service of the National Socialist Public Welfare Organization assisted mothers in 25,000 advice centers throughout Germany, providing food subsidies, housing for single mothers, and domestic help for large families. Since housemaids were in short supply, the regime instituted a Domestic Service Year for girls beginning in 1934, which became obligatory in 1938. This attempt to use teenage girls as unpaid help for large families was resisted and was largely unsuccessful.

The Nazis instituted a propaganda campaign to exalt the status of mothers and housewives. As part of this campaign, Hitler instituted the German Mother's Cross in 1938. Mothers with four children received a bronze cross, those with six a silver cross, and those with eight or more a gold cross. The Mother's Cross was portrayed as a distinction of the highest order. Although many Nazi leaders seldom practiced their own preaching, Martin Bormann's wife, Gerda, excelled with ten children. These crosses were awarded in an annual ceremony on August 12, which was Hitler's mother's birthday. The elaborate cross bore the inscription "The child ennobles the mother."

In the Third Reich the concern for the propagation of children led to a rejection of abortion except where one of the parents was of impure blood. Birth control clinics were closed and harsh penalties initiated for those performing abortions. But the regime did not succeed in eliminating abortion, especially during the war, when normal sex mores broke down entirely.

The population policies of the Third Reich, which sought to increase the number of "pure Germans," appear to have been successful. Live births increased to 1.2 million in 1934, 1.35 million in 1938, and 1.4 million in 1939. However, they never achieved the pre–World War I level of 2 million. In any event, economic recovery may have played just as significant a role as Nazi population policies in producing this increase in babies.

Toward a Pure Aryan Race

The Nazi desire to create an Aryan racial state had two effects on population policy: the need to expand the number of pure Aryans, as we have seen, and the need to eliminate inferior human stock. Hitler believed that society could improve its racial stock through sound racial hygiene. The Nazi regime had the support of a number of German doctors who had become believers in racial hygiene. They argued that the increase in the number of weak and insane people threatened the future of the German people.

The new Nazi racial policy began in July 1933 with a law for the prevention of hereditarily diseased offspring. This legislation made possible the sterilization of persons suffering from incurable hereditary problems such as schizophrenia, manic-depressive psychosis, epilepsy, and blindness. Chronic alcoholism was also viewed as grounds for sterilization. Health courts, staffed by doctors, singled out those to be treated. Between 1933 and 1939, 400,000 people were sterilized. A 1935 law prohibited marriage for those with serious infectious diseases or hereditary illnesses. The Nuremberg racial laws of 1935 sought to eliminate sexual relations between Germans and Jews for the same reasons of racial health and purity (see Chapter 9).

But Nazi population policy, aimed at the creation of a pure Aryan race, went beyond sterilization and prohibition of certain marriages. The regime portrayed the mentally ill and physically deformed as both a threat to racial purity and an unwanted expense as "useless eaters." Even school math problems were used to instill this latter point of view in children. One text contained this problem: "The construction of a lunatic asylum costs

6 million RM (Reichsmark). How many houses at 15,000 RM each could have been built for that amount?" In 1939, Hitler authorized a euthanasia program. The first phase of the program, initiated in the spring, focused on the killing of mentally deficient and physically deformed infants. Probably 6000 "racially valueless" children died as a result. One pediatrician who participated in the program later remarked, "I had the feeling that my activity was something positive, and that I had made a small contribution to human progress."[10]

A second phase of the euthanasia program began in the fall of 1939 with Hitler officially authorizing the head of his chancellery, Philipp Bouhler, to proceed with the "mercy" killing of the "incurably sick." This operation, known in code as the T-4 program (after Tiergarten Strasse 4, Berlin, the street address of the villa where the department of the Reich Chancellery was located), was considerably more complex than the killing of the children. Organizations were established for choosing and transporting the victims to six "euthanasia" installations, where they were gassed in rooms camouflaged as shower chambers. The bodies were then cremated. It has been estimated that close to 100,000 people were killed in this fashion. Christian Worth, the leader of one killing center at Hartheim, explained what was happening to his workers:

> Comrades, I've called you together here today in order to inform you about the present position in the castle and what is going to happen from now on. I have been assigned the task of running the castle from now on by the Reich Chancellery. As the boss I am in charge of everything. We must build a crematorium here, in order to burn mental patients from Austria. Five doctors have been chosen who will examine the patients to establish what can or cannot be saved. What can't be saved goes into the crematorium and will be burned. Mental patients are a burden upon Germany and we only want healthy people. Mental patients are a burden upon the State. Certain men will be chosen to work in the crematorium. Above all else, the motto is silence or the death penalty. Whosoever fails to observe this silence will end up in a concentration camp or be shot.[11]

As a result of growing public protest, including an especially powerful sermon by Catholic bishop Galen of Münster denouncing the entire euthanasia program, Hitler suspended the T-4 program in the fall of 1941. Many of the personnel from this program came from the SS and were eventually used in the killing operations of the Holocaust.

SEX AND MORALS

One of the features of the Nazi attack on the Weimar Republic was the condemnation of its sexual freedom. The Nazis viewed the Weimar era as a degenerate age in which all that was good and beautiful in the German heritage had been scorned and perverted. Hitler blamed the Weimar system of government for the cultural disintegration and moral decay of Germany. Theater, art, literature, cinema, and press would all have to be purified and used in the service of a new moral idea. As early as February 23, 1933, the Nazis had managed to ban all pornographic literature. One could hardly argue, however, that the Nazis themselves offered any new morality. Their own ideas of morality were based on their nationalist

[10]Quoted in Michael Burleigh, *Death and Deliverance: Euthanasia in Germany 1900–1945* (Cambridge, 1994), p. 100.
[11]Ibid., pp. 126–127.

and racial conceptions as well as on the moral precepts of a preindustrial, agrarian society. Hitler and the Nazis, as in so many areas of life, offered conflicting attitudes toward sex and morality. Official sex education promoted strict rules calling for self-control. Contemporary publications portrayed sex as the means of procreation, not personal enjoyment. And yet numerous Nazis, including Hitler, scornfully rejected the old "bourgeois morality" and castigated it as "prudish hypocrisy." Hitler encouraged "wholesome delight in existence" and argued that one must not attempt to restrain robust males, especially in wartime. Certainly Hitler himself had never let others' sexual patterns affect his use of those individuals. The most prominent example was, of course, his continuing support of Ernst Röhm as head of the SA despite revelations about the latter's homosexuality. Other Nazi leaders, such as Bormann and Goebbels, never allowed official Nazi views on the "mutual ties of loyalty, love and respect" in marriage to keep them from participating in numerous sexual affairs. Nor did the definition of marriage as a "lasting, life-long union" prevent Nazi leaders from divorcing their faithful wives from the earlier period of struggle and replacing them with new wives, frequently young blonds with a taste for luxury.

The Attack on Homosexuality

One of the crimes of the Third Reich was degeneracy. Although never legally defined and always vaguely worded, degeneracy was viewed as being contrary to "wholesome popular sentiment" and as infringing upon National Socialist values. Degeneracy produced crime, an especially important problem since the degenerate supposedly lacked "racial sensitivity" and hence harmed the national community instead of fulfilling his duty. The Nazis believed that according to "wholesome popular sentiment," moral purity could be achieved by harsh measures and drastic penalties, especially in the area of sexual offenses that were considered deviant. Nowhere is this more evident than in the Nazi drive against homosexuality.

Nazi ideologists saw homosexuality as a product of degenerate individuals, especially those tainted with Jewish blood. In keeping with their ideological fantasies about peasant nobility and purity of blood, they viewed rural villages as "unacquainted with such problems." This belief caused the Nazis untold grief and perplexity when cases of homosexuality did occur in these villages. Homosexuals were singled out by the Nazis as particularly destructive toward the racial community, for they failed to help preserve the race by having children. Homosexuality was thus seen as a political problem, especially by the SS. Male homosexuals were singled out for attack; at least lesbians could still bear children and thus fulfill their basic mission.

After the murder of Ernst Röhm in 1934 and the crushing of the SA, Hitler's tolerance of homosexuality quickly dissipated and he began to attack it instead. His statements focused on two major reasons. First, he feared that homosexuals in positions of leadership would undermine the ability of a government to rule effectively. Second, although homosexuality would also curb population growth, Hitler was especially concerned that its spread to the finest leaders of a community would prevent reproduction of the best people.

Heinrich Himmler, leader of the SS, used similar arguments. The SS journal *Das Schwarze Korps* (The Black Korps) emphasized that homosexuals could be rehabilitated in concentration camps and made into healthy German males by hard labor. Himmler, however, contemplated more severe measures. He viewed homosexuality as a "national plague" and stated: "For hundreds of years the Teutonic peoples and in particular the

German people have been ruled by men. But as a result of homosexuality this male state is in the process of destroying itself."[12] Therefore he felt that homosexuals should be "entirely eliminated" and even recalled the ancient Germanic practice of drowning homosexuals in bogs. He did not revive the practice, but by 1934 the Gestapo had begun to make lists of persons known to have engaged in homosexual activity. Homosexuals were sent to concentration camps, where they were forced to wear pink triangles as a sign of their "crime." They were often sadistically punished.

Himmler was especially anxious to eliminate homosexuality from the SS. Official policy was to expel members involved in homosexual activity; unofficially, they served a prison sentence, whereupon Himmler ordered that they be sent to a concentration camp and be shot while "attempting to escape." In 1941, official policy was stiffened so that SS or police members were executed for homosexual activity. Regular courts handed down the milder sentence of castration, but by 1942 they were also giving out death sentences in supposedly serious cases.

Prostitution in the Third Reich

Nazi rhetoric condemned prostitution by emphasizing the dangers of venereal disease and prostitution's lack of productive value for the national community. Although the regime threatened to send prostitutes to concentration camps, and whereas pimps were sent to the camps as antisocial parasites, in practice the prostitutes continued to ply their trade. Heinrich Himmler, the grand inquisitor of the Nazi movement, thought it was worthwhile to be broadminded, if only to keep frustrated males from sinking into homosexuality. Accordingly, prostitution was incorporated into the Nazi system and even used at times for double purposes. The most famous whorehouse in Berlin, the Salon Kitty, was really the brainchild of Reinhard Heydrich, the head of the SD. Microphones planted in the numerous bedrooms of the Salon enabled the SD to gather information from party bigwigs as well as government guests from abroad, who were encouraged to frequent the brothel.

Basically, the Nazi regime moved from official condemnation of prostitution to toleration and finally systematic organization of it, especially in wartime to serve sex-starved soldiers. By 1940, medically supervised whorehouses had been established throughout Germany. Freelance prostitution remained forbidden, however, and could result in a trip to the concentration camp.

Illegitimacy

Blatant contradictions were a regular feature of many Nazi practices. While posing as saviors of the German family, the Nazis did not feel themselves limited by Christian values, especially in regard to sexual morality. The desire to increase the German population overrode any moral concerns. Hitler, followed by other Nazi leaders, condemned the bourgeois hypocrisy that permitted pre- and extramarital intercourse by men but spurned the women involved in such unions and the illegitimate children they produced. Nazi ideology emphasized that hereditarily fit German children were crucial to the *Volksgemeinschaft* and that illegitimate children and their mothers needed support, not scorn. The Mother and

---

[12]Quoted in Peter Longerich, *Himmler* (New York, 2012), p. 233.

Child auxiliary service of the National Socialist Public Welfare Organization took responsibility for providing this support for unwed mothers and their children.

Prominent Nazis made official statements encouraging promiscuity in the cause of producing offspring. On October 28, 1939, Heinrich Himmler issued an order to the SS and the police in which he encouraged SS men to think of posterity and produce more babies, either legitimate or illegitimate. Both kinds of children would be provided for in the event of their fathers' deaths. Himmler also established the *Lebensborn* homes for mothers, both wed and unwed. Himmler's official encouragement of illegitimacy hardly produced a boom in pre- or extramarital sex that affected the birthrate. Of 12,081 children fathered by SS officers, only 1 percent were illegitimate.

Himmler's order had been addressed only to the SS and the police. Considerably more publicity was given to a letter published in the party newspaper, the *Völkischer Beobachter*, on Christmas Day 1939 and signed by the Führer's deputy, Rudolf Hess. Addressed to an unmarried mother whose lover had been killed in the war, the letter indicated that she would be given a widow's pension, as if she were married, and the official birth certificate would designate the father's name as "war-father." Hess emphasized that the highest duty of any German woman to her community was to add to the life of the nation by giving birth to "racially healthy children." This letter was officially denied, since it gave rise to the belief that the Nazis were encouraging illegitimate children. Nevertheless, Nazi leaders continued to do precisely that. One senior party official told an audience of underage League of German Girls members that they would not all be able to get husbands because of the war, but that they could "all be mothers." Gauleiter Geisler told a gathering of female students at the University of Munich that they should not stay at the university during the war but instead "present the Führer with a child." Nazi long-range plans called for even more drastic measures after the war. Himmler mentioned the need for new marriage laws that would force all German women to have children, and both Hitler and Himmler talked about legalizing bigamy, although Hitler felt that initially the latter should be reserved for war heroes. Figures indicate, however, that Nazi leaders were no more successful than Himmler in the SS in producing large numbers of illegitimate "pure Aryans."

Nazi cultural and social policies had been designed to enhance the growth of a unified national community, but not to create personal happiness. "The day of personal happiness is over," Hitler had proclaimed. If the 1000-year Reich had taken a genuine interest in the happiness of its *Volksgemeinschaft* members, then it might have lasted longer than twelve years. The real purpose of organizing the national community was to prepare for war and the ultimate foreign policy objectives of Hitler's Nazi movement. It is time now to examine Hitler's war, the world it tried to create, and the one it destroyed in the process.

SUGGESTIONS FOR FURTHER READING

A good collection of primary sources on Nazi culture can be found in George L. Mosse, *Nazi Culture* (New York, 1966). An overview of Nazi culture can be found in Jonathan Huener and Francis R. Nicosia, eds., *The Arts in Nazi Germany: Continuity, Conformity, and Change* (New York, 2006). On literature, see James M. Ritchie, *German Literature Under National Socialism* (Totowa, N.J., 1983); Karl-Heinz Schoeps, *Literature and Film in the Third Reich* (Rochester, N.Y., 2004); Jay W. Baird, *Hitler's War Poets: Literature and Politics in the Third Reich* (New York, 2008); and Christa Kamenetsky, *Children's Literature in Hitler's Germany: The Culture Policy of National Socialism* (Athens, Ohio, 1984). On the "inner emigration" of writers who chose to stay in

Nazi Germany, see Neil H. Donahue and Doris Kirchner, eds., *Flight of Fantasy: New Perspectives on Inner Emigration in German Literature, 1933–1945* (New York, 2003). For a well-illustrated survey of the arts in Nazi Germany, see Peter Adam, *Art of the Third Reich* (New York, 1992). On the Nazi coordination of the arts, see Richard A. Etlin, *Art, Culture, and Media under the Nazis* (Chicago, 2002); and Alan Steinwels, *Art, Ideology, and Economics in Nazi Germany: The Reich Chamber of Music, Theater, and the Visual Arts* (Chapel Hill, N.C., 1993). The basic survey of painting in Nazi Germany is Berthold Hinz, *Art in the Third Reich*, trans. Robert and Rita Kimber (New York, 1979). See also Henry Grosshans, *Hitler and the Artists* (New York, 1983). On excluded artists, see Stephanie Barron and Peter W. Guenther, eds., *Degenerate Art: The Fate of the Avant-Garde in Nazi Germany* (New York, 1991). On the importance of the arts to Hitler, see Frederick Spotts, *Hitler and the Power of Aesthetics* (New York, 2003); and Ines Schlenker, *Hitler's Salon: The Grosse Deutsche Kunstausstellung at the Haus der Deutschen Kunst in Munich, 1937–1944* (Oxford, 2007). A study that puts Nazi architecture into a broader perspective is Barbara M. Lane, *Architecture and Politics in Germany, 1918–1945* (Cambridge, Mass., 1968). Robert R. Taylor, *The Word in Stone* (Berkeley, Calif., 1974), discusses the importance of architecture in National Socialist ideology. The classical monumentality of Nazi architecture is considered in Alexander Scobie, *Hitler's State Architecture: The Impact of Classical Antiquity* (University Park, Penn., 1990). On the connections of Nazi architectural planning and the goal of world conquest, see Jochen Thies, *Hitler's Plans for Global Domination: Nazi Architecture and Ultimate War Aims* (New York, 2012). On the use of forced labor in the realization of Nazi architectural visions, see Paul B. Jaskot, *The Architecture of Oppression: The SS, Forced Labor and the Nazi Monumental Building Economy* (New York, 2000). The political significance of art is examined in Jonathan Petropolous, *Art as Politics in the Third Reich* (Chapel Hill, N.C., 1996); Eric Michaud and Janet Lloyd, eds., *The Cult of Art in Nazi Germany* (Stanford, Calif., 2004); and Glenn R. Cuomo, *National Socialist Cultural Policy* (New York, 1995). On key figures in the art world of Nazi Germany, see Jonathan Petropoulos, *The Faustian Bargain: The Art World in Nazi Germany* (New York, 2000).

On cinema, see David S. Hull, *Film in the Third Reich* (Berkeley, Calif., 1969); Susan Tegel, *Nazis and the Cinema* (New York, 2007); Linda Schulte-Sasse, *Entertaining the Third Reich: Illusions of Wholeness in Nazi Cinema* (Durham, N.C., 1996); Mary-Elizabeth O'Brien, *Nazi Cinema as Enchantment: The Politics of Entertainment in the Third Reich* (Rochester, N.Y., 2004); Erica Carter, *Dietrich's Ghosts: The Sublime and the Beautiful in the Third Reich Film* (London, 2004); Eric Rentschler, *The Ministry of Illuson: Nazi Cinema and Its Afterlife* (Cambridge, Mass., 1996); and the essays in Robert C. Reimer, ed., *Cultural History through a National Socialist Lens: Essays on the Cinema of the Third Reich* (Rochester, N.Y., 2000). On women and Nazi films, see Antje Ascheid, *Hitler's Heroines: Stardom and Womanhood in Nazi Cinema* (Philadelphia, 2003); and Jana Francesca Bruns, *Nazi Cinema's New Women* (New York, 2009). Still fascinating is the classic work by Siegfried Kracauer, *From Caligari to Hitler*, rev. ed. (Princeton, N.J., 1974). On Nazi film propaganda, see David Welch, *Propaganda and the German Cinema* (New York, 1985); Richard Barsam, *Filmguide to Triumph of the Will* (Bloomington, Ind., 1975); Rolf Giesen, *Nazi Propaganda Films: A History and Filmography* (Jefferson, N.C., 2003); and Hilmar Hoffmann, *The Triumph of Propaganda: Film and National Socialism, 1933–1945* (Providence, R.I., 1996).

On music during the Third Reich, see Karen Painter, *Symphonic Aspirations: German Music and Politics, 1900–1945* (Cambridge, Mass., 2007); Brian Currid, *A National Acoustics: Music and Mass Publicity in Weimar and Nazi Germany* (Minneapolis, Minn., 2006); Pamela M. Potter, *Most German of Arts: Musicology and Society from the Weimar Republic to the End of Hitler's Reich* (New Haven, Conn., 1998); Erik Levi, *Music in the Third Reich* (New York,

1994) and *Mozart and the Nazis: How the Third Reich Abused a Cultural Icon* (New Haven, Conn., 2010); Michael Meyer, *The Politics of Music in the Third Reich* (New York, 1991); Michael H. Kater, *The Twisted Muse: Musicians and Their Music in the Third Reich* (New York, 1997); and Michael H. Kater and Albrecht Riethmüller, eds., *Music and Nazism: Art under Tyranny, 1933–1945* (Laaber, 2003). On jazz, see Michael H. Kater, *Different Drummers: Jazz in the Culture of Nazi Germany* (New York, 1992). On Jewish responses to cultural exclusion, see Lily E. Hirsch, *A Jewish Orchestra in Nazi Germany: Musical Politics and the Berlin Jewish Cultural League* (New Haven, Conn., 2010).

On sports and the Nazi cult of the body, see Hans Bonde, *Niels Bukh and Male Aesthetics* (Copenhagen, 2006). On the 1936 Berlin Olympics, see Richard Mandell, *The Nazi Olympics* (London, 1971); Christopher Hilton, *Hitler's Olympics* (Stroud, 2006); Guy Walters, *Berlin Games* (London, 2006); and David C. Large, *Nazi Games* (New York, 2007). On the international response to the Berlin Olympics, see Arnd Krüger and William Murray, eds., *The Nazi Olympics: Sport, Politics and Appeasement* (Urbana, Ill., 2003). The fundamental study of the press is Oron J. Hale, *The Captive Press in the Third Reich* (Princeton, N.J., 1964), but see also Modriss Eksteins, *The Limits of Reason: The German Democratic Press and the Collapse of Weimar Democracy* (London, 1975); as well as Stephenie L. Mayer, ed., *Signal*, 2 vols. (London, 1978, 1979), for examples of Nazi illustrated magazines; and see Detlef Mühlberger, *Hitler's Voice: The Völkischer Beobachter, 1920–1933*, 2 vols. (New York, 2004), which contains numerous excerpts from the official Nazi party newspaper.

Two general social histories of the Third Reich: Richard Grunberger, *A Social History of the Third Reich* (London, 1971); and Frederic V. Grunfeld, *The Hitler File: A Social History of Germany and the Nazis, 1918–1945* (London, 1974). Both tend to be very impressionistic. A thoughtful analysis is provided in Pierre Ayçoberry, *The Social History of the Third Reich*, trans. Janet Lloyd (New York, 1999); and Detlef Mühlberger, *Hitler's Followers: Studies in the Sociology of the Nazi Movement* (New York, 1991). See also the collection of articles in David F. Crew, ed., *Nazism and German Society, 1933–1945* (New York, 1994). An insightful book about the responses of ordinary Germans to the Third Reich is Detlev Peukert, *Inside Nazi Germany: Conformity, Opposition, and Racism in Everyday Life*, trans. Richard Deveson (New Haven, Conn., 1987). Also valuable are Richard Bessel, ed., *Life in the Third Reich* (Oxford, 1987); Bernt Engelmann, *In Hitler's Germany, Daily Life in the Third Reich*, trans. Krishna Winston (New York, 1986); and Peter Fritzsche, *Life and Death in the Third Reich* (Cambridge, Mass., 2008), which emphasizes the importance of the notion of building a "national community" in attracting most Germans to Nazism, yet at the same time necessarily excluding other Germans. In this regard, see also Lisa Pine, *Hitler's National Community: Society and Culture in Nazi Germany* (London, 2007); Thomas Kühne, *Belonging and Genocide: Hitler's Community, 1918–1945* (New Haven, Conn., 2010); and Michael Wildt, *Hitler's Volksgemeinschaft and the Dynamics of Racial Exclusion: Violence Against Jews in Provincial Germany, 1919–1939* (New York, 2012). For more on those who were not accepted within this community, see the essays in Robert Gellately and Nathan Stoltzfus, eds., *Social Outsiders in Nazi Germany* (Princeton, N.J., 2001). On women, see Jill Stephenson, *Women in Nazi Society* (London, 1975) and *Women in Nazi Germany* (London, 2001); Matthew Stibbe, *Women in the Third Reich* (New York, 2003); Michelle Moulton, *From Nurturing the Nation to Purifying the Volk: Weimar and Nazi Family Policy, 1918–1945* (Cambridge, Mass., 2007); Claudia Koonz, *Mothers in the Fatherland: Women, the Family and Nazi Politics* (New York, Conn., 1987); and the oral history by Alison Owings, *Frauen: German Women Recall the Third Reich* (New Brunswick, N.J., 1993). Various aspects of youth in Nazi Germany are discussed in H. W. Koch, *The Hitler Youth* (New York, 1976); Brenda Lewis, *Hitler Youth* (Osceola, Wisc., 2000); Peter Stachura, *Nazi Youth in the*

Weimar Republic (Santa Barbara, Calif., 1975); Gerhard Rempel, *Hitler's Children. The Hitler Youth and the SS* (Chapel Hill, N.C., 1989); Lawrence Walker, *Hitler Youth and Catholic Youth, 1933–1936: A Study in Totalitarian Conquest* (Washington, D.C., 1970); Michael H. Kater, *Hitler Youth* (Cambridge, Mass., 2004); and Alan Dearn and Elizabeth Sharp, *The Hitler Youth, 1933–1945* (New York, 2006). On the BDM, see Dagmar Reese, *Growing Up Female in Nazi Germany*, trans. William Templer (Ann Arbor, Mich., 2006). A pictorial history of the Hitler Youth is Jean-Denis Lepage, *Hitler Youth, 1922–1945: An Illustrated History* (Jefferson, N.C., 2009). Also interesting is a Nazi handbook for educating Hitler Youth, edited by Fritz Brennecke, *The Nazi Primer* (New York, 1938). For a fascinating account by a Hitler Youth member, see Alfons Heck, *A Child of Hitler: Germany in the Days When God Wore a Swastika* (Frederick, Colo., 1985). On education, see Lisa Pine, *Education in Nazi Germany* (New York, 2010). Gilmer W. Blackburn, *Education in the Third Reich* (Albany, N.Y., 1985), examines how Nazi textbooks viewed race and history, while Gregory P. Wegner, *Anti-Semitism and Schooling under the Third Reich* (New York, 2002), extends this discussion, showing how Nazi racial anti-Semitism and eugenics theories became established parts of German primary education. On the impact of Nazism on academic disciplines, see Wolfgang Bialas and Anson Rabinbach, eds., *Nazi Germany and the Humanities* (Oxford, 2007); Gretchen E. Schafft, *From Racism to Genocide: Anthropology in the Third Reich* (Urbana, Ill., 2007). Steven P. Remy, *The Heidelberg Myth: The Nazification and Denazification of a German University* (Cambridge, Mass., 2002); Kristie Macrakis, *Surviving the Swastika: Scientific Research in Nazi Germany* (New York, 1993); Alan Beyerchen, *Scientists Under Hitler: Politics and the Physics Community in the Third Reich* (New Haven, Conn., 1977); Margit Szöllösi-Janze, *Science in the Third Reich* (New York, 2001); John Cornwell, *Hitler's Scientists* (New York, 2003); Ute Deichmann, *Biologists Under Hitler*, trans. Thomas Dunlap (Cambridge, Mass., 1996); Robert Proctor, *Racial Hygiene: Medicine Under the Nazis* (Cambridge, Mass., 1988); Götz Aly, Peter Chroust, and Christian Pross, *Cleansing the Fatherland: Nazi Medicine and Racial Hygiene* (Baltimore, Mass., 1994); Michael Kater, *Doctors Under Hitler* (Chapel Hill, N.C., 1989); Geoffrey Cocks, *Psychotherapy in the Third Reich* (New York, 1985); and Stephen Frosh, *Hate and the 'Jewish Science': Antisemitism, Nazism and Psychoanalysis* (New York, 2005). On the attempt to create an interdisciplinary field of Jewish Studies and thereby give academic legitimization to Nazi racial policies, see Alan E. Steinweis, *Studying the Jew: Scholarly Antisemitism in Nazi Germany* (Cambridge, Mass., 2006). On university students, see Michael Steinberg, *Sabers and Brown Shirts: The German Students' Path to National Socialism, 1918–1933* (Chicago, 1977); Geoffrey Giles, *Students and National Socialism in Germany* (Princeton, N.J., 1985); R. G. S. Weber, *The German Student Corps in the Third Reich* (Basingstoke, 1986); and Jacques R. Pauwels, *Women, Nazis, and Universities: Female University Students in the Third Reich, 1933–1945* (Westport, Conn., 1984). On Nazi efforts in public health measures, see Robert Proctor, *The Nazi War on Cancer* (Princeton, N.J., 1999); Frank Uekötter, *The Green and the Brown: A History of Conservation in Nazi Germany* (New York, 2006); and Franz-Josef Brüggemeier, Mark Cioc, and Thomas Zeller, eds., *How Green Were the Nazis?: Nature, Environment, and Nation in the Third Reich* (Athens, Ohio, 2005).

On Nazi policy toward the family, see Lisa Pine, *Nazi Family Policy* (New York, 1997). On Nazi euthanasia policies, see Michael Burleigh, *Death and Deliverance: Euthanasia in Germany, 1900–1945* (Cambridge, Mass., 1994); and Henry Friedländer, *The Origins of Nazi Genocide: From Euthanasia to the Final Solution* (Chapel Hill, N.C., 1995). Sex and morals are examined in Hans P. Bleuel, *Strength Through Joy: Sex and Society in Nazi Germany* (London, 1970); and Dagmar Herzon, ed., *Sexuality and German Fascism* (New York, 2005). The perspectives of ordinary Germans can be seen in Frederic C. Tubach, *German Voices: Memories of Life during Hitler's Third Reich* (Berkeley, 2011).

MySearchLab™ Connections

Study and Review

Hitler's vision for Nazi Germany required molding the German people into a single *Volksgemeinschaft*, or a unified national community. It was not enough to control only the political and economic engines of Germany. Hitler wanted the Nazi Party to become the cultural and social reality of every German citizen.

Read the Document

1. **Karl Pearson, "Social Darwinism and Imperialism"**
   This document expresses the theory of Social Darwinism, the misapplication of Darwin's theories about animal evolution to human societies. Social Darwinism, by other names, was a central tenet of the Nazi "total state" ideology.

Read the Document

2. **The Rise of Totalitarianism—Propaganda?**
   This document reflects the policies of two totalitarian governments contemporaneous with Nazi Germany: Stalinist Russia and Fascist Italy. In what ways are these two government ideologies similar and different?

View the Image

3. **Brandenburg Gate, Berlin, Germany**
   Although a monument of Germany's former royal rulers, the Nazis viewed the Brandenburg Gate as a symbol of the strength and glory of their Reich.

RESEARCH AND EXPLORE

In their attempt to direct every aspect of the ordinary German's life, the Nazis were tireless with propaganda and indoctrination. Art, music, radio broadcasts, and literature were heavily censored. The Hitler Youth and the League of German Girls instructed young people in Nazi values. On occasion, these efforts to control the country's culture created resentment.

1. Why were the Nazis adamantly anti-intellectual? Were the Nazis' industrial and military capabilities affected by this stance? If so, how?

2. In what way did the Nazis' rejection of modern art serve as propaganda? How was the "Battle for Art" conducive to the Nazis' "total state"?

3. To what extent did Jesse Owens' success in the Berlin Olympics affect the image of the Aryan race? Did the Nazis consider the Berlin Olympics a success?

ADDITIONAL RESOURCES

1936 Berlin Olympics

The Soviets and the Nazis Confront the Issues of Women and the Family

CHAPTER

7

Hitler's War

Only three days after he had been made chancellor, on February 3, 1933, Hitler held a secret meeting with Germany's top generals. He spoke of the need to eliminate democracy and Marxism and create a new domestic unity that would allow for rearmament as the necessary prerequisite for the "conquest of *Lebensraum*" in the east. This policy, he explained, would eventually lead to war with France. His only immediate concern, though, was whether France might choose to wage a preventive war now in order to frustrate Germany's attempt to rearm. This speech reveals that even before he had consolidated his power, Adolf Hitler had a distinct vision of his ultimate goals. Domestic reconstruction was simply the first stage in the fulfillment of his foreign policy aims, and those aims ultimately meant war. World War II in Europe was clearly Hitler's war. Other powers may have made that war possible by refusing to resist Hitler's Germany earlier, but there is no doubt that Nazi Germany's actions made it inevitable.

PRELUDE TO WAR

Hitler's Ideology

World War II had its beginnings in Hitler's ideology. Hitler believed that only the Aryans were capable of producing a truly great civilization. However, as the leading group of Aryans, the German people were threatened by a great danger from the east in the form of massive numbers of inferior peoples (Slavs) who had learned to use German weapons and technology. To complete their goals, the Germans needed more land to support a larger population. Hitler's study of history had led him to believe that nations are militarily successful only if they control a large landmass. Where could the Germans gain the land they needed? Hitler rejected the acquisition of colonies; they were unfit for large-scale European settlement, nor could they really provide national security. The land must be found in continental Europe. At the end of the second volume of *Mein Kampf,* Hitler left no doubt where a National Socialist regime would seek this land:

> And so we National Socialists consciously draw a line beneath the foreign policy tendency of our pre-War period. We take up where we broke off six hundred years ago. We stop the endless German movement to the south and west, and turn our gaze toward the land in the east. At long last we break off the colonial and commercial policy of the pre-War period and shift to the soil policy of the future. If we speak of soil in Europe today, we can primarily have in mind only Russia and her vassal border states.[1]

Hitler believed that this living space could be acquired because of the Russian Revolution of 1917. To Hitler, only its Germanic leadership had kept the Russian state powerful. Slavic peoples were inferior and could never create a civilization by themselves. Since the overthrow of that German leadership by Jewish Bolsheviks, the Russians had succumbed to weak leadership and were ripe for conquest. Once the Germans conquered that land, the native peoples could be shoved ruthlessly aside or used as slave labor while German farmers settled the land and cultivated it to support a larger German population. Intermarriage with the Slavic peoples was unthinkable since it would lower the level of the master race. *Lebensraum,* anti-Semitism, anti-Bolshevism, and his belief in the use of force led Adolf Hitler to one obvious conclusion: Germany, preferably allied with Italy and Great Britain, must prepare for the inevitable war against the Soviet Union to conquer its living space. In making their conquests, the Germans planned to establish the foundation for the flourishing of the master race. Foreign policy meant creating the right conditions for the ultimate struggle. These ideas of Hitler were not secret. They had been spelled out in *Mein Kampf* and reiterated in a book on foreign policy written in 1928. Although this so-called *Second Book* was not discovered and published until after the war, *Mein Kampf* was available to anyone who wished to read it.

The Nazis were neither the first Europeans nor the first Germans to pursue a policy of European conquest and world power. Before World War I there was considerable discussion in German elite circles about the need for expansion in Europe as well as overseas. Germany, it was argued, could not maintain itself in comparison with large states, such as the Russian Empire, the British Empire, and the United States, unless it sought world power through the conquest and annexation of lands to its south, west, and east. With these lands Germany could obtain hegemony in central Europe and acquire the land, resources, and population that would enable it to compete with these larger states. Otherwise, it was thought, Germany was doomed as a great nation. World War I presented the opportunity to pursue these goals. The peace treaty imposed by the Germans on the Russians early in 1918 included the annexation of lands that would fulfill some of these goals. Indeed, if the Germans had won the war in the west, annexations there would have completed this quest.

The defeat of Germany, however, shattered this dream of world power. But it was kept alive in conservative circles and in universities in the form of geopolitics, an academic field centered in the relationship between politics and geography. Geopolitical theory had been introduced into German universities around 1900, especially by Karl Haushofer,

---

[1]Excerpts from *Mein Kampf* by Adolf Hitler, translated by Ralph Manheim, p. 654. Copyright © 1943, renewed 1971 by Houghton Mifflin Harcourt Publishing Company. Reprinted by permission of Houghton Mifflin Harcourt Publishing Company. All rights reserved.

a professor of geography at the University of Munich. One of Haushofer's cardinal principles of geopolitics was *Lebensraum*, the belief that a nation must acquire adequate living space if it is to grow and prosper. The power of a nation depended upon the amount and kind of land it occupied. To be strong, a nation must be willing to expand. One of Haushofer's enthusiastic students at Munich was Rudolf Hess, Hitler's devoted follower. It was Hess who introduced Haushofer and his ideas to Hitler in 1921. Hitler became a dedicated believer in the *Lebensraum* doctrine.

While there are elements of continuity in German foreign policy from the imperial days to Nazi Germany, there are also obvious differences. It is true that the traditional conservative elites in the military and the Foreign Office supported Hitler's foreign policy until 1937, largely because it corresponded to their own wishes for expansion. But, as they realized too late, National Socialist policy contained dynamic elements that carried it far beyond previous German goals. The fundamental difference lies in Hitler's racial policy. His belief in Aryan supremacy led to slave labor, the beginnings of a racial empire, and even mass extermination on a scale that would have boggled the minds of previous generations of Germans.

The "Diplomatic Revolution," 1933–1936

At first glance, Germany's situation in Europe when Hitler became chancellor was not a favorable one. Germany was surrounded by enemies. Its western boundaries with France and Belgium had been set by the Treaty of Versailles and confirmed by the Treaty of Locarno in 1925. The Versailles treaty had created a demilitarized zone on Germany's western frontier that would permit the French, in case of war, to move their armies into the heavily industrialized western part of Germany without opposition. To the east the smaller states, such as Poland and Czechoslovakia, were supported by defensive treaties with France. Germany's military capacity was extremely weak. It was limited by Versailles to 100,000 troops, had almost no navy and no air force, and possessed little in the way of modern artillery and tanks. After 1929, the depression further demoralized the German people.

But Germany did have some advantages. It was the second most populous European state after the Soviet Union. Although weakened by the war, Germany had the skills and resources to be powerful again if its industrial capacity could be put into motion. Although they might have had defensive alliances, the states in eastern and southern Europe were numerous, small, and considerably weaker than Germany. The Soviet Union was a potentially powerful opponent, although for ideological reasons it had been slow to see the danger of the Nazis. The early attempts of the Soviets to approach Germany failed. Since the capitalist Western powers were still suspicious of the Communist regime, it could be contained for the time being. The Western powers themselves, Great Britain and France, could not agree on a consistent policy toward the new Nazi state. Great Britain had been so dismayed by the costs and losses of World War I that it strove above all to avoid another war. Although France was suspicious of German intentions, it was divided internally and had no energy for a policy of firmness. France had constructed its Maginot Line to repel German invaders and was unwilling to move out of its defensive shell and mentality. Hitler realized that the French army posed a threat to an unarmed Germany, but he also knew that if he could keep the French from acting unilaterally in his first years, then France would come to depend on Britain as Germany became stronger. Of course, the restrictions on Germany created by the Versailles treaty had been intended to prevent Germany from creating problems again, but once they were removed, as Hitler perceived correctly, Germany would be a strong nation again.

Hitler had an additional advantage: He was not taken seriously by other powers. André François-Poncet, the French ambassador to Berlin since 1931, warned his government that Hitler was not an ordinary conservative nationalist. The English ambassador urged his government to read *Mein Kampf* and take it seriously. Its implications were German expansion and war. The French and British governments refused to believe the "alarmist" reports of their ambassadors. They assumed that Hitler would merely seek, as other German leaders before him, a revision of the Treaty of Versailles. They believed, as Papen and other German rightist leaders had earlier, that power would tame Hitler and make him a more responsible statesman. What he had written ten years ago was of no relevance now.

Hitler worked hard to foster precisely that image of himself. He wanted to avoid creating opposition that could stop him before he had a chance to realize his goals. His initial policies seemed to be the basic revisionist policies of his conservative predecessors. He encouraged the appearance of no fundamental change in foreign policy by retaining traditional conservatives such as Constantin von Neurath as foreign minister, Bernhard von Bülow as secretary of state, and Werner von Blomberg as defense minister. In fact, he had no difficulty in keeping these ministers content by pushing a policy of secret rearmament, which would provide the means for satisfying their desire to gain a revision of the Treaty of Versailles.

Hitler was especially successful in convincing others that his intentions were peaceful. He maintained that while his only interest was in peace, he also wanted Germany to have what other nations preached—the "natural rights" of self-determination and sovereignty. Once Germany had achieved these rights, it would be a bastion of peace in Europe and a mighty bulwark against the Soviet Union and the spread of communism. Hitler played on the legacy of World War I. He knew that Europeans had been appalled at the incredible loss of life in the world war and were eager to avoid another war that would mean even greater destruction. In numerous public speeches Hitler played on these fears, emphasizing Germany's desire to revise the unfair provisions of Versailles by peaceful means. Another war, he frequently proclaimed, could mean the end of Western civilization itself and a "sinking into Communistic chaos." Hitler reinforced these public speeches of peaceful intentions in numerous interviews with foreign reporters. Undoubtedly, his frequent declarations of peace deceived many about his ultimate intentions because they wanted to be convinced that the German chancellor was a reasonable person who desired peace. Hitler demonstrated considerable diplomatic skill and cunning in playing his "peace game."

During his first two years in office, Hitler was preoccupied primarily with consolidating Nazi rule in Germany. Aware of Germany's military weakness, Hitler pursued a cautious foreign policy without excessive risks. Above all, he wanted to avoid antagonizing France and to preclude the possibility of a French preventive war against Germany. While secretly laying the foundation for rearmament with his generals, he continued Germany's participation in the European disarmament conference at Geneva that had begun in 1932 and spoke eloquently of Germany's desire for peace. In his "peace speech" to the German Reichstag on May 17, 1933, he reiterated that violence would be of no value in solving Europe's problems. Germany wanted only to live in "peace and friendship" with other European states. But it also sought equality. Hitler even offered to eliminate Germany's remaining military establishment if its neighbors would do the same. However, if the others were basically unwilling to carry out the disarmament measures stipulated in the Treaty of Versailles, then it was not just that only Germany be disarmed. Germany "demands equality." Hitler knew, of course, that the other European states would not disarm. Using the argument that his own sincere appeals for honest disarmament had been ignored, Hitler announced on October 14, 1933, that Germany was ending its participation in the Geneva Disarmament Conference. At the same time, Germany withdrew from the League of Nations, denouncing it as simply a front for France's political domination of Europe. While some government officials feared that these actions would have dire consequences, there appeared to be little risk. Hitler had violated no treaties and sensed correctly in any case that others would think that Germany was within its rights to take these steps. Although they actually accomplished very little in the eyes of the other European states, that was not their real purpose. Hitler designed these steps for domestic consumption. They gave Germans the appearance that their country was no longer being dominated by the other European states. Hitler perceived correctly that the simple act of taking action was important to German public opinion. In Hitler's Third Reich, foreign and domestic policies were always closely interwoven.

After withdrawing from the Disarmament Conference and the League of Nations, Hitler reemphasized Germany's willingness to enter into international agreements if Germany were treated as an equal. But he refused to be drawn into any multinational arrangements for collective security, stressing instead Germany's readiness to make bilateral agreements. To other nations, this seemed to confirm Hitler's willingness to cooperate for peace—an argument, however, that overlooked the simple fact that bilateral agreements were the easiest to break. They also served to divide one's enemies and destroy the principle of collective security.

Nazi Germany's first bilateral agreement—with Poland on January 26, 1934—startled European governments. Ever since Danzig had been made a free city and Poland had been given a corridor across eastern Germany at the end of World War I, Germans had planned for an ultimate reckoning with Poland that would bring these areas back to the German state. After the establishment of the Nazi government, the Poles had spoken openly of the possibility of a preventive war against Germany. Hitler knew Germany was not ready for a war in the east and opened negotiations with the Poles. Fearing the Soviet Union as well as Nazi Germany, Poland sought security and welcomed Hitler's offer of a ten-year nonaggression pact. For Germany the pact was an opportunity to overcome its general isolation and to give the appearance of sincerely seeking peace by solving a problem that had seemed insoluble. Hitler felt no compulsion to maintain the pact in any case. By this time Hitler had also made it clear to the Soviet Union that he no longer favored the cooperative policies that had existed between the Soviets and the Weimar government and was willing to accept the "natural antagonism" that existed between them. Essentially, then, by the beginning of 1934 Hitler had produced a dramatic shift in Weimar foreign policy. Instead of enmity with Poland and friendship with Russia, Hitler had created a reverse alignment.

Nevertheless, if the nonaggression pact with Poland was a diplomatic victory for Hitler, additional events in 1934 revealed considerable weakness in Nazi Germany's European position. Hitler's purge of the SA at the end of June received a very unfavorable reaction abroad. Even more devastating to the prestige of the regime was Germany's blundering policy toward Austria. Hitler hoped ultimately to annex Austria to Germany. After coming to power, Hitler provided massive support to the Austrian Nazi Party in the expectation that it might come to power as his party had done in Germany. However, the Austrian chancellor, Engelbert Dollfuss, had established his own authoritarian regime in

Austria and acted to prevent a Nazi success by banning the Austrian Nazi Party in the summer of 1934 and gaining the support of Mussolini's Italian fascist regime. The Austrian Nazis, undoubtedly with German support, attempted a coup d'état against Dollfuss's regime. Although they managed to assassinate Dollfuss on July 25, the attempt to seize power failed with the arrest and execution of the Austrian Nazi leaders. By mobilizing Italian troops on the Austrian border, Mussolini forced Hitler to deny any involvement in the attempted overthrow of the Austrian government and temporarily to abandon the Austrian Nazis to their fate. The bid for power in Austria had been a fiasco and a diplomatic defeat for Hitler. In the long run, of course, it failed to deter Hitler from the pursuit of his ultimate goals.

At the beginning of 1935, Hitler won a much-needed victory. By the Treaty of Versailles the Saar region of Germany had been put under the control of the League of Nations for fifteen years; a plebiscite was to be held there in 1935 to allow its inhabitants to choose French or German control. The Nazi regime enthusiastically supported the plebiscite, which produced a 90 percent vote for reincorporation into Germany. Hitler claimed credit for the German victory.

Although the Nazis had been rearming for some time, the government had chosen to deny all such accusations. After the Saar success, Hitler was convinced that Germany could break some of the provisions of the Treaty of Versailles without serious British or French opposition. While observing the two nations, Hitler had come to believe that their most important aim was to avoid war. Of course, they wanted to preserve the international and social order but without using force and without making any of the sacrifices that the use of force entailed. Consequently, the Führer pulled the first of his "Saturday surprises" on March 8, 1935, announcing that Germany already had a new military air force, thus openly admitting that it was violating the Treaty of Versailles. One week later the German government publicly renounced the military clauses of the Treaty of Versailles and reported the introduction of a military draft that would expand the German army from its prescribed limit of 100,000 troops to 550,000. Germany could now openly rearm, much to the delight of the military, the Foreign Office, and big business. Hitler's policies were still satisfying the revisionist wishes of the traditional conservative German elites.

These moves, however, did not please the Western powers. Reaction was swift to the realization that Hitler had unilaterally repudiated certain provisions of the Treaty of Versailles. If unopposed, these actions would create a whole new set of power relationships in Europe. France, Great Britain, and Italy held a conference at Stresa in April 1935 to discuss joint strategy. But France and Britain were in the midst of domestic problems, and the Italians were beginning to prepare for an imperialistic adventure in Africa. No combined military or even economic action was taken against Germany. The three powers issued an affirmation of solidarity, condemning Germany's reintroduction of military conscription and warning of future action if Germany were guilty of any more treaty violations. But Hitler had already learned how to disarm his opponents and undermine their resolve. On May 21, 1935, in a foreign policy address to the German Reichstag, he expressed Germany's profound desire for peace and reiterated its wish to abide by the Locarno Treaty and accept France's boundaries as unalterable. Hitler promised not to interfere in internal Austrian affairs and expressed his willingness to conclude nonaggression pacts with all of Germany's neighbors.

In *Mein Kampf* and the *Second Book* Hitler had indicated that his desire for living space in the east would be accompanied by a foreign policy aimed at gaining alliances with Great Britain and Italy. In 1935, he moved to implement that plan. Hitler considered an understanding with Britain to be extremely important to his overall policy. Hitler appointed his foreign policy adviser Joachim von Ribbentrop as a special minister to Britain to negotiate an armaments agreement. Negotiations led to the Anglo-German Naval Pact on June 18, 1935. Without bothering to discuss it with its allies, Britain agreed to a treaty in which Germany was to be allowed to build a navy that would be 35 percent of the size of the British navy, with parity established in submarine strength. The naval accord between Germany and Britain was a diplomatic victory for Hitler, since it meant British recognition of Germany's right to rearm and in effect a tacit recognition of Germany's right to break the Versailles treaty to do so. The British for their part were initiating a policy of appeasement based on the belief that Europeans' satisfaction of the reasonable demands of the dissatisfied powers would make the latter content and create European stability. Consequently, the British felt they should negotiate with Hitler and make reasonable concessions even if they undermined Versailles in doing so. From the British point of view, the Anglo-German Naval Accord had gotten the Germans to negotiate and to agree to specific armaments restrictions. Of course, the British overlooked the problem of the extent to which Hitler could be trusted to maintain the agreement. The naval accord weakened the Allied front toward Germany by making the French suspicious and alarmed about what the British were doing. Hitler had hoped this willingness to negotiate reasonably with the British would make them agreeable to an alliance with Nazi Germany. The British were cool to any such suggestion.

At the end of 1935, Hitler gained an opportunity to pursue friendlier relations with fascist Italy. Mussolini's regime had opposed Nazi policy in Austria, straining relations between the two fascist regimes. But in October 1935, Mussolini began his drive for colonial conquest in Africa with an invasion of Ethiopia. This attack created a dilemma for France and Britain. Fearful of pushing Mussolini closer to Hitler, they wished to avoid any military intervention against Italy. Public opinion, however, forced them to take some action, which took the form of partial acceptance of the League of Nations' economic sanctions against the Italian aggressor. But even limited sanctions put off Mussolini. The Italian dictator began to pull away from Britain and France and became more favorable to Hitler and the Germans, who had refused to oppose Mussolini's action. At the same time, Hitler became even more convinced by their lack of action that the Western democracies had no intention of using force to maintain either the League of Nations or the Treaty of Versailles.

This conviction led Hitler to alter his timetable for the German occupation of the demilitarized Rhineland. Hitler had indicated secretly to German leaders that he intended to remilitarize the Rhineland in the spring of 1937. Although Germany was not yet ready militarily to override any possible opposition, he decided to act earlier because he believed that political events had created the right psychological conditions for action. In addition, the pace of rearmament was beginning to lead to a labor shortage and economic complaints. Hitler needed another foreign policy success. Although part of Germany, the Rhineland had been demilitarized by the Treaty of Versailles to satisfy French security needs by enabling the French to move troops easily into the industrial heartland of Germany in the event of war.

Hitler's remilitarization of the Rhineland was the first of his lightning attacks. His own military leaders considered it a considerable gamble since the German army was not ready to oppose the French army if the French decided to use force, which they had the right to do under the Treaty of Versailles. Hitler had, in fact, made it clear to his commanders that they were to withdraw immediately if the Western powers resisted. His own guess was that they would not. The march by the German troops into the Rhineland on

March 7, 1936, was publicly justified by the argument that Germany had a right to sovereignty over its own territory. As usual, Hitler accompanied his unilateral act by another "peace speech" to the German Reichstag. European problems, he again proclaimed, could only be solved by "cool reason." Underlining his desire for peace, he offered to conclude a twenty-five-year nonaggression pact with France and Belgium and nonaggression pacts with eastern European states along the lines of his earlier pact with Poland. Since Germany's "equality of rights" and restoration of "full sovereignty" over the territory of the German Reich had been attained, Hitler even offered to rejoin the League of Nations after the questions of colonial "equality of rights" had been clarified.

The British and French reacted the way Hitler had expected. Some French cabinet ministers wished to take action and requested the opinion of the military. The French chief of staff, General Gamelin, was pessimistic. He estimated the strength of the German occupation force at 265,000 troops, when in reality it was 22,000 military troops and 14,000 policemen. Gamelin argued that France could repel the Germans only by general mobilization and the support of Britain and Italy. The British were not inclined to support French resistance in any case. The British government, disposed to accept remilitarization of the Rhineland if done peacefully, dampened French consideration of military action. The British had obviously calculated that they were militarily weak and needed to solve European problems without the use of force. Britain subsequently issued only a written protest against Germany's action. In retrospect, it is apparent that the British and French missed perhaps their last good chance to stop Hitler's policy of expansion. Unwilling to use force when they had the advantage over Germany, they found it ever more onerous to consider its use when Germany was growing militarily stronger. From Hitler's point of view, the French and British were fulfilling his image of them as weak nations unwilling to use force to defend the old order.

The remilitarization of the Rhineland was an enormous victory for Hitler and Nazi Germany. Not only did it enhance German prestige, but it caused other states to wonder about the value of French and British promises to defend them. Belgium responded by abandoning its defensive military alliance with France and returning to its former status of neutrality. Hitler was of course delighted. He proclaimed to his aides after the successful occupation that "the world belongs to the brave man. He's the one God helps."[2] Since his generals had opposed this use of German troops, Hitler became even more convinced of his own superior judgment. The Rhineland success brought Hitler more domestic success. The usual plebiscite and its 99 percent "yes" vote reinforced the image of solid German support. Hitler could truly claim that German honor had been restored and national recovery established.

After his Rhineland success, Hitler continued his search for allies. He had considerable success with Italy. Hitler had recognized Mussolini's new empire in Africa while the Western powers had not. In addition, Hitler had removed the last obstacle to German-Italian cooperation by entering into an agreement with Austria in which the Germans agreed not to interfere in Austrian domestic politics. In return, the Austrians agreed that the Austrian National Socialists could have more political responsibility. Hitler and Mussolini drew even closer together as a result of their joint intervention in the Spanish Civil War on behalf of General Francisco Franco. The German Foreign Office and military

---

[2]Quoted in Joachim Fest, *Hitler*, translated by Richard and Clara Winston (New York, 1974), p. 499.

were opposed to Germany's involvement in the Spanish conflict. The decision to become involved was clearly Hitler's. There were numerous reasons to do so. Economically, there was the hope of acquiring access to raw materials. Spain also offered a laboratory for testing new weapons and especially for the Luftwaffe, the new air force, to experiment with terror bombing of civilian targets. But the decisive factors for Hitler seem to have been two. First, there was the possibility of gaining logistical and strategic bases for future expansionist moves. Second, because of Soviet support for the Spanish Republican government, German intervention could be portrayed as a defense of Western civilization against communism. Subsequent German and Italian cooperation in the war enabled Mussolini and Hitler to conclude a secret treaty in October in which both recognized their common political and economic interests. In November the Italian leader began to refer publicly to the new Rome-Berlin Axis.

Meanwhile, British reaction to Italian-German support of Franco in the Spanish Civil War encouraged Hitler. The British opinion that this alliance was more natural than the one between the Spanish Republican government and Stalinist Russia gave Hitler the hope that the British would still come around to an alliance. In August 1936, Joachim von Ribbentrop was made the new ambassador to Britain. Hitler expressly hoped he would achieve an alliance with Great Britain, but Ribbentrop's attempt to do so by the use of threats was completely rebuffed by the British. Although Ribbentrop now came to see Britain as an enemy, Hitler was still not prepared to abandon his hopes of an alliance with Britain or at least British neutrality toward ultimate German expansion on the Continent.

In the fall of 1936, Hitler made two additional moves that had long-range consequences. In August he established the Four-Year Plan for the economy, intending that Germany be prepared for war within four years (see pp. 92–94). In November, Germany and Japan signed an anti-Comintern pact in which they agreed to maintain a common front against communism.

By the end of 1936, Hitler had to be pleased with Germany's progress. Truly, a "diplomatic revolution" had occurred in Europe. Hitler's policies had completely reversed the European scene. While consolidating his power domestically in the first two years of the Nazi regime, Hitler had pursued a cautious foreign policy, aware of the danger of foreign reaction and careful to take no excessive risks. He had also demonstrated consummate skill in taking advantage of Europeans' fear of war and strong desire for peace. He had manipulated the issue of equality and justice for Germany and used the tactic of peaceful revision as effectively as he had used the tactic of legality in his climb to power. As Nazi power increased domestically with rearmament and economic recovery, the indoctrination of youth, and the militarization of Germany and German values, Hitler could move out of isolation into a more dramatic foreign policy, taking unilateral actions, making threats, disrupting alliances, and weakening the resolve of the European states to oppose him. As Hitler recognized, if the democracies so feared war that they would not use it when they were strong and Germany was weak, then they would be even less inclined to do so when Germany was strong and there was even greater danger of a destructive war. All the same, Hitler's moves had actually made war seem more possible. What Hitler had accomplished in foreign policy from 1933 to 1936 was evident. If Europeans had believed in 1933, based on their World War I experience, that war was insane and hence impossible, by 1936 it was beginning to dawn on many people that the probability of war had dramatically increased. Ignoring the regime's domestic use of brutal force and Hitler's own words in *Mein Kampf,* many Europeans still wanted to believe Hitler's own protestations that he wanted only peace. They would continue to do so until war was upon them.

The Road to War, 1937–1939

At the beginning of 1937, Hitler made a speech in Munich to the old guard of the National Socialist Party in which he exclaimed, "Today we are once more a World Power." Indeed, Germany began to strut on the world stage in a posture of near invincibility. The year 1937 seemed tame after the events of 1936 but it would soon prove to be the lull before the next storm.

Until 1937, the conservative Nationalist ministers who ran the Defense and Foreign ministries were in virtually complete agreement with Hitler's accomplishments. Germany was being substantially rearmed and the revising of the Treaty of Versailles was being accomplished with remilitarization of the Rhineland and the establishment of military equality with the other powers. Although there may have been disagreements over timing and methods, there was no disagreement about the aims. Hitler had little respect for these conservatives and did not think that they could really comprehend his broader visions. As we have seen, Hitler had larger goals, and his real purpose in maintaining these conservatives in power had been to disguise his true plans until he was ready militarily to accomplish them. At a secret conference in Berlin on November 5, 1937, Hitler gave a detailed exposition of Germany's future plans. Present at the meeting were Foreign Minister Constantin von Neurath, Defense Minister Werner von Blomberg, and the chiefs of the army, navy, and air force—Werner von Fritsch, Erich Raeder, and Hermann Göring, respectively. Hitler's army adjutant, Colonel Friedrich Hossbach, wrote down an account of Hitler's comments. The goals that Hitler expounded were not new but essentially those expressed in *Mein Kampf.* Germany must plan on the conquest of new living space, which could come only in the east. The basic needs of the German people could not be met in any other way. Hitler conceded that Germany would have to use force and that would create the possibility of having to deal with France and even Britain. Hitler had considered an alliance with Britain, but by this time he had changed his attitude and was prepared to deal differently with the British. He expressed his determination to solve Germany's needs by 1945 at the latest because Germany would be at the height of its military capacity by then and could only decline relative to the other European states. He added that the other crucial factor in respect to timing was his own person, which he considered indispensable to the achievement of Germany's goals. If the right political circumstances ensued, Germany could move as early as 1938. Before tackling the Western democracies, however, Germany needed to eliminate Austria and Czechoslovakia on its flank and use their military and economic resources. Hitler did not indicate precisely how or when these goals would be accomplished but emphasized the need to be prepared to deal at the right time with the Czechs.

Those present at the meeting, especially Neurath, Blomberg, and Fritsch, expressed doubts about Germany's lack of preparation in the west against France and the dangers of a broader war with both France and Great Britain. At the beginning of 1938 Hitler moved decisively against the doubters. Blomberg was forced to resign and was not replaced. Instead Hitler took over as supreme commander of the armed forces. A new High Command headed by General Wilhelm Keitel, a sycophantic admirer of the Führer, was established. Fritsch was replaced by General von Brauchitsch as chief of army command. The Foreign Ministry was shaken up when the obedient Ribbentrop supplanted Neurath. By making these changes in the foreign office and the military, Hitler removed all the remaining centers of old-line conservatism—a clear indication that the Führer was prepared to abandon his "peace" orientation in favor of his expansionist policies.

Hitler had always been adept at finding weaknesses in others, and in the winter of 1937–1938 he became convinced that there might be little opposition to his eastern plans from the French and British. Hitler was especially optimistic about the new British prime minister, Neville Chamberlain. Chamberlain had been a foremost advocate of the policy of appeasement. He believed that an Anglo-German agreement on arms control could still bring European and world peace. Such an agreement was possible only if the British were willing to make reasonable concessions to Germany's continental demands, providing Germany would make those changes peacefully. To Chamberlain, appeasement was the British Empire's last real hope. Since Britain did not have sufficient means to rule a worldwide empire, it had no choice but to exclude war as a weapon of policy. To pursue a policy leading to war with Germany meant a certain end to the British Empire. In November 1937, Chamberlain sent his close friend Lord Halifax as envoy to Hitler. Halifax intimated to Hitler that the British would not oppose changes in Austria, Czechoslovakia, and Danzig provided they were reasonably presented and executed peacefully. Soon after, the French foreign minister revealed that France had no objection to the "assimilation" of some of Austria's domestic institutions with Germany's. Certainly Hitler was left with the impression that the British and French would not oppose changes in central Europe. Moreover, by November 1937, Mussolini was making it clear that in the event of a crisis in Austria, Italy would do nothing. The circumstances Hitler was looking for had seemingly appeared. *Anschluss*—or union—with Austria was next on the agenda.

The Austrian chancellor, Kurt von Schuschnigg, realized Austria's growing isolation, but was able to offer little resistance to German encroachment. At a meeting with Hitler at Berchtesgaden in February 1938, Schuschnigg agreed to accelerate the coordination of Austria's economic and military systems with Germany's and to appoint the Austrian Nazi Arthur Seyss-Inquart minister of the interior, thus giving the Austrian Nazis control of the police. To forestall a complete Nazi takeover, Schuschnigg in desperation called, on March 9, for a plebiscite to be held on March 13 in which Austrians could vote to remain independent of Germany. Hitler could not afford to be embarrassed by the plebiscite if he hoped for Austria's ultimate union with Germany. He encouraged the Austrian Nazis to take more forceful action and threatened Schuschnigg with military action if the chancellor did not cancel the plebiscite. Although Schuschnigg complied, Hitler continued to press the attack by demanding—successfully—that he be replaced as chancellor by Seyss-Inquart. When German troops marched unopposed into Austria on March 12, they did so on the "legal" basis of the new Austrian chancellor's request for German troops to assist in establishing law and order. One day later, after his triumphal return to Linz, the city of his youth, Hitler formally annexed Austria to Germany. Within two weeks Great Britain acknowledged that Austria was part of the German Reich. This ready acceptance only increased Hitler's contempt for Western weakness. For the Jews of Austria, life would never be the same. The Jewish Telegraph Agency in Paris compiled a series of reports on daily life in the new Austria in the weeks after the *Anschluss*:

> The president of the [Jewish] community, Dr. Desider Friedmann, was detained in Dachau [concentration camp]. He was released and held office in Vienna for two days only to be arrested by the Gestapo again. His current whereabouts in prison are unknown.
>
> The number of suicides since Hitler took over Austria is estimated to be 2,000; the number of Jews arrested is estimated to be 12,000; the number of Jewish workers and employees laid off without notice or further payment amounts to 8,000.

The Jewish section of the central cemetery in Vienna receives bodies in closed caskets from the Nazis on a daily basis. They ordered to bury them immediately. Opening the caskets is severely punished . . .

The inmates of the Jewish orphanage at Türkenschanz Place—there are 70 orphans between the ages of 6 months and 14 years—have been evicted. The orphanage has been seized. Even the clothes supplied by the orphanage were taken away from the children.

The Gestapo demands that 25,000 Jews emigrate by the end of 1938. Raids on Jewish homes continue. Above all, money, jewelry, silver dishes, and rugs are taken.

Every Jew wanting to emigrate from Austria has to provide a confirmation that all taxes have been paid and that he will never return to Austria or Germany, respectively. They are also forbidden from taking cash with them.[3]

This rapid destruction of Jewish life in Austria would become a model for the rest of Europe's Jews soon to be within the grasp of Nazi rule.

Hitler Enters Vienna. After annexing Austria, Hitler made a triumphal entry into Vienna on March 13, 1938. *(Corbis)*

[3]"Overview of the Persecution of Jews in Central European Countries," in Jürgen Matthäus and Mark Roseman, eds., *Jewish Responses to Persecution, Volume I, 1933–1938* (Lanham, Md., 2010), pp. 286–287. By permission of AltaMira Press. Desider Friedmann would be deported from Dachau to Theresienstadt concentration camp in 1942, and then, along with his wife Elsa, to Auschwitz in 1944, where they both died.

Anschluss with Austria considerably improved Germany's strategic position in central Europe. German power was now in direct contact with Hungary and Yugoslavia, where Germany was already making economic inroads. Western Czechoslovakia, where that country's important resources were located, was now surrounded on three sides. Hitler was in a position to pursue the next objective discussed at the November 5, 1937, conference—the destruction of Czechoslovakia, an industrialized republic of considerable economic strength.

Hitler's demands on Czechoslovakia focused on the supposedly intolerable living conditions of the 3 million Germans in Czechoslovakia, who were concentrated mostly in the mountainous northwestern border area adjoining Germany and Austria called the Sudetenland. Sudeten German opposition to Czech rule crystallized about the person of Konrad Henlein, leader of the Sudeten German Party, a right-wing nationalist political party similar in ideology to the Nazis. Naturally, Hitler and the Nazis threw their support behind Henlein and his party. Hitler urged Henlein to make demands so extreme that the Czech government could never satisfy them. By keeping constant pressure on the Czechs, Henlein could create conditions for German intervention and ultimately the complete freedom of the Sudetenland. Hitler was well aware that the Sudetenland also contained Czechoslovakia's most important frontier fortifications and significant industrial resources. Without it, Czechoslovakia was defenseless.

Hitler realized that the solution of the Czech problem might require military action. He had already on December 7, 1937, set in motion Operation Green, a German military plan for an attack on Czechoslovakia. In a new directive on May 30, 1938, Hitler stated that it was his "unalterable decision to smash Czechoslovakia by military action in the near future."[4] But Hitler also emphasized that Germany would not march until he was certain France and Britain would not intervene. Since Hitler was determined to resolve the Czech question by October 1, another European diplomatic crisis loomed large in the summer of 1938.

By that time, Hitler was convinced, with good cause, that France and Britain would not use force to defend Czechoslovakia. On paper, the Czech Republic seemed well supported by pacts with France and the Soviet Union. Yet the French made it clear that they would act only if the British supported them. Chamberlain, however, informed the French premier, Edouard Daladier, that if Hitler and the Germans wished to destroy Czechoslovakia, he did not see how they could be stopped from doing so. Soviet support depended on French backing, which became increasingly doubtful because of the lack of British support and increasing French suspicion of the Russians. Besides, Soviet military support of Czechoslovakia depended upon the movement of its troops through Poland, and it was highly unlikely that the Poles would ever voluntarily permit Soviet passage through their country.

By late August, under British pressure, the Czech government had acceded to Henlein's requests for autonomy for the Sudeten Germans. The Germans then increased their pressure on the Czechs. During a meeting with Prime Minister Chamberlain on September 15 at Berchtesgaden, Hitler demanded the cession of the Sudetenland to Germany and indicated his readiness to risk "world war" to achieve it. Chamberlain convinced his own government and the French government to accede to Hitler's wishes. Pressure was placed on the Czechs, who reluctantly accepted Hitler's (and the British and French) demands. When

---

[4]*Documents on German Foreign Policy* (London, 1956), Series D, vol. 2, p. 358.

Chamberlain returned to Germany to announce Czechoslovakian agreement to Hitler's terms, Hitler made a new demand—that the Germans be allowed to occupy the Sudetenland by October 1 and take over all its military installations. Chamberlain became angry and the Czechs now refused the new demand, deepening the crisis. Suddenly war became a genuine possibility. Even the German public became fearful. Some officers, led by Colonel Hans Oster, became so alarmed at the threat of a war they felt unprepared to fight that they began to plot the overthrow of Hitler.

To defuse the crisis, Mussolini suggested a conference of the British, French, Italians, and Germans at Munich. Neither the Czechs nor the Russians were invited. Agreement was reached on a peaceful solution to the crisis. It was basically simple. All of Hitler's demands were met. The Sudetenland was to be occupied by German troops between October 1 and October 10. The latter was Hitler's only concession, since the Germans had originally demanded complete occupation on October 1. The Munich Conference was the high point of Western appeasement of Hitler. Czechoslovakia, a democracy abandoned by its democratic friends, surrendered the Sudetenland to its enemy. Although Britain and France guaranteed the new boundaries of Czechoslovakia, the new Czech state was mortally wounded. In losing the Sudetenland it lost one-third of its population, much of its industrial capacity, and, most important, virtually all of its frontier fortifications.

Upon his return to Britain, Chamberlain made the infamous boast that the Munich agreement meant "peace in our times," since Hitler had promised him that this was his last demand and that all future problems could be settled by talks. Unfortunately Chamberlain, like scores of German politicians before him, believed Hitler's promises. The real victor of the Munich Conference was Hitler. Despite the fears of his generals and diplomats, he had once again been proved right. The Western democracies were weak and would not fight, just as he had predicted. The generals' plot collapsed. German public fears evaporated. It was easier to believe that the Führer was infallible. As one general wrote in his diary, "The hope remains that the incredulous, the weak, and the doubtful people have been converted and will remain converted."[5] Unfortunately for Germany, Hitler was now convinced that he was infallible. And he was certainly prepared to make more demands.

Hitler never intended to abide by the Munich agreement. Only three weeks after the Munich Conference, he commanded the German military to prepare for the final destruction of the Czechoslovakian state. After the German occupation of the Sudetenland, the new Czech state was plagued with internal discord and foreign pressures. Hungary and Poland laid claims to Czech territory, and with German encouragement the large Slovak minority demanded and was granted autonomy within a Czecho-Slovak union. By the beginning of 1939, Hitler was planning to create enough disorder in Czechoslovakia to justify a German occupation on the pretense of preventing anarchy. The Slovaks were pressured by Hitler to declare their independence on March 14. German troops were then sent into Slovakia to prevent a Czech response to this move. Demoralized, the president of Czechoslovakia, Emil Hacha, traveled to Germany to negotiate with Hitler. Hitler demanded that the elderly, ill, and politically inexperienced Hacha sign an agreement accepting a German protectorate

---

[5]Quoted in International Military Tribunal, *Trial of the Major War Criminals,* vol. 28 (Nuremberg, 1947–1949), p. 389.

over the remaining Czech provinces of Bohemia and Moravia. If he failed to do so, Hitler promised that Germany would invade the provinces and ruthlessly bomb the capital city of Prague. Hacha capitulated, giving Hitler his "legal" cover for German occupation. On the morning of March 15, German troops marched into Bohemia and Moravia. That evening Hitler arrived in Prague and declared that he would go down in history as the greatest German of them all. Czechoslovakia had ceased to exist.

By this act, Hitler had moved completely beyond the boundaries of simply revising the Treaty of Versailles. After all, the Czechs were not Germans clamoring to be reunited with the motherland. It was apparent that Hitler's promises were worthless. Public pressure quickly produced a change of attitude in France and Great Britain. They gave military guarantees to Poland, Romania, Greece, and Turkey. Of course, the only really important power that could help to contain Nazi Germany was the Soviet Union. Consequently the Western powers initiated political and military negotiations with the Soviets. An alliance with the Soviet Union would mean the encirclement of Nazi Germany, but the West's distrust of the Soviet regime made such an alliance virtually impossible. Chamberlain never took these negotiations seriously and left them to his subordinates. The Western states had little regard for Russia's military abilities. Obviously, Chamberlain still preferred some agreement with Germany. Stalin feared precisely that and opened himself to the possibility of negotiating with the Germans.

Shortly after the Czechoslovakian success, Hitler began to focus on Poland. By the Treaty of Versailles, Poland had been given a corridor to the sea that cut off East Prussia from the rest of Germany. The German city of Danzig had also been made a free city to serve as a seaport for Poland. Now Hitler demanded the return of Danzig and an extraterritorial passageway through the Polish Corridor. Fearful of Hitler's ultimate intentions after the Czechoslovakian experience, the Poles accepted an Anglo-French offer on March 31 of a guarantee to protect Poland's existence if it was clearly threatened. On April 3, Hitler ordered his generals to prepare a military plan to solve the Polish question by September 1, 1939. At the end of April, claiming that Poland's agreement with Britain and France violated the 1934 German-Polish agreement, Hitler abrogated the nonaggression pact with Poland.

Despite the British and French guarantees to Poland, Hitler still hoped that the Western powers would give him a free hand in the east. As we have seen, Hitler's ultimate strategy to gain living space in the east was based on his securing an alliance with Britain, or at least British neutrality. His failure to do so had led him, despite his wishes, to the realization that he might have to deal with the West. He made his own preference clear, however, to Carl Burckhardt, the League of Nations high commissioner for Danzig, on August 11, 1939:

> Everything I undertake is directed against Russia. If the West is too stupid and too blind to comprehend that, I will be forced to come to an understanding with the Russians, to smash the West, and then, after its defeat, to turn against the Soviet Union with my combined forces.[6]

For Hitler, an attack on Poland was a precondition for the ultimate assault on the Soviet Union. But if the West planned to intervene in the attack on Poland, then he would need to deal with the Western democracies. Poland would have to be eliminated quickly before

---

[6]Carl Burckhardt, *Meine Danziger Mission* (Munich, 1962), p. 272.

Germany's Expansion, 1933–1939

the clash with the Western democracies. Hitler knew that his own military preparations were far superior to those of the West. Any postponement of the ultimate clash would only benefit the West.

Hitler had already strengthened his hand with the Pact of Steel, a military alliance formed with Italy on May 28. He took an even more significant step when he decided that the only way to avoid an alliance between the West and the Soviet Union was to arrive at an agreement with the Soviet state. Although he had ranted against communism his entire career, he overcame his ideological preferences for purely opportunistic reasons. An alliance with the Soviet Union, undoubtedly only temporary in Hitler's mind, freed him from the danger of a two-front war if the West took up arms over his planned attack on

Poland. In addition, the raw materials that Russia would now ship to Germany as part of the alliance freed Hitler from worries about an economic blockade of Germany in his struggle with the West. The world was startled to learn on August 23, 1939, that Hitler and Stalin had signed a nonaggression pact. The world did not know that a secret protocol between the two states specified separate spheres of influence in eastern Europe: Finland, the Baltic states, eastern Poland, and Bessarabia (in Romania) would go to the Soviet Union while Germany would gain control of western Poland. The nonaggression pact with the Soviet Union gave Hitler a free hand to attack Poland on September 1. He exulted to his generals: "Now Poland is in the position in which I wanted her . . . . I am only afraid that at the last moment some swine or other will yet submit to me a plan for mediation."[7] Obviously Hitler was eager for war by the end of August. As he remarked to his military chiefs in November 1939, "Basically I did not organize the armed forces in order not to strike. The decision to strike was always in me."[8] Hitler would have preferred a war against Poland without French and British involvement, but he was willing to take a chance. He knew he would probably have to deal with them anyway.

WORLD WAR II

The Early Victories

Nine days before the attack on Poland, Hitler indicated to his military commanders what he expected of them in their invasion of Poland: "When starting and waging a war it is not right that matters, but victory. Close your hearts to pity. Act brutally. Eighty million people must obtain what is their right . . . . The wholesale destruction of Poland is the military objective. Speed is the main thing. Pursuit until complete annihilation."[9] Europe was stunned by the speed and efficiency of the German attack. Moving into Poland with one and a half million troops from three fronts, German forces used armored columns (the panzer divisions) supported by airplanes to break quickly through Polish lines and encircle the outnumbered and poorly equipped Polish armies. The coordination of air and ground assaults allowed effective use of Stuka dive bombers, which added a frighteningly destructive element to the German attack. Within four weeks all Polish resistance had been eliminated, and on September 28, 1939, Germany and the Soviets officially divided Poland between them.

Hitler's attack on Poland was Europe's introduction to *Blitzkrieg*, or lightning war. *Blitzkrieg's* military dimension was based on the lessons of World War I as perceived by Hitler and some of his military commanders. To avoid the trench warfare that had made World War I into a defensive slaughter, the German army created plans for a lightning warfare that depended on mechanized columns and massive air power to cut quickly across battle lines and encircle and annihilate entire armies. *Blitzkrieg* meant that an enemy could be defeated quickly, before it could completely mobilize and before others could come to its aid. But *Blitzkrieg* was also based on economic considerations. It allowed the Germans to win quick victories against individual enemies and thus avoid

---

[7]*Documents on German Foreign Policy*, Series D, vol. 7, p. 204.

[8]Ibid., vol. 8, p. 441.

[9]Quoted in Norman Rich, *Hitler's War Aims*, vol. 1 (New York, 1973), p. 129.

having to mobilize the nation's resources for a long total war. Quick victories could be cheap victories. Food and raw materials could be plundered from defeated states to bolster the German economy. Hitler's concern for the German home front, based on his World War I experience, caused him to favor cheap victories instead of making too many demands on German civilians.

Two days after the attack on Poland, Britain and France declared war on Germany, thus creating the very Europewide war that Hitler had hoped to prevent. With his quick victory over Poland, however, Hitler believed that Germany could still handle the situation. Assuming a quick victory over Poland, Hitler had deliberately weakened his forces in the west, making Germany vulnerable to a British and French attack. Even Hitler believed that an Allied offensive now would create difficulties for Germany. At the same time, he doubted that the Western democracies would assume an offensive strategy. He was correct. The Allies, conditioned by their experiences in World War I, believed that time was on their side. Once again they could use a blockade and gradually grind Germany down. There was no need to follow an offensive pattern that would simply result in unnecessary bloodshed.

If the Allies were reluctant to take the offensive, Hitler was extremely eager to do just the opposite. Already on September 27 he told the military command that he had decided to attack the West as soon as possible. His generals resisted. General Guderian, one of the main panzer leaders, believed that the armored divisions would have trouble operating in winter. There was a noticeable lack of supplies and a need to repair vehicles. Hitler pressed on, but was forced by bad weather to finally give up his hopes for a lightning attack against the West in 1939.

The winter of 1939–1940 witnessed the so-called "phony" or "bore" war, which lulled the Allies into inaction except for plans by Great Britain to mine Norwegian waters to stop the flow of Swedish iron ore from Norwegian ports. On his part, Hitler was willing to see Scandinavia remain neutral, but the commander in chief of the Navy, Admiral Erich Raeder, emphasized to Hitler the importance of Norway for naval bases as well as the danger to Germany's northern flank if the British were to use Norway for bases themselves. They could, Raeder warned, close the Baltic itself to the German fleet and seriously affect the shipment of iron ore from Sweden—a serious problem since Germany received 50 percent of its iron ore from Scandinavia. Hitler received encouragement from Vidkun Quisling, head of the Norwegian National Unification Party and a confirmed anti-Bolshevik and anti-Semite. Quisling sought German aid to establish a pro-German government and warned Hitler of Norway's strategic and economic importance to the Germans. He also emphasized the need to counter British designs on Norway. Although Hitler still seemed reluctant to push the British because of his desire for a settlement with them, he decided to attack and occupy both Norway and Denmark. On April 9, one day after the British had begun to mine Norwegian waters, the Germans struck. The Danish government immediately accepted German conditions and surrendered without a fight. But the Norwegians refused to capitulate. The Nazis undertook a dramatic invasion, landing troops at key positions along the coast and dropping paratroopers into airfields and major cities. Britain landed a force of almost 50,000 troops, but they were eventually driven out. Norway surrendered on June 9 and a new government that included Quisling was established. In the course of World War II, the name Quisling became synonymous with *traitor*. Although Germany's victory had not been easy—the pocket battleship Lützow and a number of cruisers and destroyers had been lost or damaged—its northern flank was now secure, ensuring a supply of Scandinavian iron ore. Germany could also build strategic bases for air and submarine warfare against the British. Hitler continued to hope, however, for an alliance rather than a war with Britain.

The new German victory finally brought a change of government in Great Britain. On May 10, 1940, Chamberlain, the apostle of appeasement, was replaced by Winston Churchill, a longtime advocate of a tough line toward Nazi Germany who now proved to be the inspiring leader the British needed at this critical moment in their history. The same day, Hitler struck again in the west. The attack planned earlier for the previous November had been delayed by bad weather. The Germans had plotted a new strategy during the winter, fearing that their battle plans had fallen into enemy hands. Their original plans had called for an invasion of France, similar to the Schlieffen plan used in World War I, through Belgium and into northern France. The French had expected the German attack through Belgium and placed a large force in northern France for that reason. The new German strategy was the work of General Erich von Manstein, chief of staff of Army Group A. Manstein's suggestion was to attack through Luxembourg and the Ardennes forest region. French fortifications would be weak, since the Ardennes was considered largely impassable. Once through the Ardennes, German armored divisions could race across northern France and trap the combined Allied armies in northern France and Belgium. This daring plan was distrusted by other generals. Hitler liked it and accepted it as his own.

On the eve of the battle, the opposing forces were roughly equal. The West had a combined 144 divisions to the Germans' 138. The Germans had an advantage in concentrating their armor and vehicles in the panzer divisions, while the Allies tended to diffuse theirs and not use them effectively. The Germans were superior in aircraft and used them more effectively by supporting their army's tactical operations, while the Allies used theirs for reconnaissance and defense.

One month after the invasion of Denmark and Norway, the Germans launched their attack on the Netherlands, Belgium, and France. The Netherlands fell in five days. The Dutch city of Rotterdam was devastated by a bombing attack on May 14 and subsequently portrayed as a symbol of wanton Nazi destruction of civilian life. The German forces pushed into Belgium as if to sweep through into France, as they had done in World War I. But this was only a feint. The Germans now unleashed their main offensive through Luxembourg and the Ardennes, breaking through the weak French defensive positions. The panzer divisions of generals Heinz Guderian and Erwin Rommel reached the English Channel on May 21, splitting the Allied armies and then moving to trap the forces cut off in the north. The main Belgian army surrendered on May 28, and the other British and French forces were trapped at Dunkirk. At this point Hitler stopped the advance of the German armored units, fearful of overextending them, and ordered the Luftwaffe to destroy the Allied army on the beaches of Dunkirk. The Luftwaffe proved ineffective in bombing the Allied armies. By the time Hitler ordered his armored units to advance again, the British had rebuilt their defenses sufficiently to allow for a gigantic evacuation of 330,000 French and British troops by a flotilla of small ships. The "miracle of Dunkirk" saved a well-trained army to fight another day.

The Germans then launched a major offensive into eastern and southern France on June 5. Five days later, assuming the war to be over and eager to grab some spoils, Mussolini's Italy declared war on France and invaded from the south. The French asked for an armistice, which was signed on June 22 in Compiègne in the same railway car used for the German capitulation at the end of World War I. The world was stunned. The French had been so easily defeated. Dazed by the rapidity of the German attack, they had never really been able to offer any effective resistance. In a sense, the French had been on the defensive so long that they were defeated before the battle began.

The Germans occupied three-fifths of France—the northern part, including Paris, and the seacoast down to the Spanish border. The remainder was permitted to continue under French rule. Marshal Philippe Pétain, the French hero of World War I, established the authoritarian regime known as Vichy France.

Hitler was ecstatic. He had revenged the humiliating German defeat in World War I. He had proved himself a brilliant and bold leader who had invariably been right in pursuing policies that his generals and diplomats had thought too risky or even disastrous. He had triumphed over his enemies. Germany controlled western and central Europe. Germans were elated by Hitler's success. For Hitler, success was simply a vindication of what he had always believed. He was a man with a mission, which was being fulfilled. And, like any human being who has experienced so much success in so little time, Hitler came to believe even more than ever that he was infallible. He did not have long to wallow in self-congratulation, however. The French were defeated but the British were still alive. And Hitler was not really all that confident about how to handle them.

The Problem of Britain

His victory over the French had convinced Hitler of his military genius. But the purpose of the campaign against the West had been to eliminate his enemies so he could fulfill his primary goals of gaining living space in the east and definitively annihilating the "Jewish-Bolshevik" menace. Britain was still not defeated. Hitler believed, however, that the British had learned their lesson and would now accept Germany's domination of the Continent. Hitler had considerable admiration for Britain as a fellow Nordic nation that had demonstrated its racial superiority in creating a world empire. He was prepared, at least for now, to let the British keep their empire if they would assent to Germany's victory and agree to an alliance. On June 2, 1940, Hitler told his generals if the British would now accept a sensible peace, as he believed they would, then he would be free to destroy bolshevism. He tried through interviews, speeches, and diplomatic channels to give the message to the British that he was ready to make peace. When the British did not respond positively, Hitler decided to launch an invasion. On July 16, he issued the directive for Operation Sea Lion: "Since England, despite its hopeless military position, still shows no sign of willingness to come to terms, I have decided to prepare a landing operation against England and if necessary to carry it out."[10] Hitler indicated that preparations for the invasion should be complete by mid-August. The defeat of the British air force and neutralization of the British navy were, however, the preconditions for the invasion. No crossing of the English Channel by an invasion fleet could occur without control of the skies.

Hitler was not optimistic about an invasion of Britain. He informed his military commanders that it would not be easy. Consequently, while preparations continued Hitler tried to persuade the British to come to terms. He became convinced that

---

[10]Quoted in Hans-Adolf Jacobsen and Arthur L. Smith, Jr., *World War II: Policy and Strategy* (Santa Barbara, Calif., 1979), p. 82.

Britain was remaining in the war because it was counting on the Soviet Union and the United States. As he told his military chiefs on July 31,

> England's hope is in Russia and the United States. If the hope in Russia disappears, America is also lost, because elimination of Russia would tremendously increase Japan's power in the Far East . . . . But if Russia is destroyed, England's last hope is shattered. Germany will then be master of Europe and the Balkans . . . . The sooner Russia is crushed the better.[11]

Consequently, at the end of July, Hitler asked his army leaders to begin planning for the destruction of the Soviet Union—"England's last hope." Yet Hitler had no desire for a two-front war, and he continued to push plans for the invasion of Britain. On July 31, he established September 15 as the date for the invasion.

At the beginning of August the Luftwaffe launched a major offensive against Britain, bombing air and naval bases, harbors, communication centers, and important war industries. The effort essentially failed. The British had some definite advantages. They possessed an effective radar system that provided early warning of German attacks and enabled the British to mass superior numbers of planes at crucial areas. Although outnumbered, the British were fighting over their own territory, which gave them moral and strategic advantages. The Ultra intelligence operation, which enabled the Allies to break German military codes and gain specific information about German military plans, was also important. Ultra gave the British air force specific information about when, where, and how many German planes would attack. Perhaps most important was Göring's lack of leadership as commander of the Luftwaffe. He wasted airplanes on a variety of targets instead of concentrating on the destruction of air force bases. Hitler contributed to the defeat as well. By the end of August, the British air force was suffering critical losses. But in retaliation for a British attack on Berlin, Hitler ordered a shift from attacks on air force bases to raids on London. The change to massive bombing saved the Royal Air Force bases. It also cost the Luftwaffe enormously in planes. By the middle of September Germany had lost the Battle of Britain. The failure of the Luftwaffe meant the indefinite postponement of the invasion of Britain.

As doubt developed about the invasion of Britain, the Germans began to search for another way to strike at Britain. The most obvious course was to capture Gibraltar and close the entrance to the western Mediterranean to British sea power. Hitler had realized that the Mediterranean was important to Germany's southern flank, which would be exposed to attacks by the British in the Mediterranean. By September 1940, when it had become virtually certain that there would be no invasion of Britain, Admiral Raeder urged Hitler to eliminate Britain by capturing Gibraltar and the Suez Canal and then driving through Palestine and Syria to the Turkish border. Hitler agreed in principle, although he felt that he needed the cooperation of Italy and Spain to pursue this policy. Italian cooperation was forthcoming with an offensive from Italian Libya against Egypt. But the new dictator of Spain, Francisco Franco, refused to be drawn in and made such enormous demands and dragged his feet so much that Hitler finally canceled his December 11 plans for an attack on Gibraltar. Hitler was unwilling to risk war in Spain to force Franco to cooperate.

The failure of Spain to enter the war and the consequent cancellation of the plans to capture Gibraltar led Germany to take another approach to oppose British influence in the Mediterranean, an approach considerably more difficult and costly. Hitler

---

[11]Franz Halder, *Kriegstagebuch*, ed. Hans-Adolf Jacobsen, vol. 2 (Stuttgart, 1962), p. 49.

had planned to let the Italians defeat the British in North Africa and capture Egypt. The Italians had begun their campaign against Egypt in September 1940. But by January 1941 the Italians were in full retreat in North Africa. Hitler decided that only large-scale German intervention could save the campaign. He sent General Erwin Rommel, whom he described as "the most daring general of armored forces whom we possess in the German Army,"[12] with the German Afrika Korps to Libya in February. Leading a combined force of Germans and Italians, Rommel attacked on March 30 and by the end of May had reached the Egyptian frontier. Insufficient troops and supplies finally forced a halt. Hitler had no extra troops to spare, since he was now poised for his invasion of the Soviet Union.

The Invasion of the Soviet Union

In view of his ideological aims, Hitler had no intention of maintaining his nonaggression pact with the Soviet Union. Eventually he would have to turn on the Soviet Union, but not until after the defeat of the West. Hitler had paid a considerable price for Soviet neutrality. The Soviets had been granted a large sphere of influence in eastern Europe and had taken advantage of Hitler's defeat of Poland and preoccupation with the West to establish control over eastern Poland, the Baltic states of Estonia, Latvia, and Lithuania, and strategic parts of Finland. The Soviets tried to extend their sphere of influence in the south in the Balkans, particularly in Romania, Bulgaria, and Turkey. The Germans countered this thrust by establishing their own presence in Romania and Hungary. To Hitler, Soviet territorial acquisitions posed a serious strategic threat. But the Soviets posed an economic threat as well. The Germans were especially aware of the importance of the raw materials they obtained from the Soviet Union and the Soviet control of the routes of access to other raw materials. In addition, according to their agreement, the Germans were required to provide armaments in exchange for raw materials. For both strategic and economic reasons, Hitler knew that he would have to deal sooner or later with the Soviet Union.

The decisive factor in the timing of Hitler's invasion of the Soviet Union was clearly Germany's failure to force Britain out of the war. As we have seen, Hitler became convinced that Britain was staying in the war only because it expected Soviet support. If the Soviet Union were smashed, then Britain's last hope would be gone. By July 31, 1940, Hitler had made known his decision to eliminate the Soviet Union in the spring of 1941. However, the clinching of the decision depended upon what happened with Britain. Hitler preferred to defeat Britain first. He assured himself that because of its Jewish-Bolshevik leadership, the Soviet Union could be defeated quickly and decisively. Soviet problems in the invasion of Finland had convinced him that the Soviet army and leadership were pitiful.

By the end of 1940, with no immediate hope of defeating Britain, Hitler decided to take the plunge. On December 17, 1940, he issued a directive for Operation Barbarossa—the destruction of the Soviet state. Contrary to the war in the West, the new *Ostkrieg* (Eastern War) was to be a *Vernichtungskrieg*, a war of extermination. His stated military objectives therefore were to destroy the Red Army and the centers of Soviet industrial power, to capture the chief Soviet industrial and agricultural areas, and to erect a defensive line from Archangel in the north to the Caspian Sea in the south. Hitler's directive stressed the need for surprise and speed to capture the mass

[12]*Documents on German Foreign Policy*, Series D, vol. 12, p. 29.

of the Red Army in enormous encirclement operations. The Soviet army could not be permitted to retreat into the wide spaces of the Soviet hinterlands.

Although scheduled for spring 1941, the attack was delayed because of problems in the Balkans. Hitler had not pursued direct involvement in southeastern Europe. Germany already had a favorable economic position there and was exploiting it economically for raw materials. The Romanian oil supply was considered especially important for the German war effort. By 1940, Hitler had managed to obtain the economic and political coopera-tion of Hungary, Bulgaria, and Romania. Benito Mussolini, however, became considerably upset over Germany's gains and increased influence in southeastern Europe. The Italians liked to consider the Balkans their sphere of influence. To ensure the extension of Italian importance in that region, Mussolini launched an attack on Greece on October 28, 1940. But the Italians were militarily unprepared and their invasion was quickly stopped. Since the British were supporting the Greeks with 30,000 troops, Hitler became alarmed at the critical situation Mussolini had foolishly created. British air bases in Greece could now threaten not only Italy but also the Romanian oil fields. Hitler believed he could not undertake the invasion of the Soviet Union without covering his southern flank by occu-pying Greece. To secure his Balkan flank, Hitler first invaded Yugoslavia on April 6, 1941. After its surrender on April 17, he smashed Greece in six days. The British were expelled from Greece and the island of Crete. Southeastern Europe was now secure and could provide bases for military operations against the Soviet Union.

Military Operations of World War II: The German Offensives, 1939–1942

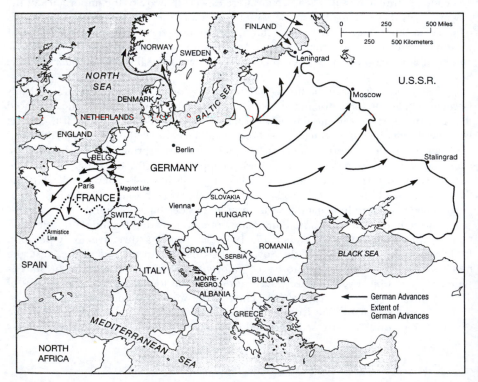

Hitler still believed that the Soviet Union could be destroyed before winter set in. He had impressed upon his generals the fact that the war in the Soviet Union was unlike any of their previous campaigns because it was a racial and ideological struggle to the end, German against Slav and National Socialism against Jewish bolshevism. Hitler explained the nature of the Eastern War to his generals on March 30, 1941 (from notes taken by General Franz Halder):

> Two world views battle one another. Annihilating judgment over Bolshevism, the same aso-
> cial criminality. Communism immense danger for the future. We must move away from the
> standpoint of soldierly camaraderie. The communist is not a comrade before and is not a
> comrade after. It is a question of a war of extermination . . . . The struggle must be waged
> against the poison of decomposition [euphemism for the Jews]. That is not a question of
> the rules of war.[13]

Per Hitler's orders, no mercy was to be given to Soviet soldiers, Communist leaders, nor any Jews caught behind the advancing army, as he believed, erroneously, they both created and controlled the Soviet system. The war against the Soviet Union and the war against the Jews were linked conceptions in the minds of the Nazi leadership. Therefore, as the Wehrmacht pushed east, atrocities against Jews would be committed by both SS units entrusted with this objective and members of the regular army.

Nazi Germany launched its attack on the Soviet Union on June 22, 1941. It was by far the largest invasion the Germans had yet attempted. The German force consisted of 180 divisions, including 20 panzer divisions, 8000 tanks, and 3200 airplanes. German troops were stretched out along an 1800-mile front. The Soviets had 160 infantry divisions but were able to mobilize another 300 new divisions out of reserves within half a year. The potential power of the Soviets had been badly miscalculated by the Germans.

The invading force was divided into three main prongs. Army Group North under General von Leeb swept through the Baltic states and on to Leningrad, which it besieged unsuccessfully in November. General von Bock's Army Group Center had the objective of taking Smolensk before moving on to Moscow, and in fact made the fastest progress. It managed to come within twenty-five miles of the Soviet's capital before being stopped by early winter and unexpected Soviet resistance. Army Group South under General von Rundstedt swept into Ukraine, took Kiev, and went on into the Crimea. The primary objective of the German armies was to destroy armies, not capture cities. The Germans used their armored divisions to break through Soviet lines, trapping large masses of Soviet troops by quickly moving infantry lines. The Germans did manage to capture over 2 million Soviet soldiers. But despite their enormous successes, the Germans failed to achieve their primary objective. They did not eliminate the Soviet army, nor did the Soviet state collapse in a few months, as Hitler and some of his generals thought it would.

Since the Germans had not been issued winter clothing because it was consid-
ered unnecessary, German soldiers were virtually immobilized by freezing temperatures. Armor and transport vehicles were stalled by temperatures of thirty below zero. Hitler's commanders wished to withdraw and regroup for the following spring. Hitler refused. He insisted on no retreat, fearing disintegration of his lines. Hitler must have realized that failure to win soon could be disastrous. The Soviet counterattack in December 1941 by an

---

[13]Quoted in Percy Ernst Schramm, ed., *Kriegstagebuch des Oberkommando der Wehrmacht (Wehrmachtführungstab) 1940–1945*, vol. 2 (Frankfurt am Main, 1961–1965), pp. 336–337.

army supposedly exhausted by Nazi victories came as an ominous ending to the year. On December 19, Hitler took over operational command of the army and cashiered generals who had ordered withdrawal or urged retreat. The Germans had failed to reach their objectives. And no doubt some of them realized the consequences. It was questionable that Hitler could win his war in the east. The Germans had also made a fundamental mistake in their treatment of civilians. In Ukraine, the Germans had been seen as liberators, which at first led to a certain degree of collaboration with the Nazis in the war not only against the Soviets, but the Jews. However, the brutal occupation policies of the Germans—a result of Nazi racial attitudes toward Slavic peoples, as well as their desire to transform parts of Ukraine into a German colony—fostered anti-German sentiment and partisan activity against the Germans. This in turn led to a so-called partisan war, which was fought with unprecedented severity throughout Nazi-occupied territories. Special forces within the SS, as well as regular army attachments, took part in these anti-Partisan campaigns. Significantly, after a meeting with Hitler on December 18, 1941, Himmler wrote in his personal calendar, "Jewish question/to be exterminated as partisans."[14] Nazi racial ideology once again took precedence over political expediency.

Another of Hitler's decisions in December 1941, the declaration of war on the United States, probably made Hitler's defeat inevitable. With Britain refusing to be eliminated, Hitler was increasingly aware that the British problem could be compounded by the American presence behind Britain. Hitler came to feel that he needed to keep America out of the war. As he told Mussolini, close cooperation with Japan was probably the most effective way to do this. But if the United States did become involved, it would pose no danger to Germany if it could be tied down in the East. Thus, in September 1940 Hitler signed a tripartite pact with Italy and Japan. The three nations agreed to help one another if attacked by a power not involved in the war in Europe or the conflict between China and Japan. Hitler's idea in signing the pact was to warn the United States to stay out of the conflict. But this agreement had the opposite effect. Germany now began to worry that Japan might seek better relations with the United States, and it began to encourage a Japanese attack on British possessions in East Asia as a way to keep America involved there. Hitler spelled out the aim of German policy on March 5, 1941. He wanted, he stated, to bring Japan into active operations in the East to tie down British forces and "divert" the United States to the Pacific. In fact, Hitler was so eager for Japanese involvement with America that he expressed his willingness to join a war against the United States if Japan became involved in one. And in fact on December 11, only four days after the Japanese attack on Pearl Harbor, Hitler declared war on the United States.

Why would Hitler have taken a step he had avoided for so long? He had used considerable restraint to avoid incidents that would draw the United States into the European war. It is possible that Hitler felt such a war was inevitable. President Roosevelt had in fact announced on December 9 that he considered Germany just as guilty as Japan for the attack on Pearl Harbor and would not divert American forces from the Atlantic to the Pacific. Hitler certainly believed that Roosevelt was determined to intervene. For that reason, he honored his pledge to the Japanese. Perhaps he also hoped he could thereby keep Japan satisfied in case he eventually wanted Japanese help against the Soviet Union. And Hitler perhaps still hoped that the Germans would defeat the Soviet Union in the spring

---

[14]Reproduced in Peter Witte, ed., *Der Dienstkalender Heinrich Himmlers, 1941/1942* (Hamburg, 1999), p. 294.

and summer of 1942. Certainly the Americans would not be ready for serious involvement in Europe for a year. With the resources of the entire European continent behind him, Hitler would be so strong that the United States and Britain combined could not harm him. But if Hitler had the intelligence to win the victories he did, he also had the intelligence to realize that if he did not knock out the Soviet Union in the spring and summer of 1942, the war was lost in any case. And one more enemy certainly did not matter then.

The Turning Point of the War, 1942–1943

Until the fall of 1942 it looked as if the Germans might still be able to prevail on the battlefield. In the spring of that year, the Germans went back on the offensive. After gaining reinforcements, Rommel and the Afrika Korps broke through the British defenses in Egypt and captured the British base at Tobruk. They then pushed on to El Alamein and were only sixty miles from Alexandria by July.

The Germans were also continuing their success in the Battle of the North Atlantic, in which their submarines continued to attack Allied ships carrying materials to Great Britain. Although the convoy system reduced ship losses, even convoys were still subject to attack. Hitler had increased the number of German submarines from 56 in 1939 to almost 250 by the beginning of 1942. German attacks led to the loss of 4.5 million tons of shipping during the first six months of 1942, causing the British to worry about being forced into submission. Not until the middle of 1943 did the Allies begin to win the Battle of the North Atlantic.

In the spring of 1942, the Germans renewed their offensive in the Soviet Union. Some of Hitler's generals advised an attack on Moscow, but Hitler listened to his economic experts, who stressed the importance of the Soviet oil resources of the Caucasus region in the south. Hitler decided to concentrate his attacks on the south. The renewed German offensive seemed to repeat the successes of the previous year. By July the entire Crimea was in German hands. But instead of concentrating then on the capture of the Caucasus and its oil fields, Hitler decided that Stalingrad, a major industrial center on the Volga, needed to be taken. By August Hitler had been buoyed again by German successes. With considerable elation Hitler told Albert Speer in his military headquarters in the Ukraine that

> for a long time I have had everything prepared. As the next step, we are going to advance south of the Caucasus and then help the rebels in Iran and Iraq against the English. Another thrust will be directed along the Caspian Sea toward Afghanistan and India. Then the English will run out of oil. In two years we'll be on the borders of India. Twenty to thirty elite German divisions will do. Then the British Empire will collapse. They've already lost Singapore to the Japanese. The English will have to look on impotently as their colonial empire falls to pieces.[15]

It was to be Hitler's last truly optimistic outburst. In the last months of 1942, the war turned irrevocably against the Germans.

In North Africa, Rommel's forces failed in the summer of 1942 to break through British defensive lines at El Alamein. The new commander of the British Eighth Army,

---

[15]Albert Speer, *Spandau*, trans. Richard and Clara Winston (New York, 1976), p. 50.

General Bernard Montgomery, launched a carefully planned counteroffensive against the Axis forces on October 23, 1942. Rommel's forces were forced back across the desert, only to be faced with another threat.

On November 8, 1942, British and American forces invaded French North Africa. This first major amphibious operation by the Allied powers was in large part a response to Stalin's demand for a "second front" that would relieve German pressure on the eastern front. The Allies landed in both Morocco and Algeria. Despite reinforcements, the Axis troops were forced to surrender in Tunisia on May 13, 1943. The Axis paid dearly for the Desert War. Nearly a million men were killed, wounded, or captured. The Allies were now ready to cross the Mediterranean into Sicily and carry the war directly into Europe.

As we have seen, it was not until 1943 that the shipping war in the Atlantic shifted to the Allies' advantage. German destruction of Allied ships reached its peak in March 1943. At the same time, the introduction of escort carriers and the development of new detection devices led to increased losses of German submarines. Admiral Dönitz, the submarine commander (who had also become commander of the navy in early 1943), reported to Hitler that the Germans could not maintain their submarine attacks due to these losses.

The years 1942 and 1943 also saw the beginning of strategic bombing of Germany. Although night raids were initially used against military and industrial targets, their lack of precision led to terror bombing or strikes against large urban targets. The American air force made daytime raids against specific military-industrial targets, which often resulted in disastrous losses of their planes.

On the eastern front, the turning point of the war occurred at Stalingrad. The German advance on that city encountered fierce resistance in early November. On November 19 and 20, the Soviets attacked German positions north and south of Stalingrad, and by November 23 they had surrounded German forces. Hitler commanded General von Paulus to stand firm with his Sixth Army and forbade attempts to break out of the encirclement. While the siege of Stalingrad was portrayed back in Germany as a heroic struggle of epic proportions, for the abandoned soldiers the war had been transformed from one of exhilaration and euphoria with rapid success in the West to frustration and hopelessness with failure in the East. Many soldiers came to believe that the only way out of Stalingrad was "to heaven or to Siberia," meaning death or a Soviet concentration camp. One soldier wrote a letter home noting that "in many newspapers you will find beautiful, high-sounding words in big black borders . . . They always pay us due honor. Don't be taken in by this idiotic to-do. I am so furious that I could smash everything in sight, but never in my life have I felt so helpless."[16] Winter privations and Soviet attacks forced the Germans to surrender on February 2, 1943. The entire Sixth Army was lost to the Soviet forces. After the defeat at Stalingrad, Hitler allowed the remaining German troops to withdraw from the Caucasus to avoid being encircled. By February 1943, the Germans were back to their lines of June 1942. On the other Soviet fronts, the Germans failed to take Leningrad and posed no more threat to Moscow. Although much fighting remained, by the spring of 1943 it was apparent that the Germans would not defeat the Soviet Union.

[16]Quoted in Stephen G. Fritz, *Frontsoldaten: The German Soldier in World War II* (Lexington, Ky., 1995), p. 68.

Hitler as Warlord

It is evident from our examination of the war that Hitler played a crucial role in German military decision making. Hitler was the supreme warlord of Nazi Germany, although there has been considerable discussion about Hitler's effectiveness in this role.

That Hitler had virtually complete control of military affairs after his reorganization of the German military is unmistakable. He created a High Command of the Armed Forces (*Oberkommando der Wehrmacht*, or OKW) headed by General Keitel as Chief and Alfred Jodl as Chief of Operations. The OKW served as Hitler's military staff under his direct command and provided the basic machinery for applying his war strategy, which he was able to impose on the three branches of the Wehrmacht. The air force, under Commander in Chief Göring, and the navy, under Erich Raeder and then Karl Dönitz, were already subject to Hitler. In December 1941, Hitler assumed control of the army as commander in chief and imposed strategy on the High Command of the Army (OKH). Hitler came to have total mastery over strategic and tactical operations. During the war, he exercised command from different places. Führer headquarters were sometimes specially constructed and fortified, as at Wolfsschanze in East Prussia, Adlerhorst in the Taunus Mountains near Frankfurt am Main, and, of course, at the end of the war in the Bunker beneath Berlin. Wherever he was, the OKW was.

In his military headquarters, daily conferences on the military situation took place twice a day, usually lasting from two to three hours. Regular participants numbered twenty and included Keitel and Jodl, representatives of the three armed forces and their adjutants, as well as Hitler's personal adjutants from each branch of the armed forces. A representative of the Foreign Office was also included. After hearing and discussing the military situation on each front, Hitler gave orders.

Hitler did possess some military talents. Many of his generals emphasized that he had a great mastery of military details. He took much delight in technical details, especially the psychological effects new weapons had on combatants and noncombatants. Although his generals contended that he acted entirely by intuition, records of military conferences suggest that Hitler weighed various aspects of positions and came to fairly rational decisions. He had a good sense for the larger questions of overall strategy. As early as 1932 he had indicated to a confidant that the next war would be different from the last one. Infantry attacks and interlocked frontal assaults would be replaced by quick, mobile operations over large expanses of territory. If Hitler is to be blamed for Germany's loss of the war, then he is to be given credit for the victories of 1939 and 1940. He pointed out the weaknesses of the French army. He seized upon General von Manstein's daring invasion plans of France and Guderian's panzer tactics. He fully grasped and developed the potential of *Blitzkrieg*. Despite the doubts of professional officers, Hitler pushed these new approaches to warfare.

His astonishing successes in 1939 and 1940 led to his undoing. He came to exaggerate his military ability and to have an especially low view of the professional military officers who had opposed his audacious plans. He particularly overestimated the role of willpower. Even the detractors among his generals considered Hitler's willpower his outstanding quality. Obviously, the power of Hitler's will in the early years of the war was bolstered by the military innovations, tactical surprise, and sheer force that brought success. Willpower, despite Hitler's protestations, proved worthless in the face of overwhelming enemy forces.

Although the sycophantic generals Keitel and Jodl praised Hitler's genius as a military commander, commanders in the field had a very different conception. General

Rommel, for example, felt that Hitler had serious shortcomings as a strategist. Other generals objected to the restraints imposed on them as field commanders. As the German wartime position worsened, Hitler increasingly interfered in daily operations down to the smallest details. Although praised for grand strategic vision, he was also criticized for failure to plan well at an operational level and to handle army groups and their components in battle. Essentially Hitler lacked the requisite professional skills for operations that come from training and experience.

A special source of conflict between Hitler and his generals was the question of retreat when faced with an overwhelming enemy force. Hitler's order for German troops to hold firm and not withdraw in the first brutal Soviet winter of 1941–1942 was costly in human lives but probably saved the German army from disintegration. Thereafter, his repeated emphasis on no retreat was foolish and led to astounding casualties. The destruction of General Paulus's Sixth Army at Stalingrad is a prominent example. Hitler came to view any request for withdrawal as being due to a lack of courage or, worse yet, as a sign of betrayal by military commanders, and he invariably rejected it. Near the end of the war, even families of generals who withdrew contrary to orders were punished. That forced stands condemned many German soldiers to death simply did not concern Hitler. As a military commander he had absolutely no respect for soldiers' lives. Once, when told that a particular battle had produced high casualties among junior officers, Hitler responded by reminding his officers that that was what "young people are there for."

Despite his belief in willpower, iron nerves, and forceful decision-making ability, Hitler made costly strategic errors because of indecision. Although he recognized the importance of the Mediterranean arena, he was unwilling to send sufficient forces to decide the outcome of the struggle there. In his invasion of the Soviet Union, he constantly shifted forces instead of concentrating on a single purpose. After Stalingrad Hitler lost any real mobility in operations, but he failed to understand this. Nor was he willing to recognize the restrictions imposed on the Germans by Allied air supremacy.

Perhaps Hitler's greatest weakness as a supreme warlord was his own ideological underpinnings. His National Socialist ideology caused him to pursue policies of racial extermination (see Chapter 9) and racial relocation (see Chapter 8) in the east that led to stronger resistance and hence greater military problems there. No doubt these abhorrent policies also caused his opponents in the war to fight even more. Then, too, his belief in the racial superiority of the Germans led Hitler to underestimate the strength of other nations and overestimate the strength of his own. This outlook also led to Germany's failure to gain military allies.

The Last Years of the War

The Western Allies' next move in 1943 was the invasion of Sicily. The American Seventh Army under General George Patton and the British Eighth Army under Montgomery landed there on July 10. Although the plan to cut off Axis withdrawal from the island failed, Sicily was nevertheless taken. Its capture led to a change in the Italian government. Mussolini was deposed and arrested at the end of July. Rescued by the Germans, Mussolini was made a puppet ruler of northern Italy by German forces, which had now seized control of Italy to prevent it from surrendering to the Allied forces.

Because of a tenacious German defense in the mountainous Italian terrain, the Allied campaign to conquer Italy turned out to be a long and bloody affair. Although this campaign has been severely criticized as unnecessary, others have argued that it served to tie down German troops that would have been used on other fronts. The invasion of Italy proper began in September with difficult landings at Salerno. The general in charge of German forces, Kesselring, proved to be an astute practitioner of defense. The Allied advance up the peninsula was painstakingly slow and entailed heavy casualties. Rome did not fall to the Allies until June 4, 1944. The Italian war now became secondary to the main Allied effort on the Western front. For on June 6, 1944, Operation Overlord was put into effect with Allied landings on the Normandy beach of France.

The Allies had begun planning in the fall of 1943 for a "second front" in western Europe, to be launched by a cross-channel invasion. Dwight Eisenhower was chosen as supreme Allied commander. The Germans had assigned General Rommel to prepare an "Atlantic Wall" and prevent an Allied invasion, although General von Rundstedt was in overall command of German forces. The Allies managed to dupe the Germans into believing that the attack would come in the Pas de Calais region and successfully landed their assault divisions on the Normandy beaches on June 6. The German response to the invasion was indecisive. Rundstedt was cashiered because he believed Germany should seek a settlement with the West. After the July 20 assassination attempt on Hitler, Rommel was suspected of involvement and encouraged to commit suicide. Rundstedt's replacement, General Kluge, also committed suicide in August after failing to stop the Allied breakout from their beachhead.

After the breakout on August 1, Allied forces moved into France. Paris was liberated by the end of August. Special emphasis was placed on the northern advance under General Montgomery. The Allies felt that control of northern Germany was the key to control of Germany itself. Eisenhower did permit a second offensive to the south. The movement of Allied troops through France to the Rhine was slowed considerably by supply problems. In December, Hitler took advantage of overstretched Allied lines to launch his Ardennes offensive, designed to capture Antwerp and reestablish German control on the Western front. Its failure made it ever more apparent that Germany was doomed.

Only Hitler continued to speak of German victory. It is doubtful that even he believed in that possibility, but he at least continued to emphasize that a last-minute split would occur between the western and eastern Allies. Hitler did not think that the West would permit the Communists to overrun large parts of Europe. In fact, even some army officers and other Nazi leaders believed they could still make peace with the West and then with their combined forces attack the Soviet troops in the east.

It was not until March 1945 that the Rhineland was taken. In the south, Patton's forces raced across Germany but were diverted by a search for a supposed Nazi fortress system that was to be the center of last-ditch German resistance. As Patton's forces discovered, it never existed. In northern Germany, Allied forces moved toward the Elbe River, where they linked up with the Soviets at the end of April 1945.

The presence of Soviet forces on the Elbe by 1945 indicates the tremendous advance they had made since 1943. In the summer of 1943, Hitler's generals were urging him to construct an "East Wall" making use of river barriers to hold back the Soviets. Hitler, however, wanted to go on the offensive near Kursk and deploy the new heavy tanks developed by the Germans. German forces attacked in July 1943, but the Soviets won a stunning victory at Kursk. Eighteen of Hitler's best panzer divisions were devastated by the Soviets. This was Germany's last major offensive on the eastern front. The Soviets now attacked on all fronts and used their own version of *Blitzkrieg* offensives to rapidly regain control of their territory. Although Hitler continued to order his "no retreat" policy, it proved to be of little value. It did not stop the Soviets, and large numbers of German troops were need-lessly sacrificed. By the end of 1943, the Soviets had reoccupied Ukraine.

By the beginning of 1944, the Soviets had lifted the siege of Leningrad and moved into the Baltic states. By April they were in Romania, where they were temporarily halted. Bulgaria collapsed and Romania joined the Soviets against Germany. Hungary was invaded, although Budapest was not reached till late December. On the northern front, the Soviets reached the outskirts of Warsaw at the end of July 1944, but did not occupy it until January 1945. The Soviets then made a major attack on all fronts in January 1945 and reached both Vienna and Berlin in April. They then linked up with American troops.

In April 1945, the Italian front collapsed. Mussolini was captured by partisans and shot on April 28. Ensconced in his Bunker, Hitler learned of Mussolini's death shortly before he took his own life.

The Bunker

On January 16, 1945, Adolf Hitler moved into the Bunker, his final wartime head-quarters. It was reached through a tunnel that led from the New Reich Chancellery building into and under the chancellery garden. Buried fifty-five feet below the ground, the Bunker was covered by a roof of reinforced concrete sixteen feet thick. Hitler and

Military Operations of World War II: The Allied Offensives, 1943–1945

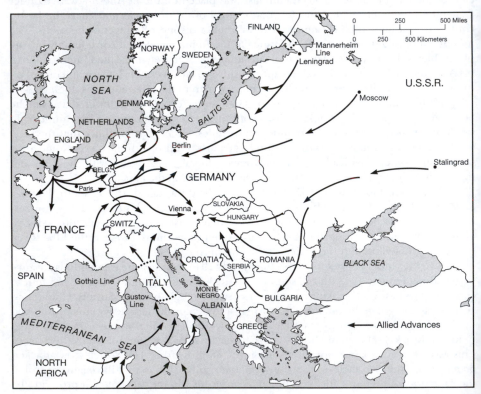

Eva Braun occupied six rooms. The remaining rooms were used for conferences, guards, a generator station, a doctor, and a cook. Joseph Goebbels and his wife and six children joined Hitler in his last days in the Bunker.

Both the physical and psychological pressures of the Bunker were oppressive. A considerable amount of Hitler's time was still occupied with the twice-daily military conferences. Hitler continued to arrange and rearrange armies as if it still made a difference. His behavior was bizarre.

> Hitler had long been accustomed, from underground bunkers, to direct the operations of non-existent armies, to dictate their strategy and tactics, dispose their forces, calculate their gains, and then to denounce the treachery of their generals when the actual results failed to correspond with his private conclusions. So in these days he would expound the tactics whereby Wenck would relieve the city. Pacing up and down in the Bunker . . . he would wave a roadmap, fast decomposing with the sweat of his hands, and explain to any casual visitor the complicated military operations whereby they would all be saved. Sometimes he would shout orders, as if himself directing the defenders; sometimes he would spread the map on his table, and stooping over it, with trembling hands he would arrange and rearrange a set of buttons, as consolatory symbols of relieving armies.[17]

Wenck's army and the others he would mention no longer existed.

In his last months, Hitler had become obsessed with destruction. He had always warned that the goal of Nazism was world domination or ruin, and if the National Socialists did not win, "even as we go down to destruction we will carry half the world into destruction with us." Beginning in March he issued a series of commands ordering the destruction of all military, transportation, communications, industrial, and food-supply facilities and all other resources that could be used by the enemy. But even Hitler was no longer able to execute such drastic commands, and some Germans, such as Hitler's armaments minister, Albert Speer, deliberately countermanded them.

The world of the Bunker was unreal. Goebbels was elated when he heard on April 13 that President Roosevelt had died. He and Hitler were now convinced that this was a turning point in the war, since the new president, Harry Truman, was an isolationist from Missouri who would withdraw the United States from the war. On April 24, Hitler ordered Colonel General Ritter von Greim to fly from Munich to Berlin. It was no longer safe to do so, and not only were some of Greim's escort planes shot down but he was wounded in the foot. Hitler informed him that he had ordered him there to tell him in person that Greim was now Hermann Göring's successor as commander in chief of the Luftwaffe. But even in this unreal world there was some clarity. At his military conference of April 22, Hitler announced that the war was lost and that he had decided to kill himself and end his struggle.

Bitter resentment and accusations of treachery occupied Hitler's final weeks in the Bunker. He ordered the arrest of Göring for high treason for his suggestion on April 23 that he take over leadership of Germany because of Hitler's decision to end his life in the Bunker. But Hitler felt especially betrayed when he heard on the evening of April 28 that Heinrich Himmler had tried to negotiate a separate peace with the Allies. Hitler had regarded Himmler as the most faithful of all the Nazis. This was the final straw, and he now

---

[17]Hugh R. Trevor-Roper, *The Last Days of Hitler* (New York, 1947), pp. 138–139.

acted to end it all. In the early morning hours of April 29, he married Eva Braun to reward her for her loyalty. After a brief celebration he dictated his will and political testament.

In his political testament, Hitler returned to the same old arguments he had first formulated in *Mein Kampf*. He, of course, had not caused the war in 1939. International Jewry would eventually be seen as the culprit. He also took a final swipe at the army:

> May it at some future time become part of the code of honor of the German officer—as it already is in the case of our Navy—that the surrender of a district or of a town should be impossible and that the leaders should march ahead as shining examples faithfully fulfilling their duty unto death.[18]

In the second part of the political testament, he made his final political arrangements. Admiral Dönitz would be his successor as president of the Reich, war minister, and supreme commander of the armed forces. Joseph Goebbels was named chancellor and Martin Bormann party minister. The last paragraph returned to the racial obsession at the heart of his ideology: "Above all I charge the leaders of the nation and those under them to scrupulous observance of the laws of race and to merciless opposition to the universal poisoner of all peoples, international Jewry."[19]

On April 30, he and Eva Braun committed suicide. Their bodies were burned, in accordance with Hitler's instructions. One week later, on May 7, German military leaders in Reims, France, surrendered unconditionally to the Allies. To the end, Hitler had characterized the Germans as unworthy of survival because they had failed their leader in their great task as Germans. We need now to examine Nazi Germany in wartime to see how and why the Germans failed.

SUGGESTIONS FOR FURTHER READING

The fundamental study of Germany's foreign policy from 1933 to 1939 can be found in Gerhard Weinberg's two classic books, now available in an updated combined edition as *Hitler's Foreign Policy: The Road to World War II, 1933–1939* (New York, 2004). Other works on foreign policy include Christian Leitz, *Nazi Foreign Policy, 1939–1941* (New York, 2004); Frank McDonough, *Hitler, Chamberlain and Appeasement* (Cambridge, Mass., 2002); Klaus Hildebrandt, *The Foreign Policy of the Third Reich*, trans. Anthony Fothergill (London, 1973); Giles MacDonogh, *1938: Hitler's Gamble* (New York, 2009). On the Munich Conference, see Igor Lukes and Erik Goldstein, eds., *The Munich Crisis, 1938: Prelude to World War II* (London, 1999); Hugh Ragsdale, *The Soviets, the Munich Crisis, and the Coming of World War II* (New York, 2004); and David Faber, *Munich, 1938: Appeasement and World War II* (New York, 2009). On the historical and ideological background of Nazi imperialism, see Woodruff Smith, *The Ideological Origins of Nazi Imperialism* (New York, 1986). A study that analyzes Hitler's early ideas on foreign policy is Geoffrey Stoakes, *Hitler and the Quest for World Dominion: Nazi Ideology and Foreign Policy in the 1920s* (New York, 1987). Specialized studies of value are Paul Seabury, *The Wilhelmstrasse: A Study of German Diplomats under the Nazi Regime* (Berkeley, Calif., 1954); John L. Heinemann, *Hitler's First Foreign Minister:*

[18] *Nazi Conspiracy and Aggression*, vol. 6 (Washington, D.C., 1946), p. 262.
[19] Ibid., p. 263.

Constantin von Neurath, Diplomat and Statesman (Berkeley, Calif., 1979); and Hans Adolf Jacobsen and Arthur L. Smith, *The Nazi Party and the German Foreign Office* (New York, 2007). On the influence of Karl Haushofer, see Andréas Dorpalen, *The World of General Haushofer: Geopolitics in Action* (New York, 1942); and David T. Murphy, *The Heroic Earth: Geopolitical Thought in Weimar Germany, 1918–1933* (Kent, Ohio, 1997). Nazi activities overseas are covered in Donald M. McKale, *The Swastika Outside Germany* (Kent, Ohio, 1977).

Studies of Germany's relations with other nations in Europe and abroad are discussed in Jonathan R. Adelman, ed., *Hitler and His Allies in World War II* (New York, 2007); and Richard L. DiNardo, *Germany and the Axis Powers from Coalition to Collapse* (Lawrence, Kan., 2005). Relations with specific nations are discussed in detail in F. W. Deakin, *The Brutal Friendship* (London, 1966); Anthony Adamthwaite, *France and the Coming of the Second World War, 1936–1939* (London, 1977); Elizabeth Wiskemann, *The Rome-Berlin Axis* (New York, 1969); MacGregor Know, *Common Destiny: Dictatorship, Foreign Policy and War in Fascist Italy and Nazi Germany* (Cambridge, Mass., 2000); Johanna Meskill, *Hitler and Japan: The Hollow Alliance* (New York, 1966); Radomîr Luza, *Austro-German Relations in the Anschluss Era* (Princeton, N.J., 1975); Robert H. Whealey, *Hitler and Spain: The Nazi Role in the Spanish Civil War* (Lexington, Ky., 1989); Wayne H. Bowen, *Spaniards and Nazi Germany: Collaboration in the New Order* (Columbia, N.Y., 2000); Stanley G. Payne, *Franco and Hitler: Spain, Germany, and World War II* (New Haven, Conn., 2008); Dietrich Orlow, *The Nazis in the Balkans* (Pittsburgh, 1968); Mario D. Fenyo, *Hitler, Horthy and Hungary: German-Hungarian Relations, 1941–1944* (New Haven, Conn., 1972); Ronald Smelser, *The Sudeten Problem, 1933–1938: Volkstumspolitik and the Formulation of Nazi Foreign Policy* (Middletown, Conn., 1975); Barry Leach, *German Strategy Against Russia, 1939–1941* (Oxford, 1973); and Francis Nicosia, *The Third Reich and the Palestine Question* (Austin, Tex., 1986). Nazi-occupied Austria is discussed in Evan Bukey, *Hitler's Austria* (Chapel Hill, N.C., 2000). The administration of Nazi-occupied Europe in general is discussed in Mark Mazower, *Hitler's Empire: How the Nazis Ruled Europe* (New York, 2008).

The basic study of Hitler's war aims and the importance of ideology to those aims is Norman Rich, *Hitler's War Aims*, vol. 1, *Ideology, the Nazi State and the Course of Expansion* (New York, 1973), and vol. 2, *The Establishment of the New Order* (New York, 1974). On the background to World War II, see P. M. H. Bell, *The Origins of the Second World War in Europe*, 2nd ed. (New York, 1997). General works on World War II include Richard J. Evans, *The Third Reich at War* (New York, 2009); Gerhard Weinberg, *A World at Arms: A Global History of World War II* (Cambridge, Mass., 1994); Max Hastings, *Inferno: The World at War, 1939–1945* (New York, 2011); Gordon Corrigan, *The Second World War: A Military History* (New York, 2010); M. K. Dziewanowski, *War at Any Price: World War II in Europe, 1939–1945*, 2nd ed. (Upper Saddle River, N.J., 1997); John Keegan, *The Second World War* (London, 1989); and John H. Campbell, ed., *The Experience of World War II* (New York, 1989). The pivotal period that saw an important shift in the scope of the war is discussed in Evan Mawdsley, *December 1941: Twelve Days that Began a World War* (New Haven, Conn., 2011). Various campaigns and theaters of operations are dealt with in the following: Allan R. Millett and Williamson Murray, *A War to be Won: Fighting the Second World War, 1937–1945* (Cambridge, Mass., 2001); Nicholas Bethell, *The War Hitler Won* (London, 1972); Alexander B. Rossino, *Hitler Strikes Poland* (Lawrence, Kans., 2003); Ronald Wheatley, *Operation Sea Lion* (Oxford, 1958); Ronald Lewin, *The Life and Death of the Afrika Korps* (London, 1977); David Stahel, *Kiev 1941: Hitler's Battle for Supremacy in the East* (New York, 2012); David Glantz and Jonathan House, *When Titans Clashed: How the Red Army Stopped Hitler* (Lawrence, Kans., 1995); Jeffrey Jukes,

Hitler's Stalingrad Decisions (Berkeley, Calif., 1985); John Erickson, *The Road to Stalingrad* (New Haven, Conn., 1999) and *The Road to Berlin* (New Haven, Conn., 1999); Antony Beevor, *Stalingrad, The Fateful Siege, 1942–1943* (New York, 1999); Anna Reid, *Stalingrad: The Epic Siege of World War II, 1941–1944* (New York, 2011); Ralph Bennett, *Ultra in the West: The Normandy Campaign* (London, 1979); Anthony Read and David Fisher, *The Fall of Berlin* (New York, 1993); and Hans Dieter Berenbeck, *Hitler's Naval War* (New York, 1974). On the Eastern War in general, see Stephen G. Fritz, *Ostkrieg: Hitler's War of Extermination in the East* (Lexington, Ky., 2011); and Rolf-Dieter Müller and Gerd R. Ueberschär, eds., *Hitler's War in the East* (New York, 2002), includes extensive bibliographies on all aspects of the Eastern War. On the turning point in the war see Robert M. Citino, *Death of the Wehrmacht: The German Campaigns of 1942* (Lawrence, Kan., 2007) and *The Wehrmacht Retreats: Fighting a Lost War, 1943* (Lawrence, Kan., 2012); and David M. Glantz and Jonathan M. House, *The Battle of Kursk* (Lawrence, Kan., 1999). On espionage, see David Kahn, *Hitler's Spies: German Military Intelligence in World War II* (London, 1978); and Zachary Shore, *What Hitler Knew: The Battle for Information in Nazi Foreign Policy* (New York, 2003). On the German army and its atrocities, see Omer Bartov, *The Eastern Front 1941–1945: German Troops and the Barbarisation of Warfare* (New York, 1986); Geoffry P. Megargee, *War of Annihilation: Combat and Genocide on the Eastern Front, 1941* (Lanham, Md., 2006); Ben Shepard, *War in the Wild East: The German Army and the Soviet Partisans* (Cambridge, Mass., 2004); and Hannes Heer and Klaus Naumann, eds., *War of Extermination: The German Military in World War II, 1941–1944* (New York, 2000). The experience of the German soldier in the war is discussed in Omer Bartov, *Hitler's Army: Soldiers, Nazis, and War in the Third Reich* (New York, 1992); and Stephen G. Fritz, *Frontsoldaten: The German Soldier in World War II* (Lexington, Ky., 1995).

On Hitler as a military leader, see Felix Gilbert, ed., *Hitler Directs His War* (New York, 1951), which contains selections from his daily military conferences; Helmut Heiber and David M. Glantz, eds., *Hitler and His Generals: Military Conferences 1942–1945* (New York, 2003); and Percy Schramm, *Hitler: The Man and the Military Leader*, trans. and ed. Donald S. Detwiler (Chicago, 1971), which includes extracts from Hitler's table talk in military headquarters. See also Ronald Lewin, *Hitler's Mistakes* (New York, 1986). Hitler's relationship with his military leaders, and their own strategic failings, is discussed in Geoffrey P. Megargee, *Inside Hitler's High Command* (Lawrence, Kan., 2000); and David Stone, *Shattered Genius: The Decline and Fall of the German General Staff in World War II* (Havertown, Pa., 2011). For biographical sketches of German military leaders, see Correlli Barnett, *Hitler's Generals* (New York, 1989). On the conclusion of the war, see Robert Stephen Fritz, *Endkampf: Soldiers, Civilians and the Death of the Third Reich* (Lexington, Ky., 2004); Richard Bessel, *Germany 1945: From War to Peace* (New York, 2009); and Ian Kershaw, *The End: The Defiance and Destruction of Hitler's Germany, 1944–1945* (New York, 2011). Hitler's last days are vividly portrayed in James P. O'Donnell, *The Bunker* (New York, 1978); Hugh R. Trevor-Roper, *The Last Days of Hitler*, rev. ed. (London, 1968); and Joachim Fest, *Inside Hitler's Bunker* (New York, 2004).

MySearchLab™ Connections

Study and Review

Inspired by racial ideology, Adolf Hitler threatened war against Russia and France to gain more land for the German people before he took control of the Reichstag. To support a larger population, Hitler believed that more space and resources were needed. For national security reasons, the land needed to be contiguous to Germany. World War II arose out of Hitler's efforts to secure Europe—and possibly the world—for the Aryan race.

View the Image

1. **Hitler celebrating French surrender**
   This image shows Hitler celebrating the conquest of France with his generals. Hitler thought that the French defeat atoned for Germany's surrender in World War I.

Read the Document

2. **Heinrich Himmler, "Speech to SS Officers"**
   This document presents the code of ethics that Heinrich Himmler, the head of the SS, expected his men to follow. It is filled with platitudes about honor and loyalty, while he does enumerate the various crimes of this group.

Read the Document

3. **Franklin D. Roosevelt and Winston Churchill, "The Atlantic Charter"**
   This document illustrates the nature of the Anglo-American alliance at the beginning of World War II. Britain, under continual attack from Germany, was able to receive support from the United States, despite stated American neutrality at the time. The Atlantic Charter lays out the war aims and ideals of the partnership.

RESEARCH AND EXPLORE

World War II was Hitler's war, and it is certainly possible that he could have won this war if his goals had been less rigid and if he had kept the nonaggression pact with the USSR. Germany suffered a second and even more disastrous defeat in this war due to political missteps, over-stretched supply-lines, and the entry of the United States and the USSR as wartime allies.

1. Was the Nazi attack against the USSR motivated by a desire for more living territory or by racial ideology? Were the Russians victims of the same level of ideological hate as the Jews were?

2. Why did Hitler engage in a two-front war? What was Hitler's rationale for breaking the nonaggression pact with the USSR?

3. What was Hitler's impression of the United States prior to the war? How did this view change after the United States joined the fighting?

ADDITIONAL RESOURCES

World War II in Europe, 1939–1945

Nazis executing Russian civilians

CHAPTER

8

Nazi Germany in Wartime

dolf Hitler's establishment of a New Order in Europe was determined largely by his racial ideology and the exigencies of war. Nazi domestic policies in wartime Germany were influenced not only by war conditions but also by Hitler's perception that Germany had collapsed in World War I because of the home front. He was determined not to repeat that situation.

THE NEW ORDER

Structure of the German Empire

The idea of a new European order was propagated by German ideological publicists and Nazi collaborators in European countries. Indeed, some Nazis, such as Germany's press chief, Otto Dietrich, spoke of a New Order based not on a privileged position for some nations but on "equal chances" for all nations. The German press favored the term *United States of Europe*.

These ideas of a European New Order were not Hitler's. Hitler saw the Europe he had conquered as being subject to German domination. He told some Nazi leaders in 1943 what the aim of their struggle was:

> All the rubbish of small nations still existing in Europe must be liquidated as fast as possible. The aim of our struggle must be to create a unified Europe. The Germans alone can really organize Europe . . . Today we are practically the only power on the European mainland with a capacity for leadership. The Reich will be the master of all Europe . . . Whoever dominates Europe will thereby assume the leadership of the world.[1]

For the time being, only Germans—and not even Germanic peoples, such as the Dutch and Norwegians, who were racial relatives of the Germans—would run the new Europe.

[1]Louis P. Lochner, ed., *The Goebbels Diaries, 1942–1943* (Garden City, N.Y., 1948), pp. 357, 359.

In reality, not only was there no new European order, but the German Empire itself could hardly be said to be organized systematically. All of that, Hitler himself emphasized, would await final German victory. Some European states, such as Spain, Portugal, Switzerland, Sweden, and Turkey, maintained autonomy through their neutral status. Germany's allies—Italy, Romania, Bulgaria, Hungary, and Finland—maintained their independence, although precariously at times. As the war progressed, these states found their freedom of action increasingly restricted by the Germans. As an ally, Finland was to be the guardian of Germany's northern flank. Due to its economic interests and concern for its southern flank, Nazi Germany sought political and economic influence in the Balkan satellite states of Hungary, Romania, and Bulgaria. Hungary's military and economic cooperation with Germany included contributing troops to the invasion of the Soviet Union. Hungary's desire to withdraw from the war led to German occupation of the country in February 1944. Romania agreed early on to the presence of large German military forces to protect the Romanian oil fields, considered crucial to the German war effort. The government of Marshall Ion Antonescu was a loyal ally of Germany, and Romania was the first Balkan state to join in the attack on the Soviet Union. The Germans used Bulgaria as transit territory for German troops invading Yugoslavia and Greece. Germany did not ask Bulgaria to participate in the war against the Soviet Union, but regarded it as a guardian of Germany's southern flank against Turkey and awarded it control of Macedonia for its efforts. Hitler had viewed Italy at least theoretically as an equal partner because of the cultural views and political values it shared with Germany. Italy, however, had become heavily dependent on Nazi Germany by 1940 and was placed under German military occupation in 1943 after its attempted withdrawal from the war.

The remainder of Europe was occupied by German forces and organized in one of two ways—either through direct annexation by Germany or through administration by German civilian or military officials combined with varying degrees of indirect control by collaborationist regimes. Almost everywhere in Europe, German civil and military administrations failed to operate according to highly touted German efficiency. The primary reason, as in the German domestic administration as well, was Hitler's propensity to establish competing lines of authority through special commissions and the tendency of those competing offices to pursue power at each other's expense. Hence civil or military administrations found themselves competing with officials from Hermann Göring's economic offices, Heinrich Himmler's SS and police forces, and, after 1942, Albert Speer's Ministry of Armaments and Munitions and Fritz Sauckel's Labor Mobilization Office. The first non-German territory to be occupied by Nazi Germany had been Czechoslovakia, which was divided into the Protectorate of Bohemia and Moravia and a semi-independent Slovakia. Bohemia and Moravia were placed under the civil administration of the office of the Reich protector, a position held first by an old-line conservative, Konstantin von Neurath. In 1941, he was replaced by the SS leader Reinhard Heydrich, who pursued considerably harsher policies.

In western Europe, direct annexation was at first limited to three small territories— Eupen, Malmedy, and Moresnet—that had been awarded to Belgium after World War I. Luxembourg was rapidly Germanized through the establishment of German language, currency, and law and the conscripting of males into the German Labor Service, Hitler Youth, and Wehrmacht. Although not officially annexed, Luxembourg was attached to a Nazi Party administrative district and treated as part of the Third Reich. In France, Alsace and part of Lorraine were also treated administratively as if they were part of Germany.

The Nordic countries were treated rather leniently because of the racial kinship of their peoples to Germans. Norway was placed under the civil administration of Joseph Terboven, a Nazi *Gauleiter.* Although Hitler insisted that the Norwegian collaborator Vidkun Quisling be made head of a national government, Terboven managed to maintain his grasp on real power. Denmark was treated even more favorably. The royal Danish government was allowed to keep control of the government and public institutions in return for its cooperation with German military and civil officials. But in the fall of 1943, after a series of strikes and a campaign of sabotage, the Nazis eliminated the Danish government and took direct control. Like Norway and Denmark, the Netherlands had a German civil administration in recognition of the Germanic character of Dutch people. The Reich commissioner for the Netherlands, the Austrian Arthur Seyss-Inquart, tried unsuccessfully to create the impression of Dutch political independence. He especially emphasized the ideological goal of Germanizing the Dutch. Plans called for settlement of the Dutch on farms in the eastern European empire, but were postponed until after the war.

Although the Flemings, who constituted 53 percent of the Belgian population, were considered Germanic by the Nazis, Belgium was placed under a military government. German-occupied France, which contained three-fifths of prewar French territory, including Paris, northern France, and the entire channel coast, was also placed under military administration. Here the military faced strong opposition to its rule by Himmler's SS, which had managed to gain control of both political and judicial authority by 1942. The remainder of France, known as Vichy France, was permitted an independent regime contingent upon its willingness to collaborate with the Nazis. Under Marshal Pétain and especially Pierre Laval, collaboration was considered necessary to gain a favorable position for France in the New Order and create the best possible situation for the French. French independence was lost, however, in November 1942, when the German military occupied all of France.

After Mussolini's failure in Greece at the end of 1940, the Germans moved into Yugoslavia and Greece to protect their southern flank. Parts of northern Yugoslavia (Slovenia) that had belonged to the Austrian Empire before World War I were Germanized in preparation for direct annexation. The rest of Yugoslavia was divided into Croatia, Serbia, and Montenegro. Croatia was placed under both Italian and German military control; a native collaborationist government ran domestic affairs. Serbia was given a German military government, and native Serbian leaders provided administrative personnel for the day-to-day running of the country. Montenegro was placed under Italian control until occupied by the Germans in 1943. Likewise, Greece was run primarily by an Italian military government until the Germans took over Italian positions with their own military government.

Since the east contained the *Lebensraum* for German expansion, German administration was both direct and considerably more ruthless there than in the west. Western Poland was annexed by the Third Reich and made into two new German provinces. The remainder of German-conquered Poland became the so-called Government General under the ruthless civil administration of Hans Frank.

German brutality was especially evident in the Soviet Union. Hitler's policies in Russia basically undermined the German position there. Germany had a wonderful opportunity to gain support from the native peoples, particularly in the Ukraine and the Baltic states where the Germans were hailed as liberators from Stalin's murderous totalitarian regime. But Hitler's policies of refusing to enlist the aid of the Slavic peoples and his deliberate treatment of them as being fit only for slave labor turned them against their German conquerors.

Nazi Terrorism. This photograph shows another Nazi act of terrorism against the Ukrainian peasants. Hitler's brutal policies cost him the support of peoples who had initially hailed the Germans as liberators from Communist rule. *(National Archives and Records Administration[242-GAV-43B])*

German administration proved especially inefficient in Russia. Hitler had delegated broad powers to four competing administrative organizations: a military administration; Göring's economic offices; Himmler's offices; and a special civil administration under the overall supervision of the Nazi Party ideologist Alfred Rosenberg. Two civil administrative provinces were established in the Soviet Union at the end of 1941. The Reich Commissariat Ostland consisted of the three Baltic states—Estonia, Latvia, and Lithuania—and White Russia. It was placed under the control of Hinrich Lohse, who was responsible to Rosenberg's Reich Ministry for the East. However, Lohse acted virtually independently of Rosenberg's authority. Hitler planned to annex this entire area after the war. The Reich Commissariat Ukraine was placed under Erich Koch. Although Rosenberg wanted to foster Ukrainian support through friendly policies, Hitler had different intentions. The brutal and arrogant Koch was more in accord with Hitler, and he alienated the Ukrainians by his harsh policies. "I did not come here to spread bliss but to help the Führer," he stated. "I will pump every last thing out of this country."[2] Hitler had planned two additional commissariats in Russia, one in the Caucasus and one in the region around Moscow, but because of the military situation they never came into being.

Resettlement and Colonization

In accordance with Nazi ideology, a major purpose of German conquest was to find the living space that would enable the German race to expand and grow. Hitler had

[2]Quoted in Norman Rich, *Hitler's War Aims,* vol. 2 (New York, 1974), p. 376.

emphasized that this land would be found in the east, and the Nazis were so eager to put their racial plans into practice that they tried to at least begin the process as soon as they had conquered Poland. On October 7, 1939, Heinrich Himmler, the SS leader, was made responsible for a Reich Commissariat for the Strengthening of Germandom (RKFVD). Its purpose was to clear away the inferior Slavic peoples from the conquered eastern lands and replace them with Germans. This policy was first applied to the new German provinces created from the lands of western Poland. Almost 1 million Poles were uprooted and dumped in the Government General area of Poland. With the invasion of Russia, Himmler's plans were expanded to include the annexation of the Government General for German colonization as well.

In order to colonize the designated areas in Poland, Hitler established selection guidelines based on sound German blood and good physical condition. Most candidates were found among ethnic Germans who had migrated years ago from Germany to different parts of southern and eastern Europe. They were now invited to "come home" and settle the new eastern German provinces. Hundreds of thousands did and were settled mostly on farms. The new German peasants in the east were viewed as political warriors who would consolidate the German conquests. By December 1940, 410,000 ethnic Germans had been resettled in the new eastern provinces. Two years later, the number had reached almost 1 million. But resettlement policies in Poland often proved counterproductive. Poles joined resistance movements and attacked the new German settlements. Even German civil administrators warned that SS policies were disastrous and that it was irresponsible to foster resettlement programs when all available manpower was needed to pursue total war.

The invasion of the Soviet Union in 1941 produced inflated visions of German colonization in the east. Hitler spoke of the ultimate aim of eastern policy as the creation of a settlement area that would support a 100 million Germans, a process that would occur over several generations. This task was simply the concrete realization of *Lebensraum* ideology: The east was the living space for the master race. Clearly, the Nazis planned an unbelievable project of social engineering. There would, of course, be economic rewards, but the real purpose was fulfillment of a grand and glorious mission laying the foundation for German mastery for all time. The Nazis involved in this planning knew that the human costs would be profound. While the east would be Germanized by German colonists, native peoples would be used as slave labor. As Himmler told a gathering of SS officers in January 1941, the destruction of 30 million Slavs, which was to be done primarily through starvation, was a prerequisite for German plans in the east. "Whether nations live in prosperity or starve to death interests me only insofar as we need them as slaves for our culture. Otherwise it is of no interest."[3] For Himmler and the SS, German strength easily justified the death of inferior peoples. Because Germany never won the war, none of the grandiose SS schemes for German colonization of Russia was realized.

Inherent in the resettlement and colonization program was the Nazi pursuit of Germanization, which meant a careful selection of peoples racially close enough to the Germans to be absorbed into the master race. Such peoples as the Dutch, Norwegians, and Flemings, given their kinship with Germans, could easily be Germanized and also

---

[3]International Military Tribunal, *Trial of the Major War Criminals*, vol. 22 (Nuremberg, 1947–1949), p. 480.

used to resettle the east. The Latin peoples, such as the French, Italians, and Spaniards, were considered a lesser breed but would still occupy some place within the New Order since they were superior to the Slavic peoples of the east. Hitler and the Nazis had no long-range plan for the west.

Economic and Labor Exploitation

Although some Germans spoke with seeming vision about the new economic unity within the new European order, reality was harsher. German policy was quite simple. The conquerors exploited conquered territory and gave no compensation for the products taken from occupied countries. This policy was based on the assumption of a quick war and the need to concentrate war production in Germany and to keep an acceptable standard of living for the German people. In this way Nazi exploitation and expropriation of foreign assets helped not only to fight the war but also to manufacture consent in Germany. Some Nazis, such as Albert Speer, favored a more rational program of exploitation. Speer urged that industrial production be encouraged in the occupied territories. What was produced should be shared with local peoples to encourage their cooperation with the regime. And in western Europe and the Czech protectorate, manufacturing enterprises for the German war effort actually kept these economies working, and subsequently made postwar recovery possible. However, in eastern Europe plunder was the rule. Most Nazis, including the decisive Hitler, were inclined to follow Hermann Göring's reasoning: "In the old days, the rule was plunder. Now, the forms have become more humane. Nevertheless I intend to plunder, and plunder copiously."[4] For eastern Europe then, the economies were devastated, and postwar recovery was next to impossible as a consequence. During the war, however, plunder served the dual purposes of supplementing the war economy and providing ordinary Germans with a higher standard of living, thus continuing their support of both the war and the Nazi party.

In eastern Europe then, economic exploitation was direct and severe. The Government General was stripped of raw materials, machines, and food and left only enough to maintain the population at a bare level of existence. In the Soviet Union, Hermann Göring was given power as plenipotentiary of the Four-Year Plan to ensure full exploitation of conquered territory, a policy based originally on short-term plundering of materials valuable for the German war economy. As the war continued, however, the Nazis realized the value of Soviet industry and agriculture and shifted to long-range plans for the reconstruction of the Soviet economy. Munitions plants in Ukraine were now rebuilt. A New Agrarian Order was proclaimed in 1942 in which collective farms, disliked by Soviet peasants, were renamed communal farms and promises were made that all communal land would eventually become private property. Attempts to allow for some private enterprise in businesses were also introduced. These efforts were generally unsuccessful, since the Germans themselves tended to sabotage their execution.

The Germans adopted legal formalities in their economic exploitation of western Europe, although military supplies and strategic raw materials were often confiscated outright. The Nazis required France, Belgium, the Netherlands, and Norway to pay the costs of the German occupation forces. Only Denmark was exempt. But figures were artificially

[4]Ibid., 39, p. 391.

inflated, giving the Germans excess credit that they used to purchase raw materials, finished products, and food from the occupied countries for use in Germany. In addition, purchases were often made with military promissory notes, which essentially gave the Germans unlimited credit. The manipulation of currency made possible German purchases at favorable rates of exchange. Business and industrial enterprises in western and southern Europe were not blatantly confiscated unless owned by Jews. However, a policy of indirect expropriation and control was pursued. German banks and businesses invested in key enterprises, gaining a foothold in management. Eventually, with government assistance, they acquired possession of foreign banks, chemical concerns, copper mines, and numerous other companies.

The Germans had virtually no regard for the consequences of their economic exploitation of occupied Europe. Such a policy might have succeeded in a short war, but in the protracted struggle that actually ensued, Germany's failure to create industrial and agricultural bases with cooperative native labor in conquered countries cost it dearly in terms of materials with which to maintain the war. The policies of exploitation also created inflation, drastic shortages, black markets, and ultimately resistance by conquered peoples. Nazi policies seemed, once again, to be ultimately self-defeating. This is especially true of the exploitation of labor.

> The demand for soldiers in the German military resulted in a severe labor shortage in Germany. The need for labor had already been felt before the war, particularly in agriculture, but the war magnified the problem, especially due to Nazi reluctance to use German women in industrial labor. Consequently, the Nazis turned to conquered territories for laborers. By 1940, the Germans were shipping Polish prisoners of war and civilians to Germany for forced labor, primarily on farms. It was in reality a form of slavery. Because of unemployment in their own countries, volunteers were also recruited from Italy, France, Belgium, and the Netherlands to add to the number of foreigners working in Germany. By the end of 1941, foreign workers numbered 4 million, half of them Polish.

The continuation of the war meant that even these 4 million were insufficient for Germany's labor needs. In March 1942, Hitler appointed Fritz Sauckel, *Gauleiter* of Thuringia, as plenipotentiary-general for labor mobilization to raise more workers. Sauckel's methods for labor recruitment were direct and brutal. Especially in the east, Sauckel's "protective squads" surrounded entire villages, cinemas, or dance halls and captured all physically fit people. These natives were then shipped to Germany. The Germans had already wasted an important source of labor by allowing 3 million out of 4 million Russian prisoners of war to perish through neglect within a year of their capture. Within a year of assuming his new office, Sauckel had raised 2.1 million foreign workers, most of them from the Soviet Union, although conscription of laborers was pursued in western Europe as well. Labor camp housing conditions for forced laborers were not much better than in the concentration camps, as one *Ostarbeiter* (eastern worker) from Ukraine recalled:

> In the camp, we were housed in barracks, you know, they were really basic structures, made of metal sheets. We were locked in at night. Completely—even the windows—everything was locked from the outside. And a guard patrolled outside. The camp was also enclosed by barbed wire.[5]

[5]Quoted in Alexander von Plato, Almut Leh, and Christoph Thonfeld, eds., *Hitler's Slaves: Life Stories of Forced Labourers in Nazi-Occupied Europe* (New York, 2010), p. 270.

By mid-1944, 7 million foreign workers were laboring in German industry and agriculture, constituting 20 percent of Germany's labor force. Another 7 million workers were providing forced labor in their native countries in agriculture, industry, and even military camps. Sauckel's labor recruitment often proved counterproductive. In occupied countries it wreaked economic chaos and disrupted production in industries that could have helped Germany. In the last years of the war, Sauckel's brutal recruitment drives drove increasing numbers of conquered peoples into resistance movements against the Germans.

Resistance Movements

The speed of German victories left the defeated little time to organize effective resistance. But after the initial success, German policies toward the conquered peoples tended to elicit resistance movements that became a notable feature of all Nazi-occupied Europe. As German failure became more apparent and German policies ever harsher, resistance movements increased dramatically in numbers and gained the support of many citizens. In fact, by 1945, many resistance movements had grown strong enough to gain control of their states after the Nazi collapse.

Already in May 1940, the first stirrings of resistance had begun in conquered western Europe. Very small groups circulated anti-German pamphlets. The Norwegian and Dutch monarchs, who established governments-in-exile in Great Britain, became rallying points for resistance. Although the king of Belgium had remained with his people, his cabinet had been sent to Britain, where it served as a focus for Belgian resistance. Charles de Gaulle performed the same function for France when in June 1940 he broadcast a plea for his fellow French to continue the struggle against the Germans. The British attempted to further these fledgling efforts by establishing a Special Operations Executive (SOE), which sent trained agents into western European countries to help establish resistance movements and aid in strategic sabotage. By mid-1941 resistance cells existed throughout western Europe, executing acts of sabotage, spreading anti-German newspapers, and even spying on German military movements and positions.

As resistance movements grew they came to have an ideological focus. Many members believed in a new political and social order within a democratic structure that would be established once the Germans were defeated. As one French underground newspaper expressed it, "from resistance to revolution." But after the invasion of the Soviet Union, resistance movements oriented toward liberalism and democratic socialism were joined by Communists. The Communists formed broad-based fronts served by armed auxiliaries. These fronts were effective and soon became very influential. The Communists were distrusted by other groups, however, and although they shared the desire to liberate their countries from the Nazis, they feared the postwar consequences. In France, Charles de Gaulle's Free French movement worked to gain control of the major French resistance groups and managed to thwart Communist attempts to dominate them.

Resistance groups became especially active in 1943 as it became more apparent that the Germans would lose. Underground newspapers now circulated in large numbers. When Sauckel's Labor Mobilization forces tried to round up more laborers, thousands of young men were hidden or joined resistance groups. Although some underground groups, especially in France, even fought pitched battles with the Germans, most were content to undermine German efforts by destroying railways, power lines, and other strategic points. Other activities included military intelligence and hiding fugitives from

German persecution. Denmark's Jews were largely saved in this fashion. Resistance movements contributed significantly to the invasion of western Europe by the Allies. And once their countries were liberated, resistance movements contributed considerable administrative leadership to the new governments.

In southern Europe, resistance movements became involved in guerrilla tactics from the beginning. In Yugoslavia two conflicting groups emerged. The forces of General Mihajlovic were oriented toward the monarchy and favored Serbian ascendancy in Yugoslavia. Josip Broz, known as Tito, was a Croat and a Marxist and led a band of guerrillas who favored radical economic and social change. Tito's forces believed in active military campaigns against the Germans and Italians and barely managed to survive in 1942 and 1943. The British government initially supported General Mihajlovic, who seemed to be clearly superior in strength to Tito by 1943. But a dramatic change occurred in that year. The capitulation of Italy enabled Tito and his forces to take over large numbers of Italian arms and gain control over significant areas of Croatia. His partisan army now swelled to 250,000, and the Allied forces switched their support to him. In the summer and fall of 1944, it was Tito's forces and not the Allies that liberated Yugoslavia from the Germans. This victory enabled Tito to establish control over a unified Yugoslavia.

In Greece, the resistance movement also divided into two groups, the right-wing National Greek Democratic Union and the Communist National Liberation Front. The British were unable to get the rival groups to coordinate their activities against the Germans. Instead, the two virtually waged a civil war. British support of the rightists prevented the Communists from gaining the upper hand. The end of the war brought renewed civil war.

Although there was an anti-Fascist resistance movement, most Italians seemed unwilling to turn against their government in wartime. But with German occupation of Italy in 1943 came a full-fledged resistance movement whose partisans sought to harass the Germans and aid the Allied liberation of their country. Despite ideological differences between the Communists and pro-monarchy forces, the various Italian resistance groups managed to unify by April 1944. Partisan forces grew to 80,000 that summer and conducted campaigns against German forces. They played an active role in the final liberation campaign in 1945 and were responsible for capturing and executing Mussolini and his mistress. After liberation, resistance leaders controlled the new Italian government.

The nature of resistance movements in eastern Europe varied considerably from nation to nation. In the Protectorate of Bohemia-Moravia, a small resistance movement began even before World War II. The Czechs were responsible in October 1939 for a public demonstration that led to the closing of Czech universities for the rest of the war. By 1940, Bohemia-Moravia had an organized underground group, the Central Committee of Internal Resistance (UVOD). A Communist underground arose after the invasion of the Soviet Union, but there was apparently little cooperation between the two groups. The UVOD suffered considerably after the assassination of Reich Protector Reinhard Heydrich by Czech agents from London, an act that brought massive German retaliation. Lacking a base for guerrilla operations, underground resistance groups concentrated on individual acts of sabotage.

The resistance movement in Poland was remarkably strong. Of course, the intensity of Nazi repression demanded extraordinary efforts from the Poles if they were to avoid capitulating entirely. A Polish government-in-exile was established first in Paris and then in London, where it worked from afar to encourage underground resistance in Poland. By 1940, the so-called Home Army was operating as a unified resistance movement responsible for gathering intelligence, performing acts of sabotage, and distributing anti-German underground newspapers. By 1944, the Home Army had reached almost one-third of a million members.

Germany's attack on the Soviet Union altered the Polish underground movement. The Soviet Union sponsored a Communist Polish Workers' Party with its own partisan guerrilla force. The Home Army refused to join forces with the Communists as the latter requested, and the two groups became bitter rivals. After the discovery in 1943 of a mass grave of Polish prisoners of war—murdered by the Soviets—in the Katyn forest, the rift between the Polish government-in-exile and the Soviet Union intensified. The latter severed diplomatic relations with the Polish government in London and established its own Polish Liberation Committee as an alternative. In August 1944, the Home Army attempted to liberate Warsaw from the Germans; the Soviet army stood by only ten miles away while German tank divisions devastated the Home Army and systematically wasted Warsaw. When the Soviets advanced in January 1945, they imposed their Polish Liberation Committee as the new Polish government.

Since the Soviet Union was not defeated by Germany, the resistance movement there became part of the country's continuing fight against the Nazis and was closely directed by the Soviet government. Soviet partisan forces consisted of Soviet soldiers who had escaped from the Germans, civilian refugees fleeing the German mobilization of labor, and villagers forced into service. Since most partisan leaders were assigned to their positions by Soviet military commanders, the resistance movement was not entirely spontaneous. By 1943, partisan forces numbered 20,000. Although they operated behind German lines, committing sabotage and harassing the German forces, this was not their only function. The partisan movement was also used by the regime to remind the German-dominated Soviet population that the Soviet government continued to rule and would someday return. Under the circumstances it would not be wise to collaborate with the Germans. As the Soviet army reconquered Russian territory, it simply absorbed the partisan bands.

THE HOME FRONT: CIVIL LIFE IN WARTIME GERMANY

The German response to the outbreak of the two world wars was considerably different. In August 1914, there had been crowds cheering in the streets, a profusion of waving flags, processions, and flowers to accompany German troops marching off to war. In September 1939, the streets of major cities were quiet. There was a feeling of apathy and, even worse for the Nazi regime, a foreboding of disaster. There was, of course, some enthusiasm from devout Nazis who believed the Führer was always right and who were eager to do battle. But the Nazi regime, even if it was still in control and could easily prevent overt opposition to war, was unable to generate any enthusiasm for war.

Nevertheless, Hitler was strongly aware of the home front. As we have seen, he believed that the collapse of the German home front had caused Germany's failure in 1918. Hitler was determined not to repeat that experience and to maintain morale on the home front. This attitude determined his economic policies and raises the basic question of whether his home-front policies might indeed have helped cost him the war.

The Economy

From the beginning of his regime, Hitler's preparations for war included concern for its economic dimensions. The government established control of the economy and instituted a massive rearmaments program. But Hitler's economic plan contained a fatal flaw. Fearing the collapse of the home front, Hitler failed to convert the German economy early enough to a total wartime economy. When this was finally done, the war was already lost and the time of defeat could only be prolonged.

German armaments production had been greater than that of any other country in the 1930s. In 1938, German spending on armaments was five times that of Great Britain. The Four-Year Plan was instituted in 1936 to create self-sufficiency by boosting production of synthetics in key areas and to prepare Germany for war in four years. But it had not been overly successful. It boosted armaments by restoring the German economy to full capacity from depression levels and stabilizing production of consumer goods after 1936. But it did not result in a systematic organization of a war economy since rational organization was contrary to the disorganized structure of the Nazi state with its overlapping authorities and bureaucratic chaos. Before the war, some state officials had pushed for an "in-depth" economic policy that favored concentration of production in heavy industry and stockpiling of strategic raw materials to ensure supplies for a protracted war effort. These suggestions meant a war economy in peacetime. Hitler was unwilling to take this step and instead pushed his "in-breadth" policy of armaments. This meant steady production of armaments to guarantee *Blitzkrieg*, or rapid conquest of an enemy. Any losses from such a war could be compensated for by ruthless exploitation of the conquered state's resources. In addition, the requirements of different campaigns could be met by shifting armament production from one kind of warfare (such as tanks and artillery) to another (such as planes or naval vessels). To Hitler, this meant the least possible disruption to the economy and consumer industries, and thus maintenance of morale at home.

From 1939 to 1941, Hitler pursued his basic economic policy. *Blitzkrieg* produced rapid conquests in 1939 and 1940, and the Germans procured massive supplies of war materials from conquered countries. It was unnecessary to increase armament production or to cut consumer goods. Wage and price controls and a system of rationing helped to keep the economy stable. Grain from Russia as part of the Nazi-Soviet pact and silks and champagnes from France, lace and chocolate from Belgium, and other goods from occupied Europe kept the German people relatively contented. Hitler even maintained the building of the autobahns and some urban renovation projects.

However, at the end of 1941, when Germany began to face both a two-front European war and a world war, a change in economic priorities was necessary. In order to step up the production of armaments, a Ministry for Armaments and War Production was established in 1940 under an engineer and old Nazi, Fritz Todt. Todt had been responsible since 1933 for the construction of the autobahns, power plants, and various military fortifications (see p. 86). Todt's new ministry was unable to accomplish anything significant until early in 1942, when Hitler at last ordered an enormous increase in the production of armaments and an increase in the size of the army. Todt's ministry now bested the Wehrmacht and gained virtually complete control over the new war economy. Todt was killed in an airplane crash in 1942, and as his successor Hitler surprisingly chose his favorite architect, Albert Speer.

Speer was enormously successful in increasing the production of armaments. By rationalizing procedures, simplifying programs, and eliminating waste, Speer tripled production in 1942 and 1943, despite massive Allied bombing attacks. Some areas experienced even more dramatic increases. Heavy tank production increased from 2900 in 1942 to 17,300 in 1944, a sixfold increase. At the same time, there was no dramatic decline in consumer goods production until the last year of the war, although Speer favored such a decrease in the interests of total war.

However, as Adam Tooze has noted, Speer's "armaments miracle" was not all of his making and not necessarily what it seemed. The rationalization of the means of production had begun before he took office and much of the increase in production resulted from investments made early in the war now coming to fruition. Furthermore, the quality of goods was often degraded to achieve the startling quantity that served both the needs of waging a two-front war and bolstering German confidence in ultimate victory. Finally, the "ruthless mobilization" of the means of production, including the exploitation of foreign resources and use of slave labor, was achieved at a horrendous human cost.[6]

But total mobilization of the German economy was not truly pushed until July 1944, when Joseph Goebbels was made Reich plenipotentiary for total war. Earlier attempts at total mobilization had largely fizzled. Goebbels made one final effort to mobilize the German war effort. Theaters, cafes, and schools were closed. Children from ten to fifteen were to help with farming and youth were to serve as antiaircraft helpers. All men sixteen to sixty-five and women seventeen to fifty were registered for compulsory labor allocations. Up to this point Hitler and the Nazis had opposed the employment of women in industries. A *Volkssturm* (people's army) was created as a last-ditch home defense force. All males from sixteen to sixty not serving in the armed forces were now enrolled in this final effort to stave off defeat. In some communities, petty restrictions were established; walking the family dog was prohibited as a waste of time. Penalties for defeatism were severely increased. Seventeen postal employees in Vienna were publicly executed for stealing chocolates from gift parcels meant for soldiers at the front. Speer was now allowed to use all remaining resources for quantity production of a few standard military items. But it was all too late. The war was lost. Even if Speer's production lines could still turn out planes and tanks, there was no fuel to run them and no transportation system to get them to the front. Total war mobilization, which might have turned the tide in Russia in 1941 and 1942, was too little and too late to stave off complete German defeat.

Women in Wartime

The necessities of war created a reversal in Nazi attitudes toward women. Although resistance to female employment could be found until 1941, there was a growing tendency after that year to emphasize the need for women to enter into productive activities. Nazi magazines exalted working women: "We see the woman as the eternal mother of our people, but also as the working and fighting comrade of the man!"[7] Articles glorified individual women, such as the test pilot Hannah Reitsch, for their contributions to

---

[6]Discussed in Adam Tooze, *The Wages of Destruction: The Making and Breaking of the Nazi Economy* (New York, 2007), pp. 552–589.

[7]Cited in Claudia Koonz, "Mothers in the Fatherland: Women in Nazi Germany," in Renate Bridenthal and Claudia Koonz, eds., *Becoming Visible: Women in European History* (Boston, 1977), p. 466.

Millionen deutscher
Frauen und Mädchen
arbeiten in Fabriken,Werk=
stätten und Büros ...
Es·ist nicht unrecht ,wenn
wir verlangen , dass sich
diese Millionen deutscher
schaffender Volksgenossinnen
noch viele Hunderttausende
andere zum Vorbild nehmen
Adolf Hitler 4.Mai 1941

Deutsche
Frau !
Hilf mit

German Women in Wartime. With millions of German men fighting in the war, the Nazis attempted to replace them with female laborers. This recruitment poster reads "German Women! Help out." It also quotes Hitler's May 4, 1941, speech where he stated that millions of German women and girls are working in factories, workshops, and offices to support the war effort, and that many hundreds of thousands of others should take that as an example. *(akg-images/Alamy Limited)*

Germany. "Women Help Win the War" became the recruiting slogan for more female labor. Although the Women's Bureau proclaimed the newfound equality of men and women, in reality women continued to receive lower wages than males for the same work. Women's wages were set at 75–80 percent of men's wages.

By 1943, in the interests of total war, women between seventeen and forty-five were being required to register for compulsory labor. Women workers came to outnumber male workers by the end of the war, but they never constituted more than 50 percent of the female population. Women in the Third Reich were remarkably skilled at avoiding compulsory labor. The wives of important party leaders were hired for jobs that never really existed. Upper-class women were usually able to find agreeable part-time secretarial positions, and some women even adopted enough children to make them exempt from full-time labor. At the same time, many Nazi leaders, and especially Hitler, added to the problem by continuing to support their belief that women should remain home as mothers and wives. They expected that women would return to their natural roles once the war was over. A Nazi pamphlet on women, written in 1943, stated: "A woman who forgets her species and her position and becomes intellectual and erotic is in a similar state of racial degeneration as a man who scorns work and action, who sings the praises of some vague notions of humanity or pacifism, or who imagines that the most desirable form of existence is one of mental or material retirement."[8]

As labor shortages became magnified, women appeared in jobs in munitions factories, foundries, and construction once considered unsuitable for females. New policies were designed to keep women happy in such jobs. The government encouraged the establishment of nurseries for children, a system of coffee breaks and free soup for lunch, and in some places an extra day off every two weeks for doing household chores. Fashion changes also occurred. Despite male disapproval, women began to wear slacks instead of dresses. By 1944, women were being moved into quasi-military jobs such as working on antiaircraft teams operating searchlights and other detection instruments.

As the war progressed, the Women's Bureau began to disintegrate. Women were still excluded from any important positions in the party. The bureau made little effort to boost morale by public speeches. Yet women were daily expected to bear the loss of husbands and sons courageously and to sacrifice everything for the Third Reich. As with World War I, food shortages eventually made life at the home front difficult. Writing her husband at the war front late in 1945, one woman explained:

> There are new regulations everywhere for every piece of bread or meat and we have to read the paper carefully to find out what is available on the ration card. When I go shopping, people in the shops talk about nothing apart from food, foraging and where goods can be obtained off the ration card, or when one should be able to get this or that again. This everyday palaver is getting increasingly on my nerves. At home there is the constant worry about what we are going to cook . . . We lack so many of the ingredients that we need. So Gusti, housewives are certainly not having it easy at the moment.[9]

These women did the best they could under extraordinary conditions to keep their families fed and save them from harm. There also existed a different kind of courageous German woman—the one who resisted Nazi rule. Women, such as Sophie Scholl, played prominent roles in the German resistance, and countless other women used Nazi males' trust of their honesty as German women to harbor Jewish refugees and perform countless other small acts of resistance.

The Nazi Party

During the war years, there were some noticeable trends in the sociological composition of the Nazi Party. The percentage of workers actually increased, although they were still slightly underrepresented compared with their proportion of the population at large. This increase was due to the positive feelings created for some groups of workers by relatively good wages and better opportunities. The lower middle class remained the core constituency of National Socialism, although variations occurred in the degree of support by various groups within this social stratum. Independent shopkeepers and retail merchants began to withdraw their support during the war. Although farmers seemed to be generally indifferent to the war, they continued to join the party at the same rate in

---

[8]Quoted in Martin Kitchen, *Nazi Germany at War* (London and New York, 1995), p. 140.

[9]From in Hester Vaizey, *Surviving Hitler's War: Family Life in Germany, 1939–1948* (New York, 2010), pp. 106–107. By permission of Palgrave Macmillan.

the period 1939–1944 as before and remained overrepresented in the party. Lower civil servants showed a decrease beginning in 1940, although they remained overrepresented until 1942. The declining fervor of these civil servants for National Socialism is probably connected to the fact that they were seriously overworked and underpaid. Of all the lower-middle-class groups, the white-collar workers (shop clerks, salespeople, business employees) continued to be the most dedicated to Nazism. They increased in membership and continued to be slightly overrepresented. They were strong supporters of the war effort and probably became even more patriotic during the war.

Of the three major social groupings, the elite (upper middle class and traditional aristocracy) clearly turned its back on Nazism once Germany became involved in world war. Although the elite remained overrepresented compared with its Reich population, it did decline in new memberships until in 1942 it was no longer overrepresented in the party. The elite was opposed to the war with Great Britain and even more opposed to taking on both the Soviet Union and the United States.

University students expressed increasing contempt for the Nazis because of their anti-intellectual stance. More and more students offered themselves for leadership roles in the military, but were unwilling to do the same in the Nazi Party. Although some professors joined the party to protect themselves from interference, the academic profession turned increasingly against the Nazis as the war developed and became critical of their lack of intelligence, morality, and social conscience. Like lower civil servants, the higher civil servants began to decline in party membership after 1939. Lawyers, like judges scorned by Nazi leaders, also declined in Nazi membership. Even doctors, who had been a major support group for Nazism, declined in membership because of drastic change in their ranks as they were drafted to serve at the front or subjected to the resultant overwork at home.

The most consistent support for the Nazis until the very end of the war came from entrepreneurs and business managers. The alliance between Nazism and big industry became especially profitable for the latter. Under the direction of Fritz Todt and Albert Speer as munitions leaders, businessmen were generally accorded considerable freedom to produce as they wished, provided they created the desired armaments at fixed prices. German conquests in Europe opened new markets and offered opportunities to improve cost efficiency through the use of cheap foreign labor. Industries even made use of concentration camp labor, since it cost much less. Although party membership gave protection to businessmen in the Third Reich, many did not join the party, feeling they had no need to do so since they had such an important role in the regime.

The number of women in the Nazi Party dramatically increased in the war years. This was a process that had begun before the war and was magnified by the necessities of the war. In 1939, as labor shortages increased and women were treated more tolerantly and as increasing numbers of males were drafted, female membership in the NSDAP increased to 16.5 percent. The demands of the war, leading to an even more serious decline in males at home, led to the encouragement of female members of the Hitler Youth to join the party. From 1942 to 1944, 34.7 percent of Nazi Party membership was female. Also noticeable was the fact that the average age of female members was dropping while that of males was rising.

As the war progressed, the party rank and file experienced considerable pressures that made the NSDAP increasingly unpopular. Expectations to serve in new ways increased spectacularly after 1941. Earlier, Winter Relief canvassing and snow removal had been burdensome but manageable responsibilities. But by 1942, party members were expected to be available for day and night service. In 1944, they were commanded to organize and direct the new *Volkssturm* (people's army), which was counted upon to do what the army could not—stop the enemy. As demands for service increased, little was provided in the way of rewards. The highest distinction in the Nazi Party, the Golden Party Badge, was given to only 508 members between 1934 and 1942. Finally, as the war worsened, the burden of criticism was placed not on the Wehrmacht but on the Nazi Party. By 1943, after Stalingrad, members were beginning to hide their party badges. By 1944, some were even beginning to deny membership in the party, although fear kept them from resigning or being vocal about disaffiliating.

The war made enormous demands on the leadership of the Nazi Party. During the war the NSDAP experienced a serious problem of leadership recruitment, which became critical in 1944 and 1945. The war was the primary factor. At the beginning of the war, party leaders discovered a considerable number of ways to gain exemptions from military service. In some areas, only 15 percent of party members were drafted, although by 1943 the overall proportion of party members drafted had increased to 42 percent. Once drafted, Nazi leaders discovered ways to avoid the front lines or managed to serve only a short time at the front, thereby sustaining fewer casualties. A favorite practice was to use influence to be appointed to positions in occupied countries. The desired locations were Poland and occupied Russia because of the opportunities there for booty and professional growth. As more party leaders found themselves outside Germany, there was a noticeable shortage of leaders in Germany itself, and especially a lack of men of "real caliber," as Hitler expressed it. People of "real caliber" tended to seek lucrative and prestigious positions in industry and the armed forces rather than seeking their fortunes in the Nazi Party. Even Hitler Youth members preferred to pursue careers in the Wehrmacht rather than in the Nazi Party. In part, this problem was exacerbated by the unwillingness of the higher echelons of Nazi leaders to step aside for younger leaders.

At the same time, many of the tendencies that had been noticeable among party leaders before the war were magnified. As failures increased in the war years, they came to exercise power even more arbitrarily and abused civilians in numerous ways. The war created plenty of opportunities for graft and corruption. Local party funds were embezzled and groceries and alcohol stockpiled. While ordinary Germans suffered more and more privations, many party leaders made use of villas staffed with servants, held private hunts, hoarded expensive wines, and threw lavish parties known for their sexual excesses. As this corruption flourished, ordinary Germans developed even more contempt for their leaders. Although appearing angry at times over reports of corruption, Hitler did little to stop it, perceiving that such corrupt men would be tied even more to his leadership. As the end came closer, especially after the July 20, 1944, plot to kill Hitler, the Führer gave even more power to the *Gauleiter* and *Kreisleiter* to organize a home defense system through the *Volkssturm*. Now Nazi leaders even used the power of martial law to execute civilians considered defeatists or shirkers of their war duties. As Germany collapsed, the *Gauleiter* and *Kreisleiter* tried to save themselves. Some simply laid down their arms and went home; others tried to flee abroad. Few felt a sense of honor or any personal responsibility for what was happening. In their final acts, the Nazi leaders proved that although they had acquired authority and prestige, they had never really become a new ruling elite, as they so often claimed. They did not last long enough to become new role models for German society. And German society certainly benefited from that.

Public Opinion, Morale, and Propaganda

From the beginning of Nazi ascendance to power, the leaders of the Third Reich had attempted to gain information about the public's opinion of the regime. During the war, an accurate assessment of the public mood was considered imperative, especially since Hitler and other Nazi leaders were determined not to repeat the collapse of the home front that they believed had caused Germany to lose World War I. Although numerous Nazi organizations and institutions collected information on German public opinion, the Security Service (SD) of the SS bore primary responsibility for this task. The SD used thousands of volunteer agents as well as full-time paid collaborators in every sector of society throughout Germany to eavesdrop on conversations in post offices, streetcars, stores, beauty shops, and other public places to gain impressions of the public mood. SD agents were commanded to present frank reports "without embellishment or propagandistic make-up, i.e., objectively, clearly, reliably, as it is, not as it could or should be."[10] Although there was some retouching, reports tended to give notice of increasingly critical attitudes. These so disturbed party leaders, especially Goebbels and Bormann, that the number of agents was reduced and the SD reports were restricted to a small group of leaders. There is little concrete evidence that Hitler himself read these reports on any regular basis. But his reactions to church opposition to the euthanasia program and his remarks about the German populace after Mussolini's fall indicate a very precise knowledge of the public mood in Germany.

The public opinion reports of the SD and other organizations were intimately related to the news and propaganda policy of the Third Reich. This policy, which was meant to mold public opinion, was also a reaction to public opinion. Propaganda and public opinion affected and limited each other. Joseph Goebbels's Ministry of Public Enlightenment and Propaganda had the major responsibility for providing information to the general public, especially through his ministerial conferences attended by the heads of government departments and representatives of the radio, press, film, party, and Wehrmacht. Although Goebbels's goal was complete control over influencing public opinion, he had too much competition from the foreign office, the military, the press bureau, and party agencies to achieve it.

Goebbels's ministerial conferences provided guidelines on how to handle the news during the war years. Initially Goebbels seemed very aware that the Germans were not enthusiastic about the war and that their mood varied from exultation over the victories to depression over the failure to achieve a final peace. Consequently, Goebbels's initial propaganda barrage took a twofold approach. The enemy, especially Britain, was blamed for the coming of the war and the failure to end it. In addition, Hitler was emphasized as a genius constructing a new world; he was infallible and deserved complete loyalty and obedience. Goebbels wove both themes together after the attempt on Hitler's life in Munich on November 8, 1939. Goebbels blamed the British Secret Service for the attempt and widely publicized Hess's speech after the attempted assassination.

The Führer lives! In boundless gratitude we all feel today as if he had been given to us anew. How many tears of joy have been shed for him! How many fervent prayers have been said on high for him! The miracle of his rescue has enhanced our belief in him. Providence has spared our Führer in the past, and Providence will spare our Führer in the future, because

---

[10]Marlis Steinert, *Hitler's War and the Germans*, trans. Thomas de Witt (Athens, Ohio, 1977), p. 14.

he has been sent on a great mission . . . To our enemies we call out: You wanted to take the Führer from us and you have only drawn us closer to him. You wanted to weaken us and you have only made us stronger.[11]

Goebbels's propaganda worked during the "phony war" in the west and the real victories in Norway, Denmark, the Low Countries, and France. The SD reports at the end of June 1940 after the victory over France emphasized a new inner resolve among the German people and revealed that traditionally leftist groups were no longer hostile to Hitler. Even previous opponents spoke admiringly of Hitler.

Such mass enthusiasm was only temporary. Goebbels's propaganda message—that this period constituted only a brief interlude before final victory—was increasingly rejected as Britain showed no signs of being defeated. Increasing fear of shortages—especially of coal, clothes, and shoes—rising prices, and the surprise British bombing of Berlin in August 1940 led to discontent and growing depression. The invasion of the Soviet Union generated some initial enthusiasm, since Nazi ideological propaganda had long pointed to the Soviets as the real enemy. But the great expectations, fueled by Hitler's own premature announcement on October 3 that the Soviet Union had essentially been defeated, dashed German hopes. The dawning realization that Germany now faced a long struggle with uncertain results brought genuine depression to the German mood.

Hitler's announcement of imminent victory in the Soviet Union was contrary to Goebbels's own policy. The propaganda minister believed it was foolish to raise expectations by announcing victories ahead of time. Unjustified optimism would simply weaken the credibility of the regime in the eyes of the people. By 1942, Goebbels had come to believe it was time to be brutally frank with the German people about the real military situation Germany faced. Only in this way was it possible to initiate total war, a total mobilization of resources and people to win the war. Hitler, however, ever fearful of the home front, refused to go this far. By the early months of 1942, the mood and morale of the German people had deteriorated noticeably. By this time, the British air force was bombing Germany on a regular basis. The home front had also become a battlefront.

The defeat at Stalingrad at the beginning of 1943 made it clear to many Germans that the war might be lost. It brought forth social and political unrest and considerable criticism of the Nazi Party leadership. But despite the disappointment over the military losses, despite the bombing, and despite the apprehensive reports, German morale remained remarkably steadfast. Likewise, German determination to continue the struggle remained strong. Nazi propaganda continued unabated, but its effectiveness now was due to Goebbels's clever combination of hope and fear. Hope was embodied in the promise of secret weapons. And the use of V-1 bombs and V-2 ballistic missiles did produce some elation, seemingly confirming the belief that wonder weapons were available. Fear was driven home by Nazi propaganda threats. Goebbels cleverly used the Allied statement of January 24, 1943, that the Allies would accept only Germany's unconditional surrender to frighten the Germans over what lay ahead if they lost the war. Especially effective was the warning that the Soviet Army would rape German women and plunder the land.

From late 1943 to May 1945, it was apparent that Nazi ideology played a less important role in maintaining German morale and the war effort. Amidst the bombing terror, the simple will to survive and the traditional values of obedience and duty became paramount.

---

[11]Quoted in Jay W. Baird, *The Mythical World of Nazi War Propaganda* (Minneapolis, 1974), p. 66.

In addition, the person of Adolf Hitler certainly remained an important factor. Hitler did little personally to sustain German morale. By 1943, he was making very few public appearances. On November 8, 1943, he delivered an address to party leaders in Munich that was broadcast to the nation. He assured his listeners that Germany would never capitulate and that their steadfastness guaranteed ultimate victory. After the war, Germany would be rebuilt with millions of new houses. Hitler made few public broadcasts after this speech. One of the last was his radio broadcast after the July 20 bomb plot to reassure the German people that he had not been injured in the dastardly attempt to kill him. Hitler did not care to involve himself in the suffering of the German people.

✶ The remarkable thing was that the German people's ties with the Führer, expressed in the phrase "Trust in the Führer," worked to hold state and people together. It appears that Hitler continued to be admired by many Germans until the last months of the war. Although there was considerable criticism of the Nazi regime, these attacks did not extend to Hitler. The bond between Adolf Hitler and the Germans remained strong.

After July 1944, Joseph Goebbels as Reich plenipotentiary for total war became the most visible Nazi leader. The indefatigable Goebbels visited bombed-out areas and managed to keep people doing their jobs. Even the July 20, 1944, attempt to kill Hitler was disavowed by many Germans, as a Foreign Ministry official serving in the information and press sections observed in his diary:

> Public reaction to the plot is less violent than one would have expected. Although July 20 brought home to the masses the crisis in our national leadership, it has not reduced their readiness to follow that leadership. Since no one has a comprehensive view of the situation that has arisen or can see any way out, and since everyone fears that any display of disloyalty might well contribute to a deterioration of the situation, the regime can continue to rely on the further support of the people. The situation today differs from that in 1918 in many respects. For today, despite the burden of the air attacks, the morale of the nation is unimpaired.[12]

While Hitler was directing nonexistent forces from the Bunker, while Nazi leaders were beginning to commit suicide or making plans to save themselves, while the slaughter of *Volkssturm* boys and old men continued, the German people waited fatalistically for the end.

Impact of Allied Bombing ✶

Although the British executed a bombing raid on Berlin in August 1940, major bombing raids did not begin until 1942 under the British air force's Bomber Command's wartime leader, Arthur Harris. This force was rearmed with four-engine heavy bombers, which provided the means for carrying the war into the center of occupied Europe. The use of improved navigational and radio/radar aids improved bombing accuracy. The first 1000-bomber attack on a German city occurred on May 31, 1942: Cologne was subjected to a ninety-minute assault and 2000 tons of explosives.

✶ Initial British strategy had aimed at daylight attacks against military targets, which would keep civilian losses at a minimum. But the heavy losses resulting from these raids forced their cancellation. The British Bomber Command changed to nighttime attacks

[12]Hans-Georg von Studnitz, *While Berlin Burns* (Englewood Cliffs, N.J., 1963), pp. 189–190.

on industrial plants and military posts. Results were meager, producing another shift—to nighttime raids on industrial cities to weaken civilian morale and cause workers to desert their jobs.

Full-time American entry into the war resulted in a dual bombing approach. American strategy called for daylight precision bombing of submarine yards, transportation facilities, aircraft industry, the oil industry, and other industrial targets. The Americans soon discovered that self-defending bomber formations were vulnerable to German fighter planes. Daylight attacks on the ball-bearing factories at Schweinfurt in southern Germany in August and October 1943 resulted in disastrous losses of planes and crews. The Americans eventually added escorts of fighter planes with auxiliary fuel tanks that enabled them to penetrate as far as Berlin.

The British Bomber Command meanwhile continued the nighttime saturation bombing of German cities. Virtually all cities over 100,000 were attacked. By 1942, German civilians were already having their lives disrupted by the war. Except for farmers, who had direct access to food, Germans, especially city dwellers, were suffering from poor diets. Clothing declined in quality and wore out. A black market arose despite government efforts to stop it with harsh penalties. Some institutions managed to flourish despite the privations. Establishments that catered to high government officials, such as the restaurant in the Hotel Adlon in Berlin, somehow continued to have access to food and expensive wines and champagnes.

Bombing raids added a new element of terror to already difficult times. Germans especially came to fear the high-explosive and incendiary bombs that produced tornado-like firestorms that would sweep through the streets destroying people and objects alike. Four raids on Hamburg in August 1943 created temperatures of 1800 degrees Fahrenheit, killed 50,000 civilians, and destroyed almost half of the city's buildings. Especially frightening to inhabitants were the phosphorus bombs, which "burst and glowed green and emptied themselves down the walls and along the streets in flaming rivers of unquenchable flames, seeping down cellar stairs and sealing the exits to the air-raid shelters."[13] A resident of Hamburg later recalled

> heaps of rubble wherever one looks, hollow ruins of houses, empty windows, lonely chimney stacks, charred remnants of furniture, high up on a bit of a wall a bathtub, a forlorn bedframe, a radiator or even a picture clinging precariously to the bombed-out shell of what was once someone's home.[14]

By 1944, these air raids were extended to the cities of southern Germany, such as Munich and Nuremberg. The last major bombing raids were made on Dresden between February 13 and 15. These attacks, which created a firestorm that may have killed over 35,000 inhabitants and refugees, became controversial after charges were levied by some Allied leaders of unnecessary terror bombing of German cities. Dresden, as these critics noted, was a thickly populated city and had little military or industrial importance.

The bombing raids made daily life dangerous and extremely stressful for many Germans. By 1945 almost 12 million people had become homeless. Many of them had lost their possessions and found it difficult, especially as the war progressed, to replace even

---

[13]Quoted in Charles Whiting, *The Home Front: Germany* (Chicago, 1982), p. 144.
[14]Ibid, p. 148.

The Bombing of Germany. This photograph shows the city of Cologne in ruins in 1945. Allied bombing raids devastated major German cities. *(© National Archives and Records Administration[239-RC-18-1])*

the bare necessities of life. In such an environment, stealing became a real temptation despite, as one historian has observed, the often severe penalties.

> Thus on 31 May 1942 Paula W., a seamstress from Cologne, took some clothes, coffee and a suitcase which did not belong to her out of the burning apartment house in which she lived. She was denounced by a neighbor, promptly arrested, hauled in front of a Special Court and guillotined on 3 June. Posters were immediately printed and posted throughout the city announcing that she had been executed for plundering. Her body was sent to the anatomical institute in Cologne so that medical students could refine their skills.[15]

Only the rural areas of southern and eastern Germany remained relatively free of the horrors created by the Allied bombing campaign.

Germany's physical response to Allied bombing proved inadequate. Hermann Göring had boasted that not one Allied bomber plane would penetrate German defenses. "You can call me Meier, [if they do]." Neither German fighter planes nor the 21,000 antiaircraft guns located throughout western Germany were sufficient to stop the Allied planes. Increasingly, antiaircraft guns were manned by teenage boys and girls as more men were drained off into the army. Germans in cities became accustomed to life in air-raid shelters, usually cellars in houses or businesses. If the shelters were directly hit, their occupants were crushed to death. Or they might survive the wreckage above yet die of suffocation below. It was not until 1943 that Nazi leaders became aware of the need for a new response to the raids and began

---

[15]Kitchen, *Nazi Germany at War*, p. 94.

mass evacuations from the most dangerous urban areas. But this was also problematic, since people in rural areas were often hostile to the newcomers.

The damage to Germany from Allied bombing was great. Over 11 million dwellings were destroyed and half a million civilians killed by the 1 million tons of bombs dropped. Although Allied bombing affected civilian morale, Nazis and anti-Nazis alike seemed united by the disasters and by a desire simply to survive. In Stuttgart, after surviving its thirty-seventh air raid of the war, Anny Haindl, leader of the local National Socialist Women's Bureau, issued the following call:

> The German woman . . . is determined not to surrender the essence of her world—her family and her home—to the enemy without a fight. On the contrary, she is resolved to defend herself with all her might and with deep fanaticism, even with weapons in her hand, if it come to that . . . Our destiny is in our hands.[16]

The city would suffer sixteen more bombing raids before the end of the war. Undoubtedly, such bombing did produce skepticism about the official bulletins that still foolishly proclaimed ultimate Nazi victory. The Allied Strategic Bombing survey showed that bombing did not stop production, which increased under Speer's direction from 1942 to 1944. Even in 1944 and 1945, Allied bombing cut German production by only 14 percent and armaments by 7 percent. But it did help to destroy the German transportation system and it eliminated fuel supplies so that the new materials could not reach the German military. Arguments will continue over the role of strategic bombing and whether it shortened the war or lengthened it by stiffening civilian resolve. But one thing is clear. There would be no stab-in-the-back myth after the war about the collapse of the home front. The German people knew that the home front had been a battlefront, and they knew they had lost on their front just as the frontline soldiers had lost on theirs.

RESISTANCE IN WARTIME GERMANY

Despite the inherent difficulties of expressing opposition to the Nazi police state, the wartime years did see the development of serious resistance to the regime. Of course, there had been resistance before the war. Groups had gathered and attempted to spread information about events in Germany. But virtually all of these groups were reluctant to use violence, especially to bring about the assassination of Hitler.

In some ways, the war made resistance more difficult. Hitler's war successes had generated intense enthusiasm and heightened patriotism with which the Nazi regime now identified itself. To resist the Nazi regime meant to harm Germany. The wartime years saw greater control by the Nazi Party and the SS state over everyday life. This control made resistance a more dangerous undertaking. But the war also created new openings for resistance. The army had become powerful, and formerly civilian enemies of the regime were now found in military positions that gave them new opportunities. This could be seen especially in the Abwehr, the army intelligence office, which had played such an important role in the 1938 plot against the regime. Its head, General Oster, deliberately

---

[16]Quoted in Jill Stephenson, *Hitler's Home Front: Württemberg under the Nazis* (New York, 2006), p. 160.

recruited people who were known to oppose the regime. Different kinds of resistance to the regime occurred from a variety of political directions and groups.

The Rebellion of Youth

Compulsory attendance in the Hitler Youth had unexpected consequences when increasing numbers of young people during the war years began to rebel against authority by forming alternative forms of community. Two groups especially stand out.

The Edelweiss Pirates first became visible in western Germany at the beginning of the war. These informal gangs, mostly of working-class youth, resented the quasi-military discipline of the Hitler Youth and sought to escape from the adult world by weekend hikes into the countryside and informal gatherings after work in abandoned buildings and local parks. But a growing number of conflicts between the Edelweiss Pirates and the Hitler Youth alarmed authorities, as this report from a branch of the Düsseldorf Nazi Party to the Gestapo indicates:

> Re: "Edelweiss Pirates." The said youths are throwing their weight around again. I have been told that gatherings of young people have become more conspicuous than ever [in a local park], especially since the last air raid on Düsseldorf. These adolescents, aged between 12 and 17, hang around into the late evening with musical instruments and young females. Since this riff-raff is in large part outside the Hitler Youth and adopts a hostile attitude towards the organization, they represent a danger to other young people . . . There is a suspicion that it is these youths who have covered the walls of the pedestrian subway with the slogans "Down with Hitler," . . . "Down with Nazi Brutality."[17]

As reports of activities by these gangs grew, so too did persecution by police authorities, who shipped hundreds of these young people to labor camps in the hope of restoring them to productive ways. Occasionally authorities tried to make a more drastic example to discourage such youthful protest; the leaders of the Cologne Edelweiss Pirates were publicly executed in November 1944. Although most gang members had no strong political convictions, some Edelweiss Pirates, especially in Cologne, joined resistance groups and even provided refuge for deserters from the German army.

Young people of an upper-middle-class background created a different kind of youth rebellion. Attracted to jazz and swing music, the *Swing-Jugend* (the swing youth), as the authorities called them, organized swing festivals in many large cities. A Hitler Youth report from 1940 discussed such a gathering of 500 young people in Hamburg:

> The dance music was all English and American. Only swing dancing and jitterbugging took place . . . The dancers made an appalling sight . . . Sometimes two boys danced with one girl; sometimes several couples formed a circle, linking arms and jumping, slapping hands, even rubbing the backs of their heads together; and then, bent double, with the top half of the body hanging loosely down, long hair flopping into the face, they dragged themselves round practically on their knees. When the band played a rumba, the dancers went into wild ecstasy. They all leaped around and mumbled the chorus in English . . . Frequently boys could be observed dancing together, without exception with two cigarettes in the mouth, one in each corner.[18]

[17]Quoted in Richard Bessel, ed., *Life in the Third Reich* (New York, 1987), p. 34. By permission of *History Today.*
[18]Ibid., p. 37.

A ban on swing festivals only led to the formation of informal gatherings in night clubs and homes, where middle-class youths pursued their new interests.

Like the Edelweiss Pirates, the swing youth were not overtly political, but their use of British and American fashions, long hair, and choice of musical styles outraged many Nazi officials. Heinrich Himmler, head of the SS, proposed that swing youth be sent for several years to a concentration camp to dampen their youthful rebellion. Nevertheless, the continued existence of both the Edelweiss Pirates and the swing youth demonstrates that the Nazis by no means had complete control of German society.

The White Rose

The university environment had not been particularly noticeable for active resistance to the Nazi movement, although there was considerable passive resistance, including withdrawal into scholarly isolation. Nevertheless, as members of the elite stratum of German society, university students had become considerably disenchanted with the Nazi regime, sharing their superiors' intellectual disdain for the anti-intellectual lower-middle-class Nazi leadership. For some students, this contempt ultimately led to acts of resistance, regardless of how futile they may have appeared. The outstanding example is the White Rose group at the University of Munich.

Hans Scholl was a medical student at the University of Munich who had been a zealous member of the Hitler Youth. Raised as a Catholic, he came to be extremely disenchanted with the Hitlerian system, especially after becoming aware of the Nazi euthanasia program for cripples and mental defectives. Hans Scholl had also seen the nature of German occupation policies in the east as a result of service in the Wehrmacht. He and the university friends who shared his attitudes did not aim their anger at the military but against the detestable behavior of leading party bosses. In May 1942, Scholl and his friends Christoph Probst, Alex Schmorell, and Willi Graf joined a professor of philosophy, Kurt Huber, to begin writing, printing, and distributing leaflets against the government. They were soon joined by Hans's sister Sophie, an undergraduate studying biology and philosophy at the university. They signed their pamphlets the White Rose as a symbol of purity.

These conspirators were aware that their opposition was not that significant. But they felt that someone had to make a beginning against such a criminal regime. German youth, they argued, had been deceived by a ruthless regime and made into godless murderers and "stupid Führer followers." Students now had a responsibility to sabotage a regime that had inflicted horrible bloodshed on all of Europe. One pamphlet stated:

> And now every convinced opponent of National Socialism must ask himself how he can fight against the present "state" in the most effective way, how he can strike it the most telling blows. Through passive resistance, without a doubt. We cannot provide each man with the blueprint for his acts, we can only suggest them in general terms, and he alone will find the way of achieving this end . . . Try to convince all your acquaintances, including those in the lower social classes, of the senselessness of continuing, of the hopelessness of this war; of our spiritual and economic enslavement at the hands of the National Socialists; of the destruction of all moral and religious values; and urge them to passive resistance.[19]

[19]Excerpt from *Students Against Tyranny* by Inge Scholl, translated by Arthur Schultz © 1970 by Inge Aicher-Scholl, pp. 83–84. Reprinted by permission of Wesleyan University Press.

For all its ultimate futility, the White Rose group hoped to revive a "badly wounded" inner spirit that could not be crushed by Nazi barbarism.

In the summer and fall of 1942, the White Rose distributed its pamphlets in Munich. By winter 1942–1943, it had expanded its operations by establishing contacts with universities in Hamburg, Berlin, and Vienna, distributing posters there as well. But circle members became too confident and went too far by passing out leaflets in daylight at the university. The Scholls and two others were caught, arrested, tried before a People's Court, sentenced to death, and guillotined. With the arrest of fourteen more members, the White Rose was completely crushed. Students at Munich did not rise in revolt, as Sophie Scholl had predicted, but adopted a wait-and-see attitude.

The Churches

Upon the outbreak of war in 1939, Nazi policy toward the churches changed. Hitler perceived that most Germans were still regular Christians. Since their support was needed for the war effort, Hitler commanded that actions against the churches cease. According to Hermann Göring, Hitler's view was that

> every German should do his duty and that every soldier should, if need be, go to his death bravely . . . If, in that connection, religious belief is a help and support to him, . . . it can only be an advantage, and any disturbances in this connection could conceivably affect the soldier's inward strength.[20]

Both Catholic and Protestant leaders themselves aided Hitler's efforts by urging their members to support the war.

Despite Hitler's wishes, new attacks on the church broke out in 1941. These involved primarily the expropriation of church properties such as entire monasteries and convents. The need for auxiliary hospitals or resettlement centers for refugees was the excuse made for these actions, when in fact they were done primarily to promote the Nazis' anti-Christian policies. There was also a notable increase in anticlerical propaganda carried out by party agencies and with special fervor by Martin Bormann, who had taken over the Party Chancellery after Rudolf Hess's flight to England in a bizarre attempt to end the war. In a secret message to the *Gauleiter* on June 9, 1941, Bormann had declared that "National Socialism and Christianity are irreconcilable"[21] and called for an end to the power of the churches. But this was on the eve of the invasion of the Soviet Union, and Hitler was optimistic that the churches could be drawn into endorsing a struggle against atheistic communism and thus strengthening the German people in this fight. This was not the time for an anti-Christian crusade, and Hitler saw to it that Bormann's circular was withdrawn.

Church resistance to Nazi policies grew in 1941, especially to Hitler's policy of euthanasia for inmates of lunatic asylums. Since the churches had had a long tradition of caring for the mentally ill in church-run institutions, reports of these killings alarmed church authorities. By summer 1940, several church leaders were protesting

---

[20]International Military Tribunal, *Trial of the Major War Criminals*, vol. 9, p. 271.

[21]Quoted in John S. Conway, *The Nazi Persecution of the Churches, 1933–1945* (New York, 1968), p. 383.

to authorities the alleged practice of euthanasia. Some clergy took their case to government offices as well, such as the Ministry of the Interior. The Protestant minister Friedrich von Bodelschwingh refused to hand over children from his asylum for retarded children and was able to survive only because of his popularity and the accidental bombing of his institution.

The most strenuous opposition to the Nazis' use of euthanasia came from the aristocratic bishop of Münster, Clemens von Galen. On August 3, 1941, Bishop Galen preached a sermon condemning the euthanasia project as murder of innocent people. Copies of these sermons were printed and distributed throughout Germany. The reaction from the public was too strong for Nazis to overlook. Some Nazi leaders were outraged by Galen's sermons. Bormann advocated executing him. Although Hitler privately expressed his dislike of Galen and indicated a desire to eventually settle accounts with him and Christianity itself, for the time being he was unwilling to take any negative action. He feared the response, especially of Catholics, to such action, and he was unwilling to create martyrs, something that might undermine the war effort. He quietly ordered the euthanasia program stopped on August 28, 1941—a rare example of Hitler being forced to change policy as a result of the mobilization of public opinion. Soon after, Hitler decreed an end to all persecution of the churches so that Germans could concentrate on the war effort. Even Bormann, perhaps the most hostile of the other Nazi leaders to Christianity, seconded this decree. Although the protests against the murder of innocent people had been effective, they were not used later against the killing of the Jews.

Socialists and Communists

The experience of the Social Democratic politicians from 1933 on taught them that the methods they had employed since 1933 were insufficient. The Nazi system could be overthrown only with the support of the Wehrmacht. After the war began, they established contact with conservative–nationalist resistance groups and opposition members in the armed forces. In 1944, the SPD resistance leaders, Julius Leber and Adolf Reichwein, even met with Communist resistance leaders in Berlin to bring them into a plot against Hitler, but before a second meeting could be held, all of them were arrested. Many of the SPD resistance leaders who had plotted with other circles against Hitler lost their lives after the July 20, 1944, assassination and putsch attempt.

At the beginning of the war, only a few elements of the Communists' illegal organization had survived the mass arrests of 1936 and 1937. Moreover, German Communists were confused when Stalin ordered them to cooperate with the Nazis and oppose French and British "capitalistic imperialists." After the German invasion of the Soviet Union, the Communists were again free to continue the struggle against the Nazi regime and began to infiltrate party officials into Germany. They established a centrally directed illegal organization and increased the output of propaganda. But by January 1943, the results had not been especially good. The Communist resistance leaders had not built up any large following. Independent Communist groups had been established as well, such as those by Robert Uhrig and Joseph Römer. They managed to issue monthly pamphlets and made plans to establish activist groups that would engage in terrorist operations but were arrested by the Gestapo before they could do so. Although many Communist resistance leaders were wiped out after the July 20 fiasco, small Communist resistance groups survived. Illegal pamphlets were already reappearing in Berlin by the end of the summer in 1944.

Conservatives and Nationalists

Conservatives and nationalists may have wanted to eliminate Hitler, but they did not necessarily wish to remove all of his foreign policy accomplishments. Hitler was viewed as a gambler who had gone too far and now endangered Germany's genuine revisionist interests. Carl Goerdeler, mayor of Leipzig and a leading conservative opponent of the Nazi regime, and others who shared his perspective, such as General Beck and Ulrich von Hassell, held to their fundamental belief that Germany had a right to Austria, the Sudetenland, Alsace-Lorraine, and its 1914 eastern frontiers, even if they did not approve of the methods Hitler had used to obtain them. These frontiers would guarantee Germany its central European empire and its rightful dominating position in Europe. Of course, the conservatives realized that to be successful they would need the cooperation of the military and civil service, and up to 1942–1943 they realized that those groups would hardly be willing to give back all conquered territories. These conservative-nationalist leaders were opposed to democracy and modern mass parties and favored the reestablishment of a strong authoritarian government.

In 1940, a group of opponents of the Nazi regime gathered at the estate of Count Helmuth von Moltke in Silesia. They continued to meet into 1943. Although known as the Kreisau Circle after the name of Moltke's estate, many of the group's meetings were actually held in Berlin. The members were generally in their thirties. Although in background they were members of the traditional civil service, nobility, or military officer corps, they were not strongly bound by conservative and nationalist opinions. Count Moltke and his relative Count Yorck von Wartenburg were both descendants of Prussian generals. The Kreisau Circle had made contacts with representatives of the Socialist resistance movement and was influenced by Socialist ideas for a post-Hitler state. It also had Christian members, who added a different perspective to their discussions. These included the Jesuit priest Alfred Delp and the Protestant pastor Eugen Gerstenmaier. The Kreisau Circle also included diplomats, professors, and local government officials.

The Kreisau Circle formulated a number of proposals for the post-Hitler era. In general, they rejected the more traditional limitations of the Goerdeler group. They favored a new European international order in which there would be no hegemony by Germany, and no controversial territorial demands, but understanding and cooperation instead. What they wanted was Franco-German or German-Polish understanding. Some Kreisau Circle members spoke of a need for a new European federalism that would respect the rights of all constituents. Some even proposed a common economic policy, common citizenship, and a European army. The Kreisau Circle's foremost exponent of European internationalism was Adam von Trott zu Solz, who, like the others, believed that nationalism was antiquated. As one member expressed it, "Europe is sickening, of a condition which no longer has any place in this world—nationalism . . . it is high time that politicians too began to draw the logical conclusions and throw overboard what is known as nationalism."[22]

After 1941, the internationalist ideas of the younger members of the Kreisau Circle began to exert an influence upon the conservative opposition. Beck and Goerdeler, for example, began to speak of a new era featuring a permanent European federation in which no nation, including Germany, would claim supremacy. At the same time, these

---

[22]Quoted in Hermann Graml, "Resistance Thinking on Foreign Policy," in Hermann Graml et al., *The German Resistance to Hitler* (Berkeley, Calif., 1970), pp. 29–30.

conservatives were unable to give up their old idea of a sovereign German state that included all the territory rightfully belonging to it. In turn, conservatives also had an impact on the thinking of the Kreisau Circle. Even Trott zu Solz became more nationalistic and concerned about German frontiers.

The Military

As in 1938, military resistance initially focused on preventing further war efforts. Resistance leaders attempted, among other things, to gain a commitment from foreign governments that they would conclude a peace with a new non-Nazi Germany in the event of a successful coup d'état. Although France and Britain made such a guarantee, the Allies became distrustful of these overtures when the German army command failed to take action in the spring of 1940. General Oster of the Abwehr even attempted to establish the credibility of the opposition to the Allies by passing on through Holland the dates for the planned German attacks on Norway and France. But he was not taken seriously, and Hitler's rapid successes meant the scrapping of immediate plans for stopping Hitler. The regime was simply too popular and powerful. In addition, many military leaders themselves were unlikely to support action against Hitler after such successes. Moreover, many younger officers were deeply dedicated to Hitler. With wartime success, SS power also grew; and so did the measures designed to protect Hitler. This created a serious obstacle, since it had become obvious to the conspirators that wartime circumstances and Hitler's role as absolute leader made it necessary to assassinate Hitler in order to change the government.

The conspirators faced a no-win situation. As long as the Nazis were successful, a coup would be seen as an act of treachery against the German people. If the Nazis began to lose the war, the conspirators might pick up domestic support, but then the Allies would perceive the opposition movement as simply the work of "nationalist opportunists" who hoped to avoid the bitter defeat Germany deserved. Moreover, what would a new government be like, and what would its positions be on the pressing problems Germany would face?

July 20, 1944: Operation Valkyrie

Some have praised the conspirators who attempted to assassinate Hitler on July 20, 1944, as being motivated by a pure and noble cause. Others have argued that the plot came only when it was obvious that the Nazis had lost, that it was an attempt to salvage something for Germany before it experienced total defeat. Certainly there was little chance of success for a military coup d'état against Hitler in the period 1940–1942, when total victory still seemed within the Germans' grasp. Nevertheless, a military resistance movement had continued despite Nazi successes. After 1941 the military opposition had been joined by a number of younger officers upset about occupation and Jewish policies. The most prominent of this younger group was Colonel Count Claus von Stauffenberg, member of the Swabian nobility and a relative of Count Yorck of the Kreisau Circle. Stauffenberg had become hostile to Hitler and his policies. In addition to conservative and military groups, he had made contact with the Socialist resistance movement, especially Julius Leber.

Stauffenberg came to believe that the conservative-nationalist circles were too busy formulating plans for the post-Hitler scene; the primary concern should have been the elimination of Hitler and the overthrow of the Nazi regime. Stauffenberg realized that to many military officers the oath of loyalty they had sworn to Hitler as supreme commander was a stumbling block to a coup. Unless it was removed by the elimination of Hitler, the army, which was the sole instrument for a coup against the Nazi state, would not be totally reliable. Stauffenberg managed to create a rather extensive circle of associates, especially fellow younger officers who were willing to overthrow the regime without having any foreign guarantees about a post-Hitler government. They knew, in any case, that by January 1943 the Allies were committed to Germany's unconditional surrender. Plans for action against the regime came from two younger generals who cooperated with Stauffenberg in the planning of a coup. These were Friedrich Olbricht, chief of the Army Office in Berlin, and General Henning von Tresckow, who tried, unsuccessfully, to persuade other military commanders on the eastern front to desert Hitler.

The conspirators' plan called for Olbricht to place procoup officers in army commands in Germany so party and SS leaders in the major German cities could be seized the day Hitler was assassinated. The code name for the planned action was Operation Valkyrie. Since they were unable to pull in any outstanding frontline commanders, the conspirators based in Berlin were crucial. Stauffenberg was transferred there in April 1943. In 1943 and 1944, various opposition groups involved in the plot drew up lists of possible leaders in the new government to be established after the overthrow of Hitler's regime.

It was Stauffenberg who really pushed the plan along. In the fall of 1943, he gained the cooperation of retired Field Marshal Witzleben to head the military operation that would have to take place after the assassination of Hitler. Witzleben signed troop orders drawn up by Stauffenberg for use after the coup was initiated. By the end of 1943 and the beginning of 1944, anxiety by the plotters mounted as the Gestapo began to close in on members of the conspiratorial group and break up the opposition. The Kreisau Circle was disbanded with the arrest of Count Moltke, and the role of the Abwehr was discounted after Admiral Canaris was dismissed in February 1944.

By the summer of 1944, with the invasion at Normandy, Stauffenberg and the conspirators knew they needed to act quickly. By now they had gained the support of Field Marshal Rommel and the army commander in France, General von Stülpnagel. At the beginning of July, Stauffenberg was promoted, enabling him to be present at the Führer's military conferences and giving him the opportunity to make an attempt on Hitler's life. Fortune seemed to be favoring the conspirators.

After two frustrated attempts on July 11 and 15, Stauffenberg succeeded in smuggling a bomb into Hitler's East Prussian headquarters at Rastenburg on July 20, 1944. Hitler's conference that day was held not in the compound's bunker but in a flimsy wooden building above ground. After leaving his suitcase in the conference room fairly close to Hitler, with the bomb set to detonate within minutes, Stauffenberg excused himself to make a telephone call. When the bomb exploded Stauffenberg was able to leave the compound and fly back to Berlin, believing Hitler had been assassinated. But although his eardrums had been shattered and he had received burns, Hitler had not been killed. Some of the force of the bomb had been dissipated by the wooden walls and open windows. A massive oak table holding the maps had also protected Hitler from the full force of the blast. Four men had been killed, but not the dictator.

Believing the bomb had been effective, the conspirators set their plan in motion. The War Ministry in Berlin was secured and orders signed by General Witzleben as the new supreme commander of the army were sent out to general commands throughout

Germany to arrest all the major Nazi officials and seize major SS offices. But the conspiracy soon began to unravel. As reports filtered in that Hitler had not been killed but only injured, some of the conspirators began to waver. In addition, the failure in Berlin to seize the broadcasting offices and the Propaganda Ministry enabled Hitler's headquarters to issue countermanding orders not to obey any order emanating from the War Ministry in Berlin. Despite the uncertainties in Berlin, some of the conspirators in Paris, Vienna, and Prague began to implement their plans. This was especially true in Paris under General Stülpnagel. When the full knowledge of what had happened in Berlin became known, the conspirators backed down. By late evening of July 20, the War Ministry had been stormed and the coup quickly smashed. Stauffenberg and a few of the chief conspirators were shot on the spot by order of General Fromm. Himself one of the conspirators, Fromm acted in this fashion to try to save himself, a ploy that ultimately failed.

A massive investigation of the German resistance movement ensued. The Gestapo made numerous arrests and used horrible tortures to gain information. The People's Court, under the notorious Roland Freisler, held sham trials and condemned thousands to death. An estimated 5000 people lost their lives as a result of the July 20 plot. Hitler wanted blood and was unwilling to grant pardons. He did allow Field Marshal Rommel, because of his popularity, to commit suicide and then be given an official funeral. Prisoners of prominence in concentration camps, whether connected to the plot or not, were also ordered executed. Not one of the chief conspirators escaped Hitler's vengeance.

Hitler was convinced Providence had saved him to yet fulfill his mission and achieve victory. Many Germans remained loyal to Hitler and considered the attack on him cowardly. German resistance had never been a mass movement. Even resistance of one kind, as that of the church, did not spill over to other areas. Hitler's survival really meant that the Germans would now experience a total unconditional surrender. In the midst of this orgy of destruction, the Nazis hastened to continue the destruction of the Jews, and it is now time to examine this last tragic chapter of the Nazi story.

SUGGESTIONS FOR FURTHER READING

The most comprehensive account of Nazi occupation policies throughout the conquered territories is Mark Mazower, *Hitler's Empire: How the Nazis Ruled Europe* (New York, 2008). See also the pertinent essays in Shelly Baranowski, *Nazi Empire: German Colonialism and Imperialism from Bismarck to Hitler* (New York, 2011). Studies of regional German occupation policies and the internal problems created by them include Walter Maass, *Country without a Name: Austria under Nazi Rule, 1938–1945* (New York, 1979); Stevan K. Pavolwitch, *Hitler's New Disorder: The Second World War in Yugoslavia* (New York, 2008); Jozo Tomasevich, *The Chetniks: War and Revolution in Yugoslavia, 1941–1945* (Stanford, Calif., 1975); Chris Bellamy, *Absolute War: Soviet Russia in the Second World War* (New York, 2007); Alexander Dallin, *German Rule in Russia, 1941–1945*, 2nd ed. (London, 1981); Wendy Lower, *Nazi Empire-Building and the Holocaust in Ukraine* (Chapel Hill, 2005); and Karel C. Berkhoff, *Harvest of Despair: Life and Death in Ukraine under Nazi Rule* (Cambridge, Mass., 2004). See Alan S. Milward, *The New Order and the French Economy* (Oxford, 1970); Harry R. Kedward, *Resistance in Vichy France* (Oxford, 1978); John F. Sweets, *Choices in Vichy France: The French under Nazi Occupation* (New York, 1986); Julian Jackson, *France: The Dark Years, 1940–1944* (New York, 2001); Alan Mitchell, *Nazi Paris: The History of an Occupation: 1940–1944* (New York, 2008); Gerhard Hirschfeld,

Nazi Rule and Dutch Collaboration: The Netherlands under German Occupation, 1940–1945 (New York, 1988); Chad Carl Byrant, *Prague is Black: Nazi Rule and Czech Nationalism* (Cambridge, Mass., 2007); Dennis Deletant, *Hitler's Forgotten Ally: Ion Antonescu and His Regime, Romania 1940–1944* (London, 2006); Mark Mazower, *Inside Hitler's Greece: The Experience of Occupation, 1941–1944* (New Haven, Conn., 1993); Jan T. Gross, *Polish Society under German Occupation: The General gouvernement, 1939–1944* (Princeton, N.J., 1979); Richard C. Lukas, *The Forgotten Holocaust: The Poles under German Occupation, 1939–1944* (New York, 1997); and Marek J. Chodakiewicz, *Between Nazis and Soviets: Occupation Politics in Poland, 1939–1944* (Lanham, 2004). The basic work on German resettlement plans is Robert Koehl, *RKFDV; German Resettlement and Population Policy* (Cambridge, Mass., 1957). See also Alex J. Kay, *Exploitation, Resettlement, Mass Murder: Political and Economic Planning for German Occupation Policy in the Soviet Union, 1940–1941* (New York, 2006). On the forced movement of population of peoples resulting from Nazi policy, see Gustavo Corni and Tamás Stark, *People on the Move: Forced Population Movements in Europe in the Second World War and Its Aftermath* (New York, 2008). On the use of forced labor, see Herbert Ulrich, *Hitler's Foreign Workers: Enforced Labor in Germany under the Third Reich*, trans. William Templer (New York, 1997); and Edward Homze, *Foreign Labor in Nazi Germany* (Princeton, N.J., 1967).

Resistance movements in Europe are covered in Michael Richard. D. Foot, *Resistance: An Analysis of European Resistance to Nazism, 1940–1945* (London, 1976); Jacques Semelin, *Unarmed against Hitler: Civilian Resistance in Europe, 1939–1943* (Westport, Conn., 1993); Jorgen Haestrup, *European Resistance Movements, 1939–1945: A Complete History* (London, 1981); and Kenneth Slepyan, *Stalin's Guerillas: Soviet Partisans in World War II* (Lawrence, Kans., 2006). David Lampe, *Hitler's Savage Canary: A History of the Danish Resistance in World War II* (Barnsley, 2010). Marko Attila Hoare, *Genocide and Resistance in Hitler's Bosnia: The Partisans and the Chetniks, 1941–1943* (London: 2006).

On the home front in Germany, see Jill Stephenson, *Hitler's Home Front: Württemberg under the Nazis* (New York, 2006); Hester Vaizey, *Surviving Hitler's War: Family Life in Germany, 1939–1948* (New York, 2010); Martin Kitchen, *Nazi Germany at War* (London, 1995); Earl R. Beck, *Under the Bombs: The German Home Front, 1942–1945* (Lexington, Ky., 1986); and the popular work by Charles Whiting, *The Home Front: Germany* (Chicago, 1982). On the plight of women during the war and immediately after, see Elizabeth D. Heineman, *What Difference Does a Husband Make?: Women and Marital Status in Nazi and Postwar Germany* (Berkeley, 1999). On the total war effort in Germany, see Eleanor Hancock, *National Socialist Leadership and Total War, 1941–1945* (New York, 1991). See also the pertinent essays in Roger Chickering, Stig Förster, and Bernd Greiner, eds., *A World at Total War: Global Conflict and the Politics of Destruction, 1937–1945* (Cambridge, Mass., 2005). A superb study of the public mood and attitudes during World War II, making use of SD reports, is Marlis Steinert, *Hitler's War and the Germans*, trans. Thomas de Witt (Athens, Ohio, 1977). Also see Jay W. Baird, *The Mythical World of Nazi War Propaganda, 1939–1945* (Minneapolis, 1974); and Aristotle A. Kallis, *Nazi Propaganda and the Second World War* (New York, 2005). The ideological linkage of the war with the extermination of the Jews is discussed in Jeffrey Herf, *The Jewish Enemy: Nazi Propaganda during World War II and the Holocaust* (Cambridge, Mass., 2006). On the Nazi propaganda effort abroad, see Horst Bergmeier and Rainer Lotz, *Hitler's Airwaves: The Inside Story of Nazi Radio Broadcasting and Propaganda Swing* (New Haven, Conn., 1997); and Jeffrey Herf, *Nazi Propaganda for the Arab World* (New Haven, Conn., 2010). The German war economy is best seen in Adam Tooze, *Wages of Destruction* (New York, 2007); but also see Richard Overy, *War and Economy in the Third Reich, 1938–1945* (Oxford, 1994). Still useful is the pioneering study by Alan S. Milward, *The German Economy at War* (London, 1965). On the Nazi exploitation of the resources of conquered territories and peoples, including the Jews, to both fund the war and satisfy the consumer needs of the home front, see Götz Aly, *Hitler's Beneficiaries: Plunder, Racial War, and the Nazi Welfare State* (New York, 2005); Hein A. M. Klemann and Sergei Kudryashov, eds., *Occupied Economies: An Economic History of Nazi-Occupied Europe, 1939–1945* (New York, 2012). On women in the war, see Leila J. Rupp, *Mobilizing Women for War: German and American Propaganda, 1939–1945* (Princeton, N.J., 1978). On the destruction of Germany by bombing raids, see Hans Rumpf, *The Bombing of Germany* (London, 1963); Stephen Garrett, *Ethics and Airpower in World War II: The British Bombing of German Cities* (New York, 1993); Randell Hansen, *Fire and Fury: The Allied Bombing of Germany, 1942–1945* (New York, 2009); and the essays found in Paul Addison and Jeremy A. Crang, eds., *Firestorm: The Bombing of Dresden, 1945* (Chicago, 2006). The human cost of World War II for Germany is the subject of Martin K. Sorge, *The Other Price of Hitler's War: German Military and Civilian Losses Resulting from World War II* (New York, 1986).

A fundamental study on resistance in Germany is Hans Mommsen, *Alternatives to Hitler: German Resistance under the Third Reich*, trans. Angus McGeoch (Princeton, N.J., 2003). See also Peter Hoffmann, *The History of the German Resistance, 1933–1945*, 3rd ed., trans. Richard Barry (Montreal, 1996). There is also a shorter study by the same author entitled *German Resistance to Hitler* (Cambridge, Mass., 1988). Other works include Roger Moorhouse, *Killing Hitler* (New York, 2006); Hans Rothfels, *The German Opposition to Hitler: An Assessment* (London, 1970); Anthony Gill, *An Honourable Defeat: A History of German Resistance to Hitler* (New York, 1994); Theodore Hamerow, *On the Road to the Wolf's Lair: German Resistance to Hitler* (Cambridge, Mass., 1997); Hermann Graml, Hans Mommsen, Hans-Joachim Reichhardt, and Ernst Wolf, *The German Resistance to Hitler* (Berkeley, Calif., 1970); Frank McDonough, *Opposition and Resistance in Nazi Germany* (Cambridge, Mass., 2001); On Operation Valkyrie see Peter Hoffmann, *Stauffenberg: A Family History, 1905–1944*, 3rd ed. (Montreal, 2008); Harold Deutsch, *The Conspiracy Against Hitler in the Twilight War* (Minneapolis, 1968); and an interesting insider's account, Philipp Freiherr von Boeselager, *Valkyrie: The Story of the Plot to Kill Hitler by Its Last Member*, trans. Steven Rendall (New York, 2010). Also, worthwhile is a collection of essays edited by Hedley Bull, *The Challenge of the Third Reich* (New York, 1986) and the articles in Wolfgang Benz and Walter H. Pehle, eds., *Encyclopedia of German Resistance to the Nazi Movement* (New York, 1997). A useful collection of primary sources is Peter Hoffmann, ed., *Behind Valkyrie: German Resistance to Hitler: Documents* (Montreal, 2011). On the White Rose, see Inge Scholl, *Students Against Tyranny*, trans. Arthur Schultz (Middletown, Conn., 1970); and Annette E. Dumbach and Jud Newborn, *Shattering the German Night: The Story of the White Rose* (Boston, 1986).

MySearchLab™ Connections

Study and Review

Hitler believed that Germany was defeated in World War I because of a lack of support on the home front. He was determined that this would not happen again during World War II. Because of this, Nazi domestic policies were shaped by wartime conditions and by their theory of a new European order. The systematically disorganized former German Empire, however, proved difficult to reassemble as Hitler had promised.

Read the Document

1. **Marc Bloch, from Strange Defeat**
   This document shows the author's attempt to come to terms with the French defeat and surrender to Nazi Germany. Like many, Bloch was surprised by the speed and totality of the French defeat, and he was searching for causes of this failure.

View the Image

2. **Civilian Refugees in Europe**
   This image depicts the aftermath of heavy Allied bombing of German cities during the advance that followed the D-Day landings. The Germans suffered heavy civilian losses during the final months of the war.

View the Image

3. **Nazi Book Bonfire, 1933**
   This image indicates the attacks on historic German culture that the Nazis imposed on the German people. The Nazis were anti-intellectuals who were determined to suppress all dissenting voices and ideas.

RESEARCH AND EXPLORE

Though the Nazis were omnipresent in German life, resistance and opposition continued even in wartime Germany. Hitler's early wartime successes and charisma initially dissuaded rebellion, but ultimately, war weariness and the virulence of Nazi repression fostered increasing resistance.

1. Big industry was a strong supporter of the Nazis until the end of the war. In what ways were the policies of the Nazis influenced by their industrial supporters? Why did big industry remain loyal to the Nazis, despite the fact that many in the elite class disliked Nazi policies?

2. Considering the timing of the Valkyrie operation, could the coup have stopped the Allied war effort? Why or why not?

3. What was the rationale behind Nazi attacks on the influence of German churches? How were these attacks on the churches perceived by the German people?

ADDITIONAL RESOURCES

Hitler and Roosevelt (Randy Roberts)

Nazi Murder Mills: WARNING: This clip is very graphic.

The Holocaust

The deliberate destruction of millions of human lives in the Holocaust makes it a highly emotional topic that is difficult to discuss dispassionately. Although historians of Nazism debate some aspects of the Holocaust, there is general agreement on the details of this tragic chapter in history. Certainly, the mass murder of millions of European Jews served no military purpose. In fact, the failure to fully use the skilled labor of the Jews, and the mobilization of railroad cars for the transference of Jews to death camps at a time when transportation was desperately needed for the war effort, served only to hasten Germany's eventual defeat. In many ways, the Holocaust seemed a logical extension of Hitler's deeply felt racial views. Surely it was no accident that Heinrich Himmler's SS, the self-appointed standard bearer of Nazi racial ideals, assumed the primary responsibility for the attempted annihilation of European Jewry.

HITLER'S RACIAL IDEOLOGY

The racial ideas of Adolf Hitler are a logical beginning for an examination of the Holocaust. It may be impossible to pinpoint when Hitler conceived of the mass murder of the Jews, but it is not difficult to demonstrate that his ideology led in that direction, twisted though the road may be. As we have seen, conflict and racial struggle were at the core of Hitler's ideology. This racial struggle consisted of a clear play of opposites: the Aryans, bearers of human cultural development, against the Jews, parasites who were attempting to destroy the Aryans. Already in 1922, at a meeting of the National Socialist Party, Hitler said, "There can be no compromise—there are only two possibilities: either victory of the Aryan or annihilation of the Aryan and the victory of the Jew."[1] Opposition to the Jews became Hitler's sacred mission. "Today I believe that I am acting in accordance with the will of the Almighty Creator: *by defending myself against*

---

[1]Adolf Hitler, *My New Order*, edited by Raoul de Roussy de Sales (New York, 1941), pp. 21–22.

the Jew, I am fighting for the work of the Lord."[2] Since the Jews, according to Hitler, were "evil incarnate," with plans to dominate the world, the Aryans must be prepared for a long and bloody struggle.

> It is the inexorable Jew who struggles for his domination over the nations. No nation can remove this hand from its throat except by the sword. Only the assembled and concentrated might of a national passion rearing up in its strength can defy the international enslavement of peoples. Such a process is and remains a bloody one.[3]

Mein Kampf, written in the mid-1920s, is replete with pronounced anti-Jewish comments. In fact, in the last chapter, while discussing the role of the Jews in Germany's defeat in World War I, Hitler made statements that, psychologically at least, foreshadowed the Final Solution of the Holocaust.

> If at the beginning of the War and during the War twelve or fifteen thousand of these Hebrew corrupters of the people had been held under poison gas, as happened to hundreds of thousands of our very best German workers in the field, the sacrifice of millions at the front would not have been in vain.[4]

Clearly, Hitler's ideological stance called for the elimination of the "evil" Jews if the Aryan race were to survive. Many contemporaries and later observers as well have maintained that Hitler did not mean these words literally but was simply expressing a popular sentiment in Germany that would gain attention and votes. But in view of the Holocaust, might it not be more reasonable to assume that just as World War II represented the ultimate result of Hitler's notions on conflict, the Holocaust was a logical outcome of his views on the Jews? Hitler expressed this possibility before World War II when he remarked candidly to the Czechoslovakian foreign minister on January 21, 1939, that "the Jews will be destroyed by us. They are not going to get away with what they did on November 9, 1918. That day will be avenged."[5] That was meant to be confidential, but Hitler returned to this theme publicly in an address to the Reichstag on January 30, 1939, the anniversary of his accession to power.

> One thing I would like to express on this day, which is perhaps memorable not only for us Germans: In my life I have often been a prophet, and I have mostly been laughed at. At the time of my struggle for power, it was mostly the Jewish people who laughed at the prophecy that one day I would attain in Germany the leadership of the state and therewith of the entire nation, and that among other problems I would also solve the Jewish one. I think that the uproarious laughter of that time has in the meantime remained stuck in German Jewry's

[2]Excerpts from *Mein Kampf* by Adolf Hitler, translated by Ralph Manheim, p. 65 (italics in the original). Copyright © 1943, renewed 1971 by Houghton Mifflin Harcourt Publishing Company. Reprinted by permission of Houghton Mifflin Harcourt Publishing Company. All rights reserved.

[3]Ibid., p. 651.

[4]Ibid., p. 679.

[5]Quoted in Hans Buchheim, Martin Broszat, Hans-Adolf Jacobsen, and Helmut Krausnick, *Anatomie des SS-Staates,* vol. 2 (Freiburg im Breisgau, 1965), p. 340.

throat. Today I want to be a prophet again: If international finance Jewry inside and outside Europe again succeeds in precipitating the nations into a world war, the result will not be the Bolshevization of the earth and with it the victory of Jewry, but the annihilation of the Jewish race in Europe.[6]

Later, in a speech during the war, Hitler recalled his earlier address to the Reichstag.

You will recall that meeting of the Reichstag in which I declared: If Jewry per-chance imagines that it can bring about an international world war for the annihilation of the European races, then the consequence will be not the annihilation of the European races, but, on the contrary, it will be the annihilation of Jewry in Europe. I was always laughed at as a prophet. Of those who laughed then, countless ones no longer laugh today, and those who still laugh now will perhaps in a while also no longer do so.[7]

Even in his last political testament, on April 29, 1945, Hitler remained consistent in his hatred of the Jews. "Above all I charge the leaders of the nation and those under them to scrupulous observance of the laws of race and to merciless opposition to the universal poisoner of all peoples, international Jewry."[8]

THE FINAL SOLUTION

World War II provided the major turning point in Hitler's "solution to the Jewish question." The war and the annihilation of the Jews became interrelated, for two reasons. One of Hitler's objectives was to achieve *Lebensraum* in the Soviet Union. Since he had always associated Soviet bolshevism with the Jews, it made sense to destroy the enemy wherever he could be found. A war against Soviet bolshevism was a war against the Jews. In addition, the disorder produced by the war created an environment in which to carry out a systematic annihilation of the Jews.

Role of the SS

Hitler's initial conquests, therefore, created the opportunity to put his racial programs into effect. His racial ideology was shared especially by the SS under Heinrich Himmler, a true believer in the development of a pure Aryan race. The SS assumed primary responsibility for the execution of the Final Solution. Within the SS, the SD under Heydrich wielded enormous power through a well-developed surveillance system that included Germany and eventually all Nazi-occupied Europe. In 1939, Himmler's reorganization plans established the Reich Security Main Office (RSHA) comprising the SD and the Security Police (Sipo). The latter consisted of the Gestapo (secret political police) and the Kripo (criminal police). Heydrich was placed in charge of this new RSHA.

[6]Quoted in Saul Friedländer, *Nazi Germany and the Jews*, vol. 1, *The Years of Persecution, 1933–1939* (New York, 1997), pp. 309–310.

[7]Lucy Dawidowicz, ed., *A Holocaust Reader* (New York, 1976), p. 33.

[8]*Nazi Conspiracy and Aggression*, vol. 6 (Washington, D.C., 1946), p. 263.

In 1934, the SD had established a separate office, known as SD-Inland, II–112, for Jewish affairs under Leopold von Mildenstein, who promptly hired Adolf Eichmann as his expert on Jews. Also in 1934, an office coded II-F–2 was established in the Gestapo to deal with Jewish matters. With the reorganization of 1939 establishing the RSHA, the Gestapo became Amt IV, or Office IV within the larger organization, and it was in Section B4 of this office (thus IV B4) that Adolf Eichmann came to control the Nazi machinery for the deportation of Jews from all over Europe to the east for the Final Solution.

Reorganization of Poland: Jewish Ghettos

The conquest and occupation of Poland in 1939 provided the territory in which the Final Solution to the Jewish question would take place. German anti-Jewish legislation was quickly imported into the conquered territory. As a Jewish woman from the town of Lipno wrote,

> On September 8, X [the Germans] entered the town. After they took control, a whole series of orders and prohibitions was issued. One could only be on the street until 5 o'clock, Jews had to wear yellow ribbons, and when these markings proved too small, Jews were ordered to pin yellow sashes onto their backs and chests. Walking on the sidewalk was forbidden; [there was] an order to walk on the road, to bow.[9]

Initial anti-Jewish actions in the wake of the invasion went beyond legislation. Similar to *Kristallnacht,* Jewish cultural life was decimated. Jews who attempted to protect their heritage often were murdered. Another observer of the conquest wrote:

> On the evening of Saturday, September 9, 1939, at the same time as in Sosnowiec, a frightening dynamite explosion was heard across town. It was soon learned that the synagogue was on fire. A number of Jews, including Rabbi Yekhil Shlezinger, his two sons, and his son-in-law, Rabbi Yekhezkel Kon, raced into the burning synagogue to rescue the Torah scrolls. The arsonists shot at them and killed all of them. The martyrs were burned together with the synagogue and its Torah scrolls. The Jews began to pour out of the surrounding houses to save themselves from the flames. The whole area, however, had been cordoned off by soldiers, and as soon as a Jew was spotted, he was shot. In a short time the streets near *schul* were filled with the bodies of dead Jews.[10]

In October, Hitler partitioned Nazi-occupied Poland by absorbing the western part into Greater Germany and establishing a civil administration called the Government General in the remaining Polish territory. At the same time, Hitler gave Heinrich Himmler overall responsibility to resettle Poland along racial lines. Actual administration of this policy was left to Reinhard Heydrich and his special strike forces known as the *Einsatzgruppen.*

The *Einsatzgruppen* had been created during the annexation of Austria in March 1938 and the invasion of Czechoslovakia in March 1939 as striking forces for the political

---

[9]Quoted in Alexandra Garbarini, ed., *Jewish Responses to Persecution, vol. II, 1938–1940* (Lanham, Md., 2011), p. 129. By permission of AltaMira Press.

[10]Ibid., p. 138.

police and security intelligence services. Their task was to track down opponents of the Nazis. Six *Einsatzgruppen* were now sent into Poland. Although attached to the regular German army, they very quickly established their independence from military control. On September 7, 1939, Heydrich referred to the "eliminating of the leading strata of the population." He clarified this the following day: "We want to spare the little people, but the nobility, the priests and the Jews must be killed."[11] Tens of thousands of Polish intellectuals, priests, communist leaders, and Jews would be murdered in months ahead. The next step in the Germanization of the conquered would be the forced relocation of over 200,000 ethnic Poles and over 100,000 Polish Jews. Regarding the relocation of the Jews, Heydrich informed the commanders of the *Einsatzgruppen* that the "first prerequisite for the ultimate goal is the concentration of the Jews from the country to the larger cities." All Jews therefore were to be expelled from the parts of Poland that were to be incorporated into Germany proper, namely Danzig, West Prussia, Posnan, and Eastern Upper Silesia. These Jews and all remaining Jews in other parts of Poland were to be concentrated in cities in the Government General, preferably in "as few concentration points as possible so that future measures may be accomplished more easily." Heydrich asserted that only cities that had rail junctions or were located along railroad lines were to be used as concentration points. The *Einsatzgruppen* were responsible for executing this directive by establishing a number of Jewish ghettos in late 1939 and 1940.

The first one was established in October 1939 in Piotrkow Tribunalski. Not until the following spring did the Nazis seal off the first major ghetto in the city of Lodz. The Warsaw ghetto was created in October 1940. In the latter, 183,000 Jews were initially sealed off by walls, barbed wire, and guarded gates from the rest of the Polish inhabitants. The chief chronicler of the Warsaw ghetto, Emmanuel Ringelblum, described the shock of the experience:

> The Saturday the Ghetto was introduced was terrible. People in the street didn't know it was to be a closed Ghetto, so it came like a thunderbolt. Details of German, Polish and Jewish guards stood at every street corner searching passersby to decide whether or not they had the right to pass. Jewish women found the markets outside the ghetto closed to them. There was an immediate shortage of bread and other produce.[12]

The loss of freedom was felt by all. A thirteen-year-old boy in Vilna stated in his diary: "I feel that I have been robbed, my freedom is being robbed from me, and my home and the familiar Vilna streets I love so much."[13] Ghettos were later established in the Soviet Union after it was invaded.

The ghettos were located in the oldest, most run-down sections of the cities. The ghetto buildings were dilapidated and lacked running water and toilet facilities. Overcrowding was the norm, as this report by a top German official in Warsaw indicates: "The Jewish quarter extends over about 1,016 acres . . . Occupancy therefore works out at 15 persons per apartment and six to seven persons per room."[14]

[11]Quoted in Helmut Langerbein, *Hitler's Death Squads: The Logic of Mass Murder* (College Station, Tex., 2004), p. 25.

[12]Emmanuel Ringelblum, *Notes from the Warsaw Ghetto*, edited and translated by Jacob Sloan (New York, 1958), p. 86.

[13]Quoted in Lucy Dawidowicz, *The War Against the Jews*, 2nd ed. (New York, 1986), p. 207.

[14]Quoted in Yehuda Bauer, *A History of the Holocaust* (New York, 1982), p. 153.

In his September directive, Heydrich had commanded the establishment of a *Judenrat* (Jewish Council) in each Jewish ghetto. These were to be executive bodies composed of twenty-four "of the remaining influential personalities and rabbis." These councils were responsible for the "exact and punctual execution" of all Nazi orders. Their duties included registration of all Jews by age and "principal occupation groups" and the internal administration of the ghetto, which included police duties, housing, and health. Believing in most cases that the Germans would lose the war, many of these councils temporarily cooperated with the Nazis in the hope of ameliorating the worst conditions and gaining eventual liberation. Sometimes, however, *Judenrat* members refused to go along with the Germans and were subsequently murdered. Those who cooperated were forced to provide labor, confiscate property, and sacrifice the lives of some people in the hope of saving others when the Nazis requested a group for deportation to a death camp. Some *Judenrat* leaders, such as Mordechai Rumkowski of Lodz, tried to make the ghetto Jews indispensable by doing work crucial to the German war machine. Rumkowski's approach almost succeeded, since the Lodz ghetto was the last one in Poland, but it too was liquidated, in August 1944, shortly before the Russians occupied the city. The Nazis, of course, realized the advantages of strengthening the role of these Jewish councils. As one German ghetto administrator stated: "When deficiencies occur, the Jews direct their resentment against the Jewish administration and not against the German supervision."[15]

Life in the ghettos was extremely harsh. In addition to a lack of fuel for heat, food provisions were very meager. Since the ghettos were sealed off, their food supply was controlled by the Germans, whose policy was virtual starvation. Only the smuggling of food into the ghettos, especially by youngsters, kept the Jews alive. Some ghettos, such as the one in Lodz, were so well surrounded that smuggling was impossible and starvation considerably higher. Deaths by hunger became increasingly frequent. In the Warsaw ghetto, there were 91 deaths by hunger at the end of 1940 and 11,000 in 1941. With hunger and physical weakness came diseases and epidemics, especially typhoid and dysentery. Typhus killed 43,000 in Warsaw in 1941 out of the 420,000 then residing in the ghetto there.

In the large-city ghettos, refugees from outlying communities and rural areas created especially difficult problems. In addition to the original inhabitants, over 600,000 Jewish refugees were crammed into the ghettos. Expelled from their communities, lacking any means of subsistence, they became totally dependent on social welfare. The *Judenrat* often did not have the resources to feed them. Uprooted, demoralized, and forced to beg for food, the refugees tended to be the first to die of starvation.

The Jewish ghetto inhabitants displayed an incredible will to survive. "Don't despair, rally yourselves, trust in God" became a typical appeal by rabbis to fellow Jews. Strategies of accommodation and adaptability were pursued with considerable flexibility. To maintain their spirit and create a sense of community and social cohesion, the ghetto inhabitants established voluntary associations. In Warsaw, the political organization *Zetos*, headed by the ghetto historian Emmanuel Ringelblum, provided social welfare services in competition with the local *Judenrat*. *Zetos* organized public kitchens, homes for children, hospitals, and especially house committees that provided aid for families living together. About

---

[15]Quoted in Raul Hilberg, *The Destruction of the European Jews*, 3rd ed., vol. 1 (New Haven, 2003), p. 241.

one-fourth of the ghetto inhabitants received some form of aid from *Zetos*. Religious life was fostered by underground religious services, since public prayer was forbidden. A Warsaw diarist noted:

> Public prayer in these times is a forbidden act. Anyone caught in this crime is doomed to severe punishment. If you will, it is even sabotage, and anyone engaging in sabotage is subject to execution. But this does not deter us . . . They pick some inside room whose windows look out onto the courtyard, and pour out their supplications before the God of Israel in whispers. This time there are not cantors and choirs, only whispered prayers. But the prayers are heart-felt; it is possible to weep in secret, too, and the gates of tears are not locked.[16]

Educational and cultural activities were undertaken in a variety of ways in the ghettos. Secret ghetto libraries were established. Writers and painters managed to find ways to continue their work. Orchestras and choirs were founded. Since education was often forbidden, Jews responded by forming small groups of four to eight children instructed by a teacher who would receive a loaf of bread as a salary. Illegal high schools were maintained in Warsaw. Numerous secret archives, some of which have survived, were constituted to preserve a record of Nazi atrocities and maintain a picture of life in the ghettos. The Jewish ghetto inhabitants discovered that the human spirit could still thrive in the midst of Nazi barbarism.

Once the Germans had established the death camps in 1941 and 1942, they began to systematically liquidate the ghettos. Jews in the ghettos were told that they were being resettled in work camps in the east. Soon, rumors developed that the trains were bound instead for annihilation camps. Many were unwilling to believe these rumors, but others responded by developing and joining resistance movements.

Physical resistance was, of course, very difficult. It was inhibited by German terror and not by passivity, as some have claimed. Being unprepared for such brutal treatment, Jews were slow to react in any coordinated fashion. Indeed, contrary to Nazi racial propaganda, Jews were not a well-organized group of conspirators preparing for world domination. Terror and starvation also weakened the social bonds that would make cooperation possible. In addition, the Jews as a distinct minority (1 percent in Germany, 10 percent in Poland) received little support from the general populace and governments abroad and hence were not able to obtain underground supplies of arms. Without such support, open resistance was extremely difficult. Finally, any thought of individual or small-group attempts at resistance, even if they succeeded in doing some harm to the Germans, would bring massive retaliation and possible death for thousands of Jews, thus making resistance a moral dilemma as well. Nevertheless, despite these obstacles to resistance, what made it feasible was the growing understanding, especially on the part of young people, that the Nazis did intend to annihilate the Jewish people. Once this thought was believable, individual Jews could fight knowing it was better to die with honor by resisting than to be gassed. Even with a fighting attitude, however, it was difficult for resistance movements to succeed without sufficient weapons. Polish and other non-Jewish sources were not willing to supply arms, forcing Jewish resistance members to purchase them or steal them from German supplies.

---

[16]Abraham I. Katsh, edited and translated by, *Scroll of Agony: The Warsaw Diary of Chaim A. Kaplan* (New York, 1965), pp. 202–203.

Despite the problems, armed resistance did occur in a considerable number of ghettos. Armed groups resisted the Nazis in twenty-four ghettos in western and central Poland, and sixty-three armed underground groups were established in the 110 ghettos of northeast Poland. Likewise, underground organizations were formed in Lithuanian ghettos and in the Soviet Union. In the areas where the ghettos were surrounded by forests, tens of thousands of resisters fled the ghettos and linked up with partisan groups.

The most famous instance of rebellion occurred in Warsaw. Attempts early in 1942 to establish a Jewish fighting organization (JFO) failed. But after the deportation of 265,000 Jews from July to September to the gas chambers of Treblinka, a JFO, consisting primarily of members of the three original Zionist youth groups, Dror, Hashomir Hatzair, and Akiva, was formed under Mordechai Anielewicz. Arms were bought, stolen, and smuggled into the ghetto. The JFO managed to gain the support of the remaining 55,000 to 65,000 Jews in the ghetto. After its first armed resistance in January 1943, the JFO was aided by a new group, the Jewish Military Organization, which brought in more weapons, including a few light machine guns. When the Nazis entered the ghetto on April 19, they met fierce resistance and had to retreat. Under their new commander, General Jurgen Stroop, the Nazis eventually overpowered their outclassed opponents, although not without considerable struggle. General Stroop's final report triumphantly proclaimed that "the Warsaw Jewish Quarter is no more." Stroop obliterated the Jewish ghetto.

> The resistance offered by the Jews and bandits could be broken only by the energetic and relentless day and night commitment of our assault units. On 23 April 1943, the Reichsführer-SS [Himmler] promulgated his order, . . . to complete the sweeping of the Warsaw Ghetto with greatest severity and unrelenting tenacity. I therefore decided to embark on the total destruction of the Jewish quarter by burning down every residential block, including the housing blocks belonging to the armament enterprises. One enterprise after another was systematically evacuated and destroyed by fire . . . Now there are no enterprises left in the former Jewish quarter. Everything of value, the raw materials, and machines have been transferred. The buildings and whatever else there was have been destroyed. The only exception is the so-called Dzielna Prison of the Security Police, which was exempted from destruction.[17]

Einsatzgruppen *Atrocities in the East*

The first stage of the Final Solution began with the assault on the Soviet Union in June 1941. As we have seen, the Nazis conceived of the *Ostkrieg*, the Eastern War, as a *Vernichtungskrieg*, a war of extermination. In the active war zone, the regular army advance into the Soviet Union was followed by four newly organized *Einsatzgruppen*. These four mobile killing units varied in size from 500 to 900 men. The officers were enlisted from the SS, the SD, the Gestapo, and Sipo, the regulars from various branches of the SS. Middle-echelon leaders of these four *Einsatzgruppen* were a curious combination of highly qualified academics (some with Ph.D. degrees), lawyers, ministerial officials, and even one Protestant minister. In addition to basic military training, they were carefully indoctrinated in National Socialist racial ideology, which emphasized, as Heydrich stated, that "Judaism in the East is the source of Bolshevism and must therefore be wiped out in accordance with the Führer's aims."[18]

---

[17]Sybil Milton, edited and translated by, *The Stroop Report* (New York, 1979), pp. 9–11.

[18]Quoted in Hans Höhne, *The Order of the Death's Head* (New York, 1969), p. 358.

Activities of the *Einsatz-gruppen.* Shown here is the execution of a Jew by a member of one of the SS killing squads known as the *Einsatzgruppen.* Onlookers include members of the German army, the German Labor Service, and even Hitler Youth. *(Mary Evans Picture Library/Alamy)*

The day after the invasion of Russia, the four *Einsatzgruppen* entered the Soviet Union, 3000 men in search of millions of Jews. Each group used basically similar methods of deception, terror, and savagery to accomplish its goals. Otto Ohlendorf, head of one group, later explained the mode of operation:

> In June, 1941, I was designated by Himmler to lead one of the *Einsatzgruppen* . . . Himmler stated that an important part of our task consisted of the extermination of the Jews—women, men, and children—and of communist functionaries . . . The unit selected for this task would enter a village or city and order the prominent Jewish citizens to call together all Jews for the purpose of resettlement. They were requested to hand over their valuables to the leaders of the unit, and shortly before the execution to surrender their outer clothing. The men, women, and children were led to a place of execution which in most cases was located next to a more deeply excavated anti-tank ditch. Then they were shot, kneeling or standing, and the corpses thrown into the ditch.[19]

The *Einsatzgruppen* were pleasantly surprised by the cooperation they received from the German army. The generals, initially reluctant to participate in the killing of Jews, became willing accomplices in many instances. The *Einsatzgruppen* were also assisted

---

[19]*Nazi Conspiracy and Aggression*, vol. 5, pp. 341–342.

by local non-Jews, sometimes under pressure, sometimes willingly. One Ukrainian Jew recalled in his diary what happened in June 1941 in Tarnopol:

> On the third day of the [German] invasion a massacre lasting three consecutive days was carried out in the following manner. The Germans, joined by Ukrainians, would go from house to house in order to look for Jews. The Ukrainians would take the Jews out of the houses where the waiting Germans would kill them, either right by the house or they would transport the victims to a particular site where all would be put to death. This is how some five thousand people found their death, mostly men.[20]

Such constant killing produced morale problems for some of the German executioners. Many resorted to frequent use of alcohol. The following paraphrase of a speech Himmler gave during a visit to Minsk illustrates how the leader of the SS tried to raise morale:

> He [Himmler] pointed out that the *Einsatzgruppen* were called upon to fulfill a repulsive duty. He would not like it if Germans did such a thing gladly. But their conscience was in no way impaired, for they were soldiers who had to carry out every order unconditionally. He alone had responsibility before God and Hitler for everything that was happening. They had undoubtedly noticed that he hated this bloody business and that he had been aroused to the depth of his soul. But he too was obeying the highest law by doing his duty, and he was acting from a deep understanding of the necessity for this operation.[21]

The effectiveness of these appeals can be judged in the words of an *Einsatzgruppen* middle-level commander: "I was continually hearing myself and my men accused of barbarity and sadism when all I was doing was my duty."[22] Some commanders, such as Dr. Otto Rasch, forced all of their men to witness and participate in the horror, using collective blood guilt as a bond of comradeship. Other soldiers, however, felt entirely justified with their actions. A Private Franzl, involved in the Tarnopol massacre mentioned earlier, wrote his parents approvingly of the action: "Up to now we have sent approximately 1,000 Jews to the other world, but this is by far too little for what they have done." He asked his parents back in Germany to inform others of these events, concluding: "If there are doubts, we will bring photos. Then, no more doubts."[23]

A second sweep by the *Einsatzgruppen* in 1942 followed the first one of the previous year. It has been estimated, based on the methodical reports of the *Einsatzgruppen* themselves, that over 1 million Jews were killed by these mobile killing units and their auxiliaries in this two-year period.

Organization of the Death Camps

The *Einsatzgruppen* approach to solving the Jewish question was soon seen to be inadequate. There emerged, then, a second approach to the Final Solution: the systematic annihilation of the Jewish population in Nazi-occupied Europe in specially constructed death camps.

---

[20]Quoted in Saul Friedländer, *The Years of Extermination: Nazi Germany and the Jews, 1939–1945* (New York, 2007).

[21]Quoted in Hilberg, *The Destruction of the European Jews*, vol. 1, pp. 343–344.

[22]Quoted in Höhne, *The Order of the Death's Head*, p. 371.

[23]Quoted in Friedländer, *Years of Extermination*, p. 214.

The general plan was simple. The rest of the European Jews in countries under German occupation or sympathetic to Germany would be shipped by train to death camps in or near the Government General of Poland. Once this basic decision had been made, only administrative and technological details remained. Hitler granted responsibility for this task to Himmler, who was in fact particularly anxious to claim it. In the summer of 1941, Rudolf Höss, commandant of Auschwitz, was told by Himmler: "The Führer has ordered that the Jewish question be solved once and for all and that we, the SS, are to implement that order."[24] In his morale-boosting speeches, Himmler emphasized that the "leaders and men who were taking part in the liquidation bore no personal responsibility for the execution of this order. The responsibility was his alone, and the Führer's."[25] Administrative responsibility for coordinating the Final Solution was given to Reinhard Heydrich as head of the RSHA. Heydrich lodged operational duties in Amt IV B4 of the RSHA, where Adolf Eichmann supervised "Jewish affairs."

Technical problems consisted of the creation of physical facilities to accommodate the efficient killing of large numbers of people. Rudolf Höss was directed in the summer of 1941 to enlarge Auschwitz, which had been chosen for the Final Solution because of its ready railroad connections and its isolation from populated areas, which made it easy to guard. At the same time, five other major annihilation camps were established in or near the General Government area of Poland: Chelmno, Belzec, Sobibor, Majdanek, and Treblinka. There were, of course, scores of other concentration camps in Germany, Austria, France, and Yugoslavia where Jews and non-Jews were sent into forced labor, starved, tortured, and murdered under horrible conditions. But these six were established for extermination and put into operation in 1941 and 1942.

After considerable discussion and experimentation, first at Chelmno with bottled carbon monoxide, Zyklon B (the commercial name for hydrogen cyanide, or prussic acid) was usually selected as the most efficient gas for quickly killing large numbers of people. After gassing, the corpses were to be burned in specially constructed crematoria. Höss was especially proud of the fact that he had made Auschwitz much more efficient than Treblinka.

> I visited Treblinka to find out how they carried out their extermination. The Camp Commandant at Treblinka told me that he liquidated 80,000 in the course of one-half year. He was principally concerned with liquidating all the Jews from the Warsaw ghetto. He used monoxide gas and I did not think that his methods were very efficient. So when I set up the extermination building at Auschwitz, I used Cyclon B . . . which we dropped into the death chamber from a small opening . . . Another improvement we made over Treblinka was that we built our gas chambers to accommodate 2,000 people at one time, whereas at Treblinka their ten gas chambers only accommodate 200 people each.[26]

Much assistance in the technical details of gassing people was provided by experts from the T-4 program for the elimination of mental and physical defectives in

---

[24]Rudolf Höss, *Commandant of Auschwitz: The Autobiography of Rudolf Hoess* (New York, 1959), p. 205.

[25]International Military Tribunal, *Trial of the Major War Criminals*, vol. 4 (Nuremberg, 1947), p. 318.

[26]*Nazi Conspiracy and Aggression*, vol. 6, pp. 788–789.

Germany. This program, which had used Zyklon B, was responsible for killing between 80,000 and 100,000 people before it was halted. But many of the personnel and even some of the apparatus, including gas chambers, were transferred to Poland for the Final Solution.

The general procedures for the Final Solution were outlined for the benefit of state and party officials by Reinhard Heydrich at the Wannsee Conference, held outside Berlin on January 20, 1942. Heydrich reported that he had be delegated to make "preparations for the final solution of the Jewish question in Europe," and discussed the steps taken to "solve the Jewish question," including the efforts at emigration. This policy, however, now had to be changed, and that "a new solution had emerged, after prior approval of the Führer." Heydrich then presented a statistical review of the Jews in Europe, which he numbered at 11 million, including those in states such as England, Ireland, and Switzerland not yet occupied by the Nazis. Heydrich reported that those Jews "fit to work" would "work their way eastward constructing roads," and as a consequence, "doubtless the large majority will be eliminated by natural causes." Reflecting Nazi social Darwinism, he remarked: "any final remnant that survives will doubtless consist of the most resistant elements. They will have to be dealt with appropriately because otherwise, by natural selection, they would form the germ cell of a new Jewish revival (See the experience of history)." Thus, all 11 million Jews were to die, by one means or another. Heydrich further explained how "in course of the practical implementation of the final solution Europe is to be combed through from west to east" for Jews. All would be included in the Final Solution. They would be brought, "group by group, into so-called transit ghettos, to be transported from there farther to the east."[27] The conference then elaborated upon the administrative details for the practical implementation of the Final Solution. Since the technical machinery had already been tested and was in the process of being constructed, the purpose of this conference was to ensure the smooth operation of the bureaucratic machinery. The German bureaucracy now assisted in the final elimination of the Jews.

Shipment of Jews to Death Camps

With the technical machinery in place and administrative affairs put in order, the Final Solution entered its last stage. "Resettlement for work in the east" was the lie perpetrated by the Germans to dupe the Jews concerning their fate. To reinforce that lie, the Nazis allowed the Jews to take along personal belongings. Amt IV B4 of the RSHA, under Adolf Eichmann, was in charge of arrests and the deportation of the Jews to the death camps. Special SS counselors on Jewish affairs, responsible to Eichmann, were attached to German embassies in satellite and occupied countries throughout Europe and instructed to smooth the way for deportations. The forced removal from the ghettos was often brutal. Fanny Miller recalled the night the Germans came to remove the women and children from the Brzeziny ghetto in 1942 for transit to Chelmno. The Germans, including

---

[27]Quotations from the Wannsee Protocol, as reprinted in the appendix of Mark Roseman, *The Wannsee Conference and the Final Solution: A Reconsideration* (New York, 2002).

drunken SS officer Franz Seifert, burst into buildings with pistols and rubber truncheons, grabbing the children first. As Miller recalled:

> I did not want to lose my two-and-a-half-year-old daughter, Hannah Miller, and I tried to hide her. The child was very agitated and I remember her crying, "Please mommy, do not let them do it—daddy is not here." Seifert must have heard this, for he came up to me and hit me in the face with his rubber truncheon, and I bled heavily. He then tore my baby away from me and she was taken outside with the rest. I was frantic and asked Seifert to shoot me. He only laughed and said, "You will die anyway."[28]

The Jews were then taken to train depots to be transported to the death camps. The Transport Ministry was responsible for trains throughout Nazi-occupied Europe. The schedules worked out by Amt IV B4 were initiated in March 1942, when a group of Slovakian Jews arrived at Auschwitz. Although the Wannsee Conference had decided to remove the Jews methodically, starting from the west, top priority was given to the elimination of the ghettos in Poland, as Joseph Goebbels commented in his diary:

> Beginning with Lublin the Jews in the General Government are now being evacuated eastward. The procedure is a pretty barbaric one and not to be described here more definitely. Not much will remain of the Jews. On the whole it can be said that about sixty per cent of them will have to be liquidated, whereas only about forty per cent can be used for forced labor.[29]

By the summer of 1942, Jews were being shipped as well from France, Belgium, and Holland. Norwegian Jews were added in the fall. In 1943, there were deportations to the death camps from the capital cities of Berlin, Vienna, and Prague, and from Greece, Luxembourg, southern France, Italy, and Denmark. Even in 1944, as the Allies were making significant advances, Jews were being sent from Greece and Hungary. The train experience was both brutal and humiliating. As a Hungarian victim recalled:

> My mother, Aunt Gisele, Sharu and I were jammed into a cattle car with about ninety men, women, and children. There was hardly any room to stand, and only the elderly and sick were allowed to sit where there was room. Soon we heard the rhythmic clanking of the train's wheels, and our unknown journey began. A lone square window barred with planks of wood prevented escape and kept fresh air from circulating in the car. The heat was stifling. I was surrounded by acrid bodies dripping with perspiration. Two pails stood in a corner to be used for human waste. At first everyone hesitated to use them, for it was so degrading to relieve oneself in public; but we soon realized that there was no alternative. Often the bucket was too full, and its contents overflowed. People sat in their own feces and urine, and the stench was unbearable.[30]

---

[28]Quoted in Patrick Montague, *Chelmno and the Holocaust: The History of Hitler's First Death Camp* (Chapel Hill, N.C., 2012), p. 74.

[29]Joseph Goebbels, *The Goebbels Diaries, 1942–1943*, edited by Louis P. Lochner (Garden City, N.Y., 1948), pp. 147–148.

[30]Quoted in Simone Gigliotti, *The Train Journey: Transit, Captivity, and Witnessing in the Holocaust* (New York, 2009), pp. 108–109.

Despite desperate military needs, the Final Solution was given top priority in using railroad cars for the shipment of Jews. German bureaucrats in charge of the deportations were particularly eager to speed along their work. They regularly made special requests to transportation officials, asking them to help free bottlenecks. And, as the following letter from the chief of Himmler's personal staff to the state secretary of the Transport Ministry demonstrates, they responded gratefully when those requests were fulfilled:

> Dear Party Member Ganzenmüller: For your letter of July 28, 1942, I thank you—also in the name of the Reichsführer-SS—sincerely. With particular joy I noted your assurance that for two weeks now a train has been carrying, every day, 5000 members of the chosen people to Treblinka, so that we are now in a position to carry through this population movement at an accelerated tempo. I, for my part, have contacted the participating agencies to assure the implementation of the process without friction. I thank you again for your efforts in this matter and, at the same time, I would be grateful if you would give to these things your continued personal attention. With best regards and Heil Hitler! Your devoted W.[31]

Even Himmler was constantly badgered by lower officials to intervene with the army and the transportation department to obtain more trains; he was usually successful.

The importance of the Final Solution to Hitler and the Nazis is also evident in the allocation of Jewish labor in the construction of armaments. The military was especially eager to allow Jews to use their specialized skills in the production of military necessities. The Jewish ghetto of Lodz, for example, located seventy-five miles west of Warsaw and consisting of 80,000 inhabitants, was responsible for 95 percent of the armaments work produced in that area of Poland. Naturally, the army had an interest in maintaining the ghetto. In June 1944, Himmler ordered the liquidation of the ghetto. Despite the army's attempt to countermand the order, the Lodz ghetto Jews were all sent to Auschwitz by August. This occurred at a time when the German military situation was becoming desperate. The victory of Himmler over the army is another indication of Hitler's perception that if he could not win his European war, he might at least be able to win his war of annihilation against the Jews.

Death Camp Procedure

A standard procedure was usually followed for Jews arriving at one of the six death camps. Rudolf Höss, commandant at Auschwitz-Birkenau, described the experience awaiting the Jews as they decamped from the trains at Auschwitz.

> We had two SS doctors on duty at Auschwitz to examine the incoming transports of prisoners. The prisoners would be marched by one of the doctors who would make spot decisions as they walked by. Those who were fit for work were sent into the camp. Others were sent immediately to the extermination plants. Children of tender years were invariably exterminated since by reason of their youth they were unable to work. Still another improvement we made over Treblinka was that at Treblinka the victims almost always knew that they were to be

---

[31]Quoted in Hilberg, *The Destruction of the European Jews*, vol. 2, p. 512.

The Extermination Camp at Auschwitz. This photograph shows a group of Hungarian Jews who have just arrived at Auschwitz. Hungarian Jews were not rounded up and shipped to the death camps until 1944. *(Library of Congress Photographs and Prints Division[130.1105 W/S #77320])*

> exterminated and at Auschwitz we endeavored to fool the victims into thinking that they were to go through a delousing process. Of course, frequently they realized our true intentions and we sometimes had riots and difficulties due to that fact. Very frequently women would hide their children under their clothes but of course when we found them we would send the children in to be exterminated.[32]

Since Auschwitz was also a labor camp, some of the arrivals were chosen for work, while the remainder were sent to the gas chambers, after undressing and being told that they were to be deloused in shower stalls. Höss described the actual killing process.

> It took from 3 to 15 minutes to kill the people in the death chamber depending upon climatic conditions. We knew when the people were dead because their screaming stopped. We usually waited about one-half hour before we opened the doors and removed the bodies. After the bodies were removed our special commandos took off the rings and extracted the gold from the teeth of the corpses.[33]

Höss's account, while coldly accurate, does not reflect the true horror of the process. Chil Rajchman, a Jew forced to work extracting gold teeth from the corpses at Treblinka,

[32]*Nazi Conspiracy and Aggression*, vol. 6, p. 789.
[33]Ibid., p. 788.

witnessed the actual effects of the process Höss described above. He observed that the size of the gas chamber used changed the appearance of the murdered victims:

> There was a difference in the appearance of the dead from the small and from the large gas chambers. In the small chambers death was easier and quicker. The faces often looked as if the people had fallen asleep, their eyes closed. Only the mouths of some of the gassed victims were distorted with a bloody foam visible on their lips. The bodies were covered in sweat. Before dying, people had urinated and defecated. The corpses in the larger gas chambers, where death took longer, were horribly deformed, their faces all black as if burned, the bodies swollen and blue, the teeth so tightly clenched that it was literally impossible to open them, and to get to the gold crowns we had sometimes to pull out the natural teeth—otherwise the mouth would not open.[34]

After processing, the bodies were then burned in the crematoria. In his autobiography, Höss gave an account of those used at Auschwitz.

> The two large crematoriums I and II . . . had five three-retort ovens and could cremate about 2,000 bodies in less than twenty-four hours . . . Crematoriums I and II both had underground dressing rooms and gas chambers in which the air could be completely changed. The bodies were taken to the ovens on the floor above by means of an elevator. The gas chambers could hold about 3,000 people, . . . The two small crematoriums III and IV were capable . . . of burning about 1,500 bodies within twenty-four hours . . . The capacity of number V was practically unlimited, so long as cremations could be carried out both day and night . . . The highest number of people gassed and cremated within twenty-four hours was rather more than 9,000.[35]

When the crematoria were unable to handle very large shipments of Jews, open pits were used for burning bodies instead, using the fat of the dead as fuel for the fire.

Starvation, beating, torture, and killing were regular features of life at the camps. Inmates were subjected to "medical" experiments that were cruel and exceedingly painful. These experiments included the testing of the effects of high altitude by putting prisoners in pressure chambers, submersion in freezing water to see how long humans could survive, and sterilization of men and women by X-rays and other methods. Inmates were shot with poisonous bullets to study the consequences and injected with viruses to test new drugs. At Auschwitz, camp doctor Josef Mengele was especially notorious for his experimental surgery.

The victims' goods and even their bodies were used for economic gain. Females' hair was cut off before and after gassing, collected, and sent to Germany to be made into mattresses for submarines. Clothes, money, and valuables were salvaged and shipped to appropriate state and SS agencies for disposition. Cash and gold fillings were sent to the Reichsbank. Ashes from the crematoria were used for fertilizer.

The statistics of the death camps are only approximate. Although precise records were made at some camps, others never fully registered their victims. The Germans were estimated to have killed between 5 and 6 million Jews, over 3 million of them in the death camps.

The gas chambers and crematoria were the final manifestation of an ideology based on racial conflict and the hatred of one man and one group of people for another. Some so-called historians, lacking in intellectual rigor or misguided by prejudices, have even

---

[34]Quoted in Chil Rajchman, *The Last Jew of Treblinka: A Memoir*, translated by Solon Beinfeld, (New York, 2011), p. 67. Reprinted with permission from Pegasus Books.

[35]Höss, *Commandant of Auschwitz*, pp. 214–215.

denied that there was a Holocaust. Heinrich Himmler knew better. He spoke of these crimes, but in terms of "glory." Thus, Heinrich Himmler, in an address to the leaders of the SS in 1943, stated:

> I also want to talk to you, quite frankly, on a very grave matter. Among yourselves it should be mentioned quite frankly, and yet we will never speak of it publicly . . . I mean the clearing out of the Jews, the extermination of the Jewish race. It's one of those things it is easy to talk about— "The Jewish race is being exterminated," says one party member, "that's quite clear, it's in our program—elimination of the Jews, and we're doing it, exterminating them." And then they come, 80 million worthy Germans, and each one had his decent Jew. Of course the others are vermin, but this one is an A-I Jew. Not one of those who talk this way has witnessed it, not one of them has been through it. Most of you must know what it means when 100 corpses are lying side by side, or 500 or 1000. To have stuck it out and at the same time—apart from exceptions caused by human weakness—to have remained decent fellows, that is what has made us hard. This is a page of glory in our history which has never been written and is never to be written, . . . We have taken from them what wealth they had. I have issued a strict order, . . . that this wealth should, as a matter of course, be handed over to the Reich without reserve. We have taken none of it for ourselves . . . We had the moral right, we had the duty to our people, to destroy this people which wanted to destroy us. But we have not the right to enrich ourselves with so much as a fur, a watch, a mark, or a cigarette or anything else. Because we have exterminated a bacterium we do not want, in the end, to be infected by the bacterium and die of it. I will not see so much as a small area of sepsis appear here or gain a hold. Wherever it may form, we will cauterize it. Altogether however, we can say, that we have fulfilled this most difficult duty for the love of our people. And our spirit, our soul, our character has not suffered injury from it.[36]

Heinrich Himmler, like Adolf Hitler a true believer in the Nazi ideology, remained convinced to the end of the greatness of Germany's achievement.

For those who experienced the atrocities, however, it was a nightmare made real. The ghetto experience had been harsh and debilitating. The final stage of the Jewish experience under the Nazis, deportation by train to a death camp and liquidation by gassing, was by comparison an incredible horror. For many Jews, it was literally unbelievable, as the survivor Elie Wiesel related from his experiences at Auschwitz:

> We did not know, as yet, which was the better side, right or left, which road led to prison and which to the crematoria. But still, I was happy, I was near my father. Our procession continued to slowly move forward.
>
> Another inmate came up to us:
>
> "Satisfied?"
>
> "Yes," someone answered.
>
> "Poor devils, you are heading for the crematorium."
>
> He seemed to be telling the truth. Not far from us, flames, huge flames, were rising from a ditch. Something was being burned there. A truck drew close and unloaded its hold: small children. Babies! Yes, I did see this, with my own eyes . . . children thrown into the flames . . . So that was where we were going. A little farther on, there was another larger pit for adults.
>
> I pinched my face. Was I still alive? Was I awake? How was it possible that men, women, and children were being burned and the world kept silent? No, all this could not be real . . . A nightmare perhaps . . . Soon I would wake up with a start, my heart pounding, and find that I was back in the room of my childhood, with my books . . .[37]

---

[36] *Nazi Conspiracy and Aggression*, vol. 4, pp. 563–564.

[37] Elie Wiesel, *Night*, translated by Marion Wiesel (New York, 2006), p. 32.

Resistance in the concentration camps was rarely possible but did occur upon a few occasions in three of the death camps—Sobibor, Treblinka, and Auschwitz—as well as in some of the smaller camps. Of the 300 inmates at Sobibor who attempted a mass escape on October 14, 1943, only 50 survived and managed to join Soviet partisan fighters. In a rebellion at Treblinka on August 2, 1943, over 200 escaped, but only half survived. Of the 650 who tried to escape Auschwitz on October 7, 1944, 450 were eventually killed. Attempts at resistance and mass escape from the death camps tended to be an exercise in futility.

Extermination of Other European Jews

The liquidation of the ghettos by "resettlement" to the death camps was paralleled by attempts to round up and "resettle" Jews from other parts of Europe. German success in achieving this goal depended on each country's wartime status under Germany. Wherever German rule was complete and supreme, the fate of the Jews was already determined. As we have seen, this occurred in "Greater Germany" and in occupied Poland and the Soviet Union, where the Jews came under the direct jurisdiction of the SS. Elsewhere, in countries allied to Germany and in those conquered by Germany but still retaining some autonomy, the fate of the Jews depended upon the willingness of their governments and their fellow citizens to protect them.

There were few Jews in Norway, and 50 percent of them managed to survive by finding refuge in neutral Sweden. The story of the 8000 Danish Jews was a heartwarming and unique episode in the Holocaust saga. The entire Danish population, from the king to ordinary fishermen, put forth a great effort to save their Jewish neighbors. After the Germans resorted to martial law in 1943, the Gestapo attempted to round up the Jews. Warned in time and hidden by their countrymen, the Danish Jews were ferried across the Baltic Sea to Sweden in a remarkable rescue operation. Finland's small population of 2000 Jews was saved by the refusal of the Finnish government to cooperate with the Nazis.

The Nazis acquired nearly 500,000 Jews when they overran France, Belgium, and the Netherlands. The settling of the western European Jewish problem, however, was much more difficult for the Nazis than that of the eastern European problem. Western Jews had really been assimilated into their communities and had no distinguishing physical or religious features. Western Jews differed from eastern ones in that Jews and non-Jews alike considered themselves nationals, possessing all the rights of citizens. Moreover, western resistance movements encouraged the involvement of Jews, and both Jews and non-Jews were solidly united against the common German enemy. The Dutch Jews suffered the most in the west simply because the German control over the Netherlands was nearly absolute. Belgian and French Jews also experienced problems, but because the German occupation of their countries was nonpervasive, there was more room for escape.

In Holland, the *Reichskommissar* in charge of the civil government, Arthur Seyss-Inquart, was also an SS officer and thus cleared the way for the liquidators. From May 1942, Dutch Jews were forced to wear the Star of David; in June deportation trains began to arrive, and by July these trains were on their way to the east. Two transit camps, Westerbork and Vught, were constructed; Jews were interned there until train schedules permitted their shipment to Auschwitz. Seventy-five percent of the 140,000 Dutch Jews were killed. In Belgium, opposition to SS policies by the army and the cooperation of Belgian police and citizens in rescuing them saved a considerable number of Jews. About 25,000 of the 52,000 Jews who had remained in Belgium were sent to Auschwitz.

Many of the 310,000 Jews in France lived in Paris and in northern and northeastern France. Thousands of them fled south as a result of the German invasion. In the northern zone of France, controlled directly by the Nazis, the Foreign Office and the SS, especially Eichmann's assistant Theodore Dannecker, assumed responsibility for Jewish affairs. Roundups of Jews began in May 1941. They were sent primarily to Drancy, the chief transit camp for Auschwitz. The first deportation train left France on March 27, 1942. The semi-independent Vichy government embarked on anti-Semitic legislation and interned foreign Jews, as the Germans wanted, but refused the more drastic request of allowing French Jews in Vichy to be deported. As a compromise, the Vichy government did hand over interned foreign Jews. After the Germans militarily occupied Vichy in late 1942, the French continued in ingenious ways to resist German deportations of native French Jews. Nevertheless, the Nazis continued their roundups of Jews, which included raids on Jewish children's homes. Klaus Barbie, Gestapo chief at Lyon, cabled on April 6, 1944: "Early this morning the children's home at Aisier-Anne was emptied. A total number of 41 children ages 3–13 was seized. We also succeeded in catching all the Jewish working personnel comprising 10 persons of whom five are women . . . I transferred them to Drancy on April 7, 1944."[38] About 25 percent of France's Jews were exterminated, mostly at Auschwitz.

Although allied with Germany, Italy under Mussolini refused to participate whole-heartedly in the German plans for the Jews. Mussolini denied German requests to allow the deportation of Jews, but did subject them to harsh legislation and deprivations. After the Germans occupied Italy in 1943, the SS managed to round up and ship to Auschwitz about 7500 of the 40,000 Jews then in Italy.

In central Europe, as we have seen, Czechoslovakia had been dismembered in 1939 into a German Protectorate of Bohemia and Moravia and a semi-independent Slovakia. Each state had approximately 90,000 Jews. In the fall of 1941, the Germans established a central ghetto at Theresienstadt (Terezin) that served two functions—as a model camp to which privileged categories of German Jews were sent and as a transit camp from which Czech Jews were shipped to Poland for annihilation. Of the 180,000 Jews in Bohemia, Moravia, and Slovakia, only 35,000 survived.

Hungary, although an ally of Germany, refused to fulfill German demands for the deportation of Jews. The Germans acted quickly, however, once they occupied Hungary in 1944. On the day of occupation, March 19, 1944, Adolf Eichmann and the SS arrived in Hungary to supervise the Final Solution. Hungary was divided into six zones for rapid roundup and transit of Jews to Auschwitz. Consequently, 450,000 of Hungary's 750,000 Jews were annihilated by the summer of 1944.

In southeastern Europe, the Nazis were very successful in their attempt to kill Jews in Yugoslavia and Greece, where they had direct control. Sixty percent of Yugoslavian Jews and almost 80 percent of Greek Jews were annihilated. The Bulgarian government, although allied with Germany, protected the Jews of Old Bulgaria while allowing the deportation of Jews in the occupied territories of Thrace and Macedonia. In Romania, the army command volun-tarily cooperated with the German *Einsatzgruppen* in exterminating Jews. Romanian army units operating in southern Russia and Romania surprised even the Germans in their enthusiasm for killing Jews and their disregard for disposal of the corpses. However, the Romanian gov-ernment managed to save half of Romania's 600,000 Jews, primarily those in Old Romania, by refusing to allow the Germans to systematically deport them to the death camps.

[38]Quoted in Bauer, *A History of the Holocaust*, p. 234.

Although figures vary somewhat, estimates of the number of Jews killed range between 5 and 6 million. The greatest losses were in Poland, the Baltic countries, and Greater Germany, where virtually 90 percent of the Jewish populations were exterminated. Overall, the Holocaust resulted in the death of nearly two out of every three European Jews. The life and culture of eastern European Jewry were irretrievably lost, and everywhere in Europe Jewish communities had been perceptibly diminished.

"Righteous Gentiles" and the Rescue of Jews

The Danish people were not alone in attempting to rescue Jews from the hands of their Nazi persecutors. There are numerous examples of "righteous gentiles," non-Jews who sheltered Jews or worked to save them from becoming additional victims of the Holocaust. "Righteous gentiles" had the "courage to care," often at the risk of their own lives or careers. Many of them shared the sentiment of one Hungarian woman who wrote, "Can we, the heirs of that generation pass judgment—or can we only mourn? History proves that it was possible to fight the evil."[39] Some rescuers used their political positions to rescue Jews. The Japanese diplomat Chiune Sugihara, aided by his wife Yukiko, and working against direct orders from Tokyo, used his office in Lithuania to produce thousands of transit visas for Jews fleeing Nazi persecution in Poland. Their actions allowed perhaps 6000 Jews to use these visas to escape certain death. A similar situation was faced by Swedish diplomat Raoul Wallenberg in Hungary. Wallenberg was funded in part by Roosevelt's War Refugee Board, which was aided by a secret extra-governmental group known as The Pond, loosely affiliated with the Office of Strategic Services (the forerunner of the C.I.A). With the assistance of these groups Wallenberg went to Hungary to save as many Jews as possible. Already the Nazis had sent over 400,000 Hungarian Jews to death camps in Poland by the time Wallenberg had arrived in Budapest in July 1944. Wallenberg began using bribes and extortion to slow down the forced relocation of Jews. He then designed a flashy and entirely fake Swedish protective pass and gave out thousands to hold off further deportations to Poland. When Nazi Adolf Eichmann began accelerating the shipments of Jews to death camps, Wallenberg set up some thirty protective houses with Swedish flags to harbor Jews from Nazis and the fascist Hungarian Arrow Cross. Due to Wallenberg's actions, some 100,000 Hungarian Jews survived the war. Unfortunately after the liberation of Hungary by Soviet forces, Wallenberg, perhaps because of his association with the U.S. secret services, disappeared into the Soviet state security system. The Soviets later claimed that he died in 1947, either by a heart attack or by having been executed by the KGB. However, undocumented reports of Wallenberg alive continued into the 1980s.

Some of those who fought seemed unlikely heroes. Oskar Schindler was a German industrialist from the Sudetenland in Czechoslovakia. It seemed to many that he lived a rather dissolute life, both as a drunkard and as a womanizer who often treated his wife badly. He seemed incapable of holding a regular job in peacetime, but after the defeat of Poland, he moved to Cracow, purchased a Jewish enamelware factory from its German "liberators," and began to produce kitchenware for the German army and the black market. Gradually, he built up a labor force of Jewish workers from the Cracow ghetto and then from the nearby Plaszow labor camp after the ghetto was liquidated. When the

[39]Quoted in Eric Silver, *The Book of the Just* (New York, 1992), p. 2.

Germans began to liquidate the Plaszow camp in the fall of 1944, Schindler received permission to transfer his factory—and about 1100 of his Jewish workers, whose names were put on "Schindler's list"—to his native Sudetenland. Schindler's willingness to take risks—by bribing German officials, forging documents, and placating SS officers with gifts of vodka—ultimately saved the lives of his Jewish workers. When asked later why he risked his own life to save those of "his Jews," Schindler replied, "I knew the people who worked for me. When you know people, you have to behave towards them like human beings."[40]

Another important rescue center was Le Chambon-Sur-Lignon, a village of 5000 inhabitants located in southeastern France. Mostly Protestants whose ancestors had once faced persecution in the French religious wars, the village residents felt drawn to help Jews who were being hounded by the Germans and their Vichy allies. From 1941 to 1945, the residents of Le Chambon and nearby villages, encouraged by the example of eleven pastors, hid thousands of Jewish refugees and helped them to escape to Switzerland, which remained neutral throughout the war. Being a resort town, Le Chambon made an ideal place to harbor Jewish refugees, who would first check in at one of the local hotels and then be sent on to one of the neighboring farms for hiding. When villagers were later questioned about the danger they faced in hiding Jews, one replied, "No one knew what the consequences of hiding Jews might be. The sense of danger was always present, but we never spoke of it."[41] Pastor André Trocmé, one of the leading figures in the rescue of the Jews, explained the villagers' response in one of his sermons: "The duty of Christians is to respond to the violence that will be brought against their consciences with the weapons of the spirit."

THE OTHER HOLOCAUST

In addition to the 5 to 6 million Jews, the Nazis were also directly responsible for the death by starvation, shooting, and overwork of probably another 9 to 10 million human beings. Nazi racial ideology encouraged German mistreatment of peoples other than just the Jews. Although originally thought to be of Aryan descent, the Sinti and Roma (Gypsies) became a matter of scientific research in Nazi Germany. The Reich Health Office, through the Research Institute for Racial Hygiene and Population Biology, began a study of the Sinti and Roma. The institute was run by physician Robert Ritter, a vocal advocate of the relatively new field of criminal biology. Ritter stated: "the aim of our work is to demonstrate with an exact methodology that sociological manifestations have their root in biology, i.e., in the final analysis in the laws of heredity."[42] If the Sinti and Roma were deemed hereditary criminals, they could not be redeemed through education or any other nonbiological means. Ritter also concluded through his research that the Sinti and Roma were so racially mixed that any possible Aryan blood was irrevocably tainted. They therefore were placed in the same category as the Jews—a rootless, unproductive, criminal, and "parasitic" race containing alien blood and consequently fit only for sterilization, and eventually, extermination. In its attempt to solve what was termed the "Gypsy plague," about 40 percent of Europe's 1 million Sinti and Roma were murdered by the Nazis.

[40]Ibid., p. 148.
[41]Ibid., p. 18.
[42]Quoted in Guenter Lewy, *The Persecution of the Gypsies* (New York, 2000), p. 48.

Slavic peoples, such as Poles, Ukrainians, and Belorussians, were not in the same category as the Jews and Sinti and Roma but were nevertheless considered inferior by the Germans and suited only for slave labor. The leading elements of these peoples—clergy, aristocracy, intelligentsia, civil and political leaders, judges, and lawyers—were arrested and exterminated soon after German invasions. The remaining population, considered subhuman, was to be treated as slave labor, permanently reduced to a lower-class status. It has been estimated that almost 4 million Poles, Ukrainians, and Belorussians lost their lives as slave laborers for the Third Reich. Hundreds of thousands of Slavic peoples were forcibly deported out of German-occupied territories as part of the Nazi colonial schemes. Moreover, during planning for the invasion of Russia in 1941, SS leaders concluded that the war economy would be dramatically affected by extending operations to the East. This would result in a shortage of grain that would have to be offset by the use of Soviet resources at the expense of the local population. A memorandum from a meeting on May 2, 1941, concluded the following:

1. The war can only continue to be waged if the entire Wehrmacht is fed from Russia during the 3rd year of the war.

2. As a result, if what is necessary for us is extracted from the land, tens of millions of people will doubtlessly starve to death.[43]

According to another economic report in relation to the forthcoming eastern campaign, the exploitation of food from south and southeast of Russia and the Caucasus would be at the expense of feeding the people of the northern "wooded zone" and the industrial centers of Moscow and St. Petersburg. As a consequence, the report concluded, "The population of these territories, in particular the population of the cities, will have to face the most terrible famine . . . . Many tens of millions of people in this territory will become superfluous and will have to die or migrate to Siberia."[44] With the invasion less than two weeks away, Himmler made it clear to SS leaders that "the purpose of the Russian campaign" was "the decimation of the Slavic population by thirty million." In July, only a few weeks after the campaign had begun, Professor Dr. Franz Alfred Six, chief of the Advance Commando Moscow (of *Einsatzgruppe* B), noted:

> Hitler intends to extend the eastern border of the Reich as far as the line Baku-Stalingrad-Moscow-Leningrad. Eastward of this line as far as the Urals, a "blazing strip" will emerge in which all life is to be erased. It is intended to decimate the around thirty million Russians living in this strip through starvation, by removing all foodstuffs from this enormous territory. All those involved in this operation are to be forbidden on pain of death to give a Russian even a piece of bread. The large cities from Leningrad to Moscow are to be razed to the ground.[45]

While the starvation plan was never fully realized due to unexpected German losses on the battlefield, Nazi exploitation of food resources in Eastern Europe did lead to the

---

[43]Quoted in Alex J. Kay, "The Purpose of the Russian Campaign Is the Decimation of the Slavic Population by Thirty Million," in Alex J. Kay, Jeff Rutherford, and David Stahel, eds., *Nazi Policy on the Eastern Front, 1941* (Rochester, N.Y., 2012), pp. 107–108.

[44]Ibid., p. 111.

[45]Ibid., pp. 112–113.

starvation of millions. The Germans also deliberately allowed between 2 and 3 million Soviet prisoners of war to die in captivity as an extension of the starvation policy.

As mentioned in Chapter 6, the Nazis also singled out homosexuals for persecution. Paragraph 175 of the German penal code made sexual relations between men, especially older men and boys, illegal. Although not uniformly enforced during the Weimar period, during the Third Reich antihomosexual efforts were viciously pursued. Himmler was particularly obsessed with homosexuality, considering it a threat to the nation's health. He estimated that there were between 2 and 4 million homosexuals in Germany, and since they were not fathering children, "our nation is going to be wiped out by this plague."[46] With heterosexual soldiers lost in war, this problem of potential child loss was only exacerbated. Himmler was convinced that for Germany to be world power, it needed more children, and homosexuals were a threat to expanding the population. When Himmler took over the German police in 1936 antihomosexual measures were intensified, including establishing the Reich Centre for the Combating of Homosexuality and Abortion, as both issues were linked through the assumed loss of potential children. The number of arrests and convictions increased dramatically, from 4000 during 1933–1934 to 22,000 during 1935–1938. While it was believed that most homosexuals could be cured through work therapy, reeducation, and institutionalization in concentration camps, so-called habitual homosexuals were treated like Gypsies and Jews as being incurable. Himmler would eventually issue a Purification Edict, introducing the death penalty for homosexual activity within the SS and police. Himmler hoped in this way that his organizations would serve as "pioneers in the fight to eliminate homosexuality among the German people."[47] Once in a concentration camp, homosexuals were treated viciously, both by the guards and by other inmates. Forced to wear a pink triangle, it was evident to everyone in the camp what a homosexual inmate's "crime" was. After his arrival at Sachsenhausen concentration camp for the crime of homosexuality, Heinz Heger noted:

> Jews, homosexuals and gypsies, the yellow, pink and brown triangles, were the prisoners who suffered most frequently and most severely from the tortures and blows of the SS and the Capos. They were described as the scum of humanity, who had no right to live on German soil and should be exterminated. Such were the oft-repeated words of the commandant and his SS subordinates. But the lowest of the low in this 'scum' were we, the men with the pink triangle.[48]

Thousands of homosexuals were physically and sexually abused in the concentration camps, and many thousands lost their lives. Tragically, even those homosexual inmates who survived until liberation of the camps often found themselves still under arrest after war, as Paragraph 175 was not repealed until 1994. Once freed, homosexuals still faced persecution as their "crime" was now public knowledge, and antihomosexual sentiment was still prevalent.

[46]Quoted in Peter Longerich, *Heinrich Himmler*, translated by Jeremy Noakes and Lesley Sharpe, (New York, 2012), p. 232.

[47]Ibid., p. 239.

[48]Heinz Heger, *The Men with the Pink Triangle* (London, 1997), pp. 32–33.

Jehovah's Witnesses, in part because of their refusal to participate in what they considered sacrilegious Nazi rituals, were also persecuted. One Jehovah's Witness recalled:

> When the times of Hitler started, they observed us not saying 'Heil Hitler' and every year it became more difficult when we didn't say this. My father wanted to teach us religion and he took us out of the religion lesson. And this one teacher said, 'These Kusserow children, they are not for Hitler, they have to go to Moscow, they are communists.' Then the children made fun of us and said, 'You go to Moscow, you are not our people, you are not for Hitler.' My father taught us that saying 'Heil Hitler' meant that salvation came from Hitler, but the Bible tells us that salvation comes from Jesus Christ. He told us that we must choose, that real Christians would be persecuted, and that one day maybe they would persecute us also, because the Bible says some will be killed because of faith, the belief in Christ. I never thought this would be in our own family, never thought about it until it came.[49]

Thousands of what the Nazis labeled "Bible Pushers" died in concentration camps.

QUESTIONS ABOUT THE HOLOCAUST

Questions about the Holocaust remain that have created considerable debate. How much did the Allies and the German people themselves know about the Holocaust? Could more have been done by the Allies to stop the Nazi extermination of the Jews?

News of the Final Solution had been received all over Europe in 1942, even though not all the details were known. The massacres by the *Einsatzgruppen* in occupied eastern areas began immediately after the invasion of the Soviet Union. However isolated the area was, many of the executions had thousands of witnesses. German Wehrmacht officers, Italian, Hungarian, and Romanian military personnel, as well as countless unobtrusive civilians observed the grisly work of the elimination squads. The Soviet government must have known within days, and the Western powers probably knew within weeks. The news of Chelmno, the first extermination camp, reached Warsaw within four weeks.

The news was transmitted to the ghettos and the West by the Polish underground resistance movement, illegal newspapers, testimony by escaped prisoners of war and Jewish internees, and ghetto wireless transmissions. Jewish leaders and the public outside of the Continent had great difficulty accepting the idea of the Final Solution. They could not believe that such a monstrosity could actually occur in civilized Europe. The ample news that reached them seemed to point to unorganized pogroms, which were to be expected in wartime. Jewish leaders in Great Britain, the United States, and Palestine simply failed to act on the evidence. Because they did not believe, or did not want to believe, the reports, they refused to publicize the atrocities. When the worst was finally confirmed by escapees in 1942, these leaders were confused as to what action they should take. A feeling of helplessness pervaded their ranks.

Millions of Germans knew by late 1942 that the Jews had disappeared. News and rumors of their fate were transmitted by German military personnel, through the underground, and by their own leaders' speeches. Many Germans probably preferred to believe that the Jews were actually being resettled eastward. At any rate, the Germans held little sympathy for the

---

[49]Quoted in Lyn Smith, *Remembering: Voices of the Holocaust*, p. 29. By permission of Perseus Books Group.

Jews and the topic did not interest them. Preoccupied with surviving the war, they merely shut their eyes to the whole thing and closed their minds to the implications.

But to what extent was the German population involved in the Final Solution? No doubt, hundreds of thousands of people in government service, the army, and business corporations played some role. In fact, some scholars have argued that there were many "ordinary Germans" who actively participated in the killing. Reserve Police Battalion 101, which was part of the regular police controlled by the SS, consisted of 500 "ordinary men" who had been trained for routine police duties in occupied Poland. Between 1941 and 1943, however, they took part in a "special action" that resulted in the killing of 83,000 Polish Jews. Most of these "ordinary men," then, became dedicated killers, causing the American historian Christopher Browning, who wrote an account of the murderous activities of Police Battalion 101, to conclude: "If the men of Reserve Police Battalion 101 could become killers under such circumstances, what group of men cannot?"[50]

The Allies and the Holocaust

The governments of the Soviet Union, the United States, and Great Britain did not show any pronounced interest in the fate of the Jews. The Soviets published many accounts of the Nazi horrors in the occupied areas of eastern Europe, yet rarely mentioned the Jews separately as a persecuted group. The initial facts of the Final Solution were known in Britain and America from an early date, probably in 1942. The information reached the highest echelons of the military, intelligence circles, and governments, but it was considered of low priority. Some officials even thought the reports were propaganda, or at least exaggerated. But even if the Allies had accepted the news at face value, the issue still would have been low on their list of wartime priorities. To them, winning the war was everything. Too much publicity about the Jews' plight might have evoked public demands to deal with it. This would remove important materials and men from the war effort when victory was still in doubt (up to late 1942). Even after the outcome seemed assured, there was little willingness to help. Churchill showed more interest and compassion than Roosevelt, but neither really acted to stop the Nazi operation. The American and British publics were informed through the media, but they were little moved. Many, of course, did not believe the stories, and others could feel little sympathy for distant Jews when their own kin were dying.

Could the Allies have done more to stop the Holocaust? The idea of reprisals against German prisoners of war was dismissed because this would only serve as a pretext for German atrocities against captured Allied soldiers. The Allies, especially Britain, could have done the most good by receiving more refugees. Once again the dilemma of policy versus pragmatics arose. The British refused to open Palestine to unlimited Jewish immigration in order to maintain strong Arab ties there. The British were also reluctant to allow wholesale Jewish immigration into the United Kingdom on the pretext that it would lead to anti-Semitism by the British population, which would feel threatened by the influx. The British, however, did receive nearly 100,000 refugees, mostly Jewish, up to 1945. The United States also opposed the idea of an open-door refugee policy. The U.S. government hoped throughout the war that the British would allow the Jewish refugees

[50]Christopher Browning, *Ordinary Men: Reserve Police Battalion 101 and the Final Solution in Poland* New York, 1992), pp. 188–189.

to settle in Palestine. The United States did offer haven to more than 5000 Jews in 1944
The United States, so the British believed, was influenced by two conflicting policies
receptiveness to immigration by the influential Jewish segment of the population and the
general hostility of Americans to any immigration.

The question of a greater Allied response to the annihilation of the Jews often raises
the question of the possible bombing of Auschwitz. It was not until June 1944 that the
Allies finally became convinced of the true nature of Auschwitz-Birkenau as a mass mur
der site and as the destination of all the trains moving east. The Jewish Agency called upon
the Allied Air Command to bomb the railway lines leading to the camps and the camp
themselves. Churchill fully endorsed the proposal and the United States had a great dea
of information concerning Auschwitz. However, in a bureaucratic muddle, the British
Air Ministry could not obtain the full cooperation of the Foreign Office and the Allied
High Command. The British Royal Air Force first rejected the demand on the grounds
of lack of precise target information (the United States had this). The U.S. governmen
deferred all requests to the British, who made target objectives. The Royal Air Force then
commented that precious planes, pilots, and bombs could not be diverted from the wax
effort at such a crucial time. Both air forces believed that bombing Auschwitz was the
responsibility of the Soviet air force, since the Polish death camp was in the Soviet theate:
of war. However, the U.S. Air Force and the Royal Air Force had both flown missions ove:
or nearly over Auschwitz on two occasions. In fact, several times in September 1944 the
U.S. Air Force accidentally bombed Auschwitz, damaging the Auschwitz-Birkenau railwa
siding and destroying Gestapo quarters.

In part the failures and negative responses to the Jewish requests for help were due
to the Allies' lack of comprehension and imagination in the face of the unbelievable
Many Jews had been thus paralyzed as well. One man, however, realized the enormity o
the situation. In a letter to Anthony Eden in July 1944 Churchill wrote: "There is no doub
that this is probably the greatest and most horrible crime ever committed in the whole his
tory of the world."[51] But Churchill did not have the final say in Allied policy, and in man
cases (Auschwitz was one of them) other voices and considerations prevailed. There wa
no one reason for this failure but many, as Walter Laqueur has noted:

> paralyzing fear on one hand and, on the contrary, reckless optimism on the other; disbelie
> stemming from a lack of experience or imagination or genuine ignorance or a mixture o
> some or all of these things. In some cases the motives were creditable, in others damnable
> In some instances moral categories are simply not applicable and there were also cases which
> defy understanding to this day.[52]

Many have lamented the difficulty in ever understanding the magnitude of the
crimes committed in the Holocaust. And yet, Heinrich Himmler could speak not o
crimes but of "glory" and the "spirit of love for our people" that motivated the Germans
And lesser functionaries, such as one Pfannenstiel, an SS officer and professor of hygien
at the University of Marburg, could say in a speech at a banquet honoring the employee
of the death camp at Treblinka that "when one sees the bodies of the Jews, one under
stands the greatness of your work!"[53] The Holocaust will always stand out historically a

---

[51]Quoted in Martin Gilbert, *Auschwitz and the Allies* (New York, 1981), p. 341.
[52]Walter Laqueur, *The Terrible Secret* (Boston, 1980), p. 208.
[53]Dawidowicz, ed., *A Holocaust Reader*, p. 109.

an awful warning of what horrors can be perpetrated as a result of slavish obedience to authority and an ideology based on hatred of one people for another.

SUGGESTIONS FOR FURTHER READING

The best studies of the Holocaust are Peter Longerich, *The Holocaust: The Nazi Persecution and Murder of the Jews* (New York, 2010); Saul Friedländer, *The Years of Extermination: Nazi Germany and the Jews, 1939–1945* (New York, 2007); Raul Hilberg, *The Destruction of the European Jews*, rev. 3rd ed., 3 vols. (New Haven, 2003); Leni Yahil, *The Holocaust, The Fate of European Jewry, 1932–1945* (New York, 1990); Lucy Dawidowicz, *The War Against the Jews*, 2nd ed. (New York, 1986); Yehuda Bauer, *A History of the Holocaust* (New York, 1982); Deborah Dwork and Robert J. Van Pelt, *Holocaust: A History* (New York, 2002); Martin Gilbert, *The Holocaust: The History of the Jews of Europe During the Second World War* (New York, 1985); and David M. Crowe, *The Holocaust: Roots, History, and Aftermath* (Boulder, Colo., 2008). Four brief works are Jack Fischel, *The Holocaust* (Westport, Conn., 1998); Rita Botwinick, *A History of the Holocaust*, 4th ed. (Boston, 2010); Frank McDonough and John Cochrane, *The Holocaust* (New York, 2008); and Robert Wistrich, *Hitler and the Holocaust* (New York, 2001). On the relationship between World War II and the Holocaust, see Donald M. McKale, *Hitler's Shadow War: The Holocaust and World War II* (New York, 2002); and Doris L. Bergen, *War and Genocide: A Concise History of the Holocaust*, 2nd ed. (Landham, Md., 2009). Attempts to examine the Holocaust by looking at the activities of the participants can be found in Raul Hilberg, *Perpetrators, Victims, Bystanders* (New York, 1992); Claudia Koonz, *The Nazi Conscience* (Cambridge, Mass., 2003); and Nechama Tec, *Resilience and Courage: Women, Men, and the Holocaust* (New Haven, Conn., 2003). See also the discussion and corresponding documents in Ernst Klee, Willi Dresen, and Volker Riess, eds., *"The Good Old Days" The Holocaust as Seen by Its Perpetrators and Bystanders* (New York, 1991); For guides to the historical literature on the Holocaust, see Dan Stone, *Histories of the Holocaust* (New York, 2010); Michael Marrus, *The Holocaust in History* (London, 1988); Lucy Dawidowicz, *The Holocaust and the Historians* (Cambridge, Mass., 1981); Paul R. Bartrop and Steven Leonard Jacobs, *Fifty Key Thinkers on the Holocaust and Genocide* (New York, 2011); and Donald Niewyk and Francis Nicosia, *The Columbia Guide to the Holocaust* (New York, 2000). Valuable reference works include Jonathan C. Friedman, ed., *The Routledge History of the Holocaust* (New York, 2011); Peter Hayes and John K. Roth, eds., *The Oxford Handbook of Holocaust Studies* (New York, 2010); Israel Gutman, ed., *Encyclopedia of the Holocaust*, 4 vols. (New York, 1990); and Martin Gilbert, *The Macmillan Atlas of the Holocaust* (New York, 1982). For good collections of primary sources, see Lucy Dawidowicz, ed., *A Holocaust Reader* (New York, 1976); and Raul Hilberg, *Documents of Destruction* (Chicago, 1971). Eyewitness accounts are included in Martin Gilbert, *Final Journey: The Fate of the Jews in Nazi Europe* (London, 1979); Lyn Smith, *Remembering: Voices of the Holocaust* (New York, 2006); and the documents found in Alexandra Garbarini, ed., *Jewish Responses to Persecution, Volume II, 1938–1940* (Lanham, Md., 2011). Good collections of essays are Michael Berenbaum and Abraham Peck, eds., *The Holocaust and History* (Washington, D.C., 1998); Omer Bartov, ed., *The Holocaust: Origins, Implementation, Aftermath* (New York, 2000); and Neil Gregor, ed., *Nazism, War and Genocide: New Perspectives on the History of the Third Reich* (Exeter, 2008). For excellent refutations of those people who claim that the Holocaust never occurred, see Deborah E. Lipstadt, *Denying the Holocaust* (New York, 1993); and Michael Sherman and Alex Grobman, *Denying History* (Berkeley, Calif., 2000).

Hitler's role in the Holocaust has been summarized in Eberhard Jäckel, "Hitler Orders the Holocaust," in Jäckel's *Hitler in History* (Hanover, N.H., 1984); Gerald Fleming, *Hitler and the Final Solution* (Berkeley, Calif., 1984); Peter Longerich, *The Unwritten Order: Hitler's Role in the Final Solution* (Stroud, 2005); and Philippe Burrin, *Hitler and the Jews: The Genesis of the Holocaust*, trans. Patsy Southgate (London, 1994). The important role of Heinrich Himmler has been examined in Peter Longerich, *Heinrich Himmler* (New York, 2012); Richard Breitman, *The Architect of Genocide: Himmler and the Final Solution* (New York, 1991). On Himmler's handpicked executioner for exterminatory policies, see Robert Gerwarth, *Hitler's Henchman: The Life of Heydrich* (New Haven, Conn., 2011). On the early stages of the Final Solution in Poland, see Catherine Epstein, *Model Nazi: Arthur Greiser and the Occupation of Poland* (New York, 2010). On the background to Nazi genocide, see Henry Friedlander, *The Origins of Nazi Genocide: From Euthanasia to the Final Solution* (Chapel Hill, N.C., 1995). The decisions that led to the Final Solution are examined in the works of Christopher R. Browning, including *Fateful Months* (New York, 1985), *The Final Solution and the German Foreign Office* (New York, 1978), *The Path to Genocide* (Cambridge, Mass., 1992), *Nazi Policy, Jewish Workers, German Killers* (Cambridge, Mass., 2000), and *The Origins of the Final Solution* (Lincoln, 2004). See also the wide-ranging collection of essays in Ian Kershaw, *Hitler, the Germans, and the Final Solution* (New Haven, Conn., 2008). For an examination of the German public's response to the Nazis' anti-Semitic policies, see David Bankier, *The Germans and the Final Solution: Public Opinion under Nazism* (Oxford, 1992); Eric A. Johnson and Karl-Heinz Reuband, *What We Knew: Terror, Mass Murder, and Everyday Life in Nazi Germany* (Cambridge, Mass., 2005); and James M. Glass, *"Life Unworthy of Life": Racial Phobia and Mass Murder in Hitler's Germany* (New York, 1997). The Jewish experience of the Nazi persecution is best seen in Marion A. Kaplan, *Between Dignity and Despair: Jewish Life in Nazi Germany* (New York, 1998). How Jewish and non-Jewish neighbors throughout Europe experienced and interacted during Nazi occupation and persecution, see Beate Kosmala and Georgi Verbeeck, eds., *Facing the Catastrophe: Jews and non-Jews in Europe During World War II* (New York, 2011). The experience of children during the Third Reich is considered in Lynn H. Nichols, *Cruel World: The Children of Europe in the Nazi Web* (New York, 2005); and Nicholas Stargardt, *Witnesses of War: Children's Lives under the Nazis* (New York, 2006). For an extension collection of documents, see Patricia Heberer, ed., *Children during the Holocaust* (Lanham, Md., 2011). The plight of the *Mischlinge* is discussed in James F. Tent, *In the Shadow of the Holocaust: Nazi Persecution of Jewish-Christian Germans* (Lawrence, Kans., 2003).

For perspectives on the role of the Catholic church in the Holocaust, see Randolph L. Braham, *The Vatican and the Holocaust: The Catholic Church and the Jews during the Nazi Era* (New York, 2000); Susan Zucotti, *Under His Very Window: The Vatican and the Holocaust in Italy* (New Haven, Conn., 2000); Michael Phayer, *The Catholic Church and the Holocaust 1930–1965* (Bloomington, Ind., 2001); David Cymet, *History vs. Apologetics: The Holocaust, the Third Reich, and the Catholic Church* (Lexington, Ky., 2010); and Paul O'Shea, *A Cross Too Heavy: Pope Pius XII and the Jews of Europe* (New York, 2011). On the Wannsee conference, see Mark Roseman, *The Wannsee Conference and the Final Solution* (New York, 2002).

The role of the *Einsatzgruppen* and police battalions are discussed in Christopher R. Browning, *Ordinary Men: Reserve Police Battalion 101 and the Final Solution in Poland* (New York, 1992); Edward B. Westermann, *Hitler's Police Battalions: Enforcing Racial War in the East* (Lawrence, Kans., 2005); Richard Rhodes, *Masters of Death: The SS Einsatzgruppen and the Invention of the Holocaust* (New York, 2002); and Helmut Langerbein, *Hitler's Death Squads: The Logic of Mass Murder* (College Station, Tex., 2004). A valuable reference source is *The United States Holocaust Memorial Museum Encyclopedia of Camps and Ghettos, 1933–1945*, two volumes of which have appeared, Volume I, *Early Camps, Youth Camps, and Concentration Camps and Subcamps under the SS-Business Administration Main Office (WVHA)*, edited by Geoffrey P. Megargee (Bloomington, Ind., 2009) and Volume II, *Ghettos in German-occupied Eastern Europe* (Bloomington, Ind., 2012), edited by Geoffrey Megargee and Martin Dean. On the horrific transport to the death camps, see Simone Gigliotti, *The Train Journey: Transit, Captivity, and Witnessing in the Holocaust* (New York, 2009). The death marches are analyzed in Daniel Blatman, *The Death Marches: The Final Phase of Nazi Genocide*, trans. Chaya Galai (Cambridge, Mass., 2011). The Nazi concentration camps are described in Eugen Kogon, *The Theory and Practice of Hell* (London, 1950); Wolfgang Sofsky, *The Order of Terror: The Concentration Camp*, trans. William Templer (Princeton, N.J., 1997); Konnilyn G. Feig, *Hitler's Death Camps: The Sanity of Madness* (New York, 1981); Michael Thad Allen, *The Business of Genocide: The SS, Slave Labor, and the Concentration Camps* (Chapel Hill, N.C., 2002). Also useful is the collection of readings in Eric Katz, ed., *Death by Design: Science, Technology, and Engineering in Nazi Germany* (New York, 2006); and Jane Kaplan and Nikolaus Wachsmann, eds., *Concentration Camps in Nazi Germany: The New Histories* (New York, 2010). There are separate accounts of various camps. On the first extermination camp, see Patrick Montague, *Chelmno and the Holocaust: The History of Hitler's First Death Camp* (Chapel Hill, N.C., 2012). On Auschwitz, see Sybille Steinbacher, *Auschwitz: A History* (New York, 2005); and the survivor account, Wielaw Kielar, *Anus Mundi: 1500 Days in Auschwitz/Birkenau*, trans. Susanne Flatauer (New York, 1972); and the remarkable collection of photographs in *The Auschwitz Album* (New York, 1981); Jules Schelvis, *Sobibor: A History of a Nazi Death Camp*, trans. Karin Dixon, (New York, 2007); Yitzhad Arad, *Belzec, Sobibor, Treblinka: the Operation Reinhard Death Camps* (Bloomington, Ind., 1987). Chil Rajchman's *The Last Jew from Treblinka: A Memoir*, trans. Solon Beinfeld (New York, 2011) presents a powerful and insightful survivor's account. Good insight into the psychology of concentration camp doctors is provided in Robert J. Lifton, *The Nazi Doctors* (New York, 1986). See also the essays in Francis R. Nicosia and Jonathan Huener, eds, *Medicine and Medical Ethics in Nazi Germany: Origins, Practices, Legacies* (New York, 2002).

There is a growing historical literature and debate on whether the democracies could have done more to help the Jews. Most recently see Alexander J. Groth, *Accomplices: Churchill, Roosevelt, and the Holocaust* (New York, 2011), who argues that the Allies were complicit in the Holocaust through inaction. Theodow S. Hamerow, in *Why We Watched: Europe, America, and the Holocaust* (New York, 2008), argued that anti-Semitism was the prevailing cause of such inaction. On the failure of allied attempts to first help and then rescue Jews, see Schlomo Aronson, *Hitler, the Allies, and the Jews* (New York, 2006). On American policy in general, see the early revisionist study by Arthur D. Morse, *While Six Million Died* (New York, 1968); and the scholarly studies by Henry L. Feingold, *The Politics of Rescue* (New Brunswick, N.J., 1970); Saul Friedman, *No Haven for the Oppressed* (Detroit, Mich., 1973); David Wyman, *The Abandonment of the Jews: America and the Holocaust* (New York, 1984); and Robert N. Rosen, *Saving the Jews: Franklin D. Roosevelt and the Holocaust* (New York, 2006). On Britain, see A. J. Sherman, *Island Refuge: Britain and Refugees from the Third Reich, 1933–1939* (Berkeley, Calif., 1973), who views the British as compassionate and even generous in their policy. See also the interesting discussions found in Michael J. Neufeld and Michael Berenbaum, eds., *The Bombing of Auschwitz: Should the Allies Have Attempted It?* (New York, 2000).

The subject of the Jewish ghettos is covered in Gustavo Corni, *Hitler's Ghettos: Voices from a Beleaguered Society, 1939–1944* (New York, 2003); Leon Poliakov, *Harvest of Hate*

(New York, 1979); Isiah Trunk, *Lódz Ghetto*, trans. Robert Moses Shaprio (Bloomington, Ind., 2006); Tim Cole, *Holocaust City: The Making of a Jewish Ghetto* (New York, 2003); Eric Sterling, ed., *Life in the Ghettos during the Holocaust* (Syracuse, N.Y., 2005); and Gordon J. Horwitz, *Ghettostadt: Lódz and the Making of a Nazi City* (Cambridge, Mass., 2008). Mendel Grossman's *With a Camera in the Ghetto* (New York, 1977) gives a visual portrait of life in the Lodz ghetto. An inside account of the latter is Lucjan Dobroszycki, *The Chronicle of the Lodz Ghetto 1941–1944*, trans. Richard Lourie et al. (New Haven, Conn., 1984). The Jewish councils are discussed in Isiah Trunk, *Judenrat: The Jewish Councils in Eastern Europe Under Nazi Occupation* (New York, 1972). On the Warsaw ghetto, see Abraham I. Katsh, ed. and trans., *Scroll of Agony: The Warsaw Diary of Chaim A. Kaplan* (New York, 1965); and Emmanuel Ringelblum, *Notes from the Warsaw Ghetto*, ed. and trans. Jacob Sloan (New York, 1958). An important account on those who managed to escape life in the ghettos, see Gunnar S. Paulsson, *Secret City: The Hidden Jews of Warsaw, 1940–1945* (New Haven, Conn., 2002).

The most detailed and thorough study of Jewish resistance to the Nazis is Reuben Ainsztein, *Jewish Resistance in Nazi-Occupied Eastern Europe* (London, 1974). See also Nechama Tec, *Defiance: The Bielski Partisans* (New York, 1993); James M. Glass, *Jewish Resistance during the Holocaust: Moral Uses of Violence and Will* (New York, 2004); Steven B. Bowman, *Jewish Resistance in Wartime Greece* (Portland, 2006); and Barbara L. Epstein, *The Minsk Ghetto, 1941–1943: Jewish Resistance and Soviet Internationalism* (Berkeley, Calif. 2008). The best study of the Warsaw Rebellion is Yisrael Gutman, *Resistance: The Warsaw Ghetto Uprising* (Boston, 1994). Resistance in the camps is discussed in Hermann Langbein, *Against all Hope: Resistance in the Nazi Concentration Camps, 1939–1945* (New York, 1996) and Richard Rashke, *Escape from Sobibor* (Urbana, Ill., 1995).

The roundup and extermination of Jews outside of Germany and eastern Europe is discussed in: Jacob Press, *The Destruction of the Dutch Jews* (New York, 1969); Michael Marrus and Robert Paxton, *Vichy France and the Jews* (New York, 1981); Susan Zuccotti *The Holocaust, the French, and the Jews* (New York, 1993); Renée Poznanski, *Jews in France during World War II* (Hanover, N.H., 2001); Meir Michaelis, *Mussolini and the Jews* (Oxford 1978); Joshua D. Zimmerman, *Jews in Italy under Fascist and Nazi Rule, 1922–1945* (New York, 2005); Michele Scarfatti, *The Jews in Mussolini's Italy: From Equality to Persecution* (Madison, Wisc., 2006); Livia Rothkirchen, *The Jews of Bohemia and Moravia: Facing the Holocaust* (Lincoln, Neb., 2005); Yitzhak Arad, *The Holocaust in the Soviet Union* (Lincoln 2009); Wendy Lower, *Nazi Empire-Building and the Holocaust in Ukraine* (Chapel Hill, N.C. 2005); Martin Dean, *Collaboration in the Holocaust: Crimes of the Local Police in Belorussia and Ukraine, 1941–1944* (New York, 2000); Randolph Braham, *The Politics of Genocide* vol. 1, *The Holocaust in Hungary* (New York, 1981); and with Brewster S. Chamberlain, eds. *The Holocaust in Hungary: Sixty Years Later* (New York, 2006); David Cesarini, *Genocide and Rescue: The Holocaust in Hungary, 1944* (New York, 1997); Ivan Kamenec, *On the Trail of Tragedy: The Holocaust in Slovakia* (Bratislava, 2007); Anton Weiss-Wendt, *Murder without Hatred: Estonians and the Holocaust* (Syracuse, N.Y., 2009); Adrej Angrick and Peter Klein *The "Final Solution" in Riga: Exploitation and Annihilation, 1941–1944*, trans. Ray Brandon (New York, 2009); and Frederick Chary, *The Bulgarian Jews and the Final Solution, 1940–1944* (Pittsburgh, 1972). For Nazi policy in the Middle East see Edwin Black, *The Farhud: Roots of the Arab-Nazi Alliance in the Holocaust* (Washington, D.C., 2010); and Klaus-Michael Mallmann and Martin Cuppers, *Nazi Palestine: The Plans for the Extermination of the Jews in Palestine* (New York, 2010). For brief portraits of the thousands of ordinary citizens who rescued Jews during the Holocaust, see Israel Gutman, ed., *The Encyclopedia of the*

Righteous Among the Nations (Jerusalem, 2004–2007); and Mordecai Paldiel, *The Righteous Among the Nations: Rescuers of Jews During the Holocaust* (New York, 2007). See also Carol Rittner and Sondra Myers, eds., *The Courage to Care* (New York, 1986); Eva Fogelman, *Conscience and Courage: Rescuers of Jews During the Holocaust* (New York, 1994); the oral history by Eric Silver, *The Book of the Just* (New York, 1992); Nechama Tec, *When Light Pierced the Darkness: Christian Rescue of Jews in Nazi-Occupied Poland* (Oxford, 1986); Charles Fenyvesi, *When Angels Fooled the World: Rescuers of Jews in Wartime Hungary* (Madison, Wisc., 2003); Martin Gilbert, *The Righteous* (New York, 2003); Richard Unsworth, *A Portrait of Pacifists: Le Chambon, the Holocaust and the Lives of Andre and Magda Tracme* (Syracuse, N.Y., 2012); Andrew Handler, *A Man for All Connections: Raoul Wallenberg and the Hungarian State Apparatus, 1944–1945* (Westport, Conn., 1996); Hillel Levine, *In Search of Sugihara: The Elusive Japanese Diplomat Who Risked His Life to Rescue 10,000 Jews from the Holocaust* (New York, 1996); Thomas Keneally, *Schindler's List* (New York, 1982); and David Crowe, *Oskar Schindler: The Untold Account of His Life, Wartime Activities, and the True Story Behind the List* (Cambridge, Mass., 2004).

The "other Holocaust" is discussed in Bohdan Wytwycky, *The Other Holocaust* (Washington, D.C., 1980); and Richard Lukas, *Forgotten Holocaust. The Poles under German Occupation, 1939–1944* (Lexington, Ky., 1986). On the Nazi deportation of Poles in Western Poland, see Philip T. Rutherford, *Prelude to the Final Solution: The Nazi Program for Deporting Ethnic Poles, 1939–1941* (Lawrence, Kan., 2007). On the Eastern Front and the enforcement of Nazi racial policy, see Alex J. Kay, Jeff Rutherford and David Stahel, eds., *Nazi Policy on the Eastern Front, 1941: Total War, Genocide, and Radicalization* (Rochester, N.Y., 2012). On the "partisan war," see French MacLean, *The Cruel Hunters: SS-Sonderkommando Dirlewanger: Hitler's Most Notorious Anti-Partisan Unit* (Atglen, PA, 1998); and the essays in Ben Shepard and Juliette Pattinson, eds., *War in a Twilight World: Partisan and Anti-Partisan Warfare in Eastern Europe, 1939–1945* (New York, 2010). On the plight of the Sinti and Roma, see Guenter Lewy, *The Nazi Persecution of the Gypsies* (New York, 2000). On the persecution of persons of African descent, see Clarence Lusane, *Hitler's Black Victims: The Historical Experience of Afro-Germans, Aftro-Europeans, African-Americans, and Africans during the Nazi Era* (New York, 2002); Tina Campt, *Other Germans: Black Germans and the Politics of Race, Gender, and Memory in the Third Reich* (Ann Arbor, Mich., 2004). On the Nazi mistreatment of the disabled, see Suzanne E. Evans, *Forgotten Crimes: The Holocaust and People with Disabilities* (Chicago, 2004); and Carol Poore, *Disability in Twentieth-Century German Culture* (Ann Arbor, Mich., 2007). On the persecution of homosexuals, see Richard Plant, *The Pink Triangle: The Nazi War Against Homosexuals* (New York, 1986); Heinz Heger, *The Men with the Pink Triangle* (London, 1997); and Günter Grau, Claudia Schoppmann, and Patrick Camiller, eds, *Hidden Holocaust?: Gay and Lesbian Persecution in Germany, 1933–1945* (Chicago, 1995). On the persecution of Jehovah's Witnesses, see M. James Penton, *Jehovah's Witnesses and the Third Reich: Sectarian Politics under Persecution* (Toronto, 2004); and Detlef Garbe, *Between Resistance and Martyrdom: Jehovah's Witnesses in the Third Reich* (Madison, Wisc., 2008).

Works on who knew what about the Holocaust include Richard Breitman, *Official Secrets: What the Nazis Planned. What the British and Americans Knew* (New York, 1998); Walter Laqueur, *The Terrible Secret* (Boston, 1980); and Martin Gilbert, *Auschwitz and the Allies* (New York, 1981). Gilbert's account tends to be more sympathetic to the Allies, but still points out their faults. See also the wide-ranging essays found in David Bankier, ed., *Secret Intelligence and the Holocaust* (New York, 2006).

MySearchLab™ Connections

Study and Review

The systematic murder of millions of European Jews during the Holocaust served no military purpose and offered no military gain. The destruction of such a large portion of the workforce and the diversion of the resources needed to conduct such an operation weakened the German war effort and contributed to Nazi Germany's defeat. The Holocaust was purely an extension of Nazi ideology—the annihilation of Europe's Jews—and remains the greatest single act of genocide in modern history.

Read the Document

1. **The Holocaust: Memoirs from the Commandant of Auschwitz (1940s) Rudolf Hoess**
   This document presents an almost clinical description of the brutality and inhumanity of the extermination process.

View the Closer Look

2. **Envisioning Evidence: Deciphering the Holocaust**
   This presentation shows the distribution of the Jewish people who died in the Holocaust by nation of origin. This presentation also illustrates the survival rate of the European Jewish people by nation.

View the Map

3. **The Holocaust**
   This map depicts the percentage of each European country's Jewish population that was murdered in the Holocaust. It also makes it possible to compare percentages across national borders.

RESEARCH AND EXPLORE

While the Nazis bear responsibility for their atrocities, many argue that the Allies didn't do enough to stem the massacre. It can be argued that had the Allies allowed increased immigration and protested more vigorously, the percentage of surviving Nazi victims might have been higher.

1. Do the Allies deserve any blame for the Holocaust because of their immigration policies? Why or why not?
2. How might the course of World War II have been different if the Nazis had foregone extermination of the Jewish people in favor of forced labor of the entire captured population?
3. Jehovah's Witnesses were selected for extermination due to their refusal to swear allegiance to Hitler. How did other groups show resistance to the Nazi regime?

ADDITIONAL RESOURCES

The Holocaust I

The Holocaust II

10

Conclusions

THE WAR CRIMES TRIALS

Before the end of 1943, Allied leaders had begun to discuss the fate of Nazi leaders once the war was over. Allied opinions divided over the use of trials or courts-martial with summary executions. By the summer of 1945, the United States, Great Britain, and the Soviet Union had agreed to pursue "legal forms" and hold a trial of the major criminals. The charges against them were gathered under four chief headings: common conspiracy, or the use of government power to plan foreign aggression; crimes against peace, or the planning and waging of wars of aggression; war crimes, or the murder of civilians and prisoners of war, the conscription of slave labor, and the wanton destruction of cities and private property; and crimes against humanity, or the deliberate extermination of people on political, racial, or religious grounds.

The International Military Tribunal met in Nuremberg beginning in October 1945 before judges from the United States, Great Britain, the Soviet Union, and France. The Americans took primary responsibility for preparing evidence, rounding up defendants, and getting witnesses. The twenty-one defendants included the party leaders Göring, Hess, and Streicher; the state ministers Frick, Ribbentrop, Schacht, Papen, and Funk; the two leaders of armament and labor mobilization, Speer and Sauckel; the military leaders Keitel, Jodl, Dönitz, and Raeder; two representatives from the SS and Propaganda Ministry, Kaltenbrunner and Fritzsche; and territorial leaders Rosenberg, Hans Frank, Schirach, Seyss-Inquart, and Neurath. Three other prominent Nazis were already dead: Heinrich Himmler and Joseph Goebbels had committed suicide and Martin Bormann was killed trying to escape from Berlin.

An incredible quantity of documentation was used to bolster the arguments against the defendants. The materials served the additional purpose of demonstrating to the world the appalling crimes of the Nazi regime. The defendants generally used two basic arguments in their defense. They claimed that they knew nothing about the murder of the Jews and that they were only obeying orders. Hitler, they said, had such a "power of hypnotic suggestion" on them that they were not responsible for what had happened. Hermann Göring, after years of lethargy, reasserted himself and now acted again as a leader of the group. After twelve grueling months the trial ended on October 1, 1946. Ten Nazis—Göring, Streicher, Frick, Ribbentrop, Sauckel, Keitel, Frank, Rosenberg, Kaltenbrunner, and Jodl—received the death penalty. All were executed on October 15 except Göring, who managed to commit suicide a few hours before his scheduled execution by swallowing a poison capsule he had kept hidden on himself. Three were acquitted—Schacht, Papen, and Fritzsche—and the remainder received prison sentences varying from ten years to life.

Criticism was made, especially by the Germans, that the victors were simply trying the losers. The victors argued, however, that the enormity of the crimes committed dictated some attempt to deal with the problem. An additional question was how to deal with the prosecution of Nazi officials below the top echelon of leaders. Although all four powers pursued these "lesser" officials, the Americans were the most avid and consistent in doing so.

Additional Allied tribunals were held in Nuremberg beginning in October 1946 and lasting for years. The defendants included medical doctors who had conducted "scientific" experiments on camp inmates, judicial officials, administrators of the death camps, industrialists who used concentration camp labor, *Einsatzgruppen* commanders, and some military leaders. Death sentences were passed on members of only three of these groups: the doctors, the *Einsatzgruppen* commanders, and the death camp bureaucrats. Others received jail sentences, and about 20 percent were totally exonerated. By 1950, as the developing Cold War with the Russians produced a shift in American attitudes, an increasing number of convicted Nazis were being given reduced sentences or freed completely. By this time, German courts, as empowered by the Allies, had begun to take over war crimes trials. Although there was little effort during the Cold War years to pursue Nazi criminals, the German legal machine persisted in prosecuting cases. The vast majority of perpetrators, however, were never tried. Many Nazis managed to escape Europe entirely, in some cases aided by the Red Cross, the Catholic Church, and even the victorious governments themselves, now eager to mine German intellectual and scientific assets to fight the Cold War. The focus on the Holocaust in the 1970s, however, brought a considerable revival of interest in justice for the victims of Nazism. The search for perpetrators has not yet ended.

THE SIGNIFICANCE OF NAZISM

The war crimes trials brought to the world's attention the enormity of Nazi crimes against humanity. For many years, scholars sought to find the roots of Nazism in German history by looking for the forces in the German past that led to Nazi militarism, authoritarianism, and racism. Others have rightfully warned that one can arrive at a very unbalanced picture of German history by emphasizing only the elements that led to Nazism. That the Nazis could perpetrate their barbarities in the land of Bach and Beethoven not only reveals serious problems in the development of Germany but also causes us to examine the veneer of civilization that exists in all societies. Nazi Germany shows that there are no simple guarantees of a nation's civilized character. Eternal vigilance is the price not only of liberty but of civilization itself. Historians of modern Germany have long debated the significance of the Nazi era in German history. But we need to also ask what the significance of the Nazi era is to us.

Many of Hitler's contemporaries overlooked a crucial aspect of Hitler and the Nazi movement. *Mein Kampf* may have been a dreadfully written book that could be shrugged off as the product of a political radical who would become more respectable and responsible once he was in power. However, in viewing Hitler in this way, many forgot that how people view their world often determines the world they try to create. Hitler's view of the world was based on struggle as a way of life, the right of the strong leader to dominate, and the missionary need to create the Aryan racial state that would dominate Europe and perhaps the world. Of course, these could be seen as the fanciful ideas of an ill-educated Austrian provincial and not be taken seriously. Nevertheless, they did form the foundation for a movement that consciously contradicted what many believed were some fundamental assumptions of Western civilization. Nazism attacked the liberal tradition, with its belief in individual freedom and limited state power, and democracy, with its emphasis on universal suffrage and equality. Both were products of the Western rational tradition. In opposing these movements, Nazism was expressing its contempt for the shared values of Western civilization.

Instead of equality and liberty, Nazism favored hierarchy and obedience. A movement of integration, mass collectivism, and totalitarian order, it advocated a leadership principle that permitted only obedience to the will of the leader. Above all, Nazism was a movement that exalted a new collective ideal, that of the racial community based on blood. The Nazis never tired of proclaiming their new *Volksgemeinschaft*, the national community. Many contemporaries thought they found the basis for a social revolution in Nazi Germany. After all, didn't Nazi propaganda constantly downplay class, regional, and religious differences? Didn't Aryan blood mean that all Germans were united by common bonds and shared a common national destiny? However, as historians have frequently pointed out, the Nazis certainly failed to create a true social revolution, despite their rhetoric. Class consciousness remained. Regional and religious differences were not eliminated, as German urban refugees discovered when they fled their bombed-out cities only to experience the hostility of fellow Aryans in the countryside who did not wish to share their food supplies with them. As one perceptive youth observed near the end of the war,

> The Labor Service once was organized for every German boy and every German girl . . . Was it not originally founded so that members of all occupations could unite to perform the same type of work, where the young would see no difference between high and low, poor and rich? To this day we see no indication whatsoever that this has happened.[1]

German society had not been fundamentally altered by Nazism.

An important question remains, however: Did the Nazis really set out to transform the German social structure? Hitler's ideal *Volksgemeinschaft* was a racially homogeneous community. All Germans were equal because of blood. The Nazi ideal of community was to be based on the willingness (forced or unforced) of Germans to submerge their individual wills into a single-minded community of will that was well disciplined, obedient to the leader, and willing to sacrifice individual lives for the sake of the community. "The time of personal happiness is over," Hitler had said. And indeed

---

[1]Quoted in Michael Kater, *The Nazi Party: A Social Profile of Members and Leaders, 1919–1945* (Cambridge, Mass., 1983), p. 165.

it was meant to be. The Nazis essentially wanted to establish a new consciousness of national community, not a new social structure. In the new racial community there was no room for "alien blood" or "bad blood." Elimination of the Jews and the euthanasia program for the mentally retarded take on their proper and logical significance in this context. The eagerness to create this new consciousness also explains why the Third Reich placed so much emphasis on propaganda. It is not social programs but new values that achieve a change of consciousness. To the Nazis that meant indoctrination. The task of propaganda was clear—to produce a new unity of people and leader, a community that would "think in unison" and "act in unison."

Not all Germans accepted the Nazi propaganda about their new community, but enough did to create a powerful German state. Why so many did might be related to Nazi appeals to the traditional German forces of authoritarianism, militarism, and nationalism, as many historians have argued. But Nazism was also a movement that took root as a result of certain economic, social, and political conditions, primarily the shattering of traditional society and the unsettled situation created by the devastation of World War I and the shock of the Great Depression. The German sense of security, community, and common decency was weakened. Rootlessness, aimlessness, and the alienation of individuals and classes from one another permeated the social fabric. Ultimately, then, Nazism was, as Hitler never tired of saying, a "spiritual" movement that offered a new sense of security, meaning and purpose in life, and community. That these benefits, which are best secured in freedom, were achieved in an atmosphere of violence, hatred, and loss of individual freedom seemed insignificant at the time.

They are, however, important to our understanding of Nazism. In the final analysis, Hitler and the Nazis never intended to create a new national community to meet the Germans' real need for security, meaning and purpose in life, and community. Their organized and uniformed community was simply an instrument to achieve a larger goal of conquest that would assure domination by the Aryan racial community for centuries to come. As historians have constantly repeated, there were no redeeming virtues in Nazism. The future Nazi empire that Hitler envisioned was fundamentally demoniacal, based on nothing less than constant repetition of inhumane acts.

Nazism, then, was a movement that filled a vacuum in modern times when a traditional society disintegrated. Therein lies our need to understand it. The present period of unsettled conditions and apparent disintegration makes it appropriate to remind ourselves anew of the true nature and ultimate products of Nazism.

SUGGESTIONS FOR FURTHER READING

Works on the war trials include Joseph Persico, *Nuremberg: Infamy on Trial* (New York, 1994); Eugene Davidson, *The Trial of the Germans* (New York, 1966); Bradley F. Smith, *The Road to Nuremberg* (New York, 1981); Ann Tusa, *The Nuremberg Trial* (New York, 1984); Robert Conot, *Justice at Nuremberg* (New York, 1983); and Norbert Ehrenfreund, *The Nuremberg Legacy: How the Nazi War Crimes Trials Changed the Course of History* (New York, 2007). Also of interest is Michael Salter, *Nazi War Crimes, U.S. Intelligence and Selective Prosecution at Nuremberg: Controversies Regarding the Role of the Office of Strategic Services* (New York, 2007). On the trial of Adolf Eichman, see Deborah E. Lipstadt, *The Eichman Trial* (New York, 2011). On the prosecution of Nazi doctors for human experimentation, see Horst H. Freyhofer, *The Nuremberg Medical Trial: The Holocaust and the Origin of the Nuremberg Medical Code* (New York, 2004); Paul Julian Weindling, *Nazi Medicine and the Nuremberg Trials: From Medical War Crimes to Informed Consent* (New York, 2004); and the personal account of Vivien Spitz, *Doctors from Hell: The Horrific Account of Nazi Experiments on Humans* (Boulder, Colo., 2005). It is also interesting, however, to use the proceedings and documents from the Nuremberg trials themselves. See *Trial of the Major War Criminals Before the International Military Tribunal*, 42 vols. (Nuremberg, 1947–1949); *Trials of War Criminals Before the Nuremberg Military Tribunals*, 15 vols. (Nuremberg, 1946–1949); and *Nazi Conspiracy and Aggression*, 8 vols. (Washington, D.C., 1946). For a brief collection of documents, see Michael R. Marrus, *The Nuremberg War Crimes Trial, 1945–1946: A Documentary History* (Boston, 1997). A selection of interviews of defendants and witnesses by psychiatrist Leon Goldenstein can be found in Robert Gellately, ed., *The Nuremberg Interviews* (New York, 2004). On the occupation of Germany and the denazification process, see Frederick Taylor, *Exorcising Hitler: The Occupation and Denazification of Germany* (New York, 2011). On those Nazis who managed to escape justice, see Gerald Steinacher, *Nazis on the Run: How Hitler's Henchmen Fled Justice* (New York, 2011); and Donald M. McKale, *Nazis After Hitler: How Perpetrators of the Holocaust Cheated Justice and Truth* (Lanham, Md., 2012).

MySearchLab™ Connections

Study and Review

After the defeat of Germany, efforts were made to understand the enormity of Nazi crimes. Nazi war criminals were tried and convicted for their participation in planning and carrying out atrocities. The Nazi regime had forced the world to deal with the consequences of ideologies of extreme nationalism and hatred.

Read the Document

1. **The United Nations, Universal Declaration of Human Rights, 1948**
   This document, written partly as a response to the Holocaust and the actions of the Nazis and Stalinist USSR, was created as an ideal to which all nations could aspire.

Read the Document

2. **Israel's Proclamation of Independence, 1948**
   This document declares the steps to the creation of the Jewish State of Israel in 1948. Displaced European Jews sought a country of their own, and the Allies' response to the Holocaust convinced the Jewish people that they needed to reclaim Palestine for their own national identity.

Read the Document

3. **Winston Churchill, from the Iron Curtain Speech (1946)**
   This document reflects the beginnings of the Cold War, the prolonged period of heightened animosity between the Western nations and the USSR. The Cold War distracted attention from the Nazi atrocities, postponed major war crimes trials for years, and deprioritized investigations into and reparations for Nazi depredations.

RESEARCH AND EXPLORE

Some historians have argued that the power vacuum within the Weimar Republic made the emergence of an extremist party inevitable. However, it was Hitler's specifically racist ideology that led Germany into genocide and the Holocaust.

1. Did the Allies' loss of commitment to Nazis' war crimes trials as a result of the Cold War represent a betrayal or a refocusing of priorities? Why?

2. Without Hitler's leadership, would the Nazi Party have had the same racially polarizing agenda? If any of the assassination attempts on Hitler had succeeded, could the "Final Solution" have been avoided?

3. If the Nazis did not rise to prominence in Germany, would another extreme party have taken its place? Why or why not?

ADDITIONAL RESOURCES

Tokyo and Nuremberg war crimes trials, I

The Big Three Confer—Yalta Conference

Glossary

Adolf Hitler SS Guards: SS Leibstandarte Adolf Hitler
Ancestral Heritage Organization: Ahnenerbe
Criminal Police: Kriminalpolizei (Kripo)
Faith and Beauty: Glaube und Schönheit
German Communist Party: Kommunistische Partei Deutschlands (KPD)
German Democratic Party: Deutsche Demokratische Partei (DDP)
German Labor Front: Deutsche Arbeitsfront (DAP)
German National People's Party: Deutschnationale Volkspartei (DNVP)
German People's Party: Deutsche Volkspartei (DVP)
German Social Democratic Party: Sozialdemokratische Partei Deutschlands (SPD)
German Workers' Party: Deutsche Arbeiterpartei (DAP)
Guard Squadrons: Schutzstaffeln (SS)
High Command of the Armed Forces: Oberkommando der Wehrmacht (OKW)
High Command of the Army: Oberkommando der Heeres (OKH)
Hitler Youth: Hitlerjugend
Investigation and Arbitration Committee: Untersuchungs- und Schlichtungs-Ausschuss (USCHLA)
League of German Girls: Bund deutscher Mädel (BdM)
National Socialist German Student Union: Nationalsozialistischer Deutscher Studentenbund (NSDStB)
National Socialist German Workers' Party: Nationalsozialistische Deutsche Arbeiterpartei (NSDAP)
National Socialist Public Welfare Organization: Nationalsozialistische Volkswohlfahrt (NSV)
National Socialist Teachers' Association: Nationalsozialistischer Lehrerbund (NSLB)
National Socialist Women's Association: Nationalsozialistische Frauenschaft (NSF)
People's Army: Volkssturm
Reich Governor: Reichsstatthalter
Reich Labor Service: Reichsarbeitsdienst (RAD)
Reich Security Main Office: Reichssicherheitshauptamt (RSHA)
Secret State Police: Geheime Staatspolizei (Gestapo)
Security Police: Sichersheitspolizei (Sipo)
Security Service: Sicherheitsdienst (SD)
Spring of Life: Lebensborn
Stormtroopers: Sturmabteilung
Strength Through Joy: Kraft durch Freude (KdF)

Index

Note: Page numbers followed by *f* and *m* indicate figures and maps respectively.

A

Abortion in Third Reich, 175
Abwehr, 241, 247–248
Activities of the *Einsatzgruppen,*
    261*f*
Adlerhorst, in Taunus
    Mountains, 211
Admiral Dönitz (submarine
    commander), 210
Advent of Nazism, 1
Affirmation of solidarity, 189
Afrika Korps, 205, 209
Aftermath of *Kristallnacht,* 107
Agrarian community, 99
Agriculture, 75, 99–100, 156
Ahlwardt, Hermann, 5
Ahnenerbe, (Ancestral Heritage
    Organization), 112
Air force (Luftwaffe), 118
Akiva, 260
Algeria, 210
Allen, William S., 120
Allied bombing of Germany
    and Third Reich, 238–241
Allied offensives, 1943–1945,
    214*m*
Allied response to, 278
Allies and the Holocaust,
    277–279
Alsace-Lorraine, 246
Amann, Max, 88, 153
America and Allied bombing
    of Germany, 238–241

American air force, 210
American isolationism, 8
Amt IV B4 (Gestapo), 263–265
Anglo-German Naval Pact,
    119, 190
Anielewicz, Mordechai, 260
Annexation of Poland by
    Third Reich, 222
Anschluss with Austria,
    117, 196
Anti-Bolshevik, 201
Anticlerical propaganda by
    Bormann, Martin, 244
Anti-Comintern pact, 192
Anti-Fascist resistance
    movement, 228
Anti-intellectualism,
    of Nazis, 152
Anti-Jewish
    activity in Nazi Germany,
        105*f*
    policies of Third Reich, 105
Anti-Nazi Prussian state
    government, 65
Anti-Semite, 201
Anti-Semitism
    in Germany, 254
    and Hitler racial ideology,
        253–255
    Hitler views on, 131
    Kristallnacht and, 256
    nationalism and, 2
    "Nuremberg laws"
        and, 102–103

Völkisch ideology and, 6
    See also Aryan ideology
Antonescu, Ion, 221
Appeasement policy of Great
    Britain, 202
Architecture, 157
Ardennes, 202, 213
Armor, 207
Army
    German democracy and, 3
    clash with SA and, 76–79
    presidential government,
        58–60
    support for Nazi party, 36
    in Third Reich, 117
    Weimar republic
        and, 13, 16
Art in Weimar republic, 154
Artamanen, 108
Artisans' guilds, 98
Arts in Third Reich,
    154–158
Aryan ideology
    basic concepts of, 6
    Liebenfels and, 29–30
    Population policy and,
        175–176
    racial ideas of Hitler
        and, 253–255
    SS and, 111
    Thule Society and, 32–33
    World war II and, 184–186
Aryan racial community,
    140, 288

Aryan racial state, 83,
  175–176, 287
Aryan Versus Jew, 135–138
Assassination attempt on
  Hitler, 241–249
  and Gestapo, 248–249
  by Rommel, 213
Atomization of society in
  Third Reich, 120
Atonal music, 20, 159
Attack on degeneracy, 177–178
Auschwitz concentration
  camp, 111, 263, 266–270
Auschwitz-Birkenau, 266, 278
Austria, 246
  Anschluss with Austria, 117
  Germany's blundering
    policy towards, 188
  Nazi Party in, 188
Austrian National
  Socialists, 191
Autarky, 92
Authoritarianism, Nazi, 286
Autobahns (superhighways), 86

B

Bachem, Karl, 75
Badenweiler march, 142
Balkans, 205–206
Baltic states, 200, 205, 207,
  214, 222–223
Bandwagon effect, 76
Barbie, Klaus, 271
Barmen Confession, 115
Barth, Karl, 115, 168
Battle of Britain, 204
Battle of the North
  Atlantic, 209
Bauer, 99
Bauhaus architecture, 20
Bauhaus school of architecture,
  23, 66, 157
Bavaria, 16
Bavarian Alps, 128
Bayreuth, 159
Beauty of Labor, 94
Beck, Ludwig, 246
Becker-Kohen, Erna, 103
Beckmann, Max, 151
Beer Hall Putsch, 41–43
Belgian resistance, 227
Belgium, 202
  Jews in, 270
  Nazis in, 222

occupation of the Ruhr
  region, 40
remilitarization of the
  Rhineland and, 190
Belorussians, 274
Belzec concentration camp, 263
Benn, Gottfried, 152
Berchtesgaden meeting,
  194, 196
Bergas, Hanna, 101
Berghof, 128
Berlin (Weimer capital), 26
  decadence of in Weimar
    Republic, 20
  1936 Olympic games in,
    104, 162
  secret conference in, 193
Berlin Alexanderplatz, 22
Berlin Bunker in World War II,
  214–216
Berlin SS barracks, 79
Bessarabia (in Romania), 200
Bigamy, 179
Birth control clinics, 175
Birthrate, 174
Black market, 239
Blitzkrieg (lightning war),
  200–201
  concept of, 118
  economic policy and, 230
  in Poland, 200
Blockleiter, 84
Blomberg, Werner von
  as defense minister,
    69, 187, 193
  Hitler and, 118
  purge of the SA and, 79
  Party Chancellery and, 86
Blood Flag ceremony, 131
"Blood purge" of the SA, 79
"Blood and Soil theory," 55,
  75, 99, 156
Blue Angel, The, 23
Bock, General von, 207
Bodelschwingh,
  Friedrich von, 245
Bohemia, 198, 221, 271
Bolz, Eugen, 71
Bombing of Germany, 240*f*
Bormann, Martin, 84, 86, 175,
  216, 244, 285
  anticlerical propaganda
    by, 244
  death of, 286
  goals of, 87

as Hess chief of staff, 87
vs. Lammer, 87
National Socialist German
  Workers' Party (NSDAP)
  and, 87
Party Chancellery and, 87
SA Insurance Office and, 87
sexual affairs of, 177
Bouhler, Philipp, 176
Brauchitsch, Walter von, 193
Braun, Eva, 127, 215–216
Brecht, Bertolt, 151
Breker, Arno, 157
Britain, Great
  France invasions over
    Germany and, 202
  World War II and, 201–202
British Royal Air Force, 278
British Secret Service, 236
Browning, Christopher, 277
Broz, Josip (Tito), 228
Brüning, Heinrich, 16, 20, 60,
  63–65, 68, 173
Buchenwald, 105, 111, 117
Bülow, Bernhard von, 187
Bulgaria, 205–206, 214,
  221, 271
Bund Deutscher Mädel (BDM,
  League of German Girls),
  165–166
Bunker beneath Berlin, 211
Burckhardt, Carl, 198
Burden, Hamilton, 147
Burning of books, 152
Business classes in Third
  Reich, 97–99
Business, 97–99
Businessmen in the Third
  Reich, 234

C

*Cabinet of Dr. Caligari,
  The* (film), 23
Campaign of sabotage, 222
Canaris, Wilhelm, 248
Capitalism, Hitler views
  on, 136
Castle Wewelsburg, 112
Catholic Bavarian People's
  Party (BVP), 55
Catholic Youth Sports, 115
Catholics in Third Reich,
  114–115
Caucasus region, 209

Censorship, 153, 160
Center Party, 75
Central Committee of Internal
    Resistance (UVOD), 228
Central-Verein, 101
Chamberlain, Neville, 124,
    129, 194
Chancellorship, The, 1993, 67–68
Chelmno concentration camp,
    262–264, 276
Choral groups, 120
Christian Worth, 176
Chronic alcoholism, 175
Churches
    Himmler and, 111–112
    in Third Reich, 114–117,
        244–245
Churchill, Winston,
    202, 219, 290
Cinemas in Third Reich, 160
Civil liberties, 7
Civil life in wartime Germany,
    229–241
Clash with the army and SA,
    76–78
Cloud of Doom or *Heaven and
    Earth*, 155
Coarse jokes, 159
Cold War with Russia, 286
Cologne, Allied bombing,
    Germany, 238–241
Colonization, German, 224
Combat League for German
    Culture, 88, 152
Communist National
    Liberation Front, 228
Communist party of Germany
    (KPD)
    elimination of, 73, 75
    founding of, 9
    in Reichstag, 59
    Spanish Civil War and,
        191–192
    in Third Reich, 245
    Weimar republic and, 12–16
Communist Polish Workers'
    Party, 229
Communist putsch (coup), 16
Concentration camps, 106,
    262–270
    at Buchenwald, 105–107
    at Dachau, 105–107
    and Goebbels, Joseph, 265
    and Holocaust, 262–270
    at Sachsenhausen, 105–107
Conference at Stresa, 189

Confessional church, 115–116
Conflicts in National
    Socialism, 156
Conquest of *Lebensraum*, 184
Conservatives. *See* German
    National People's Party
    (DNVP)
Consolidation of Hitler power,
    69–80
Coordination, 73
Coordinating free time, 95*f*
Coordination of Labor, 74*f*
Cowherd, 156
Cracow ghetto, 272
Croatia, 222
Cubists, 155
Cultural Bolshevism, 154
Culture
    and society in Nazi
        Germany, 151–179
    in Third Reich, 151–162
Czecho-Slovak union, 197
Czechoslovakia, 193, 194
    destruction of state, by
        Hitler, 196–197
    Germany taken over of,
        195–196
    Jews in, 271

D

Dachau concentration
    camp, 113
Dadaists, 155
Daladier, Edouard, 196
Danish government, 201
Danish Jews, 270
Dannecker, Theodore, 271
Danzig, as seaport
    to Poland, 198
Darré, Walter, 75, 85, 99,
    112, 174
Darré's innovations in
    agriculture, 99
Das Schwarze Korps (The Black
    Korps), 177
Dawes, Charles, 19
Day of National Labor, 73
Death camp bureaucrats, 286
Death camp procedure,
    266–270
Death of Hindenburg, 79
Death of Mussolini, 214
Decadence, 136
Decline of the West, The,
    (Spengler), 20–21

Decree for the Protection of
    People and State, 71
Defense Economy and
    Weapons Bureau, 91
Degeneracy, attack on,
    177–178
Degenerate art, 154–155
Degree of "authoritarian
    anarchy," 87
Delbrück, Hans, 21
Delp, Alfred, 246
Democracy, Hitler views
    on, 133
Demographics of Nazi party,
    35–36, 56–57, 66–67,
    233–235
Denmark and Norway,
    invasion of, 202
Denmark, 222
Desert War, 210
Dictator, Hitler as, 125–147
Dietrich, Marlene, 23
Dietrich, Otto, 88, 148, 220
Dietrich, Sepp, 109
"Diplomatic Revolution,"
    1933–1936, 186–193
Döblin, Alfred, 22
Dollfuss, Engelbert, 188–189
Domestic Service Year, 175
Dönitz, Karl, 211, 216, 285
Doppelverdiener (double
    earner), 25
Dresden, Germany, 239
Drexler, Anton, 33, 34
Dror, 260
Dualism, 85–88
Düsseldorf Industry Club, 138
Duesterberg. Theodor, 64
Dunkirk, France, 202
Dutch, 202, 222, 270

E

Eastern Europe and Jews,
    270–272
    economic exploitation
        of, 225
    resistance movements
        in, 228
Early German victories and
    World War II, 200–203
Early economic policy of Third
    Reich, 90–92
Early Nazi economic policy, 90
Ebert, Friedrich (Weimar
    president), 9, 14, 59

Eckart, Dietrich, 126
Economic and labor
exploitation in Third
Reich, 225–227
Economic crisis by 1935, 91
Economic Exploitation in
Europe, 225
Economic exploitation of
Western Europe, 225
Economic policy
of Third Reich (1933–1939),
89–93
of Third Reich (1939–1945),
230–231
Eden, Anthony, 278
Education in Third Reich,
166–169, 172–173
Egypt, 204–205, 209
Eichmann, Adolf, 256,
263–264
and shipment of Jews to
death camp, 264–266
Eicke, Theodor, 111
Einsatzgruppen
Atrocities in the East,
260–262
commanders, 286
and Holocaust, 256–260
Einstein, Albert, 168
Eisenhower, Dwight, 213
Electioneering techniques of
NSDAP, 61–62
Elections and Nazi
propaganda, 59–62
Electoral campaigns of Nazi
Party, 61
Elimination
of DNVP, 75
of KPD, 75
of SPD, 75
Elite and National
Socialism, 234
Elites, war with Great
Britain, 234
Employment in Third Reich,
170–172
Enabling act and Nazis, 71–73
End of Weimar democracy,
59–60
Enemies of *Völkisch* ideology, 6
Entry in to World War II,
200–202
Epp, Ritter von, 41
Esser, Hermann, 38
Establishment of one-party
state, 75–76

Estonia, 205, 223
Eupen, 221
Europe, 1–3, 189, 220–229
antidemocratic
movements, 2
anti-Semitism in, 2
civilization of, 2
imperialism in, 2
industrial revolution, 2
internationalism, 246
liberalism, 1
Marxian socialist movement
and, 2
nationalism, 1
new order and Italy, 221
political life of, 1–2
urbanization, 2
World War I and, 2–3
Euthanasia, 245
Euthanasia program, 176
Expressionism, 20–21
Extermination Camp at
Auschwitz, 267*f*
Extermination of other
European Jews, 270–272

F

Factors affecting public
opinion, 119
Fahnenweihe (consecration of
the flags), 143
Family policy in Third Reich,
174–176
Farmers, 75, 99–100, 155
Fascist movements in
Europe, 1
Fate of Nazi leaders, 285–286
Fatherland, 134
Fear of Great Depression, 83
Female employment, 171–172
Female Hitler youth and
women, 164–165
Female nudes, 155–156
Female in the Nazi party, 234
Films in the Third Reich,
160–161
Führer of Germany, final step
of, 79
Final victories of Soviet Union,
213–214
Finland, 200, 205, 221, 270
First stage of Nazi conquest, 69
Foreign policy plans and
Hitler, 78
Fortresses of Our Time, 155

*Foundations of the Nineteenth
Century, The*, 6
Four Elements, 156
Four-Year Plan, 92–94,
225, 230
chief objective of, 93
for economy, 192
and Third Reich, 92–94
France, 189
de Gaulle and, 227–228
entry in to World War II,
201
German-occupied, 222
Jews in, 271–272
and Maginot Line, 186
nonaggression pact
with, 191
occupied the industrial
Ruhr region, 18, 40–41
Poland agreement with
Britain and, 198
remilitarization of the
Rhineland and, 191
resistance movements
and, 227
Franco, Francisco, 191, 204
François-Poncet, André, 129,
146, 187
Frank, Hans, 112, 222, 285
Frank, Walter, 169
Free Corps Recruitment
poster, 17*f*
Free French movement, 227
Free Love, 26
Freedom of the press, Hitler
views on, 136
Freisler, Roland, 249
Frick, Wilhelm, 41, 68–69, 71,
85, 110
Fritsch, Werner von, 193
"Führer power" of Hitler, 84
Führerprinzip (leader
principle), 51, 115, 138
Funk, Walter, 93, 120, 285
Futurists, 155

G

Galen, Clemens von (bishop
of Münster), 176, 245
Gamelin, Maurice, 191
Gauleiter (Nazi party leader), 51
Gauleiter, 73, 84, 235
Gaulle, Charles de, 227
Gebrauchsmusik (utilitarian
music), 22

Generals' plot to overthrow
  Hitler, 197
Geneva Disarmament
  Conference, 188
Genre painting, 155–157
  realism, lack of, 156
Geopolitics and *Lebensraum,*
  185
German Christians, 115–116
German Communist Party
  (KPD)
  founding of, 7
  and resistance to Nazi
    regime, 227
  in Weimar Republic, 16
German Democratic Party
  (DDP), 90
German Earth, 155
German export trade
  in 1935, 92
German folk music, 159
German imperial
  authoritarianism, 8
German labor force, 171
German Labor Front (DAF),
  75, 94
German Labor Service, 221
German morale, 237–238
German Mother's Cross, 175
German National Community,
  157
German National People's
  Party (DNVP), 5, 15
  elimination of, 75
  in Third Reich, 246–247
  in Weimar Republic, 14
  Young-Plan and, 56
German offensives, 1939–1942,
  206*m*
German People's Party (DVP),
  14–15, 59, 60
German political
  anti-Semitism, 5
German politics, 7
German Press Agency, 153
German women in
  NSDAP, 237
German women in
  wartime, 232*f*
German Women's Bureau,
  170–171
German's attack on
  Netherlands, 202
  Belgium, 202
  France, 202

Germanic order, 32, 35
German-Italian cooperation
  and Mussolini, 191
German-occupied France, 222
German-Polish agreement, 198
Germany after World War I,
  13*m*
Germany take-over
  Czechoslovakia, 221
Germany's
  expansion 1933–1939, 199*m*
  expenditures on
    rearmament, 91
  need for raw material and
    food stuffs, 92–94
  salvation, 60
Gerstenmaier, Eugen, 246
Gestapo (secret state police),
  110
  arrest of orthodox Lutheran
    bishops, 115
  assassination attempt on
    Hitler and, 248
  Göring, Hermann and, 110
  Holocaust role of, 255,
    260–263
  homosexuals and, 177
  religious targets of, 117
  role of, 110
Ghettos and Holocaust,
  256–260
Ghettos and Poland, 256–260
Gibraltar, 204–205
Giesler, Gauleiter Paul, 179
Gleichschaltung (coordination),
  73–74, 98, 114
Gleichschaltung, internal
  consolidation of power,
  73–76
Goal of Jews, 136
Goebbels, Joseph, 50, 52, 61,
  65–66, 72, 105, 141–142,
  151–152, 160
  Berlin Bunker in, 215
  concentration camps
    and, 265
  Hitler and, 60
  Kristallnacht and, 105
  Nazi cultural policy control
    and, 152, 159
  popular culture and,
    160–162
  and public opinion and
    propaganda, 236–238
  sexual affairs of, 177

in Third Reich (1939–1945),
  236–238
war economic policy and,
  231
Goebbels, Magda, 127
Goebbels's, Joseph and public
  opinion and propaganda,
  236–238
Goerdeler, Carl, 246
Göring, Hermann, 38, 66,
  68–70, 72, 85, 92–93, 98,
  110, 118, 193, 215, 221,
  225, 240, 244, 285
  as air force chief, 211
  Allied bombing of Germany
    and, 240–241
  arrest of, 215
  as art collector, 154
  churches and, 244
  and Four-Year Plan, 92–94
  Gestapo and, 110
  labor exploitation, and, 225
  Luftwaffe and, 118
  minister of the interior in
    Prussia, 68
  police in Prussia, 69
  president of the
    Reichstag, 65
  secret conference in Berlin
    and, 193
  suicide of, 285–286
Government's anti-Christian
  campaign, 117
Graf, Willi, 243
Great Britain
  Allied bombing of Germany
    and, 239
  appeasement policy of, 202
  Elites, war with, 234
  Ribbentrop, Joachim von
    and, 190
  World War II and, 203–205
Great coalition collapse, 59
Great economic depression,
  58–60
Great German Art Exhibition,
  154
Greece, 206, 222, 271
Greim, Ritter von, 215
Gropius, Walter, 23, 151
Growth of Nazism, 48–80
Gruber, Kurt, 162
Guderian, Heinz, 202
Gypsies and Holocaust,
  273–276

H

Hacha, Emil, 197
Hadamovsky, Eugen, 161
Haindl, Anny, 241
Halifax, Lord, 135, 194
Hamburg and Allied bombing
    of Germany, 238–241
Harnisch, Paul, 156
Harris, Arthur, 238
Harvest festival, 75, 142
Hashomir Hatzair, 260
Hassell, Ulrich von, 246
Hauptmann, Gerhard, 152
Haushofer, Karl, 185–186
Heidegger, Martin, 152
Heil salute, 35
Heines, Edmund, 36
Henlein, Konrad, 196
Hess, Rudolf (Political Central
    Commission), 33, 38,
    48, 84, 86–87, 96, 179,
    186, 244
  devotion to Hitler, 38
  and flight to England, 244
  and *Lebensraum,* 186
  Party Chancellery and, 86
  trial of, 285–286
  in Thule society, 32
Hesse, Hermann, 20
Heydrich, Reinhard, 107,
    109, 178, 221, 228, 256,
    263–264
  assassination of, 228
  Bohemia and Moravia
    in, 221
  Einsatzgruppen and,
    256–260
  Kitty, Salon, and, 178
  Kristallnacht and, 106
  as SD leader, 109
High Command of the Armed
    Forces, 211–212
Himmler, Heinrich, 99, 107,
    174, 177–179, 221, 224
  and anti-Semitism, 268–269
  and Christianity, 112
  and churches, 114
  and growth of SS, 107–110
  Heydrich and, 110
  Holocaust role of, 262, 266
  homosexuality and, 177
  peasants and, 108
  Poland and, 256–260
  promiscuity and, 179

and racial ideology of,
    268–269
  resettlement program
    and, 224
  and SS, 107–110
  suicide of, 285
  and swing youth, 242
Hindenburg, Paul von (Reich
    president), 8, 14, 51
  and Weimar system, 59
Hitler, Adolf
  anti-Semitism and, 28,
    134–138
  assassination attempt on,
    213, 238–239, 241, 248
  assessment of, 129
  assumption of Party
    Leadership, 34–35
  Bavarian politics and crisis
    of 1923, 40–41
  Beer Hall Putsch, 41–43
  Blood Flag and, 54*f*
  chancellorship, 67–68
  as charismatic leader, 85
  early life of, 26–27
  early Nazi party, 34–40
  emergence of the Nazi party
    and, 26–34
  emphasis on racial purity,
    102–103
  Enabling act and, 71–73
  establishment of single-party
    regime, 73–76
  as Führer of Germany, 79
  German Workers' Party
    (DAP) and, 32–34
  as an ideologist, 134–140
  influences on, 28–30
  and Jews, 135–138
  leadership, 88–89
  Mass spectacles and,
    141–143
  as messiah figure, 116, 119
  as messianic leader, 130–131
  as military commander and
    World War II, 211–212
  Munich and World War I,
    30–32
  New order in Europe and,
    220–229
  outbreak of World War I,
    31*f*
  political power of, 40–43
  and power of community,
    139*f*

and Quisling, 201
  racial ideology of, 135–138,
    186
  rebuilding of Nazi Party
    and, 48–48
  significance of Nazism and,
    286–288
  as a spiritual movement, 137
  Stalin, nonaggression pact
    and, 200
  and *völkisch* ideology, 89
  in Vienna, 27, 195*f*
  Young Plan and, 56–57
  See also Mein Kampf;
    National Socialist German
    Workers' Party (NSDAP);
    Third Reich (1933–1939);
    Hitler's
Hitler Youth (*Hitlerjugend*),
    162–165, 163*f*, 242–243
Hitler Youth organization
  and National Socialism,
    164–165
Hitler, Alois, 26–27
Hitler, leadership and, 88–89
Hitler's
  acceptance of autarky, 91
  appointment as
    chancellor, 89
  attack over Poland, 198–199
  belief in Darwinian
    struggle, 89
  character traits, 125–130
  concept of *völkisch* state,
    138–140
  foreign policy, 186
  grandiose plans, 120
  home front policies,
    229–241
  idea of struggle, 134–135
  ideological goals, 89,
    184–186
  leadership of Third Reich,
    89, 138–140
  mind, 126
  nonaggression pact,
    188–189
  personality, 125–130
  plan against Soviet
    Union, 204
  policies in Soviet Union,
    222–223
  racial ideology in *Mein
    Kampf,* 135–138, 187
  Social Darwinian belief, 90

Hitler's (*continued*)
  views on National
    Socialism, 131
  vision of Nazism as a
    "spiritual crusade," 85
  war, 184–216
Hitlerjunge Quex, 161
Hitler–Papen government, 68
Hoffmann, Heinrich, 31, 127
Hohenzollern monarchy, 14
Holocaust
  Allies and the, 277–279
  concentration camps and,
    262–270
  Einsatzgruppen and, 256–260
  ghettos and, 256–260
  Gypsies and, 276–277
  of Himmler, 262–263, 266
  Jews outside Germany and,
    270–272
  Resistance movements
    and, 270
  "*Righteous gentiles*" and,
    272–273
  role of Heydrich, Reinhard
    and, 255
  role of Gestapo and, 255,
    260–263
  role of SD and, 255–256
  SS role of, 255–256
  and Third Reich, 253–279
Home Army, 229
Home defense system, 235
Homosexuality, 177–178, 275
Homosexuals and Gestapo, 178
Honor, greatness, and *power,* 134
Höss, Rudolf, 111, 263–264
  and concentration camp, 266
Hossbach, Friedrich, 193
House of German Art, 154,
    157–158, 158*f*
Hoyer, Hermann, 155
Huber, Ernst, 84
Huber, Kurt, 243
Hugenberg, Alfred, 15, 56, 68,
    75, 129
Hungary and deportation of
    Jews, 271
Hungary, invasion of, 214

I

Ich Klage an (*I Accuse*), 161
Idea of struggle, 134–135
Ideology of Hitler, 216
IG Farben, 93, 99

Illegitimacy in Third Reich,
    178–179
Im Westen nichts Neues (*All Quiet
    on the Western Front*), 22
Impact of Allied Bombing,
    238–241
Impact of World War I on
    Germany, 7–9
Imperial Germany, 2–7
  Bismark and
    new Germany, 3
Importation of raw
    materials, 92
In the Beginning Was the Word
    (painting), 155, 156*f*
Inflation effects, 18–19, 19*f*
Informers and SD, 119
Institute for the History of the
    New Germany, 169
Institutional control,
    152–153
Intellectuals in Third Reich,
    151–152
Intentionalist historians,
    88–89
International Military
    Tribunal, 285
Internationalism, Hitler views
    on, 136
Invasion of
  Czechoslovakia, 256–257
  Finland, 205
  France, 202
  Italy, 212
  Poland, 198–199
  Soviet Union and World
    War II, 205–209, 224,
    261–262
  Western Europe,
    by Allies, 227
Iron ore, 201
Island of Crete, 206
Italians attacked Greece, 206
Italians campaign against
    Egypt, 204–205
Italy, 189
  attacked Greece, 206
  and deportation of Jews, 271
  entry into World War II, 202
  European New order
    and, 220
  German-Italian cooperation
    and, 191
  and Hitler, 190
  invasion of, 213
  and pact of steel, 199

  and resistance movement,
    227–229
  tripartite pact (Germany,
    Japan and), 208

J

Jagow, Dietrich von, 72
Japan, 192
Japanese attack on Pearl
    Harbor, 208
Jazz, 159, 242
Jehovah's Witnesses,
    117, 276
Jewish
  art, 154
  emigration from Germany,
    103–104
  fighting organization
    (JFO), 260
  ghettos, 256–260
  military organization, 260
  modern art, 136
  See also Jews
Jewish-Bolshevik intelligentsia,
    Hitler task and, 209
Jewish-Bolshevik menace, 203
Jews
  and allegations of Nazi
    Party, 55
  as dangerous enemies of
    völkisch state, 110
  emigration to Palestine, 104
  fate of outside Germany,
    270–272
  and Germany, 5–6
  Gleichschaltung and, 73
  and Hitler's racial ideology,
    253–255
  Luther and, 5
  mass murder under Nazi
    regime, 253–279
  outside Germany and
    Holocaust, 270–272
  See also Anti-Semitism;
    Holocaust
*Jews and Their Lies,
    The* (Luther), 5
Jodl, Alfred, 211, 285, 286
Johst, Hans, 158
Journey to the East, The, 20
Joy movement, 125
Jud Süss (film), 161
Judenrat (Jewish Council), 258
Judicial system of Third Reich,
    112–114

Jüdische Rundschau
 (newspaper), 101
Jung, Edgar, 79
Jungmädel (Young Girls), 165
Jungvolk (Young People), 131,
 163–166
Junkers, 64, 68, 69

K

Kahr, Gustav von, 32, 41, 79
Kaiser (Emperor) William II, 3
Kampfbund (Combat
 League), 41
Kapp Putsch, 16, 73
Kapp, Wolfgang, 16
Katyn forest, murder in, 229
Keitel, Wilhelm, 193, 211,
 285, 286
Keppler, Wilhelm, 91
Kerrl, Hans, 85, 116
Kesselring, Albert, 213
Kitty, Salon, 178
Kluge, Hans Günther von,
 suicide of, 213
Koch, Erich, 223
Kokoschka, Oscar, 151
Kommunistische Partei
 Deutschlands (KPD), 9
Krauch, Carl, 93
Krebs, Albert, 52
Kreisau Circle, 246–248
Kreise (districts), 52
Kreisleiter, 52, 84, 235
Krieg (*War*), 22
Kristallnacht (night of glass),
 104–107
Kubizek, August, 27–28,
 127–128
Kursk, Soviet Union, 213

L

Labor exploitation and Third
 Reich, 225–227
Labor Front, 94–97
Labor mobilization forces, 227
Labor mobilization office, 221
Labor Service for girls, 172
Lammers, Hans Heinrich,
 85, 87
Land-reclamation projects, 96
Landscape paintings, 155
Landwirt, 99
Lang, Fritz, 151
Laqueur, Walter, 21, 278

Latvia, 205, 223
Laval, Pierre, 222
Law against Malicious Attack,
 113, 119
Law for the Protection of
 German Blood and
 Honor, 103
Law for the Reduction of
 Unemployment, 171–172
Le Chambon-Sur-Lignon,
 France, 273
Leadership and *völkisch*
 ideology, 138
League of Nations, 188, 189,
 190–191
Lebensborn (Spring of Life),
 112, 179
Lebensraum (living space), 25,
 49, 89, 133, 168, 174
 as goal for Hitler, 89
 and Poland, 222
 and Soviet Union, 224
 and *Völkisch* ideology,
 89, 223
Leber, Julius, 245
Leeb, Ritter von, 207
Legal revolution, 69–73
Legal source of a reign of
 terror, 71
Legal systems in Third Reich,
 112–114
Leibstandarte SS Adolf Hitler, 109
Leipzig, worse scene in, 106
Leningrad, Soviet Union,
 207, 214
Ley, Robert, 75, 84, 87, 94
Liebenfels, Lanz von, 29–30,
 32, 35
Liberalism, Hitler views
 on, 136
Literature in Third Reich, 160
Lithuania, 205, 223, 260, 272
Lithuanian ghettos, 260
Locarno Treaty, 189
Lodz (Poland), 104, 257
Lodz ghetto, 258, 266
Lohengrin, 28–29
Lohse, Hinrich, 223
Lossow, Otto von, 41
Loudspeaker, 161
Lublin (Poland), 104, 265
Ludendorff, Erich, 8, 38, 42
Lüdecke, Kurt, 131–132
Lufthansa airlines, 118
Luftwaffe, 118, 192, 204
 and Goring, 118

Lüttwitz, Walther von, 16
Luitpold Arena, 144
Luther, Martin, 5, 11
Luxembourg, 202, 221, 265

M

Majdanek concentration
 camp, 263
Malmedy, 221
Manipulation of youth in
 Third Reich, 162–166
Mann, Heinrich, 151
Manstein, Erich von, 202
Marinus van der Lubbe, 71
Marriage loan scheme,
 171, 174
Martial law, 270
Marx, Karl, 135
Marxism, 136–137, 184
Marxist revolutionary
 orthodoxy, 16
Mass meetings, 140–147
 and radio, 161
 of the election campaign, 62
Mass spectacles and Hitler,
 141–143
Mein Kampf (Hitler)
 as best seller, 160
 as a dreadfully written
 book, 287
 dedications of, 35
 and François-Poncet,
 André, 187
 German Workers' Party
 (DAP) and, 32–34
 Hitler's ideological goals
 and, 192–193
 Hitler's racial ideology,
 135–138, 187
 Hitler's methods and, 28
 on *Lebensraum*, 184–185
 oratory and, 131–134
 propaganda and, 140–147
 radio and, 160–161
 and the *Second Book*
 (Hitler's), 185, 189
 and sports, 161
Mein Kampf (*My Struggle*),
 27, 48
Meissner, Otto, 59, 86
Mengele, Josef, 268
Mihajlovic, General Draza, 228
Milch, Erhard, 118
Mildenstein, Leopold von, 256
Militarism, Nazi, 286

Military
  assassination attempt on
    Hitler, 247–249
  Hitler as supreme military
    commander, 211–212
  and Luftwaffe, 118, 204–205
  operations of World War II,
    206m, 214m
  resistance to Nazi regime,
    246–247
  in Third Reich, 118–119
  See also Army
Ministry of Armaments and
  Munitions, 221
Ministry of Church
  Affairs, 116
Ministry of Economics, 120
Ministry of Food and
  Agriculture, 97
Ministry of Foreign Affairs, 120
Ministry of Labor, 97
Ministry of Public Enlighten-
  ment and Propaganda,
  152, 236
Miracle of Dunkirk, 202
Mischlinge (mixed blood),
  102–103
Mit Brennender Sorge
  (Pius XI), 117
Moltke, Helmuth von,
  246, 248
Montenegro, 222–223
Montgomery, Bernard, 210,
  212–213
Morals and sex, in Third
  Reich, 176–179
Moravia, 198, 221, 271
Moresnet, 221
Morocco, 210
Moscow, 207, 210, 214m, 223,
  274, 276
Mother and Child auxiliary
  service, 175
Mother's Cross, 175
Movies in the Third Reich,
  160–161
Müller, Hermann, 20
Müller, Ludwig, 115
Munich conference, 197
Munich politician and the
  early Nazi party, 34–40
Munich, Germany, 239–240
Munitions plants
  in Ukraine, 225
Murr, Wilhelm, 72

Mussolini, Benito, 206
  arrest of, 215
  death of, 214
  and Dollfuss, 188–189
  German-Italian cooperation
    and, 191
  invasion of Ethiopia, 190
  Italian fascist regime
    and, 189

N

National Bank for Germany
  (private bank), 90
National Greek Democratic
  Union, 228
National Physical Education
  Union, 161
National racial comrades, 119
National revolution, 70
National Socialism (Nazism)
  conflicts in, 156
  Hitler's views on, 131
  Hitler youth organization
    and, 164–165
  racial ideology of, 111,
    112–114
  völkisch ideology and,
    138–140
  in wartime, 231–233
National Socialist Factory Cell
  Organization (NSBO), 94
National Socialist German
  Student Union, 57
National Socialist German
  Workers' Party (NSDAP),
  34–40
  assumption of party
    leadership, 34–35
  Beer Hall Putsch, 39–41
  campaign themes of, 61
  early organization of the
    Nazi Party, 35–36
  early party leaders of, 37–39
  elections and, 60–63
  expansion strategies of,
    52–54
  German women in, 234
  Hitler's control, 49–51
  legal revolution and, 69–73
  mass movement, 1928,
    54–56
  Mein Kampf, 48
  members and leaders of,
    57–58

organization of (1925–1929),
    51–54
  party–state relations, 85–88
  rebuilding of the Nazi party,
    48–58
  Reichstag elections and, 55
  single-party regime and,
    73–76
  social analysis of the party,
    39–40
  social composition of,
    35–36, 57–56, 66–67,
    84–85
  Sturmabteilung role and, 36
  working class and, 94–97
  See also Hitler, Adolf; Nazi;
    Nazis
National Socialist ideological
  goals, 155
National Socialist Lecturers'
  Association, 169
National Socialist Physicians'
  League, 87, 120
National Socialist Professional
  Dentists' Group, 120
National Socialist Public
  Welfare Organization,
  175, 179
National Socialist racial
  ideology, 260
National Socialist state, 94, 98
National Socialist style of
  architecture, 157
National Socialist Teachers'
  Association (NSLB), 166
National Socialist Teachers'
  League, 120
National Socialist Women's
  Association (NSF), 144,
  166, 170, 171
National Socialist Women's
  Bureau, 241
National Socialist Women's
  League, 53
Nationalism, 5
Natural antagonism, 188
Navy League, 6
Nazi
  barbarism, 118
  euthanasia program, 245
  fortress system, 213
  Germany in Wartime,
    220–249
  Germany's bilateral
    agreement, 188

indoctrination, 116
mass spectacle, 143*f*
members and leaders,
57–58
organization for women,
170–171
policy (1935–1939), 97,
116–117
power over SA, 72
pursuit of Germanization,
224
racial ideology, 273–274
state (1933–1939), 83–120.
See also One-party state
stormtroopers, 8
student league, 169
terrorism, 223*f*
Nazification of Germany,
114–117
Nazis
and DNVP, 71
defeat over Reichstag, 66
economic and social
developments, 89–100
in Belgium, 221
success, 76
Nazi party, 84–85
and state relationships,
85–88
and Third Reich, 233–235
on the eve of power, 66–67
Nazism in Europe, 1–3
Netherland, 202, 222, 270
Neue Sachlichkeit
(new objectivity), 21
Neurath, Konstantin von, 86,
120, 187, 193, 221, 285
New Agrarian order, and
Soviet peasants, 225
New order in Europe and
Hitler, 220–229
New Plan trade policies, 91
Niedergang (defeat), 129
Niemöller, Martin, 115, 117
Night of the Long Knives, 79
Nolte, Ernst, 128
Nonaggression pact
with Belgium, 191
with France, 191
with Soviet Union, 199–200
Nordic racial traits, 159
North Africa, 205, 219–210
Norway, 201, 222, 270
Norwegian National
Unification Party, 201

Norwegians, 201, 224
NSDAP, 48–80. *See also*
Socialist working-class
party
"Nuremberg laws", 102–103
Nuremberg laws and
anti-Semitism, 102–103
Nuremberg Party Rallies,
143–147, 145*f*, 149, 155
Nuremberg racial laws of
1935, 175
Nuremberg trials, 285–286
Nuremberg, Germany, 239

O

Oberkommando der Wehrmacht,
(OKW), 207, 211
Obersalzberg, 128
Office for the Supervision of
Ideological Training and
Education, 152
Office of the Führer's Deputy
(Party Chancellery),
86–87
Office of Strategic
Services, 272
Ohlendorf, Otto, 261
OKH (*Oberkommando der Heeres,*
Army High Command),
211–212
OKW (*Oberkommando der
Wehrmacht,* Armed
Forces High Command),
211–212
Olbricht, Friedrich, 248
Olympic Games, 1936 in
Berlin, 104, 162
One-party state, 75, 84, 86
Operation Barbarossa, 205
Operation Green, 196
Operation Overlord, 213
Operation Sea Lion, 203
Operation Valkyrie,
247–249
Opposition sources for Hitler, 76
Orator and Mein Kampf,
131–134
Oratory and Hitler, 131–134
Origin of SD, 109
Ortsgruppen (chapter), 52, 84
Ortsgruppenleiter (chapter
leaders), 52, 84
Oster, Hans, 197
Owens, Jesse, 162, 193

P

Pacifism, 160
Pact of Steel, 199
Pan-German League, 6–7
Panzer divisions, 202, 207
Papen, Franz von, 65, 67,
78, 129
Parliamentarianism, 136
Parliamentary Paralysis, in
Weimar Germany, 58–61
Parteitage (party days), 143–147
Party rallies in Nuremberg,
157
Pastors' Emergency
League, 115
Patriotic societies, 120
Patton, George, 212
Paulus, Friedrich von, 210
Peasants, 68, 108, 121, 156
Penalties for defeatism, 231
People's car (Volkswagen),
95*f*, 96
People's Court, 113, 244, 249
Pétain, Philippe, 202, 222
Physical Education
in schools, 167
in Third Reich, 161
Piotrkow Tribunalski, ghettos
and, 257
Pirates, Edelweiss, 242–243
Pius XI, pope, 117
Plaszow labor camp, 272
Plebiscites, 120, 189, 191, 194
Pöhner, Ernst, 41
Poland, 198, 199*f*, 200
Poles, 274
Police state, 107–112
Pölzl, Klara, 27
Polish Liberation
Committee, 229
Polish underground resistance
movement, 276
Political Maneuvering, 63–66
Political stability in
Germany, 19
Popular consent for Third
Reich, 119–120
Popular culture in Third
Reich, 160–162
Population growth in Third
Reich, 174–175
Population policy in Third
Reich, 174–176
Postwar financial security, 7

Prague, 198
Presidential Chancellery, 86
Presidential government
  and army, 59
  and Hindenburg,
    Paul von, 59
  in Weimar Germany, 58–60
Press, in Third Reich, 153–154
Problem of Britain, 203–205
Probst, Christoph, 243
Promiscuity and SS, 178–179
Propaganda
  elections and, 60–63
  Hitler and, 140–147
  and mass spectacles in Third
    Reich, 141–143, 236–238
Prostitution in Third Reich,
  178
Protectorate of Bohemia-
  Moravia, 228
Protestants in Third Reich,
  115–116
Protocols of the Elders of Zion,
  The, 37
Psychoanalysis, 20
Public opinion in Third Reich,
  119–120, 236–238
Purge of Jews, Communists,
  and Socialists in 1933, 86
Psychoanalysis, in Weimar
  Republic, 20
Pupils' League, 53

Q

Quisling, Vidkun, 201, 222

R

Racial anti-Semitism, 5–6
Racial ideology, 108, 135,
  138, 148, 167, 208, 220,
  253–255, 260, 273. *See also*
    Aryan ideology
Racism, Nazi, 286
Radio in Third Reich, 160–161
Radio/radar aids, 238
Raeder, Erich, 193, 201, 204,
  211, 285
Rasch, Otto, 262
Rathenau, Walter, 18
Raubal, Geli, 127
Realpolitik, 3
Rearmaments, 90–92
Rebellion of Youth, 242–243

Red Army, Hitler task and,
  205–206
Reelection of Hindenburg, 64
Reich Agency for Economic
  Consolidation, 93
Reich Association, 104, 153
Reich Association of
  German Newspaper
  Publishers, 153
Reich Association of the
  German Press, 153
Reich Central Office for Jewish
  Emigration, 107
Reich Chamber of Culture,
  153, 155, 157, 160
Reich Chamber of Film, 160
Reich Chamber of
  Literature, 160
Reich Chamber of Visual Arts,
  155–156
Reich Chancellery, 85–87,
  176, 214
Reich Church, 115
Reich Citizenship Law, 102
Reich Commissariat for the
  Strengthening of German-
  dom (RKFVD), 224
Reich Commissariat
  Ostland, 223
Reich Commissariat
  Ukraine, 223
Reich Committee of German
  Youth Associations, 162
Reich Council of Brethren,
  115
Reich director of
  broadcasting, 161
Reich Food Estate, 99
Reich Hereditary
  Farm Law, 99
Reich Labor Service (RAD), 96
Reich Lawyers' Association,
  112
Reich Minister of Education
  Rust, 168
Reich Ministry of Education,
  167
Reich Mother's Service, 170
Reich Nutrition Estate, 75
Reich press chamber, 153
Reich Propaganda Office, 61
Reich Representation of Ger-
  man Jews, 101–102, 104
Reich Security Main Office
  (RSHA), 255

Reichenau, Walter von, 118
Reichsbank, 91, 102, 268
Reichskommissar, 270
Reichsleiter (party leaders), 84
Reichstag during 1931,
  63–64
Reichstag election, 60
Reichstag fire, 71
Reichstatthälter (Reich
  governors), 73, 88
Reichswehr, 109, 118
Reichwein, Adolf, 245
Reign of Wilhelm II, the, 3–4
Reinhardt economic plan, 90
Reinhardt Plan, 90
Reitsch, Hannah, 231–232
Religious anti-Semitism, 4
Religious holy days in Third
  Reich, 142
Religious targets of Gespato,
  117
Remilitarization of the
  Rhineland, 190–191
  and Belgium, 191
  and France, 191
Reorganization of Poland,
  256–260
Rosenberg and Soviet Union,
  222–223
Reserve Police Battalion
  101, 277
Resettlement and Colonization, of Third Reich,
  223–225
  to concentration camps,
    270–272
  of Nazis, 223–225
  and Poland, 223–225
Resistance
  in the concentration
    camps, 270
  to Nazi regime, 230–231,
    241–249
  and Third Reich, 119–120,
    241–249
  in wartime Germany,
    241–249
Resistance movement
  in Czechoslovakia, 228
  in eastern Europe, 228
  in Poland, 228
  in Third Reich, 227–229,
    241–249
Revolution Devours Its Own,
  76–79

Rhineland, remilitarization of, 190–191, 193

Ribbentrop, Joachim von, 86, 88, 120, 190, 192, 285–286

Ribbentrop's entry into foreign affairs, 86

Riefenstahl, Leni (actress/ director), 146, 161

Rienhardt, Rolf, 153

"Righteous Gentiles", 272–273

Righteous gentiles and Holocaust, 272–273

Ringelblum, Emmanuel, 257–258

Rise and Fall of the City of Mahagonny, The, 22

Rise of political anti-Semitism, 4–7

Road to War, 1937–1939, 193–200

Robert Ley and DAF, 94

Röhm, Ernst, 37, 41–42, 77–78, 107, 162, 177

  arrest of, 78

  Beer Hall Putsch, 41–42, 107

  early Nazi party and, 37

  murder of, in 1934, 177

  SA chief of staff, 52

  second revolution and, 77

  suppression of, 78

Role of Gestapo, 110, 111

Role of Himmler, 107–110

Roma peoples, 273

Romania, 214

Romanian oil fields, 206

Rome-Berlin Axis, 192

Römer, Joseph, 245

Rommel, Erwin, 202, 205

  assassination attempt on Hitler and, 213, 248

  invasion of France and, 202

  North Africa and, 204–205, 209–210

  suicide of, 213, 249

Roosevelt, Franklin Delano, 208

  death of, 215

  War Refugee Board, 272

Rosenberg, Alfred, 33, 38, 49, 78–79, 86, 88, 126, 148, 152, 223

  Combat League for German Culture, 152

  and cultural policy control, 152–153, 159

  execution of, 286

  foreign policy office and, 86

  ideology of, 38, 50

  liaison between Hitler and Ludendorff, 38

  Röhm's arrest and, 78

  and Soviet Union, 222–223

  Thule society and, 32

Rumkowski, Mordechai, 258

Rundstedt, General von, 207, 213

Russian Revolution, 8

Rust, Bernhard, 167

S

SA (Storm Troops)

  clash with army and, 76

  growth of, 36, 57

  Hitler and, 53*f*, 77

  Nazi party and, 36

  refounding of, 52

  Separation of SS from, 109

  student group of, 38

  tactics of, 63

  trade unions and, 73

Saar region, 189

Sachsenhausen concentration camp, 117

Sacrifice, Labor, Readiness, and *Comradeship,* 157

Salomon, Franz Pfeffer von, 52, 53*f*

Sauckel, Fritz, 221, 226, 227, 286

Saxony, 41

Scandinavia, 201

Schacht, Hjalmar, 90, 102, 286

  and Hitler, 90

  new plan of, 91

Schindler, Oskar, 272–273

Schirach, Baldur von, 162–163, 285

Schlageter, 158

Schleicher, Kurt von, 59, 64, 79

Schlieffen plan in World War I, 202

Schmitt, Carl, 152

Schmitz-Wiedenbrück, Hans, 156

Schmorell, Alex, 243

Scholl, Hans, 243

Scholl, Sophie, 233, 244

Scholtz-Klink, Gertrud, 170–171

School reform in 1938, 173

Schools in Third Reich, 166–168

School teachers, 62, 164

Schroeder, Kurt von, 67

Schuschnigg, Kurt von, 194

Schutzstaffeln (SS-protection squads), 53, 107

Schweinfurt, 239

Sculpture in the Third Reich, 157

SD (Security Service), 107, 160, 236

  and public opinion reports, 236

  role in Holocaust, 260–262

Second Book, 185, 189

Secret conference in Berlin, 193

Security Police (Sipo), 255, 260–262

Seldte, Franz, 68

Serbia, 222

Sex in Third Reich, 176–179

Seyss-Inquart, Arthur, 194, 222, 270, 285

Shipment of Jews to death camps, 264–266

Shirer, William (American journalist), 131

Shooting societies, 120

Shortage of Nazi party leaders, 235

Sicherheitsdienst. See SD (Security Service)

Sicily, invasion of, 212–213

Significance of Nazism, and National Socialism, 286–288

Single party regime, 73–76

Sinti people, 273

Skilled-labor positions, 97

Slave labors for Third Reich, 274

Slavic peoples, 224–225

Slovakia, 221, 271

Slovenia, 222

Smolensk, 207

Sobibor concentration camp, 263, 270

Social composition of the Nazi Party, 57

Social Democratic Party
    (SPD), 4, 94
    early growth of, 4–5
    elimination of, 75
    Great Coalition collapse
        and, 59
    in Third Reich, 245
    in Weimar Republic, 12–14
Socialist working-class
    party, 55
Sources of Anti-Semitism, 4–5
Soviet Union
    final victories of, 213–214
    Hitler's plan against, 204
    Hitler's policies in,
        222–223
    invasion of, 205–209, 224,
        257–259, 261–262
    Lebensraum and, 224
    nonaggression pact
        with, 200
    raw materials, 205, 206
    Rosenberg and, 223
    resistance movement in, 229
Spain, Gibraltar and, 204–205
Spanish Civil War, 191–192
Spanish Republican
    government, 192
Special Bureau for Organiza-
    tion of Festivals, 142
Special Operations Executive
    (SOE), 227
Speer, Albert, 127–128, 148,
    157, 209, 215, 221, 225,
    230, 234
    big business and, 234
    and Labor exploitation, 225
    and war economic policy,
        230–231
Spengler, Oswald, 20
Sports and *Völkisch*, 161
Sports clubs, 120
Sports in Third Reich,
    161–162
Spur production of raw
    materials, 93
SS (Protection Squads)
    establishment of, 53
    freedom from SA, 79
    growth of, 107–110
    homosexuality and, 177
    ideology, 111–112
    monastery, 112
    police state, 107–112
    promiscuity and, 179

rituals and symbols, 112
role in Holocaust, 260
seperation of, from SA, 109
trade unions and, 73
in Third Reich (1933–1939),
    107–112
St. Louis (steamship), 104
Stalingrad, 209–210, 212
Stauffenberg, Claus von,
    247–249
Sterilization, 175–176
Strasser, Gregor, 50, 66, 79
Strasser, Otto, 148
Strength Through Joy (KdF),
    94–95, 125
Stresemann, Gustav (founder
    of DVP), 14–15, 19, 41,
    51, 59
Stroop, Jurgen, 260
Structuralist historians, 88
Structure of German empire,
    220–223
Student's coordination, 169
Stülpnagel, Karl von, 249
Stuka dive bombers, 200
Submarines, 209–210
Sudeten German Party, 196
Sudetenland, 117, 196–197,
    246
Suez Canal, 204
Sugihara, Chiune, 272–273
Suicide of Braun, Eva, 216
Suicide of Hitler, 215–216
Swastika flags, 72, 161
Sweden, 201, 270
Swing-Jugend (swing youth),
    242
Synthetic fuels production, 93
Synthetic materials
    development, 91
Synthetics production, 230
System of terror, 110–111

T

T-4 program, 176, 263
Tarnopol massacre, 262
Tempel, Wilhelm, 57
Terboven, Joseph, 222
Textbooks in schools, 167
Theater in Third Reich,
    158–159
Theresienstadt (Terezin)
    ghetto, 271
Thingspiel, 159

Third Reich (1933–1939)
    Abortion in, 175
    agriculture in, 99–100
    army in, 118–119
    arts in, 154–158
    atomization of society
        in, 120
    business classes in, 97–99
    Catholics in, 114–117
    churches in, 114–117,
        244–245
    cinemas in, 160–161
    culture in, 151–162
    economic policy of, 89–92
    education policy of,
        166–169, 172
    employment in, 170–172
    family policy in, 174–176
    films in, 160–161
    Four-Year Plan and, 92–94
    Hitler's leadership of,
        88–89
    illegitimacy in, 178–179
    intellectuals in, 151–152
    judicial system of, 112–114
    legal systems in, 112–114
    literature in, 160
    manipulation of youth in,
        162–165
    mass spectacles in,
        141–143
    military in, 118–119
    morals in, 176–179
    movies in, 160–161
    physical education in, 160
    popular consent in, 119
    popular culture in,
        160–162
    population growth in,
        174–175
    press in, 153–154
    propaganda in, 140–141
    prostitution in, 176
    protestants in, 115–116
    religious holy days in, 142
    resistance to, 119–120
    schools in, 166–169
    sculpture in, 157
    sex in, 176–179
    sports in, 161
    SS police state in, 107–112
    theater in, 158–159
    Universities in, 168–169
    visual arts in, 154–158
    women in, 169–174

Third Reich (1939–1945)
  Allied bombing of Germany and, 238–241
  annexation of Poland and, 224
  anti-Jewish policies of, 100–107
  business classes in, 234
  communist party of Germany in, 245
  churches in, 244–245
  economic and labor exploitation in, 225–227
  German National People's Party (DNVP) in, 5, 15, 259
  Holocaust and, 253–279
  labor exploitation and, 225–227
  morals in, 236–238
  Nazi Party and, 233–235
  propaganda in, 236–238
  public opinion in, 236–238
  resettlement and colonization of, 223–225
  resistance movement in, 227–229, 241–249
  slave labors for, 274
  Social democratic party in Third Reich, 245
  women in Third Reich, 231–233, 234
Thomas, Colonel, 93
Chorak, Joseph, 157
1000-bomber attack, on Germany, 238
Three Faces of Fascism, 128
Thuringia, 41, 56, 66, 226
Tobruk, 209
Todt killed, in an airplane crash, 230
Todt, Fritz, 86, 90, 230
Tokyo, 272
Tooze, Adam, 231
Trade unions
  and Hitler, 73–74
  and SA, 74
  and SS, 74
Transport vehicles, 207
Treaty of Locarno, 19, 186, 189
Treaty of Versailles, 12, 33, 92, 125, 186–190, 193, 198
Treblinka concentration camp, 263, 270, 278

Treitschke, Heinrich von, 5
Tresckow, Henning von, 248
Tripartite pact (Germany, Italy and Japan), 208
Triumph des Willens (*Triumph of the Will*), 161
Triumph of the Will, 146, 161
Trocmé, André, 273
Troost, Paul Ludwig, 157
Trott zu Solz, Adam von, 246–247
Truman, Harry, 215
Tschammer und Osten, Hans von, 161
Turning point of the war, 1942–1943, 209–210

U

Uhrig, Robert, 245
Ukraine, 207–209, 214, 222–223, 225–226
Ukrainians, 223, 262, 274
Ultra intelligence operation, 204
Underage League of German Girls, 179
Unemployment figures, 91
United States Air Force, 278
United States, 208–209, 234, 267, 276, 277–278, 285
Universities in Third Reich, 168–169
University of Marburg, 78, 278
University of Munich, 36, 38, 179, 186, 243
University students in Nazi Party, 234
Uschla (party tribunals), 50, 52

V

V-1 bombs, 237
V-2 ballistic missiles, 237
Verlag, Eher, 153
Vernichtungskrieg (war of extermination), 205, 260
Versailles treaty, 7, 16, 33, 42, 63, 186, 190
Vichy France, 203, 222
Victory of Nazism, 48–80
Vienna (1909–1913), 134, 231

Visual arts in Third Reich, 154–158
Volk ohne Raum (people without space), 25
völkisch ideology, 6
  architecture and, 157–158
  early Nazi party, 34–36
  enemies of, 110
  Hitler and, 89
  Hitler's concept of, 138–140
  leadership and, 88–89
  Lebensraum and, 89
  in Munich, 30–32
  and National Socialism, 138
  origin of, 6
  See also Aryan ideology
Völkischer Beobachter (newspaper), 36, 38, 41, 49, 153, 179
völkisch-Nationalist Groups, 6
Volksgemeinschaft (national community), 6, 63, 74, 90, 107, 110, 119, 147, 151, 165, 178–179, 287
Volksstaat (racial state), 138
Volkssturm (people's army), 231, 235
Volkstod (death of the people), 25
Vught concentration camp, 270

W

Waffen-SS (armed SS), 110
Wage-price inflation spiral, 97
Wagner, Richard, 28–29, 144, 159
Wagnerian theatrical motifs, 146
Wallenberg, Raoul, 272
Walter, Bruno, 151
Wannsee Conference, 264
War crimes trials, 285–286
War economy, 93, 96, 120, 225, 230, 274
War-guilt clause, 12
Warsaw (Poland), 104, 257–258
Warsaw ghetto, 257–258, 260, 263
Wartenburg, Yorck von, 246
Weimar Germany, 12–43, 155, 161, 171

Weimar republic, 12–26
  architecture of, 23
  art in, 23
  basic institutional structure
    and, 17–18
  Beer Hall Putsch and, 41–43
  culture in, 20–24
  economic problems of,
    18–20
  German army and, 14
  Great depression and, 58–60
  manners and morals of, 26
  Marxist revolutionary theory
    and, 14
  and modern architecture,
    157
  and modern art, 154
  Parliamentary Paralysis in,
    58–60
  political problems in, 14–17
  Presidential Government in,
    58–60
  repercussions of defeat in
    early, 12–14
  social divisions of, 24–26
  social problems of, 18–20
  stability of (1925–1929), 51
  Treaty of Versailles, 12–14
  womens in, 25–26
  Young Plan and, 56–57
Weissler, Friedrich, 117
Weltanschauung, 28, 136
Weltbühne, 21
Weltmacht (world power), 129
Weltpolitik, 4
Wessel, Horst, 62, 159
Westerbork concentration
  camp, 270
Western Europe and resistance
  movements, 225

Western powers, 189–190
Westphalia, 112
White Rose, 242–244
White Russia, 223
Wiesel, Elie, 269
Wilde cliques, 25
Winter Relief program, 171
Witzleben, Erwin von, 248
Wolfsschanze, in
  East Prussia, 211
Women
  education, 172
  employment, 171–172
  League of German Girls,
    165–166
  as professionals, 173–174
  Third Reich, 169–174,
    231–233, 234
Workers, Farmers, and Soldiers,
  156
Working class, 94–97
  and NSDAP, 94–97
World War I (1914–1918)
  impact over Europe, 7
World War II, 200–216,
  238–241
  Allied bombing of Germany
    and, 238–241
  Aryan ideology and,
    184–186
  Berlin Bunker in
    World War II, 214–216
  Britain and, 201–202
  early German victories in,
    200–203
  France entry into, 202
  Great Britain and, 203–205
  Hitler as military
    commander and,
    211–212

Hitler foreign policy
    and, 186
  Hitler's ideology and,
    184–186
  invasion of Soviet Union
    and, 205–209
  Italy entry into, 202–203
  last years of, 212–214
  military operations of,
    206*m*, 214*m*
  turning point of the war,
    1942–1943, 209–210
Wozzeck, 22
Württemberg Germany,
  71–72
Würzburg, 130

Y

Young people in the Nazi
    party, 61–62
Young plan issue, 56–57
Youth activities, 165–166
Youth rebellion, 242–243
Youths, 162–165
Yugoslavia, 196, 206, 221–222,
  228, 263, 271

Z

Zeitoper (topical or contempo-
    rary opera), 22
Zellenleiter (cell leaders), 84
Zeppelinwiese, 144
Zetos, 258–259
Ziegler, Adolf, 156
Zionist movement, 104
Zionist youth groups, 260
Zyklon B, 263–264